THUNDERSTICKS

THUNDERSTICKS

FIREARMS AND THE VIOLENT TRANSFORMATION OF NATIVE AMERICA

DAVID J. SILVERMAN

The Belknap Press of Harvard University Press
Cambridge, Massachusetts
London, England
2016

Library of Congress Cataloging-in-Publication Data
Names: Silverman, David J., 1971– author.
Title: Thundersticks : firearms and the violent transformation of native
    America / David J. Silverman.
Description: Cambridge, Massachusetts : The Belknap Press of Harvard
    University Press, 2016. | Includes bibliographical references and index.
Identifiers: LCCN 2016014834 | ISBN 9780674737471 (alk. paper)
Subjects: LCSH: Indians of North America—Warfare—History. | Firearms—
    North America—History. | Indians, Treatment of—North America.
Classification: LCC E98.W2 S55 2016 | DDC 970.004/97—dc23
    LC record available at https://lccn.loc.gov/2016014834

To Julie Alexis Fisher

CONTENTS

LIST OF ILLUSTRATIONS

A NOTE ON TERMINOLOGY, STYLE, AND CITATION

This book is a continental history of indigenous people on a continent where there are sometimes profound disagreements about which terms are appropriate to refer to them. Within the United States, most educators and media use the term "Native Americans," even as indigenous people themselves (with important exceptions) generally continue to prefer "Indians." In Alaska, however, indigenous people call themselves "Native Alaskans" collectively. In Canada it is widely judged to be insensitive and even racist to use the word "Indians," though some indigenous people (particularly older ones) continue to do so. North of the border, "First Nations" is the appropriate phrase. These differences pose significant challenges to an author from the United States writing for a diverse audience that hopefully will include Native people of various backgrounds, Canadians, and people even farther afield.

Another problem is which terms to use when referring to indigenous tribal and ethnic groups. Many tribal communities did not (and do not) call themselves by the names by which the general public has come to know them. A number of the tribal names most familiar to general readers originated with the group's indigenous neighbors (including enemies), then passed through English, French, or Spanish into current parlance (Mohawk and Sioux are examples). In other cases, colonists themselves made up their own names for groups of indigenous people (as in the case of the Creeks or the Hurons). Canadians often refer to the Piikani (or Piegan/Peigan), Kainai (or Blood), and Siksika (or Blackfoot proper) peoples collectively as the Blackfoot or the Blackfoot confederacy. In the United States one often hears them called by the plural,

Blackfeet. The Blackfeet/Blackfoot themselves use the term Niitsitapi (meaning the Real or Original People).

My guiding principle is to write in language that will be understood by the widest audience. At the risk of offending my Canadian readers, I use the terms "Indians," "Natives," and "indigenous people" interchangeably. My explanation (or excuse) is that most people in the United States are completely unfamiliar with the phrase "First Nations," and most (albeit not all) of the Native people I know personally do not use it. Wherever possible, I refer to specific tribal or ethnic groups. At the risk of offending my indigenous readers, I tend to err on the side of familiar tribal names, such as using "Iroquois" or "Five Nations" instead of "Haudenosaunee," and "Navajo" instead of "Diné." I hope readers who disagree with these choices will find a source of forgiveness in my mission to bring historical indigenous actors to the fore and respectfully treat the complex challenges, concerns, and priorities that shaped their lives.

My interest in making this work as accessible as possible has also led me to modernize spelling and punctuation in the many quotations that flavor this narrative. For the same reason, I have restricted notes to the end of paragraphs. Readers who want to locate the source of a particular quote will find a portion of that quote included in the notes alongside the appropriate citation.

THUNDERSTICKS

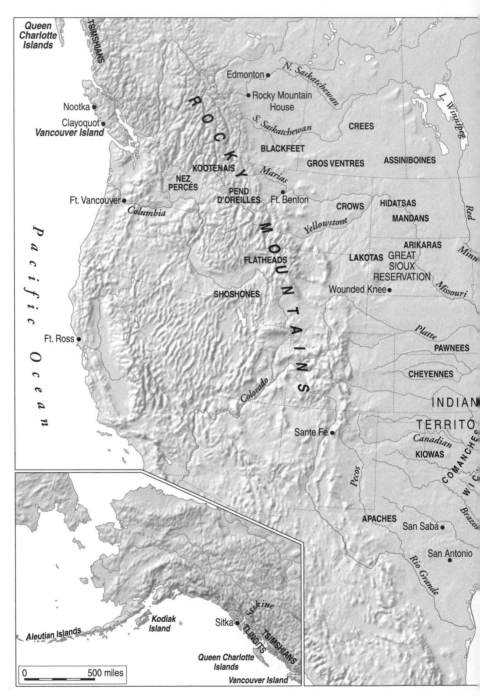

Queen
Charlotte
Islands

TSIMSHIANS

Edmonton

N. Saskatchewan

L. Winnipeg

R
O
C
K
Y

Rocky Mountain
House

S. Saskatchewan

CREES

Nootka

BLACKFEET

Clayoquot
Vancouver Island

KOOTENAIS

GROS VENTRES

ASSINIBOINES

NEZ
PERCÉS

Marias

Ft. Vancouver

Columbia

PEND
D'OREILLES

Ft. Benton

CROWS

HIDATSAS

Red

MANDANS

Minn

M
O
U
N
T
A
I
N
S

Yellowstone

ARIKARAS

FLATHEADS

LAKOTAS

GREAT
SIOUX
RESERVATION

Missouri

SHOSHONES

Wounded Knee

P
a
c
i
f
i
c

O
c
e
a
n

Platte

Ft. Ross

PAWNEES

CHEYENNES

Colorado

INDIAN

TERRITO

Sante Fe

Canadian

COMANCHE

KIOWAS

WIC

Pecos

Brazos

APACHES

San Sabá

San Antonio

Rio Grande

Aleutian Islands

Kodiak
Island

Sitka

Stikine

TLINGITS

TSIMSHIANS

Queen Charlotte
Islands

Vancouver Island

0   500 miles

Gun Frontiers in North America.

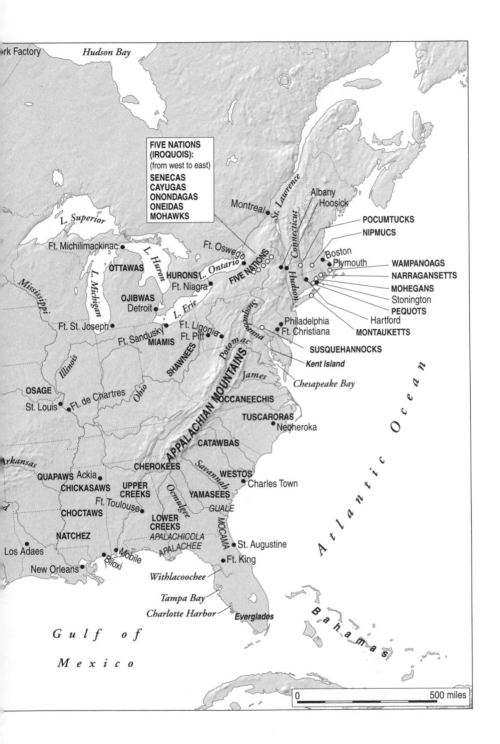

rk Factory

Hudson Bay

**FIVE NATIONS
(IROQUOIS):**
(from west to east)
**SENECAS
CAYUGAS
ONONDAGAS
ONEIDAS
MOHAWKS**

L. Superior

Ft. Michilimackinac

OTTAWAS

L. Huron

L. Michigan

HURONS

Ft. Niagra

L. Ontario

Ft. Oswego

FIVE NATIONS

Montreal

St. Lawrence

Albany
Hoosick

Connecticut

POCUMTUCKS

NIPMUCS

Boston
Plymouth

WAMPANOAGS

NARRAGANSETTS

MOHEGANS

Stonington

PEQUOTS

Hartford

MONTAUKETTS

Hudson

Mississippi

OJIBWAS
Detroit

L. Erie

Ft. St. Joseph

Ft. Sandusky

MIAMIS

Ft. Ligonia
Ft. Pitt

Susquehanna

Philadelphia
Ft. Christiana

Potomac

SHAWNEES

APPALACHIAN MOUNTAINS

James

SUSQUEHANNOCKS

Kent Island

Chesapeake Bay

Illinois

OSAGE

St. Louis

Ft. de Chartres

Ohio

OCCANEECHIS

TUSCARORAS

Neoheroka

CATAWBAS

Arkansas

QUAPAWS Ackia

CHEROKEES

Savannah

WESTOS

Charles Town

CHICKASAWS

**UPPER
CREEKS**

Ft. Toulouse

Ocmulgee

YAMASEES

GUALE

CHOCTAWS

**LOWER
CREEKS**

APALACHICOLA

MOCAMA

NATCHEZ

APALACHEE

St. Augustine

Los Adaes

Mobile

Biloxi

Ft. King

New Orleans

Withlacoochee

Tampa Bay

Charlotte Harbor

Everglades

Atlantic Ocean

Bahamas

G u l f   o f

M e x i c o

0   500 miles

WHAT CRAZY HORSE AND SITTING BULL KNEW

On May 6, 1877, Crazy Horse, the great warrior chief of the Oglala Lakotas, finally surrendered to the United States, effectively symbolizing the end of his people's quarter century of resistance to white American hegemony along the upper Missouri River and Great Plains. Though the Lakotas had welcomed the trade goods accompanying U.S. expansion, practically everything else about it constituted a disaster. Even before the invasion of white ranchers and farmers, the Lakotas had been plagued by an unending succession of American transients, some of them violent, nearly all of them wasteful. First there were the overland migrants, tracing rutted trails from Missouri to the golden fields of Oregon and the gold strikes of California and the Rocky Mountains. These travelers and their livestock stripped precious river bottoms and grasslands of materials the Lakotas needed to build and heat their homes, construct their tools, and feed their horses. Furthermore, their long wagon trains disrupted the buffalo's normal migrations, which sometimes forced the Lakotas who depended on this game to go hungry. Close behind them were white hunters, who slaughtered the buffalo wantonly, usually only for their robes, leaving their carcasses to rot on the Plains. It was as if they were eager to starve Indians who relied on these animals for practically everything. Yet at least the overland migrants and hide hunters tended to only pass through Lakota territory. The railroad-building and mining industries, by contrast, delivered

1

some of the roughest, most lawless, and environmentally destructive segments of American society directly into the Lakota heartland, including the sacred Black Hills. Whenever Lakota warriors drove them out, it seemed only to entice more of them to return, with blue-coated soldiers in tow for their protection.[1]

To be sure, Lakota men, expert horsemen often armed with the best rifles on the market, were more than a match for these troops. Most notably, on June 25, 1876, Lakota and Cheyenne warriors wiped out an invading force of 262 men under the command of General George Armstrong Custer at the Battle of the Little Bighorn. But the Americans always seemed to have more warm bodies to march into Lakota country. As some Indians put it, they were as numerous as the blades of grass on the Plains, and like grass grew back every time they were mowed down.[2]

Lakota warriors could handle U.S. cavalry in anything resembling a fair fight, but they could not cope with their relentless hounding of civilian camps, including the massacre of women, children, and the elderly, and the destruction of the people's horses and food stores. This punishment came when the Lakotas were already suffering acute hunger because of the dwindling buffalo herds, and a population freefall as epidemic diseases accompanying the Americans tore through their tents season after season. By 1877 the people could take no more. One by one, desperate Lakota bands came to the wrenching conclusion to move onto the reservations that the federal government had assigned them, where, its agents promised, at least there would be something to eat and the soldiers would stop pursuing them. Probably no one felt more anguish over this decision than Crazy Horse, who as a mature man in his mid-thirties had spent his adult life battling to avoid just this moment.[3]

Crazy Horse could hardly bring himself to utter a word when he and his band turned themselves in at Camp Robinson, an American military outpost at the southwest doorway to the Great Sioux Reservation. Though he was introverted under normal circumstances, there was no mistaking that his silence this time was rooted in despair. One might assume it was the site of the reservation that struck him speechless, but that was not the case. More moderate chiefs, such as Red Cloud and Spotted Tail, conceding the necessity of negotiating with the United States, had managed to get the reservation located squarely in Lakota country, on the vast, undulating Plains of what is now South Dakota and Nebraska. This was an achievement for which earlier generations of Native people, forced by the government to relocate from their eastern homelands to Oklahoma or Kansas, could only have wished. Instead, Crazy Horse was bitter about capitulating to American soldiers he did not respect, and anxious about how the Lakotas would be able to live in this place. He knew that Washington no longer asked but demanded that they end their raids against indigenous enemies, and against the white Americans overrunning their territory. Even more ominously, in the long term, the U.S. government planned to force the Lakotas to adopt a sedentary, agricultural life, hemmed in by farm fences and the lines of the reservation.

This prospect was especially bleak for the men. Lakota men had been hunters and warriors since time out of mind. That was how they defined themselves as individuals, as men, and as Lakotas. To them it was the sacred order of things. Fulfilling these roles also meant a life full of excitement and glory, played out across an expansive territory of beautiful, powerful places. All of this would change under American rule. A man's life would be reduced to the monotonous routines of tilling the soil and tending to livestock, day in and day out on the same tract of land. Crazy Horse could see little that was good and meaningful in this future, so what could he say in yielding to it after years of fending off the blue coats? What words could possibly capture the worry, humiliation, and sadness of this event?[4]

It would take a ceremony, and an improvised one at that, to manage such raw emotions. The proceedings began with Crazy Horse, some 200 warriors, and approximately 12,000 of their horses, gathering half a mile outside Camp Robinson, enough distance to guard against unplanned incitements by either side. U.S. commanding officer Lieutenant William P. Clark came out to meet them, whereupon the Lakotas dressed him in a feathered war bonnet and a buckskin war shirt, and presented him with a gift of a pony, to represent that they were shedding the state of war. Then Crazy Horse delegated Red Cloud, who had entered the reservation years earlier and received the dubious distinction of having an agency named after him, to ask Clark for permission "to surrender their arms at the agency voluntarily, and not have them forcibly taken away from them." The Lakotas' reasoning was "that neither Crazy Horse nor his warriors were defeated or cowed into submission, but that he

[Crazy Horse] deemed it best as a matter of policy to surrender." Warriors did not permit their rivals to count coup (or claim honor) at their expense by seizing their weapons, which ranked among the most prestigious martial achievements on the Plains. Only after receiving Clark's approval did Crazy Horse and his people begin to enter the U.S. camp in a line some two miles in length, escorted by an advance guard of sixty Lakota, Cheyenne, and Arapaho soldiers from the reservation. Along the way the new arrivals could be heard "chanting songs suited to the occasion," which was to say, reflective of their "sullen, discontented look."[5]

Hours later, after the people had erected their teepees and refreshed themselves, the men gathered in the center of camp to conclude their surrender. First Crazy Horse, then other chiefs such as Little Big Man, He Dog, and Little Hawk, and finally fifty more men of lesser rank, placed 147 guns in a pile, most of them "first-rate sporting rifles or else Springfield carbines, caliber .45, the same as now issued to United States troops." Crazy Horse himself relinquished "three fine Winchester rifles," a repeating gun that held between ten and fourteen rounds. Clearly, a lack of weapons had nothing to do with the Lakotas' capitulation to the Americans. Clark, however, refused to believe that these were all the arms they had. Rejecting the offer, he calmly but directly explained that he would accept only their complete arsenal, "and to save trouble they had better go out and find those guns at once."[6]

The people had been on edge all day, and so with this impasse the camp began panicking that "the military was about to pounce upon them and kill them all because a few of their evil spirits had hidden guns." They had fresh memories of how U.S. soldiers had massacred peaceful Cheyennes and Arapahos at Sand Creek, Colorado, in 1864 (and there were representatives of both groups in Crazy Horse's camp), and Cheyenne and Lakota noncombatants in several attacks during the winter of 1876–1877. To restore calm, Crazy Horse accompanied the reservation's Indian guard as it went tent to tent gathering weapons, sometimes in exchange for horses in the case of an unwilling donor. An additional 50 rifles and muskets and 31 pistols surfaced, making 120 rifles and muskets and 75 pistols in all—probably still less than the absolute total, but enough to satisfy the lieutenant. On May 11, with the crisis averted, the chiefs held a feast of half a dozen large dogs, a custom to signal great transitions such as war, or, in this instance, the beginning of the struggle on the reservation for the future of the Lakota people.[7]

———

Sitting Bull, the illustrious Hunkpapa Lakota warrior chief and holy man, was as loath as Crazy Horse to relinquish his gun to the Americans. Born in the early to mid-1830s, Sitting Bull, like Crazy Horse, had spent his adult life distinguishing himself in battle against the Lakotas' enemies like the Crows, Assiniboines, and Pawnees. His heroic reputation reached even greater heights during the 1860s and 1870s as he forcibly evicted Americans who trespassed on his people's land and fended off the U.S. Army, which sought to corral the Lakotas like cattle. In 1869, a grand meeting of the Lakota bands even appointed him to lead their collective resistance against the Americans. Years later, during the sacred Sun Dance, Sitting Bull's vision of dead soldiers piled high in his people's camp presaged the warriors' decimation of Custer's unit at the Little Bighorn. Sitting Bull's Winchester repeating rifle and six-shooting pistol, like those of Crazy Horse and so many other Lakota and Cheyenne warriors, cut down many of the blue coats that day.[8]

Sitting Bull's early life coincided with the Lakotas reaching the pinnacle of their strength. Over the previous century they had transformed themselves from pedestrian hunters and gatherers of the Minnesota woodlands and prairies to become the dominant equestrians of the northern Plains, with a hunting range extending from the Missouri River to the north and east, west to the Yellowstone River, and south to the Republican River. Their ascendency was a testament to the power Native people could harness from colonialism by combining horses from the Southwest (a Spanish introduction) with guns from the East. Yet their chance to exploit that opportunity depended on actual colonists residing far away. When white people arrived in large numbers, the consequences for Indians were disastrous and swift. Thus, as a mature adult, Sitting Bull had also experienced the equally dramatic collapse of the Lakotas' power under the strains of white encroachment, war with the United States, epidemic disease, and the near extinction of the buffalo. Faced with the choice between entering the reservation or dying at the hands of U.S. troops, Sitting Bull and hundreds of other Lakotas designed a third option: they headed just north of the U.S./Canadian

Sitting Bull Pictograph. This drawing was made by Sitting Bull in a ledger book shortly after his surrender. It captures the centrality of firearms to his own life and to the Lakotas and other equestrian Indians on the Plains. Smithsonian Institution National Anthropological Archives, Image MS 1929b.

border into the Cypress Hills of what is now southern Saskatchewan and Alberta, where they were safe from American forces and one of the last great buffalo herds remained. Here in the land of Queen Victoria, the Great White Mother, Sitting Bull believed he could retain at least some semblance of life as he knew it.[9]

Yet in this instance even Sitting Bull's clairvoyance failed him. He could not have anticipated how quickly the bison would disappear from the Canadian Plains too. Beset by white and Indian hunters alike, the Canadian herd finally reached its breaking point in the summer of 1878, when a raging prairie fire scattered it into several small bands and forced them south across the international line. Hungry Lakota hunters, now based in Canada, followed the animals into U.S. territory, rustling horses and cattle from civilian ranches and clashing with American troops along the way. Finally the Canadian government, unwilling to compromise its relations with Washington over the fate of refugee Lakotas, told Sitting Bull and his followers it was time to return home. With red-coated Mounties ready to force the issue, even Sitting Bull had to concede that entering the reservation was the best of several bad options, at least for the women, children, elders, and generations to

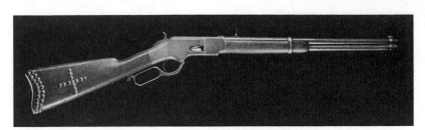

Sitting Bull's Winchester Model 1866 Carbine. This is thought to be the rifle surrendered by Sitting Bull in 1882. Note the brass tacks used to add a personal signature to the weapon. Smithsonian Institution Archives, Image E384119–0.

come, if not for him. As he said, he would rather hunt prairie mice than become a farmer.[10]

When Sitting Bull turned himself in at Fort Buford, Montana, on July 19, 1882, he understood that this was a watershed akin to his ancestors' decision to mount the horse and ride onto the Plains as buffalo hunters. This time, however, the future held far less promise. His people would have to give up their warfare, hunting, and independence, all indelibly tied to the gun, to become peaceful farmers under the rule of their American conquerors. There was no worth in this for a Lakota warrior; it was life without living. Like Crazy Horse, who maintained a dignified silence at his surrender, Sitting Bull would not deign to hand over his weapon himself. Instead, he appointed his son, Crow Foot, to perform the deed, thus preserving his own honor while acknowledging that his posterity would have to follow the new path. However, unlike Crazy Horse, Sitting Bull marked this occasion with eloquence, saying, "I surrender this rifle to you through my young son, whom I now desire to teach in this manner that he has become a friend of the Americans. I wish him to learn the habits of the whites and to be educated as their sons are educated. I wish it to be remembered that I was the last man of my tribe to surrender my rifle. This boy has given it to you, and he now wants to know how he is going to make a living." The Lakotas admired Sitting Bull for his prognostication, but even he was incapable of answering this dreaded question.[11]

The ceremonialism of Crazy Horse and Sitting Bull at the time of their surrenders captured a lesson that has too often been lost and even denied in accounts of North American Indian history. From the early days of Atlantic coast colonization in the seventeenth century, through the end of the Plains wars in the late nineteenth century, one group of Indians after another used firearms to revolutionize their lives. The first groups to adopt these weapons sought a military advantage over their rivals. Those who managed to seize temporary control of an emerging gun market transformed themselves into predatory gunmen, terrorizing entire regions to seize captives, plunder, land, and glory. In the face of such gun-toting expansionist powers, neighboring peoples had little choice but to respond in kind. They could plainly see that the groups most at risk of subjugation, forced adoption, enslavement, displacement, and death were the ones who failed to provide their warriors with guns and ammunition. Their experience taught that differential access to guns had become an essential factor in the rise of some Native peoples and the fall of others. The result was the serial eruption of regional arms races across the continent over the course of more than 200 years. The kind of predatory raiding that spurred these arms races would not subside until a rough balance of power was achieved through the widespread distribution of guns.

Most Native people participated in these arms races well before the advent of repeating rifles and pistols in the mid- to late nineteenth century—though as the Lakotas' arsenals attest, they certainly appreciated these sophisticated weapons once they became available. For the better part of two centuries, the smoothbore, muzzle-loading, flintlock musket was the stock Indian firearm. Modern opinion is sometimes too quick to dismiss these early modern shoulder weapons as crude and ineffective. Indians found them to be marvelous tools for predation, and an absolute necessity for defense against enemy gunmen.

They reached this decision not because the mere sound, flash, and smoke of firearms instilled terror—the supposed psychological effect so often cited to explain why Native people demanded slow-loading, hard-to-maintain muskets when they had perfectly serviceable bows and arrows. Indians adopted firearms because hard experience taught them that lethal wounds followed the pyrotechnics of gunfire, and that warriors outfitted with guns routinely trounced poorly armed rivals in clashes ranging from ambushes, to pitched battles, to sieges. In this the gun never displaced the bow and arrow, hatchet, or club, but it did become an essential part of the Indian arsenal.

For some Natives the gun became an important and even necessary tool for hunting. This was especially the case among deer-hunting peoples east of the Mississippi River and for caribou/moose hunters near Hudson Bay. It took only a generation or two before Indians claimed that their young people had become so accustomed to hunting with these weapons, and so out of practice at using and manufacturing bows and arrows, that they would starve without ammunition and gun-smithing services. Though readers today might view these statements as cynical bargaining ploys, they are often corroborated by archaeolog-ical evidence of Indians hunting game with guns coterminous with a decline in arrowhead production. On the Plains, only a minority of In-dians hunted buffalo with smoothbore muskets, largely because they were so difficult to load on horseback, but in the 1860s they avidly em-ployed breechloaders, repeating rifles, and six-shooter pistols in the chase. The fact that so many different indigenous peoples used guns in their hunting is a testament to their confidence in the efficiency of these weapons, for their purpose certainly was not to scare their prey.

The centrality of guns to Native warfare and hunting made them symbols of Indian manhood, for these were the most basic male respon-sibilities. Men went to war for a variety of reasons. These included the defense or expansion of territory; the seizure of captives for enslavement and adoption; the negotiation of tributary relationships between com-munities; the revenge of insults; the protection of kin from outside ag-gressors; and the plunder of enemy wealth. The people's destiny hinged on these goals, and therefore their cultural practices emphasized war as a foundation of male identity. Almost any man who aspired to social esteem, a favorable marriage, and political influence first had to prove himself as a warrior and hunter. As the weapons market spread, achieving this status required him to become a capable gunman as well. Firearms grew so essential to masculine achievements that, in many times and places, an Indian man was rarely, if ever, seen out on the hunt or on the warpath without a musket and an ammunition bag slung over his shoulder. Wielding guns filled Native men with destructive vigor, em-powering them to kill enemy warriors, seize foreign women and children as captives, overrun their settlements, and loot their treasure. Among the Blackfeet of the northwestern Plains, capturing an enemy warrior's gun became the greatest honor a man could accomplish in battle, which

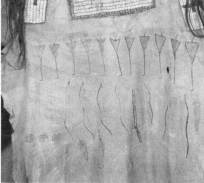

Blackfeet War Shirt. Plains Indian war shirts, particularly among the Blackfeet people, sometimes depicted the martial exploits of the wearer. The center of this particular example contains the painted image of a musket to symbolize the capture of an enemy gun, the highest Blackfeet war honor. The warrior himself would have painted this image, but his wife or another female relative would have prepared and sewed the hide from which the shirt was made. Copyright Pitt Rivers Museum, Oxford University, Ascension No. 1893.67.1.

he then memorialized in ceremony and art. Beyond being able to shoot the weapon accurately, learning to make basic gun repairs and mold lead shot joined the list of things a Native man needed to know. Indians turned firearms into a constituent part of manhood as they conceived of it, and, by extension, basic to the good and ill men brought to the people around them.[12]

It is equally telling of the role guns played in Indian constructions of gender that Native women rarely used firearms, even when their lives were in peril. The general rule was that women gave and sustained life but did not take it. This principle held firm even when the threat of enemy gunmen was imminent and the community at risk had enough resources to put muskets in the hands of adults of both sexes. It did not seem to matter that women faced special dangers from enemy raiders and armies, insofar as Indian war parties usually killed their adult male opponents but marked able-bodied women for forcible adoption or slavery. The only exceptions to this pattern were among groups that permitted biological females who identified as a gender variant "two spirit" to join the men on war and hunting expeditions. Still, such figures were so rare as to prove the rule that Native women did not handle guns. Overall, Indian gun use reinforced conventional definitions of masculinity and femininity.[13]

Indigenous people gave firearms names reflecting their ideas about the weapons' power. For instance, the Narragansett word for gun, *pésckunk,* means "Thunderstick" or "Thunderbolt"; the equivalent Lakota expression, *mázawakan,* is a compound of the terms for metal *(maza)* and lightning *(wakan).* Clearly these peoples associated the noise, flash, smoke, and lethality of guns with some of the most fearsome natural elements and, it followed, their spirits. Many Native North Americans believed that thunder was produced by the flapping wings of a giant bird streaking across the sky. That same Thunderbird shot lightning bolts from its eyes, which then crystalized on the ground into such forms as mica and ancient stone arrowheads. Calling guns Thundersticks or Metal-Lightning was a way of saying that they embodied the awesomeness of the Thunderbird.[14]

At the same time, Native people associated guns with Thunderbird's cosmological analog and rival, the Horned Underwater Serpent or Panther (the Serpent's alter ego). The Thunderbird and Horned Underwater Serpent were locked in everlasting contention, but together they formed a binary that kept their opposite, yet complementary, forces in balance. The Thunderbird inhabited the Sky World, the upper tier of the three layers of the Indian universe. The Horned Underwater Serpent, by contrast, dwelled deep beneath the earth. The Thunderbird carried associations of light, the sun, and life, while the Horned Underwater Serpent connoted darkness, the moon, and death, including success in hunting. The Horned Underwater Serpent protected himself from Thunderbird's talons and lightning bolts by growing horns made of copper and scales made of either flint or copper. Copper, with its red hue, symbolized fire, heat, blood, and animation; flint, as the raw material for arrowheads, connoted the taking of life. In a number of Native societies, experiencing a vision of the Horned Underwater Serpent was a condition for becoming a shaman, a person of spiritual power, which included the ability to implant poisonous charms in another person's body.[15]

For Indians, firearms were a manifestation of the Horned Underwater Serpent as well as the Thunderbird. To wield a gun, with its power to shoot bullets, was akin to the shamanistic ability to penetrate an enemy with lethal objects from afar. Likewise, bullets and gun barrels evoked the Horned Underwater Serpent's metallic scales. The flint of a gun's firing mechanism was another substance used by the Horned Underwater Serpent to defend himself from the Thunderbird. Indians represented these associations in a number of ways besides the names they gave to guns. Most strikingly, their preferences led Europeans and Americans to manufacture trade muskets decorated with a brass side plate of a scaled serpent. This feature first appeared on Dutch guns in the seventeenth century, then became a trademark of weapons commissioned by the British Hudson's Bay Company and North West Company in the eighteenth century, before finally appearing on guns carried by American fur trade firms in the nineteenth century. French firearms manufactured for the Native American market also occasionally contained a version of the serpent side plate. At various points in time it could be found on Indian muskets across the entire continent. Additionally, Indian gun bags and ammunition pouches sometimes carried images of the Horned Underwater Serpent, Thunderbird, or both, with these figures placed on opposite sides of the container to reflect their binary relationship. It was probably no coincidence that Indians were known to favor gun barrels with a blue finish, a color (like black and purple) representing Horned Underwater Serpent/Panther and death. Indians might have made these associations from their very first, terrifying, encounters with firearms. It is critical to remember that they sustained these beliefs because Thundersticks proved to be lethal weapons when put to the test.[16]

———

As Indians' need for munitions grew, they developed political economies to secure their people's supplies of arms and gunsmithing services

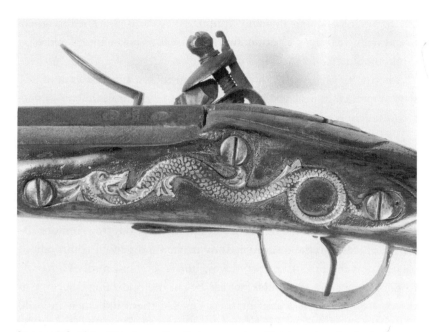

Serpent Side Plate. This decoration first appeared on Dutch muskets for the Indian market in the seventeenth century and eventually became a feature of Indian trade guns manufactured by the British and Americans well into the nineteenth century. The serpent likely appealed to Native buyers as a symbol of death and shamanism, and an allusion to the Thunderbird (the spirit behind thunder and lightning). This example comes from a 1751 Hudson's Bay Company gun in the collections of the Museum of the Fur Trade, Chadron, Nebraska.

and restrict their rivals' access to such essential things. Indigenous political economies of guns followed a common pattern across the continent over the course of 250 years. Repeatedly, Indian polities harvested resources sought by gun suppliers, and then cultivated trade with more than one weapons dealer to ensure dependable flows of munitions at low costs, even in the event of war with the societies of the arms merchants. Indians used their arsenals to cut off indigenous enemies from the arms trade and seize hunting grounds, slaves, and horses from them which could be converted into more guns. Sometimes the Indians' gun dealers hailed from different nations, such as England, France, the Netherlands, or Spain, or different colonies of the same nation, in the case of the English provinces of the Atlantic seaboard. At other times (or simultaneously), munitions came from one or more Native groups playing the role of middlemen between colonial markets and Indians of the interior.

The point of opening so many trade lines was to prevent foreigners from turning the people's dependence on firearms into political and economic weakness.

The multipolar nature of these strategies, and the vast geographic stage on which they played out, is particularly evident in the role of Native middlemen in the munitions trade. Unlike the expansionist powers that tried to monopolize the flow of arms, the middlemen accumulated earnings and allies by trafficking guns to people isolated from the Euro-American arms market. Generally the middlemen came from small communities unable to compete independently with the most formidable tribes and confederacies. They made themselves valuable to these groups by delivering them munitions and other goods from remote colonial sources. On the return trip they carried indigenous commodities such as beaver pelts, otter pelts, slaves, horses, and bison robes for trade to Euro-American merchants, which began the cycle anew. Serving as the conduit between distant markets enabled the middlemen to build political and economic alliances with peoples at both ends of the transaction, thus giving them influence disproportionate to their numbers and military strength. This role also gave middlemen a cut of the profits, thereby enhancing their own ability to purchase foreign weaponry.

Indian polities used commercial and military leverage to shape these relationships to their advantage. They threatened gun dealers that they would take their trade elsewhere unless they received gunsmithing, powder, and shot at reduced prices or even for free. They also required gunrunners who did business with them not to supply their rivals. Traders who bent to these demands often found themselves with customers so loyal that they could be trusted to repay large extensions of credit, even in the absence of a formal legal system to enforce these agreements. By contrast, traders who ignored the Indians' conditions suffered a loss of business, at best, and sometimes the loss of their lives. Such tactics were basic to the intertribal and Indian-colonial weapons economy throughout its lengthy history.

———

The danger for Indians was that American colonies and nation-states exercised their own leverage over the flow of guns and ammunition, albeit within often underappreciated limits. In wartime it was axiomatic for Euro-American governments to ban the arms trade to Indians in hopes of breaking indigenous resistance. After all, Indians never possessed the technological ability to manufacture guns and gunpowder, so in theory it was possible to exhaust their martial stores through economic embargo. This was when the Indians' emphasis on multiple sources of supply became most important. At no point in time did any one colonial or imperial polity control enough of the continent or even one region to cut off Indians completely from guns, powder, and shot. They could and did interfere with Indian supply lines, but never to the extent they wished.

Indeed, the widespread success of Indians at building and maintaining large arsenals of firearms reveals the extent of indigenous economic and political power, the limits of state authority, and the high degree of interdependence between Indians and Euro-Americans. This interdependence stemmed from a number of factors. For one, Indians were the main suppliers to colonists of beaver pelts, otter furs, deerskins, and buffalo robes. The fur trade was central to the economy of nearly every colony in its opening decades, and throughout the existence of some colonies, as in New Netherland, New Sweden, New France, and Russian Alaska. Numerous colonial and early national communities were founded on this trade, including prominent towns such as Montreal, Detroit, Springfield (Massachusetts), Albany (New York), Savannah, St. Louis, and Edmonton, and smaller settlements like Oswego, Niagara, Kaskaskia, Natchez, Natchitoches, and Benton. There were also powerful fur trade enterprises like the Hudson's Bay Company, North West Company, and American Fur Company, with commercial and political networks that stretched into the vast interior of the continent, and influence that reached the upper ranks of colonial and imperial government. Thus, Indians sold valuable resources to weighty interests. What they insisted on receiving in exchange, above all else, were high-quality, low-cost firearms, gunpowder, shot, and gunsmithing services. Indians demanded other types of goods too, particularly woolen blankets, linen, shirts, metal tools, and liquor; in fact, Indians purchased cloth in greater volume and value (determined monetarily) than any other type of commodity. Yet they could make do without manufactured cloth or nonmilitary tools if they had to do so, whereas guns and ammunition became a military necessity, an actual matter of life and death. The

Indians' Euro-American trade partners could either supply these wares or lose their Native customers and risk turning them into enemies.

Indian values and interests determined the protocols of the gun trade and gun diplomacy every bit as much as, and probably more than, those of their European and American counterparts. Indians tolerated colonial trade posts, missions, and even settlements in their territory to the extent that Euro-Americans traded them the goods they wanted, on terms they accepted, and provided political and military support in their affairs with other indigenous people. In many cases Indians framed these relationships in kinship terms, calling the Euro-Americans "brother" when their power was more or less equal and both groups remained politically independent. Brothers were expected to meet each other's material needs and come to each other's aid. When Euro-Americans fell short of these expectations, particularly when they tried to scale back or even sever the Indians' supply of guns and ammunition, or when they suddenly raised prices, Indians took it as a hostile act. To them, changes in the cost of trade goods was a gauge of the state of their relationship with their European trading partner rather than a value-neutral response to supply and demand. Colonial and imperial authorities, knowing all too well the high cost of warring against Indians in terms of lives and treasure, tried to avoid giving unnecessary offense by instituting price controls (or tariffs) over traders, even private ones.

Yet the main concession of Euro-American governments and even major trade firms to Indian demands was to make gifts of guns, powder, shot, and gunsmithing a routine part of their diplomacy with Indians. Oftentimes, presents of these goods and services were so common that powerful Indian groups no longer had to pay for them to any significant degree. In the diplomatic gift economy, the quality, quantity, and timeliness of arms-related gifts became the symbols of the health of the relationship between giver and recipient. Price was taken out of the equation. The fact that Europeans delivered these presents in ritual settings structured by Indian customs of feasting, smoking, dancing, singing, and speeches, reflected the leverage Indians exercised over colonial states even as they needed European guns to defend themselves.

Indians might have grown dependent on firearms, but their dependence on the technology of Europe did not translate into political subservience to particular empires, colonies, or nations. The lengthy condition of interdependence between Indians and Euro-Americans, and the Indians' cultivation of multiple sources of supply beyond the control of any particular government, meant that indigenous peoples' reliance on guns rarely made them captive to a single Euro-American state. Euro-American states were never able to exploit the Indians' need for munitions to force them to cede their land or extradite their people to colonial jurisprudence. What those states could do with varying degrees of effectiveness was reduce, but rarely halt, the arms trade during periods of Indian-colonial warfare and thereby pressure enemy Indians to end their campaigns. Additionally, they could use their trading policies and gift diplomacy to influence Native people toward peace or war with other tribes or colonies and to deliver warriors to imperial military campaigns. That sway was quite significant at times, but it fell short of constituting domination by any reasonable standard. The Indians' dependence on Euro-American weaponry did not make them tools of Euro-American governments.

Euro-American polities, including the United States, always struggled to control the arms trade to Indians. In the founding years of colonies, when they were most vulnerable, and during periods of war with Indian peoples, Euro-American governments typically banned the sale of munitions to Indians, but usually to little effect. There were always traders who refused to honor such restrictions. Most alarming were examples of government officers and military men who turned to the black-market trade with Indians to line their own pockets. The arms trade to Indians was one of the prime examples of American "rogue colonialism," in which colonists of all ranks pursued their own interests, often illegally, in opposition to the directives of central authorities and even against the interests of their neighbors. Government could seem fictional when it was incapable of keeping its own people from providing their enemies with martial stores.[17]

Most Indian nations remained well armed right up to the moment of their subjugation to Euro-American authority. In some instances they wielded better guns and were better shots than the Euro-American forces that confronted them. Though Indians grew dependent on firearms, gunpowder, and shot, that condition never prevented them from rising against Euro-American authority, nor did it become the deciding factor in most of their wars with Euro-Americans. The most common element in the sequential collapse of Indian military resistance to Euro-America was starvation and war-weariness stemming from the enemy's scorched-earth tactics and killing of women, children, and the elderly. Another key factor was their harassment at the hands of other indigenous people who allied with Euro-Americans in the hopes of dealing a blow against their intertribal rivals and gaining supplies of munitions. More generally, Indians lost a numbers game, with their own ranks thinned by repeated bouts of epidemic disease and warfare, while Euro-Americans were strengthened by centuries of high birthrates and large-scale migrations to North America. To the extent that Indians held back this tide, it was in no small part because of, not despite of, their adoption of firearms, a point Crazy Horse and Sitting Bull understood all too well.

———

Our story follows what might be called the "gun frontier," or the opening of indigenous markets to the gun trade, as it spread throughout North America. It pauses occasionally to examine how various Native groups faced the challenge of warring against the same colonial and imperial societies that supplied the bulk of their arms. The term "frontier," in its traditional usage, has fallen out of favor because it suggests that the history of Indian/Euro-American relations involved a triumphalist east-to-west sweep of Anglo-Americans and their institutions. Such a perspective risks compressing the timeline of the Anglo-American rise to dominance, muting the dynamism and importance of indigenous people in their own histories, and ignoring Indian relations with other Europeans elsewhere on the continent. My reference to the gun frontier seeks to disinvest the "f word" of such ideological freight. It conceives of a frontier as a zone of contact in which indigenous people exercised significant and sometimes even disproportionate power and the outcome was uncertain and contested. This kind of frontier involved indigenous people confronting long-distance forces unleashed by colonization, such as epidemic disease, slave raiding, new manufactured goods, or horses, sometimes well in advance of colonial settlement because colonial influences passed along lengthy indigenous networks.[18]

The concept of a gun frontier builds on this perspective to highlight the various means by which firearms reached Native North Americans and the complex ways indigenous people transformed their lives with these weapons. Certainly the Atlantic coast was the strongest base of the arms trade, and in broad strokes the gun frontier tended to move from east to west, but firearms arrived in Indian country from multiple directions along the twisting routes of rivers and ancient pathways. Throughout the eighteenth century, munitions flowed south from the Hudson's Bay Company's base in the Canadian subarctic into the northern Plains and Rocky Mountain regions. Weapons unloaded at French ports on the Gulf of Mexico circulated north, west, and sometimes east, often for hundreds of miles. In a striking reversal of the east-to-west movement associated with the traditional American frontier, during the late eighteenth and early nineteenth centuries shipboard traders sold guns to indigenous people along the Pacific Northwest coast, who then carried these weapons eastward to Natives of the interior. Most Indians in the continental Southwest did not possess guns in significant numbers until the mid- to late nineteenth century, because Spanish policies and economic underdevelopment stifled the arms trade out of colonial New Mexico and Texas. Nevertheless, munitions reached the hands of the Comanches of the southern Plains through their eastern neighbors, the Wichitas of the Arkansas and Red River Valleys, who in turn had obtained them from French, British, and American sources based along the Mississippi. By calling attention to the multivalence of where, when, and how firearms entered Native America, this use of the term "gun frontier" seeks to highlight, not mute, the complexity of indigenous people's experiences with colonialism.

This history of the movement of guns to Native Americans across the continent over the span of more than two centuries demonstrates how indigenous people used guns to reshape their world. This development was one of the essential features of their history with colonialism. Some Indians, for greater or lesser periods of time, used guns to accumulate wealth, power, and honors, which is to say, to become ascendant. Their stories offer an important counterpoint to the long-standing assumption that Indians generally plunged into a downward trajectory of death, land loss, and impoverishment at contact with Euro-Americans. They also challenge the notion that a disadvantage in arms somehow accounts for indigenous people's ultimate subjugation to Euro-American authority. Native economic power, business sense, and political savvy ensured that was not the case. However, it is equally critical to acknowledge that gun-toting Indian groups nearly always arose at the expense of other Natives, sometimes many others. Just as the story of the United States should not be told simply as the triumphant rise of a democratic nation-state of liberty-loving people, neither should the advantages Indians wrested from colonialism overshadow the costs. Perhaps no one grasped that point better than Crazy Horse and Sitting Bull, for whom the surrender of their guns represented the closing of a momentous chapter in their people's history and the ominous start of a new one.[19]

1. LAUNCHING THE INDIAN ARMS RACE

"Allese Rondade! Shoot!"

Everywhere Harmen van den Bogaert went in Iroquois country in the winter of 1634–1635, he encountered Native people shouting the same demand. As perhaps the first person from the colony of New Netherland to venture west of the Mohawks to meet with other Iroquois League (or Haudenosaunee) nations, he had been charged to investigate whether French competition explained a sudden decline in Dutch-Iroquois trade (the actual cause turned out to be a smallpox epidemic). The Iroquois were happy to talk business, particularly to complain about having to travel long distances to Fort Orange (renamed Albany in 1664) only to be greeted with high prices and a meager selection of goods, but most of all they wanted van den Bogaert and his companions to fire their guns. In practically every community he visited, "there were many people here who walked along with us shouting *Allese Rondade,* that is to say, 'Shoot!'" He had tried to put off the crowds, for "we did not want to shoot," apparently out of fear that Iroquois warriors would attack his men as soon as they had emptied their slow-loading muskets. Yet eventually the Dutchman realized that he could not continue to reject his hosts' demands without undermining his mission and even his safety. Finally, on December 30, after a week of equivocating, he and his men capitulated to the public pressure and shot a volley into the air. Now there was no stopping. The following day the Oneidas again prevailed on van den Bogaert to "fire three shots in this evening," which he dedicated to God, Jesus, and the New Year. Little did he know that he was also witnessing the dawn of a new era in the Northeast.[1]

Certainly the Iroquois wanted van den Bogaert to shoot because of their astonishment at the pyrotechnics of gunfire, but they also had more practical matters on their minds. Ever since the Mohawks, Oneidas, Onondagas, Cayugas, and Senecas of what is now upstate New York had formed their League sometime between the fourteenth and late sixteenth centuries, they had been at war with indigenous neighbors near and far. For most of this time the main purpose of these campaigns had been to seize captives for adoption (the fate of most women and children) or death by torture (the fate of adult men) to sustain the Iroquois population and answer the need of mourners for catharsis. Such "mourning wars," as they have come to be known, were probably responsible for the disappearance of large indigenous communities at the sites of modern Quebec and Montreal that had been visited by French explorer Jacques Cartier during his explorations of the Saint Lawrence River during the 1530s and 1540s. Seventy years later, when the French returned to the area to found a permanent colony, there was no trace of them. As European fishermen, explorers, and then fur traders began to appear along the lower Saint Lawrence with greater regularity after the mid–sixteenth century, this warfare also began to focus on controlling access to European goods. The Iroquois appear to have enjoyed the upper hand in these conflicts, at least initially. The common European term for the Haudenosaunee, "Iroquois," might very well derive from a Basque phrase meaning "killer people," in reference to their marauding. But with the founding of French Quebec in 1608, the balance of power had begun to shift to the League's enemies, the Algonquins, Montagnais, and Hurons, because of their trade and military alliance with the newcomers. Most famously, in 1609 French leader Samuel de Champlain and two of his gunmen determined the outcome of an open-field battle between those tribes and the Mohawks by firing into the Mohawk ranks and killing several chief men, producing a rout. Iroquois' calls for van den Bogaert to "*Allese Rondade!* Shoot!" reflected their ambition to acquire this technology themselves and regain the initiative.[2]

Champlain's gunshot has often been held up as a paradigmatic event. The story goes that Europeans blasted their way into the North American woods, overawing Indians with their technological prowess. The Natives, fearful of getting shot, then abandoned their customary open-field clashes in favor of ambushes, to make themselves more difficult targets. The ironic result of the colonists' superiority in arms, then, was the Indians' so-called skulking way of war, which plagued Euro-American society throughout the colonial era. One might call this line of reasoning the Champlain thesis. Missing in this perspective is the fact that early clashes with the French served less to intimidate the Iroquois than captivate them about what they could accomplish with European weaponry. Not until the mid-1620s would a market develop to feed that hunger, but once it did, and particularly once efficient Dutch flintlock muskets became available in the 1630s, League nations began trading for munitions with a fury. By the mid-seventeenth century, this armament had enabled the Iroquois to transform themselves into the preeminent military power of the Northeast and Great Lakes regions as far west as the Mississippi River. Bands of their gunmen fanned out over this range to capture foreign women and children for adoption, sometimes followed by armies of several hundred and even a thousand men to crush the enemy once and for all. Champlain might have fired the first major shot in the eastern woodlands, but it was Iroquois warriors who followed with a hail of lead.[3]

The Champlain thesis obscures that it was the threat of Iroquois, not colonial, gunmen that galvanized an arms race throughout the Native Northeast, involving new technologies, stratagems, and politics. By the mid- to late seventeenth century, arms traders had reached the Five Nations' rivals in the Chesapeake, New England, and the Great Lakes, enabling them to answer the Iroquois musket for musket. In turn, gun violence erupted across this vast geographic zone. The limits of the historical and archaeological records prevent testing the part of the Champlain thesis positing that gun-toting warriors employed ambush more often than the bowmen of earlier times, though it is clear that they favored this tactic. The reason, however, had less to do with fear of enemy firepower than an eagerness to exploit the offensive capabilities of their own weapons. It is also true that indigenous people facing enemy gunmen avoided open-field battles because of the risk of getting shot, and abandoned customary wooden armor because it reduced a warrior's mobility without protecting him against bullets and metal-edge weapons. Yet too much emphasis on the decline in pitched battles can miss the fact that sieges of fortified villages were on the rise because an invading force with an advantage in firearms and steel-cutting tools possessed the means to breach its enemy's defenses. Indigenous people answered this threat by replacing their circular palisades with straight-wall fortifications that gave defensive gunmen clearer shots at attackers. Sometimes they even mounted cannons atop their bastions. Politically, their decision making increasingly focused on securing their people's access to arms and directing arms away from their rivals. To these ends they entered multilateral alliances with shifting lineups of indigenous and colonial polities and even relocated their people closer to gun entrepôts. These innovations constituted a new epoch in Indian life.

The results were terrible, with intertribal wars and related outbreaks of epidemic diseases dramatically reducing the population of nearly every Native group in the region. Some groups were completely wiped out. In the long term, however, the growing balance of power, and recognition of the high cost of gun warfare, produced something of a détente. By the end of the century, people who expected their young men to prove themselves as warriors would have to look outside the region for victims among the poorly armed tribes of the continental interior. As they did, the gun frontier spread with them, leaving a trail of devastation that was becoming a signature of colonialism in indigenous North America.

The Rise of Iroquois Gunmen

The opening of Dutch trade and colonization on the Hudson River gave the Iroquois their counterweight to the French alliance with the tribes of the Saint Lawrence. In 1614, five years after Henry Hudson's famous voyage of exploration, the Dutch erected Fort Nassau, a tiny blockhouse and trade post, on an island near the site of modern-day Albany, just to the east of Mohawk territory and less than ten miles south of the confluence of the Mohawk and Hudson Rivers. Seven years later, in 1621, the West India Company obtained a monopoly of the Dutch Republic's North American Indian trade, spurring the establishment of Fort Orange on the upper Hudson in 1624 and New Amsterdam on Manhattan Island in 1626. Together these settlements formed the colony of New Netherland, the purpose of which was captured in its seal of a beaver surrounded by a string of indigenous wampum beads. Trade with Indians was the purpose of this enterprise. Guns, powder, and shot would soon become bases of that commerce.

Yet it would take another decade to launch the Dutch-Iroquois arms market, a decade in which League nations acquired fresh incentives to war against their neighbors and in which gun technology advanced to meet the needs of Indian users. Politically the 1620s and early 1630s witnessed a renewal of Iroquois warfare against the so-called French Indians (the Algonquins and Montagnais) of the Saint Lawrence River and the Mohicans of the Hudson River Valley. The Five Nations found themselves in a biological war as well. Between 1633 and 1634, smallpox tore through Indian communities along the New England coast and Connecticut River Valley and then up into Iroquoia. The Mohawks alone might have lost two-thirds of their population, with their absolute numbers dropping from an estimated 7,700 to 2,800 people. As the death toll mounted, the cries of mourners built into an irresistible call for the people's warriors to raid their enemies for scalps and captives. Only then would the ghosts of the dead and the hearts of their survivors find peace.[4]

Fortunately for the Iroquois, their Dutch trading partners were able and willing to supply them with Europe's best firearms technology. The Dutch were not only Europe's greatest manufacturing and trading nation, boasting supply lines of raw materials from the Baltic, Mediterranean, and Asia, they were also the continent's main producer and exporter of weapons of every sort, including shoulder arms. The Netherlands' long war for independence from Spain (1569–1648) had stimulated its gun industry, while the demand for military wares elsewhere in Europe during the Thirty Years' War (1618–1648) and subsequent conflicts sustained it into the early eighteenth century. By the time of New Netherland's founding, the Dutch Republic was manufacturing an estimated 14,000 muskets annually, most of them for export, a figure that grew larger by the year. No other European nation came close to this production level until decades later. Furthermore, Dutch gunsmiths were introducing technological innovations to their weapons that made them even more attractive to Indian customers, the Iroquois foremost among them.[5]

Initially Dutch guns came with serious drawbacks, which limited Indian demand for them despite their destructive power. In the 1620s and early 1630s these weapons would have been mostly matchlock muskets. Loading the matchlock was time-consuming and cumbersome, requiring twenty to thirty seconds for a trained hand. It involved using a worm (or metal screw attached to a handle) to clear the barrel of residue from the previous shot; blowing on a wick (or match) treated in saltpeter solution to make sure it was lit; pouring a measure of priming powder into a tiny basin (or pan) on the right-hand base of the barrel and then closing the pan cover; pouring a larger measure of gunpowder into the muzzle, then using a rod to tap down a musket ball nestled in wadding cloth until it rested on top of this charge; and, finally, securing the match in a clamp (or hammer) on top of the gun. Upon completing these steps, actually firing the weapon took only a split second. The gunner flipped open the pan cover and pulled on the gun's trigger to lower the wick into the pan. With this, the priming powder ignited (or flashed), sending a stream of flame through a small opening (the touch hole) between the pan and the barrel, which in turn set off the main charge and shot the musket ball. This weapon was well suited for the wars of Europe fought by massive armies on open battlefields, for it was easier to teach infantry in line formation to fire their matchlocks in unison at a similarly massed force than to train them as archers. Additionally, bullets fired from matchlocks, unlike arrows, could penetrate armor at a distance of up to a hundred yards. For Indians, however, the problem was that the smell and sight of smoke from the match could reveal ambushes and the wick was unreliable in wet weather. Furthermore, loading and firing a matchlock was agonizingly slow compared to shooting a bow and arrow, which would remain true of all guns until repeating breech loaders superseded single-shot muzzle loaders in the nineteenth century. This is not to say that Indians did not want matchlock muskets in lieu of better alternatives, or that Indians did not find ways to use these weapons effectively. The remains of matchlock muskets from archaeological sites indicate that some indigenous warriors learned how to employ them. At the same time, the small number of those parts, and scant mention in the documentary record of Indians wielding these guns, suggests that most Indians judged matchlocks not to be worth their cost.[6]

The weapon used by Champlain against the Mohawks, a wheel lock, redressed these issues with a self-igniting mechanism in which pulling the trigger lowered a hammer containing a piece of pyrite against a rotating serrated wheel, producing sparks that ignited the priming powder and then the main charge in the barrel. Yet wheel lock technology was fragile, prone to clogging with gunpowder residue, and expensive to buy and fix. Consequently, the wheel lock was a weapon of the European elite, not of common soldiers. It was also incompatible with the wear and tear that accompanied the activities of Indian hunters and warriors. Few colonists in the Indian trade included wheel locks in their inventories, to judge from the small number of wheel lock remains in Indian archaeological sites.[7]

The emergence of the flintlock in the 1630s introduced to the Indian market guns that were dependable and relatively easy to maintain. Flintlock technology began with the Dutch snaphaunce in the 1620s, in which pulling the trigger thrust a clamp (or "cock," as the piece looked and functioned like a pecking rooster) holding a piece of flint against a small metal plate (the "steel"), creating a shower of sparks that lit the priming powder and then the main charge. The "true flintlock," which began to appear in Europe in the 1630s, continued the evolution by combining the steel and pan lid (separate pieces in the snaphaunce) into a single "battery," thereby allowing the pan to remain covered (and thus protected from the elements) until the very moment that the flint struck the steel. Whereas gun remains from Mohawk archaeological sites dating from the 1620s and 1630s come from a mix of matchlocks and snaphaunces, by the 1640s the majority of parts derive from "first-quality snaphaunces or flintlocks" that were "up to date even by European standards." Sites from the other Iroquois nations demonstrate a similar pattern.[8]

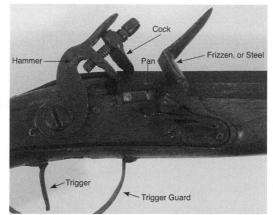

Flintlock Mechanism. Flintlock firing technology, which superseded the matchlock, was the standard on Indian trade guns from the early seventeenth century well into the early 1800s. The Iroquois, supplied by the Dutch, eagerly traded for guns possessing this cutting-edge mechanism from as early as the 1630s. This example comes from a Dutch gun in the collection of the Museum of the Fur Trade, Chadron, Nebraska.

By the 1660s it appears that the Dutch were manufacturing guns specifically for the Indian market, especially the Iroquois. These Indian trade muskets were lighter (about 7.5 pounds) and shorter (50 to 67.5 inches) than most European guns (which often weighed as much as 16 pounds and extended more than five feet in length) in order to facilitate use in the bush and long-distance travel. Some examples included a back-catch (or sear) that kept the firing mechanism at partial cock and allowed warriors and hunters to fire even quicker than normal at moving targets. The Dutch were producing weapons tailored to the needs of their Iroquois trade partners, and it is clear that the Iroquois were eager to buy them.[9]

The primary reason for this demand was that the gun was remarkably effective in Iroquois warfare, particularly as a first-stage weapon in ambush. Small parties of warriors would station themselves at places where enemy travelers were most vulnerable, such as river narrows, portages, bends in the road, or places where cliffs, tree stands, and swamps provided cover for the attackers and blocked the retreat of their targets. The goal in these assaults was to unleash one or two volleys, raise a bloodcurdling war cry, and then rush on the enemy for hand-to-hand combat with tomahawks and clubs. Such ambushes must have been common before the advent of firearms, but the new weapons encouraged the tactic, as the Iroquois demonstrated with lethal efficiency.

The superiority of the gun over the bow and arrow in ambushes was obvious to Iroquois warriors for reasons that included but exceeded the psychological effect of the weapon. Certainly the explosion, flash, and smoke from muskets shocked enemies, temporarily paralyzing them just as their attackers set upon them with hand weapons. Yet firearms had even greater utility than this function. Unlike arrows, which needed a clear path to their target, bullets could pass through the camouflage of tall grasses and even thickets without being diverted. Whereas arrows shot from long distances could be dodged, musket balls could not. The damage inflicted by a bullet wound was far greater than that of an arrow. Killing an enemy with an arrow shot required hitting a vital organ. For the most part, minor arrow injuries would heal with proper treatment, at which Native medical practitioners were masters. By contrast, when a lead ball struck its victim, it carried roughly six times more kinetic energy than an arrow, expanded to the size of a large fist, and left behind a medical disaster of shattered bone, mangled soft tissue, and internal and external bleeding many times greater than an arrow could cause. Even when the victim managed to survive the initial impact, there was a high risk of death by infection. At especially close range, gunners could load their weapons with small shot (or grape shot) consisting of several small lead balls instead of a single bullet. What this approach sacrificed in terms of accuracy and kinetic energy, it compensated for in the large, cloud-shaped area covered by the blast, which could injure and even kill more than one person at a time. Clearly, guns were valuable for far more than their ability to terrify.[10]

The Iroquois further displayed their confidence in guns by using them to hunt deer through the same ambush technique of lying in wait and firing at close range. For instance, one French captive of the Mohawks in the early 1650s told of going out with a hunting party of three men, each of whom carried a musket. Dutch and French accounts from the same period began to emphasize that whereas Indians "used to catch deer only in traps or shoot them with arrows; now they also use guns." No accounts address whether the Iroquois employed guns in their ceremonial deer drives in which hundreds, even thousands, of people would use fire and noise to flush out deer from a large area of woods into a narrow enclosure or stream, where men would be waiting to slaughter them. In individual and small group hunts, however, Iroquois hunters appreciated that a musket ball would drop a deer in its tracks, whereas an arrow wound might require pursuing the wounded game for long distances. The slow rate of reloading and firing a gun was not an issue because a hunter was not going to get the opportunity to fire more than once at a deer before it bounded away, regardless of whether he used a musket or a bow and arrow. Similar considerations influenced the Iroquois decision to employ guns in their ambushes against enemy people.[11]

Firearms had definite shortcomings, which the Iroquois and eventually other Indians mitigated in the novel ways they used these weapons. Certainly seventeenth-century guns were often undependable at distances of more than fifty yards because of a variety of issues; these included the condition of the barrel (such as whether it was bent or dented or clogged with powder residue), the fit of the musket ball to the barrel (sometimes shooters used bullets of smaller caliber, causing them to brush along the inside of the barrel before exiting and thus sending them off-target), and whether the shooter had properly loaded the weapon (particularly the main charge). Yet long-range accuracy was not much of an issue in ambushes in which the unsuspecting enemy was usually just a stone's throw away. Another challenge was that firearms required routine cleaning to prevent them from getting clogged with black powder, which reduced bullet velocity and ran the risk of the barrel bursting, with attendant injuries to the shooter such as burns and mangled fingers and hands. Tending to the maintenance of guns on the trail was difficult unless there were Indian villages, colonial settlements, or trade posts along the way where the warriors were welcome. In the mid-seventeenth century, such issues were probably of minor concern to Iroquois war parties because the raiders usually returned straight home after one or two engagements to deposit their captives, scalps, and plunder, and tend to other responsibilities. By the early eighteenth century, when they were often away for several months at a time on raids against distant peoples, warriors learned to make their own minor fixes and negotiated with colonial authorities to receive blacksmithing services at forts and villages along their route of travel.

During long-running sieges of fortified settlements, the lengthy twenty to thirty seconds it took to fire muskets by conventional European methods was a problem for both attackers and defenders. To reduce this time, Indian gunmen often measured powder by the handful rather than by the canister. They might spit a slug into the barrel from a mouthful of lead bullets or drop in several balls of small caliber without any wadding. Holding the musket upright and knocking the butt against the ground then settled the shot upon the charge without having to use a rod. Next, raising the musket to a horizontal position, tilting it on its side, and giving it a rap, sent powder from the barrel through the touch hole into the pan, thus priming it. The weapon was then ready for firing. This method shaved off precious seconds from reloading, though it also compromised the reliability of the charge and the accuracy of the shot. Native people obviously thought the tradeoff was worth it, for they routinely used these shortcuts in battle when their very lives were at stake.[12]

By the mid- to late 1640s the Iroquois as a whole, and not just the Mohawks closest to Fort Orange, had enough guns to outfit the majority of their adult warriors. Dutch, French, and English sources alike agree that the Mohawks alone, never mind the rest of the Iroquois

League nations, had 300 to 400 guns by this period. Yet this was far from a full accounting of the Iroquois armament. Colonist Symon Groot recalled that when he was working at Fort Orange during the late 1630s and 1640s, the Dutch carried on "a great trade with the Senecas," by which he meant any of the four Iroquois nations west of the Mohawks. The archaeological record agrees. Sites of the Seneca tribe proper dating from the mid- to late seventeenth century are littered with gun-related remains such as firing mechanisms, musket balls, bullet molds, detached musket barrels, cocks, springs, butt plates, and tools manufactured from gun parts. There is also a marked increase of firearms materials at Onondaga sites from these years. Not coincidentally, as early as the 1640s French and Dutch colonists sounded the alarm about Iroquois warriors who used guns "as well as our Europeans" and could even be said to "excel many Christians."[13]

Iroquois men learned not only how to shoot straight, but also how to maintain their guns so they could shoot straight. The Iroquois developed expertise in basic gun maintenance and the manufacture of lead shot and gun flints. Archaeologists have found spare gun parts throughout Mohawk and Seneca sites from the mid-seventeenth century, including a collection at the end of an excavated longhouse suggesting that the Senecas had a tribesman or resident European who specialized in making minor repairs. Additionally, these locations contain bar lead and molds for casting musket balls, stem cutters to round these slugs, and indigenous gunflints crafted by the same lithic techniques as used in the making of stone arrowheads. Neither the Iroquois nor any other Indian nation had the vast mining and industrial infrastructure and engineering knowledge to manufacture firearms and gunpowder, but they did assume some control over the production of gunshot and flints, thereby reducing their need to deal with the Dutch.[14]

It took only a few short years before firearms became a part of Iroquois rituals. By at least 1642 it was Mohawk ceremony to fire salutes at the coming and going of foreign delegates, a courtesy that surrounding nations promptly adopted as well. Volleys in honor of "the Sun" also marked the celebration of military victories. A minority of male burials began to contain grave goods of firearms, powder, shot, and flints for the spirit to carry on the journey to the afterworld. Though this practice never became widespread because the living needed the weaponry, its symbolism was poignant. Firearms had become fundamental to the operation of Iroquois society.[15]

Dutch authorities realized the danger inherent in their arms trade to Indians, but there was little they could do about it because the economy and security of New Netherland depended on the Mohawks in particular, and the Iroquois in general. During the 1630s the colony exported as many as 15,000 furs a year (mostly beaver pelts), including almost 30,000 in 1633, a disproportionate amount of which came from the Iroquois. There were only about 300 people in the colony at the time. According to Dutch sources, New Netherland's arms trade originated in the fur trade outpost of Rensselaerswyck, southwest of Fort Orange, during the late 1630s in response to a Mohawk threat that they would take their furs to New England unless they received guns. The fact that these Mohawks conspicuously displayed English muskets underscored what they said. Another incentive for the Dutch was that the Iroquois "gave everything they had" for firearms, reportedly paying twenty beaver pelts for a single weapon in the early days of this commerce. To put these figures in perspective, whereas muskets cost the Dutch about 12 guilders each, twenty beaver pelts could be sold in Europe for as much as 120 guilders. The trade received an additional boost in 1639 when the ruling Dutch West India Company abandoned its formal, but leaky, monopoly on the fur trade in favor of requiring anyone exporting furs to pay a 10 percent duty on them. The purpose was to increase the company's profits, which were being undercut by smuggling, and to encourage migration to New Netherland. The unintended consequence was a rush into the Indian gun market by nearly every sector of Dutch colonial society, from common farmers all the way up to the director-general (or governor) himself.[16]

New Netherland authorities soon thought better of this trade, at least publicly. An uprising by Munsees on the lower Hudson River in 1643–1645, known as Kieft's War, which almost wiped out colonial settlements around Manhattan, suggested that the Dutch might be signing their own death warrants by arming the Iroquois. At the same time, this war taught the Dutch a countervailing lesson that Indians interpreted weapons bans as hostility. The Munsees' grievances had included the colonists' refusal to trade munitions to them on the same liberal terms that the Mohawks enjoyed. Fearful of the Iroquois but aware that "the trade in contraband goods cannot easily be cut short or forbidden without evident danger of [a] new war," the West India Company tried to have it both ways, decreeing in 1649 that the director-general alone could sell arms to Indians, and only with "a sparing hand." Yet fur traders were simply unwilling to forgo what had become the lifeblood of their business, especially when their superiors failed to lead by example.[17]

Contemporaries denounced an "incredible amount of smuggling and fraud" in New Netherland's weapons trade, and they appear to have been right. Reportedly Director-General Willem Kieft, and then his successor, Peter Stuyvesant, confiscated illegal firearms only to trade them to the Indians on their personal accounts. At the same time Stuyvesant prosecuted lesser officers who followed his lead. In 1648 he arrested the armorer of Fort Amsterdam in Manhattan for selling company guns and gun parts to a pair of private traders, Joost Teunisen and Jacob Reynsen, who in turn had shipped the goods to a pair of merchants at Fort Orange, Jacob and Reynsen Schermerhorn, for exchange with Indians. Smugglers sometimes bribed officials to look the other way—a trade "by contrivance or winking," as the towns of Gravesend and Hempstead on Long Island complained. On other occasions black-market traders disguised enormous shipments of contraband as legitimate cargo. In 1647 a merchant named Westerhowse or Westinghouse was caught bringing in 500 to 600 guns in cases plus 500 pounds of gunpowder hidden in a brandy wine cask. Three years later the directors of New Netherland stopped Wouter van Twiller from importing 600 pounds of lead and 600 pounds of gunpowder for fear "he might make bad use of it" instead of supplying colonists, as he claimed to intend. One Dutch military officer caught trafficking arms to the Indians in 1656 tried to justify his lawbreaking with the old excuse that everyone else was doing it. "So many guns are sold here to the wilden [Indians]," he appealed, and "in the south [probably the Delaware River] they sell [guns] to the wilden by the whole shipment." A widespread but quieter trade with Indians by colonists of small means contributed to the sense that New Netherland was being "overrun" by gunrunners. The weapons trade constituted "the greatest profit" of any commerce in which the colony engaged.[18]

Iroquois military might and commercial leverage meant that their customs shaped trade and diplomacy with the Dutch. The Iroquois expectation was for the Dutch to keep the price of trade goods low regardless of market conditions and for bartering to be preceded by a series of indigenous protocols. To the Iroquois, trade was not an impersonal business transaction in which one side tried to extract maximum profit from the other. They likened commerce to family members meeting each other's needs out of affection and the pursuit of mutual well-being. It followed that political conferences began with an exchange of gifts between leaders, a historic recounting of the two people's relationship, feasting and smoking together and addressing each other as metaphorical kin, all in the Mohawk language. Hard-driving, time-conscious Dutch businessmen and officers would have preferred to dispense with such ceremony but realized they had little choice. Their concessions included accepting that politics with the Iroquois "must be carried on chiefly by means of gunpowder." In 1655 Dutch officers presented the Mohawks with a gift of twenty-five pounds of powder, followed in 1659 by another gift of seventy-five pounds of powder and a hundred pounds of lead. The latter came in response to Iroquois complaints that the Dutch practice of charging them for gun repairs and making them wait too long while the work was done was "unbrotherly." By 1660 Iroquois spokesmen had raised their demands to include the Dutch outfitting League warriors with free powder and lead in times of war.[19]

The Five Nations' favorite point person in commercial and political dealings with the Dutch, Arent van Curler, embodied their principle that "the trade and the peace we take to be one thing." As commissary for his great uncle's patroonship (or manorial estate) of Rensselaerswyck, van Curler engaged in a robust trade of guns and liquor to the Iroquois while also conducting sensitive diplomacy for New Netherland. Eventually he built a house on the so-called Flatts four miles north of Fort Orange, doubtless with an eye toward intercepting Mohawk traders heading south. Moreover, in 1652 van Curler fathered a daughter with an unidentified Mohawk woman, thereby strengthening his own and his colony's trading and political ties with people who conceived of trade and kinship as intertwined. Van Curler's success in the Mohawk trade by conforming to Mohawk rules reflected that it was the Dutch who were dependent on the Iroquois for fur and peace and, in turn, that sustaining a supply of guns, powder, and shot was not a problem

Dutch Trade Gun. This Dutch flintlock is an example of the kind of gun the Iroquois used to become the preeminent military power of the Northeast during the mid-seventeenth century. This artifact might be the only surviving intact Dutch trade gun of the era. It comes from the collection of the Museum of the Fur Trade, Chadron, Nebraska.

for the Iroquois. Iroquois abundance was, however, a lethal dilemma for their enemies.[20]

From the late 1630s well into the 1650s, the Iroquois put Dutch firearms to use in ambushes up and down the Saint Lawrence and Ottawa Rivers connecting New France and Huronia. The usual pattern was for Iroquois armies to break into bands of ten to fifty men and take positions at various points of ambush along the rivers, sometimes on both sides. When enemy boats passed by, or canoeists unloaded at portages, hidden Iroquois gunners would open fire until they had driven their victims to shore, whereupon they would set upon them with hatchets and clubs, killing some and capturing others. One Jesuit put it, "The Iroquois now use firearms, which they buy from the Flemings [Dutch] . . . A single discharge of fifty or sixty arquebuses [muskets] would be sufficient to cause terror to a thousand Hurons who might be going down in company, and make them the prey of a hostile Army lying in wait for them as they pass." In the spring of 1644 alone, ten companies of Iroquois gunmen headed to the Saint Lawrence to lie in wait for their enemies, making the river nearly impassable. The same pattern played out year after year.[21]

In addition to captives, these raids netted the Iroquois plunder in furs that they could then trade to the Dutch for more firearms. In June 1643, for instance, a Huron flotilla of thirteen canoes carrying sixty men and a large supply of beaver pelts came under attack by forty Iroquois musketeers hidden behind trees on Montreal Island, a league west of the French settlement. The Hurons landed their canoes while absorbing gunfire and tried to escape on foot, but the Iroquois managed to capture twenty-three of them plus their canoes and pelts. Attacks like this raise the question of whether plunder motivated Iroquois raiders as much as captive taking and cutting off their enemies from the French trade; European accounts mention them seizing furs in only 10 percent of their riverside ambushes, though this figure certainly understates such cases, probably vastly. The question of how the Iroquois ranked the various goals of these raids cannot be answered with certainty, but the effect of them pirating Huron and Algonquin beaver pelts was to give them more resources with which to build on the arms advantage that netted the booty in the first place.[22]

French Jesuits, from their close vantage living daily alongside the Hurons, were certain that Iroquois superiority in firearms was what made these assaults so lethal. Even when the Hurons, Algonquins, and Montagnais carried guns, Five Nations attackers seemed to possess twice as many. Consequently, the lucky few allied Indians who managed to return from trade missions to Montreal "have come back entirely naked, or pierced with arquebus [musket] balls, after having escaped seven or eight times from the hands and the cruelties of those barbarians." Father Jérôme Lalement bemoaned, "Our sharpest thorn is, that the enemies of [our] tribes have the advantage over them through the arquebuses [muskets] that they obtain from certain Europeans." By the early 1640s, Iroquois attacks had nearly choked off the French fur trade to the point that some Frenchmen began lobbying for an invasion of New Netherland to punish Dutch gun merchants.[23]

In the meantime the French settled for the more tepid response of rewarding baptized Indians with presents of guns and the opportunity to trade for more. Everyone agreed that this policy was a powerful attraction to win Indians to Catholicism and critical to organizing Huron defenses against the Iroquois. Even then, the French limited the amount of weaponry available to Native neophytes because they were reluctant to surrender their military advantage to a much larger indigenous population whose loyalties they still doubted. "We have always been afraid to arm the Savages too much," bemoaned Father Paul Le Jeune in 1641. "Would to God that the Hollanders had done the same, and had not compelled us to give arms even to our Christians."[24]

Throughout the late 1630s and early 1640s, the Hurons redesigned their forts to give their meager force of gunmen a fighting chance against an Iroquois invasion that seemed to grow more imminent by the day. The village of Ossossane erected a squared palisade with bastions at opposite corners to permit clear shots along two entire lengths of the walls. Other communities followed with diamond-shaped fortifications. The reason, as Father Jean de Brébeuf put it, was that "we have told them . . . henceforth, they should make their forts square, and arrange their stakes in straight lines; and that, by means of four little towers at the four corners, four Frenchmen might easily with their arquebuses or muskets defend a whole village."[25]

That hope was ill-placed. Beginning in the summer of 1648 and lasting into late 1649, Iroquois armies of up to 1,000 men invaded Huronia repeatedly, overrunning the forts, torching the communities, and killing and capturing thousands of people. Battered, demoralized, and starving, the remaining Hurons scattered in all directions. Some retreated northwest to the Straits of Mackinac and Green Bay, and others eastward to the protection of French guns near Quebec or even to Iroquoia to join their captive relatives. Those who sought refuge among the Hurons' close neighbors to the west, the Tionnontatés, absorbed yet another blow in December 1649, as 300 Iroquois warriors struck the village of Etharita or St. Jean, killing and capturing a large but indeterminate number of people. It had taken less than two years for the Iroquois to conquer one of the largest Indian confederacies in North America.[26]

Muskets were critical to the Iroquois victory. First and foremost, years of ambushes by Iroquois gunmen had set the stage for the invasion by making the Hurons prisoners in their own towns, too afraid to venture beyond their fortified walls to patrol their country, raise food, or protect their confederates, at least not to any effective degree. By the time the invasion began, Iroquois bands moved almost freely throughout Huronia. As for the campaign itself, the thousand-man force that devastated Huron country in 1649 was reportedly "well furnished with weapons,—and mostly with firearms, which they obtain from the Dutch, their allies." By contrast, the Hurons were poorly armed, to which at least one Jesuit directly attributed their defeat. With the Jesuits having watched their charges and colleagues die in heaps from gunshot wounds, it was difficult to conclude otherwise. The Hurons reached the same judgment, demanding the Jesuits to "speak to the Captain of France, and tell him that the Dutch of these coasts are causing our destruction, by

37

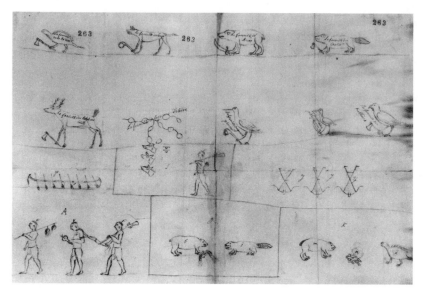

Iroquois Captive March. The lower left portion of this French drawing, circa 1666, depicts two Iroquois warriors with a captive warrior in tow. The captive is bound by a collar and leather cords. He carries a gourd rattle with which to sing his death song. The captor in front carries a pole with two scalps hanging from it. The captor in back wields a flintlock musket, the weapon that permitted the Iroquois to seize thousands of captives from other indigenous peoples throughout the seventeenth century. Courtesy Bridgeman Art Library.

furnishing firearms in abundance, and at low price, to the Iroquois, our enemies."[27]

During the early 1650s the Iroquois also rode their advantage in guns to a series of victories over the remaining tribes of the eastern Great Lakes, most of which harbored displaced Hurons. In quick succession the Iroquois shattered the Petuns in 1650 and the Neutrals in 1651, the latter with an invasion of 1,500 men. Their next target, beginning in 1653–1654, was the Eries (or Cats), a people some 2,000 strong. As they did with the Hurons and Neutrals, the Iroquois systematically broke down the Eries' perimeter with gunfire ambushes to prepare for a large-scale invasion. The Eries, who had "no firearms," nevertheless had a fearsome reputation because of their arsenal of poison arrows, which they could fire "eight or ten times before a musket can be loaded." The Iroquois neutralized this weapon during their sieges of Erie forts with a combination of thick wooden shields (or mantlets), large portable wooden walls, and even canoes, which they carried over their heads to approach enemy fortifications, then used as ladders to scale the palisades. Collectively these campaigns had netted the Iroquois thousands of captives, produced the deaths of thousands of others, and effectively cleared the region of rival nations.[28]

Balancing the Scales

The Five Nations' neighbors and rivals to the south and east, particularly the Susquehannocks of the Susquehanna River Valley, the Mohicans of the Hudson and Housatonic River Valleys, and the so-called River Tribes of the Connecticut Valley (Pocumtucks, Norridgewoks, and Squakheags), learned the lesson before it was too late and built up arsenals that gradually tipped the scales away from the Iroquois. Like the Hurons, Algonquins, and Montagnais, these groups had a long history of conflict with the League. The Susquehannocks, for example, appear to have trafficked shells from Chesapeake Bay to the Iroquois throughout much of the sixteenth century, but the relationship went sour at some point in the late sixteenth and early seventeenth centuries, which is to say, just as European traders began to appear on the east coast. The Susquehannocks then withdrew from the upper Susquehanna River Valley on the southern flank of Iroquoia and relocated first to the upper Potomac River Valley and then to the lower Susquehanna in what is now Lancaster County, Pennsylvania. These new sites provided the Susquehannocks not only with a buffer against Iroquois attack but also with easy access to the Chesapeake Bay and Delaware River, which were about to become some of the greatest gun marts in eastern America.[29]

The Susquehannocks were among the first groups to answer the Iroquois gun for gun, largely because they had access to traders at a variety of locations, beginning with the Chesapeake. English shipboard merchants were active all along the bay within years of the founding of Jamestown in 1607. By 1631 Virginian William Claiborne had established a year-round trading post on Kent Island, by water just seventy-five miles south of the main Susquehannock fort on the Susquehanna River. This establishment did a substantial amount of business, taking in 7,500 pounds in weight of beaver pelts in just three years, and in exchange it supplied the Susquehannocks with guns, powder, shot, and smithing services. Yet in the late 1630s the recently founded colony of Maryland asserted its jurisdiction by shutting down Claiborne's enterprise on Kent Island and then a second Claiborne outfit on Palmer's Island at the mouth of the Susquehanna. No one in the Maryland leadership seemed to realize that they could not capture Claiborne's trade by hijacking his posts, not as long as the Susquehannocks considered him to be a friend.[30]

In protest the Susquehannocks rebuffed Maryland's overtures and took their business east to the Delaware River, which was becoming the site of a cutthroat multinational competition for Indian furs. In 1624 the Dutch West India Company established a short-lived trading post, Fort Nassau, on the Delaware River, at the site of modern Gloucester, New Jersey, 120 miles east of the main Susquehannock settlements. Though the Lenape (or Delaware) Indians of the lower Delaware River initially contested Susquehannock trade in their territory, after some clashes they appear to have conceded their western neighbors' right of access. European interests then began vying to dominate this market. By 1638 Swedes were on the Delaware too, establishing Fort Christiana on the site of modern Wilmington, from which they launched their own trade-post building campaign. Eventually the Swedes and Dutch found themselves elbow to elbow on the Schuylkill River, near the site of modern Philadelphia, with the Swedes going so far as to construct their store barely twelve feet in front of the rival Dutch establishment to block its visibility from the water. In short time the English joined the fray. Merchants from the colony of New Haven first tried to form a settlement on the lower Delaware, and then, after Swedish and Dutch opposition foiled the attempt, began making periodic trading voyages up the river. Prime anchorages were at a premium, however, because rival ships based out of Maryland, Virginia, and even Amsterdam proper were also on the river each trading season. New Sweden, always woefully undersupplied by its parent company, ultimately found its niche as a middleman for the floating warehouses, which had ample supplies of arms, wampum, and cloth, but no ties to the fur-rich Susquehannocks. Clearly, Susquehannocks seeking firearms and ammunition were not lacking for options.[31]

Such competition all but guaranteed a favorable arms trade for Indians, which each European nation accused the others of starting.

Maryland authorities even charged the Dutch with encouraging Susquehannock depredations along the Chesapeake as a way of drumming up additional demand for their munitions. Yet even when colonial magistrates actually tried to police the flow of arms (or at least claimed to try), they confronted the limits of their authority on the Delaware. After the Dutch conquered New Sweden in 1655, Swedish gunrunners shifted from English to Dutch suppliers, then carried the weapons inland to Susquehannock country for sale, far from inspectors stationed along the river. The Delaware was an even greater river of rogues than was the Hudson.[32]

The real blame or credit for the renegade character of the Delaware Valley gun frontier belonged to the Indians themselves, who exploited the competition at every opportunity. In 1647 the Susquehannocks goaded Dutch traders by telling them that Swedish governor Printz had said "he could sell them powder, lead, and guns enough, but the Netherlanders, being poor, tattered nations, could not do so." Three years later the Dutch commissary on the Delaware apologized to his superiors for giving a Susquehannock delegation a present of arms and ammunition, contrary to orders. He knew that such actions "will earn blame for me and the Company," but he protested that "it could not be helped this time" because the Susquehannocks had claimed that their people's loyalties were divided between the Swedes and the Dutch and whichever side offered arms on the best terms would determine the outcome. Meanwhile, the Susquehannocks demanded that the Swedes provide them with gunsmiths, French flintlocks instead of Swedish matchlocks, and leather bandoleers to hold powder charges. The Lenapes squeezed the Swedes by making peace contingent on presents of trade goods, which they then carried to the Susquehannocks to trade for beaver pelts and deerskins, only to bring their haul to Dutch Manhattan, where they fetched better prices than at Fort Christiana. All this "before our eyes," exclaimed Swedish governor Johan Rising.[33]

The Susquehannocks also built up their arsenal through war, diplomacy, and eventually trade with Maryland. Lord Baltimore's colony engaged in intermittent hostilities with the Susquehannocks throughout the late 1630s into the 1650s over Maryland's treatment of Claiborne and its protection of Susquehannock enemies like the Piscataways and Nanticokes of Chesapeake Bay. The Susquehannocks' raids against outlying Maryland plantations netted them plunder in guns, powder, and shot, as in 1641 when their warriors attacked the Patuxent River house and trading factory of John Augwood (or Augud), killing Augwood and some of his men and pillaging his arms and ammunition, probably as revenge for him provisioning their indigenous rivals. After several false starts, Maryland appears to have responded by sending armed expeditions against the Susquehannocks in the summers of 1643 and 1644 (the records are quite vague), only to have the second force come under fire by Susquehannock gunmen hiding in a cover of reeds, likely using some of the very guns seized from Augwood's storehouse. To add insult to injury, the Susquehannocks captured two of the Marylanders' artillery pieces and then mounted them atop their riverside fort, "with which they shoot and defend themselves."[34]

By 1652, however, a changing political landscape encouraged rapprochement between the Susquehannocks and Maryland. For one thing, the colony was temporarily under the leadership of a Protestant faction made up of close associates of their old friend Claiborne. Furthermore, the Susquehannocks were more desperate than ever to secure military hardware, as Five Nations raiders had targeted them from 1652 until 1654 in between campaigns in the Niagara River Valley and Ontario peninsula. Most importantly, the Iroquois had emerged as enemies of Maryland too, once Seneca and Oneida warriors had begun to target Maryland's Indian protectorates (perhaps at the instigation of Susquehannock adoptees), with collateral damage to nearby English farms. Viewing the Susquehannocks as the best line of defense against Iroquois aggression, Maryland stationed fifty soldiers in the Susquehannocks' fort, furnished the Susquehannocks with powder, lead, and two more artillery pieces, and helped them redesign their palisade to maximize their growing firepower. Whereas the Susquehannocks formerly built their enclosures in a circular shape, their new fort, like those of the Hurons, contained straight walls flanked with "two bastions erected in the European manner" to give Susquehannock gunners clear shots at their besiegers. Maryland also opened a new Susquehannock trade post near Palmer's Island run by Jacob Claeson (or Clawson, also known to the English as Jacob Young), a Dutchman with some Susquehannock language skills and a close relationship with the Susquehannock leader, Wastahanda-Harignera. Maryland had concluded that it was more politic and profitable to seek alliance with the Susquehannocks through the arms trade than to continue trying to resist them. It was the Susquehannocks, not any colonial polity, who were the most formidable power in this region. Given the Susquehannocks' many options when it came to obtaining European wares, weak colonies like Maryland had the choice to supply them with guns or face their guns. The Susquehannocks, for their part, placed newfound value on Maryland as a trade partner, having lost New Sweden to Dutch conquest in 1655. Peace with the Chesapeake colony was a means of keeping their trade options open.[35]

Thus, the Susquehannocks were well prepared by the time the western Iroquois nations turned their raids back against them in the early 1660s. Though the Mohawks and Susquehannocks remained at peace during these years, perhaps because neither of them wanted to imperil their relations with the Dutch (who counted both groups as fur trading partners), the western Iroquois had no such scruples. Their populations (and the Susquehannocks') had suffered enormously from a recent smallpox epidemic, and, following the destruction of the Lake Erie and Ontario peninsula tribes, there were no major Iroquoian-speaking peoples left to raid for replacements other than the Susquehannocks. The western Iroquois' campaign began in May 1663, when a mostly Seneca force of 800 men marched 300 miles south to lay siege to the great Susquehannock fortress on the northeast bank of the Susquehanna River, a few miles south of modern Columbia, Pennsylvania. This was the same kind of large-scale invasion that had served the Iroquois so well in the recent past, except now the Iroquois lacked an advantage in arms. Confronted with a redesigned Susquehannock palisade defended by cannons and plenty of gunmen, the Senecas abandoned their hope of capturing the fort and then failed to lure Susquehannock warriors outside into an ambush. The Susquehannocks emerged only when they spied the advantage, forcing their attackers to retreat to Iroquoia empty-handed. With another Iroquois attack expected in August 1663, Maryland strengthened the Susquehannocks' defenses even further with a July gift of two barrels of gunpowder, 200 pounds of lead shot, another cannon, and four colonists to man the fort's big guns. The Hurons could only have wished for such resources from the French when they had faced the Five Nations' invasion of their country.[36]

The Five Nations' Algonquian-speaking rivals to the east, the Mohicans of the Hudson and Housatonic River Valleys and the Sokokis of the Connecticut River, also began to close the arms gap through multilateral trade. Dutch Fort Orange, with its brisk market in arms and ammunition, anchored this commerce in the western portion of the Algonquins' territory. To the north were the French on the Saint Lawrence, who, after witnessing the Iroquois dispatch the Hurons in the 1640s, opened up the gun market to Christian and non-Christian Indians alike. The Abenakis of what is now Vermont exploited this policy to become middlemen between the French on the Saint Lawrence and the Connecticut River tribes. Farther south were a range of options. The Dutch were active on the lower Connecticut River intermittently as early as the 1620s, and between 1633 and 1653 they operated a small, permanent post known as the House of Good Hope, even as it became enveloped by the English town of Hartford. During the mid-1630s it faced competition from a trading station Plymouth colony ran just a few miles to the north, on the site of what became the town of Windsor. More significantly, in 1636 William Pynchon founded the town of Springfield in the mid-Connecticut River Valley, from which his family not only managed a licensed trade house but subcontracted to seven itinerant traders, who ventured out into Indian country to intercept furs before they reached competitors. The New England colonies had strict laws against gunrunning during this period, and the Pynchons' account books contain no record of them having violated these restrictions, but it is doubtful that the family's associated traders could have competed to the extent they did (the Pynchons brought in 9,000 beaver pelts between 1652 and 1658) without dealing in arms. There were certainly plenty of Dutch smugglers in the neighborhood to supply them. The lack of a historic record of such activity is probably a reflection of its illegality rather than of its nonexistence.[37]

This multifront gun frontier set the stage for a failed Iroquois attack on a Sokoki fort at Fort Hill at the site of modern Hinsdale, New Hampshire, in December 1663, just months after the Susquehannocks repulsed the Senecas. From the safety of their palisade, Sokoki gunmen warded off a daybreak assault by the Iroquois, including extinguishing a fire the Iroquois had set to the enclosure with a rudimentary bomb comprised of a lit bag of gunpowder. Ultimately the invaders decided to retreat after suffering a hundred or more casualties. It was their second major setback in just a matter of months at the hands of enemies who had caught up to them in the regional arms race.[38]

Emboldened by their arsenals, the Five Nations' enemies began launching their own expeditions into Iroquoia from the south and east, and setting ambushes along Lake Champlain, which was the Mohawks' outlet to the north and east. Conditions in Iroquoia grew so dire that the Senecas felt compelled to organize caravans as large as 600 people in order to make it safely to Fort Orange, even though the route went exclusively through League territory. They had good reason to worry. Sometime in 1668–1669 a Mohican force lurking outside a Mohawk fort killed a hundred of the inhabitants when they exited the walls in the morning to tend to their fields. Most of the victims would have been women and children. The Five Nations' own tactics against the Hurons were coming back to haunt them.[39]

To be sure, League warriors gave as well as they got in their conflict with the New England tribes, even as the fight spread into Iroquoia. Relentless pressure from Iroquois war parties forced the Sokokis to abandon their fort in the winter of 1663 and disperse among their allies. Then in the fall of 1664 or winter of 1664–1665 a massive Iroquois army fell on the Pocumtucks' stronghold and scattered that people too, removing the last major obstacle to Five Nations' forays east of the Connecticut River. By the following spring, the Mohawks were raiding Christian Indians in eastern Massachusetts and Wabanakis in Maine. Boston-area colonists described Mohawk warriors they encountered as "stout and lusty young men, and well armed . . . for they had every one of them a firelock [flintlock] gun [or musket, for long-distance firing], a pistol [for close combat], a helved hatchet, a long knife hanging about their necks, and every one had his pack, or knapsack, well furnished with powder and bullets, and other necessaries." No wonder the name "Maqua" (Mohawk) became a cry of terror among the Christian Indians during these years.[40]

However, ongoing ambushes by Iroquois enemies around the periphery of Five Nations territory had made Iroquoia vulnerable to invasion in much the same way as Iroquois warriors had once broken down the Hurons' defenses. A striking symbol of the shifting balance of power was the Algonquins' August 1669 assault against the fortified Mohawk

45

town of Gandaouagué. The Algonquin force, made up of over 300 heavily armed men from the Mohicans, several Christian Indian communities in Massachusetts, and probably the Connecticut River Indians, was able to march unhindered right into Mohawk country by virtue of earlier raids along the eastern approach. The battle for Gandaouagué was, according to French and English accounts, a firefight in which the Algonquins initially inflicted heavy losses on the Mohawks, beginning with "so furious a discharge of musketry that the balls, piercing both the stockade and cabins, awakened men, women, and children." Yet after two hours of fighting, and failing to breach the walls, the attackers began running short of gunpowder, whereupon they lifted the siege and retreated eastward toward the Hudson. At this the Mohawks rallied, tracking the Algonquins to their nighttime camp just west of the river and then flanking them in order to lay an ambush at "a very advantageous spot, from which all the road leading toward the Dutch was commanded." They struck in the morning shortly after the enemy took to the trail. The first Mohawk volley, described as a "shower of balls," dropped numerous Algonquins—perhaps dozens—followed by another firefight with heavy losses on both sides. By the end of the engagement, some fifty Algonquins and forty Mohawks lay dead. Historians have characterized this battle as a Mohawk victory, but the Mohawks themselves were less sanguine. As their resident Jesuit realized, "these wars weaken the Agnieronnon [Mohawks] terribly; and even his victories, which always cost him bloodshed, contribute not a little to exhaust him." Without the advantage in firearms, the Iroquois no longer enjoyed the lopsided victories they had come to expect and that were their measure of a successful campaign. There was little purpose in raiding foreigners for captives to buttress the League's population if that meant losing large numbers of valuable fighting men along the way and inviting reprisals on the home front.[41]

The Five Nations' French and Indian enemies to the north and west were building up their arsenals, too, after decades of suffering the attacks of Iroquois gunmen. Not only had the French loosened their restrictions on the weapons trade, but they began to manufacture their own gun for the Indian market to answer the light, durable arms of the Dutch. It was probably no coincidence that in the spring of 1662 the Ojibwas decimated a hundred-man Mohawk-Oneida war party on the southern shore of Lake Superior. The French crown added to the pressure on the Iroquois by seizing direct control of New France in 1663 and then sending 1,000 troops of the storied Carignan-Salières Regiment with the charge to "exterminate" the Five Nations. It took until the fall of 1666 to put the massive campaign in motion, and even then the French and their Indian allies managed to kill only a few people and had to be satisfied with plundering and burning Mohawk towns. Yet the Five Nations had received another harsh notice that they could be struck in Iroquoia by enemies who had caught up in the regional arms race.[42]

Even in advance of this invasion, most Iroquois leaders had concluded that they needed to end their exhausting, decades-long conflict with the French and their indigenous allies so they could open another supply line of munitions and focus their energies on their buckling southern and eastern frontiers. Indeed, some of them feared that their rivals now had the advantage in military resources. In 1664, a year after the Five Nations' failed attacks against the Susquehannock and Sokoki forts, the Senecas reached out to the French with a request to "surround their Villages with flanked palisades, and furnish them with the munitions of war," just as Maryland did for the Susquehannocks. The next year an Onondaga delegation led by the sachem Garacontié offered to host a Jesuit mission in exchange for Quebec providing them with a gunsmith gratis (the Iroquois had been complaining to the Dutch for years about charging them for smithing services) and a surgeon to tend to gunshot wounds. As the Iroquois told Pierre-Esprit Radisson, a fur trader and one-time captive of the Mohawks, the French "should have given us [guns to] kill the Algonquins," for if they had, it would have brought peace and mutually beneficial commerce. Now was the time to set things right between the people. The Dutch were no longer a diplomatic option, for in September 1664 the English made a bloodless conquest of New Netherland and renamed it New York. Dutch merchants remained in control of Albany for many decades to come, and there is no evidence that the change in flags seriously interrupted shipments of supplies of arms and ammunition from Europe. Yet it would take several years for the Iroquois to develop a relationship with the new English authority in which they could leverage the kind of formal armed assistance they were now seeking. In the interim even the Mohawks joined the other

47

League nations in agreeing to host French Jesuit missionaries and allow Catholic Iroquois to relocate to new Christian Indian towns near Montreal. At the same time, the Mohawks prepared, in case peace negotiations with New France and its Indian allies failed, by purchasing from Albany two swivel guns (which could fire three pounds of shot each) and redesigning their palisades with straight perimeters. The end of the Iroquois' superiority in arms required a new politics.[43]

The Outer Edge of the Gun Frontier

The Five Nations' truce with the French and their indigenous allies achieved the immediate goal of permitting League warriors to concentrate on their southern and eastern flanks. Despite suffering five epidemics between 1668 and 1682 and losing some 2,200 people, the Five Nations' forcible adoption of captives permitted them to man a steady stream of war parties against the Susquehannocks, who appear to have suffered even worse from these diseases. By the mid-1670s the Susquehannocks had retreated to the Potomac River, where in 1676 they wound up fighting a war against Virginia and Maryland that served as the last blow to their status as a distinct people. A few years later, mutual exhaustion and political pressure from New York led to peace between the Iroquois and the New England Algonquins. Five Nations warriors in search of captives, plunder, and glory now had to pursue their ambitions elsewhere.[44]

One of those directions was westward against the Algonquian-speaking Miamis and Shawnees of the Ohio River Valley and the Illinois of the upper Mississippi River Valley, to take advantage of those people's weak armament. Father Jacques Marquette and fur trader Louis Joliet, in their explorations of the region, judged that the Shawnees remaining in Ohio (many of them had already left for the Savannah River) were "a very harmless people" whom the Iroquois harassed "without any provocation, because they have no firearms, and carrying them into captivity." The Illinois, who considered themselves to be "more expert in the use of bows and arrows than the Iroquois," agreed that it was the Five Nations' superiority in munitions that made them so bold. That advantage was stark indeed. Father Jean de Lamberville's best guess, from his perspective as a missionary among the Onondagas in 1682, was that the Iroquois boasted "nine hundred men armed with muskets" and "have never had a larger store of weapons and munitions of war than they have this year"; French governor Frontenac put the number even higher, estimating that the Senecas alone had "fifteen hundred warriors, well armed." By contrast, the Illinois had few muskets and barely enough powder and shot for those, most of which they obtained from Great Lakes tribes such as the Ottawas rather than directly from the French. In what would soon become a common pattern farther to the south, this trade involved the Illinois sending their few gunmen to seize captives from tribes to the west who were even more poorly armed than they were, and then, in exchange for munitions, giving the Ottawas those captives for eventual sale into slavery among the French. However, the volume was not enough for the Illinois to equip themselves sufficiently against the Iroquois.[45]

The Iroquois aimed to keep it that way. In the late 1670s and early 1680s their warriors repeatedly waylaid and plundered French traders who attempted to reach the Illinois directly. As the Onondaga spokesman Otreiouti (the French called him Grangula, or "Big Mouth") explained to New France's governor Joseph-Antoine Le Febvre de La Barre, his people would not tolerate anyone "who supplied the Illinese [Illinois] and Oumamis [Miamis] (our Enemies) with Powder and Ball." It took until the mid- to late 1680s for the French to provide adequate defenses for their canoe convoys to Illinois country, by which time the Illinois had already suffered devastation at the end of Iroquois guns. In September 1680 the Iroquois successfully intimidated the Miamis into joining them against the Illinois, creating an army reportedly 900 men strong, "all Fusiliers [or gunmen]; these two nations being well provided with Guns and all sort of ammunitions of war." This force inflicted steep losses on an Illinois army and overran the town of Tamaroa to seize an estimated 800 captives. Some Iroquois warriors remained in the area for several more months, raiding up and down the Mississippi and even west of the great river. The following year the Fox Indians of southern Michigan and Wisconsin told some Frenchmen out hunting bear that they were terrified at the sound of the gun, not because of the noise itself, but "knowing that none of the neighbors use Fire Arms, they thought we were a party of Iroquois, and were come with a design to murder them." Guns, the Iroquois, and murder went together in the minds of Indians throughout the region.[46]

The Iroquois also redirected their attacks southward along the Great Warrior Path running along the east side of the Appalachian Mountains into the Virginia and Carolina Piedmont, which was another place their weaponry gave them an advantage. To some degree these attacks were an extension of their wars in the eastern Great Lakes and Ohio River Valley, as they sometimes targeted Eries (soon to be known in the Southeast as Westos) and a group of Shawnees (or Savannahs) who had migrated to the south and west. Eventually their circle of targets grew to include the Cherokees of southern Appalachia, the Catawbas of the Piedmont, and other groups ever farther afield. There were several reasons for this shift. Certainly the Iroquois wanted their raids for captives to avoid poisoning relations with New France and northeastern English colonies, as had so often been the case during the 1660s. Also they were pulled southward by their adoptees from the Susquehannocks, Shawnees, and various Maryland and Virginia tribes. Each time Iroquois warriors ventured south, they risked armed encounters with area tribes that could easily descend into a cycle of revenge warfare. Yet too often one of the most important factors has been overlooked: the southern Indians' weak armament, the same kind of consideration that influenced League attacks in Illinois country. Elsewhere the cost of victory had become too great.[47]

———

By the turn of the century the Iroquois found themselves in the same predicament that had plagued them in the 1660s. Once again their enemies had caught up in the regional arms race, with the French outfitting nations in the western Great Lakes with 700 to 1,000 guns a year, and the southern nations accumulating munitions through the trade of indigenous slaves and deerskins to South Carolina and Virginia. Iroquois deaths mounted in turn. Renewed warfare against New France, extending largely from Iroquois attempts to keep French arms out of the Illinois country, proved even less successful than in the recent past. In 1687, 1693, and 1696 the French and their Indian allies subjected Iroquoia to scorched-earth campaigns, which, though claiming few lives directly, produced famine after famine. The people could not endure this pressure indefinitely. It was time to seek security through diplomacy, not war.[48]

The time was ripe for such an approach because the onset of more than a century of imperial warfare between France and England encouraged the empires to compete for Iroquois favor to seize the strategic initiative. The Iroquois, in turn, took advantage of their newfound leverage to extract concessions from both sides. One might call the Natives' political strategy the play-off system, in the sense that they played one rival imperial power off of the other by exploiting its fear that they would throw their support to the enemy. In 1701, for instance, Iroquois leaders pledged neutrality in all future conflicts between the English and French, all the while dropping hints to both sides that their loyalty could be bought. It is debatable whether this multilateral diplomacy was coordinated or an unintentional by-product of decentralization and factionalism. Regardless, the benefits soon became apparent. In 1724 the Onondagas granted the English permission to build a trade post, Fort Oswego, on the southern shore of Lake Ontario as a counterweight to French Fort Niagara in Seneca territory. A quieter, parallel development involved Iroquois from the Saint Lawrence missions smuggling goods between Anglo-Dutch Albany and French Montreal, as well as trading their own furs in both towns, thereby asserting their right to deal with whomever they chose, regardless of imperial claims. Farsighted Iroquois leaders were setting up a means for their people to remain well armed even as their military and economic leverage declined from the heights of the mid-seventeenth century.[49]

This arrangement opened up a brisk diplomatic market in arms and gunsmithing for Indians throughout the Northeast. English and French fur trade posts alike offered free or subsidized smithing to Indian allies and gifts of powder and shot to traveling hunters. New York and New France also paid for gunsmiths to reside in Iroquois villages in the houses of Iroquois leaders, who saw these arrangements as a means to enhance their chiefly influence over young warriors. Sometimes smiths bid against one another to take the job for free, willingly sacrificing a guaranteed salary for a chance to trade from within Iroquois villages. Imperial officers promised Native leaders, "We should provide them . . . with a Blacksmith and a Gunsmith to mend their guns, axes, etc." whenever they wanted approval to build military posts in Indian country. In all likelihood Indians' free access to gunsmiths is what accounts for their almost complete lack of interest in learning the smithing trade, at least as far as one can tell from the documentary record. Furthermore, they could plainly see that this complimentary service was an acknowledgment by colonial authorities of their importance, something they would have been loath to give up. They also appreciated the free munitions. English authorities in New York, advised and often represented by Dutch Albany merchants, accepted that their meetings with Iroquois leaders would have to include lavish gifts of muskets, powder, and shot, in addition to other goods. The colony's gifts to the Iroquois in 1693 included a July installation of ninety guns, 810 pounds of gunpowder, 800 bars of lead, and 1,000 flints, and another present two months later of fifty-seven guns, 1,000 pounds of gunpowder, and 2,000 pounds of lead. Two hundred pounds of powder and lead followed in 1699, and 400 light guns in 1700. Gifts of this sort became so common that Five Nations warriors seem to have obtained a sizable portion of their arms and ammunition gratis, for the surviving account books of Albany fur traders contain scant evidence of the Iroquois purchasing such items in appreciable volume.[50]

New France's Indian allies enjoyed similar benefits as the French expanded their fur trade and military posts into the western Great Lakes in the late seventeenth and early eighteenth century. In 1716 New France's governor-general, Philippe de Rigaud de Vaudreuil, recommended to Paris that "to maintain peace with the Indians and to prevent them trading with the English" the colony needed an annual distribution of Indian presents in the amount of 600 guns, 40,000 pounds of powder, and 60,000 pounds of lead, never mind gunsmithing. During imperial wars (1702–1713, 1744–1748, 1753–1760) the colony imported thousands of guns for diplomatic gifts and the provisioning of warriors. By the early to mid-eighteenth century, these presents constituted 5 to 10 percent of imperial spending on New France. Indians also had access to French trade in guns, some of it subsidized by the crown to stabilize the price of goods. In the 1730s and 1740s, this trade in munitions probably matched the amount of gifts and quite possibly exceeded it, to judge by the scanty records of *voyageurs* (legal traders) and their *engagés* (subcontracted traders) and anecdotal evidence relating to the activities of *coureurs de bois* (unlicensed, illegal traders). The combined volume of gifts and trade would have been enough to permit the warriors from New France's core Indian allies, which French estimates put at some 4,000 men in 1736, to replace their guns every three or four years.[51]

Indians were less grateful for these gifts and subsidized trade than insistent on them as conditions of friendship. In 1693 Five Nations headmen turned down a large gift of muskets from New York, finding them too heavy, whereupon Governor Benjamin Fletcher immediately placed a rush order in London for 200 light guns. "They will not carry the heavy firelocks," he explained, "being accustomed to light, small fuzees in their hunting." A year earlier Iroquois delegates had asked Captain Richard Ingoldsby of Albany what he expected them to do with New York's gift of powder and shot in lieu of guns. "Shall we throw them at the Enemy? We doubt they will hurt them so. Before this we always had guns given [to] us." Then they turned the screw: "It is no wonder the Governor of Canada gains upon us, for he supplies his Indians with guns as well as powder." This practice of contrasting one imperial power's stinginess with the other's generosity, and emphasizing that the people's friendship had to be earned, was the normal Indian response when gifts were scanty or of poor quality, when gunsmiths were in want, and trade goods were in short supply or too expensive. Sometimes these warnings also contained barely veiled threats of war, with headmen observing that a colonial power that failed to arm its Indian allies would be seen as conspiring to weaken and then destroy them. Almost invariably, presents of arms and ammunition followed.[52]

Over the course of the seventeenth century the Iroquois and their indigenous neighbors had become dependent on guns, powder, and shot for their military activities and to a far lesser degree for their hunting; however, the role of guns in the play-off system illustrates that dependence on these European technologies and even European gunsmithing did not translate into domination of Indians by colonies or imperial governments. It took until the mid–eighteenth century for the number of Anglo-Americans to eclipse that of Indians in the trans-Appalachian West, and even then whites did not begin wresting serious land cessions from the Iroquois until after the American Revolution. In the lightly populated French and Spanish colonies, that day never came for Native

people. One reason is that Indians almost always possessed the weaponry to defend their claims.

In the early stages of the trade, a number of factors contributed to
Indians' maintaining a steady supply of arms and ammunition at reasonable rates. These included colonial-Indian interdependence in trade,
politics, and war, as well as an expansive, multidirectional gun frontier
permitting Indians to do business with traders from different polities.
Indian political decisions had as much to do with these conditions as
any directives from colonial and imperial powerbrokers. Another important influence was rogue colonialism, with colonial regimes exercising
little control over their gunrunners. In the era of French-English warfare beginning in 1688, indigenous people added to this list an imperial
play-off system in which colonial authorities competed for Indian favor
with gifts of guns, powder, shot, and gunsmiths out of fear that failure
to do so would tip Indian loyalties toward their imperial rival and, with
this, shift the North American balance of power.[53]

The results for Indians were decidedly mixed. Their demand for firearms was based on indigenous priorities, particularly intertribal rivalries, so no one was complaining when their own people enjoyed an un-
equal access to arms. The problem was other people. For every force
like the Five Nations that rose on the strength of its armament, there
were numerous other groups on whose fall that rise was predicated. This
added up to tens of thousands and perhaps even hundreds of thousands
of eastern woodlands Indians killed, captured, tortured, forcibly adopted,
and maimed over the course of the seventeenth century. Innumerable
others suffered the misery of losing loved ones over and over again and
living in constant fear. Even the Iroquois eventually had their own tactics turned against them as their rivals acquired their own arms and fine-
tuned their defenses. The region had degenerated into a running gun
battle in which no one was safe.

Women and children suffered tremendously along the way. Men were
the ones who wielded firearms, who cut the deals with colonial gunrunners and governors, who planned the invasions and ambushes, who
took to arms to defend their people, and who garnered the honors when
their side was victorious. Certainly women were critical parts of political decision making in many communities, including whether to send
young men on revenge raids, though there is little trace of this role in

colonial documents; women also reaped the benefits of the plunder and captives their men brought home. They processed the beaver pelts that men traded not only for arms and ammunition but for clothing, pots, scissors, needles, beads, and innumerable other things that made women's lives easier and more fulfilling. Yet looming behind these roles was the fact that women were prizes for gun-toting enemy warriors, restricted by their people's gender conventions from wielding arms to defend themselves alongside their male kin. Women who made it out of an enemy attack alive but captive would serve the captor's people for a greater or lesser time as slaves before being adopted with the expectation of marrying and producing children—that is, if no one killed them beforehand. Child captives suffered similar ordeals. The misery of untold numbers of women and children fitting this description, and of thousands of men who also died along the way, were among the legacies of the arming of the Native Northeast, where in the end "there really were no winners . . . only survivors."[54]

One might conclude that guns had transformed Indians, but that would have the causation wrong. From a modern perspective, inanimate objects, even weapons imbued with the power of the Thunderbird, cannot act independently upon human beings. A more accurate way to explain this history is to say that Indians had used guns to transform their lives and those of their neighbors. Putting the matter this way highlights Native people making choices for their own futures instead of suffering as passive victims of colonial decisions, abstract economic forces, or foreign technology. Yet the point can be pushed too far. The fact of the matter is that the rise of Native gunmen, beginning with the Iroquois, dramatically circumscribed the choices of other indigenous people. They could either obtain arms by engaging in trade and diplomacy with colonial states, or become easy targets of marauding indigenous gunmen. This was an Indian-directed transformation, to be sure, but that point probably would have come as cold comfort to many of the people caught up in it. For them the colonial era and the gun age were one and the same, a period of terror and high-stakes gains and losses.

2. A VICIOUS COMMERCE

SLAVES AND ALLIANCE FOR GUNS

Sometime during the 1670s a young woman from the Yuchis of what is now the Tennessee/North Carolina/Virginia border region experienced the horror of being captured and sold into slavery by a band of gun-toting warriors from the Chichimecos, a group her people barely knew. Whether her ordeal began during an attack on her village or an ambush along the trail is unknown, but what came next probably followed what was becoming a well-worn pattern. The Chichimecos, after keeping her in a holding pen until they had accumulated enough captives for the colonial market, would have attached a leather collar around her neck connected to cords tying her wrists behind her back, and then tethered this restraint to a long leash guiding other similarly bound prisoners, most of them women and children. Marched in this constrained position throughout the day and staked to the ground at night, eventually she found herself some 300 miles east to the coast. The destination was the young English colony of Carolina, anchored by the community of Charles Town along the Ashley and Cooper Rivers. Carolina was an offshoot of the Caribbean colony of Barbados, which already had developed an insatiable appetite for cheap bound labor to do the grueling work of growing, harvesting, and processing sugarcane to satisfy Europe's sweet tooth and thirst for rum. Carolinians hoped one day to discover their own cash crop, but in the meantime they saw their most lucrative opportunity in the export of Indian slaves to Barbados and other island plantations. The Chichimecos were their first supplier, enticed by deals such as the one they got for the captive Yuchi woman:

they "sold her for a shot gun." This woman's name remains a mystery. Nevertheless, some details of her story survive because she managed to escape the English and make it back to her people. Her chief then used her story to alert Spanish authorities to the Chichimeco threat. Her fellow captives were less fortunate.[1]

The arming of the Indian Southeast took place through the trade in Indian slaves. Indian captors and their colonial customers robbed as many as 50,000 people of their freedom during the heyday of this enterprise from 1660 to 1720, and killed many more along the way. The scale of this commerce and the devastation it unleashed was infinitely greater than in the trade of Native people for arms that was developing in the Great Lakes and upper Mississippi River Valley during the same period. Southeastern slave raids wiped out numerous communities and dislocated others from the Virginia-Carolina Piedmont, deep into Florida, and all the way west to the Mississippi River Valley. South Carolina's profits from the labor of Indian slaves and their resale to the West Indies produced much of the seed money for the development of the colony and emptied indigenous people from territory that would later host plantations run on the toil of African slaves. The danger of slave raiders forced survivors to band together in defensive confederacies and take up slave raiding themselves, for one was either an aggressor or a victim in this terrifying new world. This was a new type of warfare, focused less on satisfying revenge or obtaining captives for adoption than on acquiring people to sell. The southeastern slave trade was fundamentally a trade of humans for munitions in which marauding Indian slavers grew ever more formidable by selling captives for arms, while previous victims became raiders themselves in order to obtain guns for protection and predation. The slave trade and the gun frontier marched hand in hand. The misfortune of the unnamed Yuchi woman, captured and exchanged for a musket, was but one of tens of thousands similar stories that collectively transformed the region.[2]

The kind of cascading gun violence that marred the Southeast during this period has obvious parallels to the Northeast and Great Lakes regions between the 1630s and early 1700s. Competition for captives (albeit largely for slaves instead of future adoptees) and control of European markets galvanized intertribal arms races in the Southeast as they had in the North. Rivalries between English Virginia, English South

Carolina, Spanish Florida, and French Louisiana involved using trade and gifts of military hardware to bid for Indian trade partners and allies, as was the case among New France, New Netherland, and the various English colonies of the Northeast. Most of the Southeast colonies proved just as incapable of policing gunrunners as their northern counterparts had been, and few of them made much of an effort in the first place. The raids of indigenous groups boasting a temporary advantage in arms forced their enemies to seek political alliances and trading relationships to build up their own arsenals. As in the North, within a few decades guns were more or less evenly distributed throughout the region, which ended runs of dominance of predatory raiders in favor of a balance of power maintained by the fur/deerskin trade and diplomacy with rival European powers. In many critical respects, then, the gun frontier looked similar in the northern and southern woodlands.

Human actors connect the stories of these regions, too, demonstrating the long reach of colonial violence in Indian country. The Chichimecos, as some Indians and the Spanish called them, first appear in the records of Virginia during the 1650s under the name of Rickahockans. By the 1670s the English referred to them as Westos. These Rickahockans/Westos were none other than the Eries, who had retreated from the Great Lakes to the falls of the James River to escape Iroquois gunmen. They then continued their migration into what is now South Carolina. Within a few years their neighbors included a portion of the Savannahs (or Shawnees) from the Ohio Valley, who had left the region seeking European trade and escape from indigenous slave raids out of Virginia and then Five Nations attacks, before settling on the southern river to which they gave their name. Given that the Westos were an Iroquoian-speaking people (though not a member of the Iroquois League), in all likelihood they had their own "mourning war" tradition of adopting enemy captives into their population. But that was not the primary motive of their raiding in the Southeast. Their most compelling reason to relocate this far south was the opportunity to arm themselves by trading people, deerskins, and furs to the colonies of Virginia and then South Carolina. The Westos and Savannahs knew through hard experience that guns were the key to their defense as long as rival groups had access to the colonial weapons market. Seizing captives from southeastern tribes to exchange for arms and adopt into their ranks was their way of ensuring that no one would overawe their people ever again. In this they became the same kind of menacing force that Iroquois gunners had formerly been to them. And they too, like the Five Nations, forced one group after another to build up their munitions and turn these weapons against others, part of the thunderous storm rumbling across Indian country.[3]

The Scourge of the Southeast

The Eries' move south from the Great Lakes into the Virginia Piedmont drew on a combination of old trading ties and new trading opportunities. During the sixteenth century a trade corridor had funneled seashells and shell jewelry from the Algonquins of Chesapeake Bay up the Potomac River, through the Massawomecks of the upper Ohio River Valley to Ontario Iroquoians, including the Eries. The Eries probably had friends and relatives all along this route, which made it a natural place of retreat from Five Nations' violence. The Eries also would have been drawn to the area by the prospects of trade with Virginia. By the 1640s the colony had finally defeated the Powhatan confederacy after three brutal wars, giving it control of territory from Chesapeake Bay a hundred miles westward to the fall lines of the major rivers. This growth carried the opportunity to establish contact with indigenous people of the southern Piedmont, whose furs, deerskins, and slaves had been reaching the colony indirectly for several years. With an eye toward increasing this commerce and defending the colony's western flank, Virginia ordered the construction of four posts up the James (Fort Charles), Appomattox (Fort Henry), Pamunkey (Fort Royall), and Chickahominy (Fort James) Rivers, which henceforth became trade centers and supply depots for horse trains heading south and west into Indian country. Soon weapons flowing through these sites would enable the Eries to transform themselves from a defeated people into the scourge of the Southeast.[4]

The Eries' relationship with Virginia did not get off to a good start, but eventually the parties established a mutually beneficial exchange of slaves and deerskins for munitions. When Virginia learned in 1656 that 600 to 700 strangers called Rickahockans (or Richahecrians) had suddenly appeared at the falls of the James River, its initial response was to attack them. Little did Virginia know that this group was battle tested and, judging from the Rickahockans' victory in the subsequent fight, perhaps better armed than one might have expected, possibly via the Susquehannocks and that tribe's weapons trade with Maryland and New Sweden. Thinking the better of entering yet another Indian war with such a formidable opponent, Virginia sued for peace and by 1658 had authorized an open trade in guns, powder, and shot with any "friendly Indians." A year later there were reports out of St. Augustine of "northern" Indians wielding English muskets, sometimes accompanied by Englishmen, terrorizing the missions of Guale, the northernmost province of Spanish Florida on what is now the Georgia coast. These raiders were certainly the Eries, seeking captives to sell as slaves to Chesapeake tobacco planters and probably also to buttress their population, thinned by war with the Iroquois. Virginians even began referring to the Eries by the name "Westos" after a James River plantation named Westover owned by arms traders.[5]

The Westos' prey were the bow-and-arrow Indians of the Florida missions, Carolina coast, and adjacent Piedmont. Spain's southeastern mission system was extensive, consisting of thirty-five stations along what today is the shoreline of Georgia and northeast Florida and across the Florida panhandle. Yet it was also vulnerable. One of the principles of the missions was that the Spanish would provide military support and European goods to uphold the authority of local chiefs. However, that protection and trade did not include firearms in any appreciable volume, not because the Spanish refused to trade guns to Indians, but because the Spanish crown invested few resources in the marginal Florida colony and tightly restricted its economy. Additionally, in the 1670s the number of Spanish soldiers stood at just a few hundred men out of a Spanish population of less than 1,000. Such a small, concentrated, poorly armed population was precisely what raiders wanted. Indians elsewhere in the region were also relatively easy targets. The South Carolina coast was inhabited by various Siouan-speaking communities of just a few hundred people each, weakened by successive outbreaks of epidemic disease and war. Even the large, town-dwelling Muskogean-speaking groups west and south of the Savannah River enticed Westo slavers because they were easily reached and defended only by bowmen. The Westos viewed them all as potential slaves.[6]

The Westos' advantage in arms enabled them to devastate these populations. In the fall of 1659, news arrived in St. Augustine from the interior province of Apalachee that villages eighty leagues to the north had suffered "much damage" by an army of up to 1,000 men consisting of "some striped [painted] Indians, and with them white people, and that they bought some firearms and among them two campaign pieces [or artillery guns]." Coastal Guale was next, suffering an invasion in June 1661 by "a great number of Indians" estimated at 2,000 men, "who said they were Chichimecos [and among] them some Englishmen with firearms." Another account specified that this army included "more than 500 men . . . that use firearms." Overwhelmed, the survivors abandoned the northernmost missions and fled south, only to be followed there by the Westos.[7]

It was probably no coincidence that half a dozen or so villages of a previously unknown group called the Yamasees appeared just north of the Guale missions shortly after these reports. Though the origin of the Yamasees is cloudy, they seem to have been comprised of various peoples displaced by Westo gunmen. Soon the Yamasees would move directly into the mission districts and begin contributing to Spanish labor drafts in the hope of receiving protection. Their retreat was part of a larger diaspora of peoples throughout the Piedmont and lower Southeast, including Tutelos, Saponis, Yuchis, and Coushattas, seeking refuge from the slavers.[8]

Soon the Westos were also on the move again, because their slaving, coupled with the spread of Virginia trade, spurred an arms race throughout the upper Piedmont in which they lost their military advantage. Though the first historical documentation of Westo slave raiding comes from Florida, archaeological evidence suggests that the Westos' arrival in the Piedmont was accompanied by the displacement of several groups southward to the lower Catawba River. The migrants were probably fleeing the Westo threat. Other Piedmont nations responded to the Westos by acquiring firearms from the Virginia trade forts and especially from pack trains that were probing deeper into Indian country. By the 1660s the Occaneechis inhabiting the confluence of the Roanoke and Dan Rivers along the major Piedmont trade path had established themselves as middlemen between Virginia gunrunners and indigenous slave raiders and deerskin hunters, a position they jealously guarded.

Their town became known as "the mart for all the Indians for at least 500 miles." The Tuscaroras of the North Carolina coastal plain and Piedmont carved out a similar niche for themselves, transforming one of their towns into "a place of great Indian trade and commerce." By 1670 firearms had become so common in the region that Monacans by the falls of the James and the Saponis of Otter Creek (by modern Lynchburg, Virginia) greeted English traders with celebratory "volleys of shot" and other signs that "guns, powder, and shot, etc., are commodities they will greedily barter for." If the Westos wanted to maintain their superiority in arms over their neighbors, they had to find a new home. Consequently, less than a decade after arriving in Virginia, the Westos had relocated to the Savannah River, the modern border of South Carolina and Georgia, within easier striking distance of their intended victims.[9]

The coastal Indians' need for allies against Westo gunmen provided the wedge for the founding of English South Carolina in 1670. Scouting expeditions by the colony's organizers repeatedly encountered Indians exclaiming that they were "afraid of the very foot step of a Westo," who they called "man eaters." Stephen Bull, one of the colony's first Indian agents, understood that the Westos, "having guns and powder and shot . . . do come upon these Indians in the time of their crop and destroy all by killing, carrying away their corn and children, and eat them." Initially the hope of the Sewees, Winyaws, Congarees, Stonos, and Cusabos (whom the English would soon refer to collectively as "Settlement Indians") was that the colonists would provide them with arms and discourage Westo attacks. With South Carolina's population reaching 1,000 people by 1672, it might very well have served as a defensive bulwark for nearby Indians. However, ultimately the colony would become a driving force behind the suffering of the region's indigenous people at the hands of slave raiders.[10]

If South Carolina wanted to maximize its profits from the Indian trade, it needed to deal with interior groups like the Westos, whereas the Westos saw South Carolina as a source of European goods located closer to their Savannah River base than Virginia. Additionally, Virginia had alienated the Westos by opening an arms trade with the Cherokees, who were among the Westos' enemies, and then by instituting a temporary ban on the sale of munitions to Indians in response to a number of murders. In October 1674, just a month after this ruling, a delegation of Westos visited Carolina and met with Henry Woodward, the colony's point man for Indian affairs, signaling their desire for trade and inviting him to visit their main town near the site of modern Augusta, Georgia. Along his way to the Westo settlement, Woodward could not help but notice trees decorated with effigies "of a beaver, a man on horseback, and guns." Just in case he missed the point, the Westos celebrated his arrival with a salute of "fifty or sixty small arms" and exhibited that they were "well provided with arms, ammunition, trading cloth, and other trade from the northward," which they had acquired for "dressed deerskins, furs, and young Indian slaves." They seemed to be saying that they wanted Carolina's trade but did not need it.[11]

For a time the Westos and Carolina enjoyed a profitable relationship, but to the detriment of nearly everyone else in the region. The same Yuchi woman who managed to escape her captivity told the Spanish that there were Carolinians in the Westos' town "teaching them to use firearms with the purpose in view of coming to attack this garrison." In the face of this threat, the Guales moved southward and consolidated into four mission towns clustered within eight leagues of one another after previously living in ten towns spread over forty leagues. Probably most of the Westos' raids during this period went unrecorded because they took place in the Piedmont and what is now west-central Georgia, remote from colonial scribes. In the spring of 1680, however, Westo marauders burst back into view, as a force of 300 warriors "all with long guns" marched against the Indian town of Colon on St. Simon's Island and the mission of Santa Catalina de Guale. The defenders, with just sixteen guns, were practically helpless as the Westos burned their settlements to the ground and marched away with an unspecified number of captives in tow.[12]

Yet even as the South Carolina–Westo alliance was thriving, elements within the colony were working to undermine it. The eight lords proprietor, who technically governed Carolina from England, claimed a monopoly on the interior Indian trade, including that with the Westos, but colonists, even the proprietors' own appointees, had little respect for their authority. A faction of councilors soon to be known as the "Goose Creek Men," led by James Moore, Maurice Mathews, and Arthur Middleton, began encouraging the so-called Settlement Indians and

Savannahs to raid the Westos for captives to sell into slavery. When the Westos retaliated, as predicted, the Goose Creek Men used it as an excuse to have the assembly declare war, despite the proprietors' orders to stop. In this the Goose Creek Men simultaneously dealt a severe blow to proprietary authority and weakened the most threatening indigenous power in the region. Details of the war are murky, but by 1682 the Westos were said to be "ruined" and "not 50 left alive and those Divided."[13]

With the Westos shattered, the Goose Creek Men partnered with Indians near and far to expand the hunt for slaves. The Savannahs (or Shawnees) were the first group to step into the Westo vacuum, relocating to the Savannah River and then raiding interior peoples such as the Cherokees. The Yamasees followed, abandoning the Spanish missions for territory just east of the Savannahs, after concluding that it was better to go slaving for arms than to remain the prey of armed slavers. Even Indians who thought of themselves as allies of Carolina were vulnerable to slave raiding. Shortly after the Westo War, the colony used a trumped-up excuse to declare war on the Winyaw community of Settlement Indians, then successfully urged the Savannahs to conquer and enslave them.[14]

For all their outrage, the proprietors could not figure out how to rein in the Goose Creek scofflaws. In 1680 they issued a ban on the enslavement of any Indians within 200 miles of Carolina, then in 1682 extended that range to 400 miles. In 1683 they ordered that all Indians about to be sold out of the colony should first be interviewed to determine their identities and how they were taken. Yet these laws remained no more than words on paper when the proprietors' agents in the colony, the governor and his council, were among the very ringleaders of the "dealers of Indians." In 1683 and 1685 the proprietors instructed their governor to keep Mathews and Moore off the council for having "most contemptuously disobeyed our orders about sending away of Indians and have contrived most unjust wars upon the Indians in order to the getting of slaves," only to have their will ignored. When the proprietors finally installed a governor, James Colleton, who tried to go after these rogues, the assembly managed to have him arrested and banished. Such recalcitrance led one of Mathews's opponents to denounce him as "Machiavelli, Hobbes, and Lucifer in a huge lump of Viperish mortality

[with] a soul [as] big as a mosquito." Some governors were not only impotent but just as corrupt as the Goose Creek Men; Joseph Blake, twice governor in the 1690s, was said to have taken six barrels of gunpowder sent to the colony for defense against the French and traded them to Indians on his own account.[15]

The slave traders' control of the assembly gave them leeway to pursue their criminal interests under the color of law. The proprietors accused Goose Creek Men in the legislature of banning the sale of arms to Indians only to apply the rule selectively against their commercial rivals while they "brook it themselves for their private advantage and escaped the penalty." Worse yet, the slavers provoked wars with Indians not as a matter of public good but "as best suited their private advantage in trade." Indians cooperated in these schemes, the proprietors charged, because "you induce them through [their] Covetousness of your guns, powder, and shot and other European commodities to make war upon their neighbors, to ravish the wife from the husband, kill the father to get the child and to burn and destroy the habitations of these poor people." It could only have deepened the proprietors' sense of scandal that much of their colony's importation of guns and export of Indian slaves appears to have flowed through pirates. Coastal Carolinians, including authorities, thought of pirates less as terrors than as partners in their black-market trade. From 3,000 miles away the proprietors were toothless, given that the colony's lawmakers and lawbreakers were one and the same.[16]

The Slave Wars

In the late seventeenth and early eighteenth centuries, slavers and gunrunners marched together deeper into the continent, their power channeled by the political reorganization of their home societies. Within South Carolina, the Goose Creek Men had effectually neutered the lords proprietor, taken over the Carolina government, and thrown open the Indian trade to anyone connected with their faction. Commerce in slaves and deerskins from the Indians, and munitions and other manufactured goods from Europe, became the key to riches at a time when the colony was still searching for a cash crop. For their part, Indians in an area extending for hundreds of miles were coming to the realization that unless they did business with South Carolina, they would lack the weapons to defend themselves from the growing ranks of marauders. Sensing the opportunity and danger, heretofore autonomous communities, their populations thinned by epidemic disease and foreign attacks, began to confederate to protect themselves from the slavers and to man their own armies to go slaving. By the early eighteenth century, two of the most significant of these coalitions were known as the Catawbas and the Creeks. Though anchored by a particular language family, Siouan in the case of the Piedmont Catawbas and Muskogean in the case of the woodland Creeks, these groups incorporated people from diverse linguistic and cultural backgrounds. Their cohesion was in its tentative early stages as the turn of the seventeenth century approached, contributing to the sense of regional upheaval.[17]

Competition between militant slavers meant that even groups raiding for Carolina might themselves become captives. The Westos had been merely the first group to fall victim to this trap. The Savannahs were next. In the early 1700s Catawbas attacked the Savannahs' main town, killing a reported 450 people. The survivors retreated to the Susquehanna River Valley of Pennsylvania, then sent warriors on revenge raids against Carolina's Indian protectorates. The colony encouraged the Catawbas to retaliate by giving them a gift of fifty guns, 1,000 flints, 200 pounds of gunpowder, and 400 pounds of bullets. Any Catawba who brought in a Savannah scalp or captive could keep the gun without charge, an arrangement premised on the assumption that repeat Indian customers would hold true to the bargain. Carolina was developing a pattern of turning on its friends as soon as it was profitable, but Indians facing the threat of enslavement could not resist the pull of its arms market.[18]

The imperial politics of Europe also shaped these American dynamics. South Carolinians had always been driven by profits to sponsor slave raids, but they got an additional spur in 1688 with England's Glorious Revolution and the ascension of William and Mary to the throne. By securing England's Protestant succession, this event inaugurated more than a century of on-again, off-again warfare between Britain and the Catholic powers of France and Spain. In turn, Charles Town gained political cover to enslave the Indian allies of England's imperial enemies. Queen Anne's War (or the War of the Spanish Succession), stretching between 1702 and 1713, was especially critical in this respect. It legitimized and incentivized South Carolina's long-running, de facto state of war with Florida. Furthermore, it permitted the slave traders to justify slave raids against Indians far to the west who had become associated with the young French colony of Louisiana. Founded in 1699 around the Gulf Coast settlements of Biloxi (Fort Maurepas) and Mobile, then expanding in 1718 to include the Mississippi River town of New Orleans, Louisiana was and always would be lightly populated and economically weak. However, it was a threat to Carolina's commercial expansion by virtue of its alliance with the powerful Choctaws of what is now southern Mississippi. At the same time the Choctaws' partnership with the French gave Carolina slave merchants a convenient excuse to direct slave raids against them. When authorities in London demanded an explanation, the slavers easily maintained that they acted in the interest of the empire. After all, they expounded, South Carolina was "a frontier, both against the French and Spaniards," and enslaving the Indian allies of those powers "serves to lessen their numbers before the French can arm them."[19]

Like a hurricane feeding off the warm waters and winds of the Caribbean, the slave raiders gathered political capital, manpower, and weapons, and then slammed into Florida with irresistible force, pummeling it mercilessly from the mid-1680s into the early 1700s until they had practically emptied the entire peninsula of indigenous people. Already by 1684 the slavers had shattered the missions of coastal Guale and Mocama, with the residents finally dispersing after the defection of the Yamasees and attacks by European pirates made further resistance against the slavers impossible. Some mission Indians fled toward the protection of St. Augustine; others joined the Yamasees. The latter group made the wiser choice, for the Yamasees were about to become South Carolina's newest favorite partner in the slave trade. In February 1685, fifty Yamasees made a startling attack on the Timucua mission of Santa Catalina de Afuyca, nearly a hundred miles inland from St. Augustine, burning the town, killing eighteen, and seizing twenty-one. Reportedly Carolinians at Port Royal had advanced this band thirty guns and cutlasses in return for their captives. It was but a foreshadowing of things to come.[20]

If Yamasees were the stick, Carolina trade was the carrot for mission Indians to abandon Florida and join the ranks of slavers. In 1685, the year of the Santa Catalina strike, Spanish officials learned that Woodward and other Carolina traders had been active on the Chattahoochee River, which today forms the border between Georgia and Alabama. Unable to compete economically with Carolina, Florida's response was to send six Spanish soldiers and some 200 Apalachees against four Apalachicola communities, Tuskegee, Coolame, Coweta, and Cussita, that refused to surrender the traders. The Spaniards then torched the towns and confiscated munitions and dressed deerskins. Undaunted, the Apalachicolas hosted Woodward again the next year after he appeared accompanied by 150 Indian burden bearers carrying guns, powder, and shot for trade. The Spanish countermove of erecting a fort next to Coweta was just as ineffective as burning it down had been, as it served only to drive the Apalachicolas out of Florida's orbit, northeastward to Ochese Creek (now known as the Ocmulgee River), near a Carolina trading post where Macon, Georgia, stands today. The Apalachicolas then became the southern edge of the gun frontier and another phalanx in the growing army of Indian slavers.[21]

The Apalachicolas along Ochese Creek (leading the English to refer to them collectively as "Creeks" or "Lower Creeks") became eager partners in the trade of slaves for guns. Shortly after their move, St. Augustine received an alarm that "Ocheses, Yamasees and Englishmen" had struck Timucua towns throughout north-central Florida in addition to making smaller-scale raids throughout the province. General Spanish complaints about "infestations" of slavers indicate that other incursions went without being documented. An elderly Chacato woman who managed to escape captivity among these brigands understood their motivations. She related that they "told her that they seized them [the Chacatos] to sell them to the English for muskets," which they intended to turn "against the Spanish and Apalachees." There was no mistaking that this slave trade was primarily an exchange of people for guns.[22]

A fresh opportunity to put those guns to use arose when the start of Queen Anne's War coincided with the appointment of none other than the slave trader James Moore to the governorship of Carolina, after the sitting governor died. Moore saw his term as the Goose Creek Men's chance to deal a fatal blow against the Spanish while accumulating a windfall in slaving profits. For Carolina's Indian trade partners, it was an opportunity to build up their musketry. Between 1703 and 1705, armies of up to 1,000 Yamasee, Creek, and Cherokee gunmen marched against the missions of Apalachee and Timucua, carrying away upward of 1,300 captives in just one expedition. The only way mission Indians escaped these attacks alive and unshackled was to "agree" to relocate to the Savannah River under the supervision of the Ochese Creeks. By the time this campaign was over, Spanish Florida and its once extensive mission system were reduced to the fort at St. Augustine, small indigenous villages within range of its guns, and the garrison of Pensacola. These losses, combined with deaths from a vicious smallpox epidemic beginning in 1696, which tore through the Southeast along the routes of slaving and the arms trade, meant that by 1711 slavers had to extend their raids all the way to the Florida Keys to find populations large enough to make the effort worth it.[23]

The slavers' superiority in arms was the critical factor in their conquest of the missions. Florida officials complained endlessly that enemy raiders were "being aided by the English with guns, ammunition, cutlasses, and pistols" and "have become so expert in the handling of arms that they use them as if they were born in this service." Mission Indians were no match. To be sure, some military hardware reached the Apalachees through a black-market trade with Cuban fishermen working Florida's Gulf Coast and sailors docked at St. Augustine, and a handful of warriors received Spanish weapons in recognition of exemplary military service. However, the overall number of guns among the mission Indians was small and their effectiveness was diminished by shortages of powder and shot. The largest armament by far employed in the defense of any Florida mission, San Luis in 1704, was ninety-three muskets, each one accompanied by twenty shots' worth of ammunition, and even that fell far short of the need. Florida governor Joseph de Zúñiga's report on the fall of Apalachee concluded that "for lack of munitions, my people were defeated." Indians agreed. When a band of Apalachees fled to Louisiana in the wake of the 1704 attacks, they explained that the Spanish "did not give them any guns at all but that the French gave them to all their allies." It had become a matter of life and death for Indians in the slaving zone to have a European partner willing and able to arm them.[24]

The strikes against Florida's interior missions began a phase of significant growth in the number of militant slavers and the geographic reach of their attacks. Indeed, these developments were reciprocal, for as more communities acquired guns for defense and slaving, slavers directed their attacks farther west and south against people with weak or nonexistent armaments and became even better armed in the process. Initially the Cherokees suffered slave raids by the Savannahs, Catawbas, and Esaws, but once the Cherokees began trading with Carolina in the late 1690s that became a more dangerous proposition. Muskogean-speaking communities on the Coosa and Tallapoosa Rivers, which would later become known as Upper Creeks, were also hosting Carolina traders by at least 1704. "The English were in those nations every day," Louisiana officials brooded, "and they take pack horses burdened with clothing, guns, gunpowder, shot, and a variety of other goods . . . the greatest traffic between the English and the savages is the trade of slaves . . . each person being traded for a gun." By 1715 most Tallapoosa and Alabama warriors wielded firearms and the Alabamas were said to have a warehouse containing 10,000 pounds of gunpowder. Slave raiders were wise to bypass communities with such weaponry in favor of more vulnerable targets deeper in the interior, far from the gun frontier.[25]

With the destruction of the Florida missions by Yamasee, Creek, and English slavers, the gravitational center of slaving shifted west, driven by the fears and ambitions of the Chickasaws of what is now northern Mississippi. For years the Chickasaws had suffered intermittent attacks by gunmen from the Iroquois, Great Lakes tribes, and southeastern slavers without the ability to respond in kind because those same nations blocked their access to eastern arms markets. However, eventually the gunrunners found their way to the Chickasaws. Chickasaw territory was fairly easy to reach from Carolina via the Tennessee River and the Upper and Lower Trade Paths, the major east–west arteries through Creek country. Following these routes, Carolina pack trains had reached the Chickasaws as early as 1686, and by the early to mid-1690s their visits were becoming routine, much to the chagrin of neighboring peoples. In the spring of 1699 Louisiana governor Jean-Baptiste, Sieur Le Moyne de Bienville, met with the leaders of the Colapissas, one of several small communities along the Gulf Coast known to the French collectively as *petites nations,* who told that just days earlier 200 Chickasaws accompanied by Englishmen had surprised their village and "carried off a great number of their men." Bienville also learned that the Chickasaws had killed more than 1,800 Choctaws and enslaved some 500 over the previous decade, and the problem was only growing worse. In 1706 a Chickasaw army said to have numbered as many as 4,000 men (almost certainly an exaggeration unless this force included many foreign allies) attacked the Choctaws and seized more than 300 women and children. Underlying the ferocity of these campaigns was the Chickasaw determination "never to return" to the days when they were defenseless against enemy gunmen.[26]

The inflated prices offered by the English for captives explains how and why the Chickasaws armed themselves so fast and took up slaving so enthusiastically. Thomas Nairne, a Scots trader from Carolina, wrote in 1703, "No employment pleases the Chickasaws so well as slave catching. A lucky hit, at that besides the honor, procures them a whole estate at once. One slave brings a gun, ammunition, horse, hatchet, and a suit of clothes, which would not be procured without much tedious toil a hunting." Nairne might have been overstating things, but not by much. Thomas Welsh, the ringleader of the 1706 raids on the Choctaws, recalled advancing the Chickasaws 300 muskets in exchange for the promise of just fifteen slaves. Almost overnight the Chickasaws became capable of marshaling an army of gunmen. Louisiana's Indian agent, Pierre Le Moyne d'Iberville, estimated that 700 to 800 out of 2,000 Chickasaw fighting men possessed firearms and that they killed three Choctaws for every one they enslaved. Their raids, combined with those of the Creeks, threw the Gulf Coast and lower Mississippi River Valley into turmoil, leaving towns destroyed, hundreds of people killed and carried into captivity, and the survivors fleeing their home territories to congregate near the French. But nowhere was safe. By the early eighteenth century, slavers sometimes ranged as far as 150 miles west of the Mississippi River.[27]

Louisiana's relations with area Indians hinged on arming them against this threat. The most important group in this respect was the Choctaws of the Pearl, Leaf, Pascagoula, and Tombigbee River watersheds, just south of Chickasaw territory. Unlike small Gulf Coast nations, the Choctaws, with more than 1,000 households and an estimated 4,000 warriors, had more than enough population to contend with the Chickasaws, who were less than half their number. What they needed were muskets, powder, and shot, "the most precious merchandise that there is for them," in the judgment of Diron d'Artaguette, Louisiana's commissary general. Yet the French were incapable of outdealing English gunrunners. Louisiana's supply lines from Europe and Canada were just too long, its support from the crown too scanty, and its economy and population too small, to compete on the basis of free trade. So instead the French gave away munitions as payment for political services and as diplomatic gifts. For instance, when the French gathered a force of 220 Choctaws, Pascagoulas, Tohomes, and Mobilas to attack the Alabamas in September 1704, they distributed guns to the principal warriors only, and powder and shot more generally. Louisiana then offered payment of a gun for every enemy scalp and 400 livres in goods for enemy captives, an incentive program that had produced 400 scalps and a hundred slaves by 1723. The cumulative effect of these measures was to give Louisiana's Indian allies a fighting chance against foreign raiders, a point of which the French never tired of reminding them. By 1726 the Choctaws even felt bold enough to send out thirty small parties to fire on the Chickasaws whenever they left their forts. At the same time, chronic French shortages meant that the option of dealing with the English always remained enticing.[28]

Anticolonial Resistance

The slaves-for-guns trade was inherently unstable amid its remarkable growth because the spread of firearms made raids ever more costly to the aggressors while continuing to increase indigenous demand for munitions. The trade in deerskins, which always operated alongside the slave trade, was an uncertain fallback because deerskins had far less purchasing power than slaves. As colonial traders pressured Indian customers to make good on their debts, sometimes even threatening them with enslavement, tensions mounted. At the same time, English and French settlements encroached on Indian communities already bitter over their losses to the slave trade and epidemic disease. The mix proved explosive, and between 1710 and 1730 Indians throughout the Southeast began rising up against the colonies.

The decision to go to war rested, in part, on the Indians' confidence that arms and ammunition would continue to reach them through in-

digenous middlemen and along the fault lines of imperial and intercolonial rivalries. It was dangerous for Indians to war against their arms
dealers. Once stockpiles ran out, new supplies would have to be obtained
either by plunder or by trade with another partner. No one was under
any misconception that French Louisiana, Spanish Florida, or Indian
middlemen were substitutes for the Carolina trade over the long term,
but Native people trusted that they had enough resources to supply
themselves temporarily. Access to the English arms market certainly emboldened the Natchez to rise against the French and the Chickasaws
and Creeks to war against the Choctaw-French alliance. Thus, the
southeastern Indians' anticolonial wars were an opportunity to test
whether their growing dependence on European firearms meant the
same thing as dependence on particular Euro-American states.

The Tuscaroras of the Carolina coastal plain and Piedmont were
the first to rise after years of serving as both perpetrators and victims
of the slave trade. Though the immediate spark of this war was North
Carolina's founding of a Swiss–Palatine settlement on the lower Trent
and Neuse Rivers, followed by land surveys auguring further expansion into Tuscarora territory, the Tuscaroras' fear of land loss was
indelibly tied to their fading economic power and the risk of enslavement. Tuscarora returns on the slave trade had been declining for years
as the region's other Indians grew better armed and Virginia began
importing ever greater numbers of African slaves. As the Tuscaroras
brought in fewer Indian captives, colonial traders began dealing ever
more sharply to collect on debts the Tuscaroras had accumulated by
buying European goods on credit. Tuscaroras knew, and traders probably threatened, that if these debts remained unpaid, colonists would
not hesitate to enslave their people and seize their land. North Carolina's encroachment on their territory suggested that the time was nigh.
Unwilling to brook these conditions any longer, the southern Tuscaroras and neighboring Coree Indians began attacking colonial settlements along the Neuse on September 22, 1711, killing 130 people in a
matter of days and sending the survivors in a panicked flight to the
safety of New Bern.[29]

The southern Tuscaroras had built up a substantial arsenal before their
attacks and then resourcefully exploited every avenue of supply as the
war continued. Virginia governor Alexander Spotswood understood that

the Tuscaroras "were better provided with ammunition than we our-
selves" when the conflict began. He responded by prohibiting Virginia
traders from dealing with the Tuscaroras, but it was difficult to police
violations. In the early spring of 1712 South Carolina colonel John Barnwell heard from an English captive of the Tuscaroras that traders from
"Virginia furnished them [the Tuscaroras] with 400 buckskins worth of
ammunition." Barnwell also suspected rogues from his colony of dealing
with the tribe for plunder that Tuscaroras had seized from North Carolina homesteads. Indian middlemen circumvented the ban even when
colonial traders honored it. By December 1712, complaints reached Williamsburg that the Meherrins of the Virginia/North Carolina border
were a source of the Tuscaroras' powder and shot. Tuscarora prisoners
of the English confessed that the Senecas had counseled their people not
to worry about running out of ammunition because they "would come
twice a year, and furnish them with it." What the Tuscaroras could not
obtain from such outlets, they robbed from Virginia pack trains heading
out to western nations like the Cherokees. Spotswood feared that they
"have by this means got a greater quantity of ammunition than I could
have wished." Suffice it to say, the Tuscaroras had the means to fight a
long campaign.[30]

During the war the Tuscaroras constructed several impressive forts
that maximized their firepower. On a high bluff above Catechna Creek
was "Hancock's Fort," so-called after the Anglicized name of its *teetha*
(or chief). Surrounded by a trench and an embankment lined with sharp
river cane, the fort's thick log palisade contained upper and lower firing
ports and bastions at the corners mounted with "some great guns," probably meaning swivel guns or light artillery pieces. Inside was "a great
deal of powder, and 300 men." Another nearby fort, Nooherooka, was
even more formidable. Its palisade and trench enclosed one and a half
acres, with loopholes and firing platforms all around. Each of three separate corners contained an elevated blockhouse (or reinforced room)
from which to fire down on attackers and withstand enemy volleys. A
covered trench extended from the fort to a nearby creek of drinking
water, while another trench ran from the gate to a series of outer defense works. Within the gates were fallback positions, including two underground bunkers connected by a tunnel. "The enemy says it was a
runaway negro who taught them to fortify thus," seethed Barnwell. The

Tuscaroras' use of this slave, as in their employment of firearms, was another stinging example of them appropriating the colonists' strengths to mount their own resistance to colonialism.[31]

Over the course of two years of fighting, both of these forts fell to large armies comprised of South and North Carolina militia and hundreds of Indian allies, but not because the Tuscaroras lacked munitions. By most accounts the Tuscaroras repeatedly drove foot soldiers back from their palisades by unleashing "terrible fire" and fighting like "desperate villains." When the English finally took possession of these strongholds after wearing down the defenders, they discovered sizable amounts of stored powder and shot. The problem for the Tuscaroras was that they were unaccustomed to European siege warfare. Days and weeks of bombardment exacted more psychological stress and casualties than they were willing to endure. Judging it more important to preserve life than hold territory, the Tuscaroras who survived these assaults and escaped enslavement fled either to Virginia or to Iroquois country, where they soon became the sixth nation of the League.[32]

Hundreds of Indians fought alongside the English in this war, less out of enmity for the Tuscaroras than with an eye toward obtaining slaves to pay off their debts. Indeed, the roster of Indians in this force reads like a roll call of slaving nations, including Yamasees, Apalachees, Cherokees, and Catawbas. Though they returned home triumphantly with dozens, even hundreds, of Tuscarora captives, they could not escape the haunting realization that they shared many of the same problems that had driven their victims to war. Wiping out the Florida missions had robbed these nations of their main source of slaves, while the creation of well-armed coalitions like the Catawbas and Creeks was making raids in the interior increasingly dangerous. The Yamasees, for instance, were said to have lost half of their 800 warriors in the course of slaving between 1702 and 1713. Louisiana's arming of the Choctaws and other Indians in the lower Mississippi River Valley threatened to cut off the last remaining sector of people vulnerable to captivity. The dilemma for Indians who traded with Carolina was that they had fallen into the habit of buying massive amounts of goods on credit—not only guns, but cloth, clothing, metal tools, copper kettles, and liquor—in the expectation that they could eliminate their balances with high-priced slaves. This hope was not unreasonable. Though by 1715 the Yamasees alone owed Carolina traders 100,000 deerskins, or about 250 deerskins a man, a single slave was worth 200 deerskins. The drop in the supply of slaves, however, confronted Indian hunters with debts they might never pay off. The robust turnout of warriors from slaving communities for the campaign against the Tuscaroras was a reflection of their predicament. They were growing beholden to the political agenda of colonial gun suppliers with a track record of turning suddenly on their indigenous trade partners.[33]

———

The Carolina traders' rough treatment of Indian debtors, who they mistakenly believed had become their pawns, was the main grievance behind the subsequent Yamasee War. As Indians fell behind on their payments, traders began confiscating their property and even seizing members of their communities as slaves. The likelihood that most of the victims of these kidnappings were captive foreigners whom the traders viewed as slaves to the Indians, albeit regardless of whether they had married or been adopted into local families, does not appear to have softened the offense to the host societies. Such aggression, combined with mounting cases of traders perpetrating sexual assaults, drunken brawls, and property thefts, increasingly made traders intolerable to the people with whom they dealt. Amid this acrimony Carolina made an ill-timed decision to take a census of its Indian allies, which the Indians thought to be in preparation for their enslavement. It took only a matter of weeks for Indians who did business with Carolina—Yamasees, Lower Creeks, Cherokees, and Catawbas—to kill nearly all of the one hundred traders in their towns and begin attacking outlying English settlements. By August these strikes had practically emptied the Carolina countryside outside of Charles Town, and those taking refuge in the city panicked that it might be next.[34]

One source of the Carolinians' fright was that their Indian enemies were, according to several accounts, "extremely well armed and provided with ammunition and other necessaries." Carolina's own traders were most responsible for this situation, but the colony pointed fingers at others too. Indian sources said that Virginia traders were furnishing Piedmont Indians with weapons, knowing they would pass them on to the warring tribes. The French and Spanish also drew suspicion, for good reason. Florida received an uncharacteristically large royal donation of 1,000 firearms during the war, some of which it used to outfit the Yamasees. Overall, though, neither the Spanish nor the French had the means to equip a region-wide Indian resistance movement. In July 1716 Louisiana officials bemoaned that they were wasting a precious opportunity to draw off Carolina's indigenous allies because the Indians did not see "any means of obtaining from the French the things they needed." The militants' will to sustain the war began to ebb within the first year as their weapons fell into disrepair and stockpiles of gunpowder and shot began running short. Before 1715 even came to a close, colonists began to notice that growing numbers of the Indians they warred against "had only bows and arrows."[35]

The Cherokees were the first to break, less out of fear of attack by the English than out of a need for munitions to fend off raids by the Iroquois and other indigenous enemies. To that end, in December 1715 they negotiated a peace in which Carolina restored trade and they took up arms against the Creeks. This decision, followed by a Cherokee slaughter of a Creek political delegation, inaugurated forty years of warfare between the nations, but it also opened an unprecedented flow of Carolinian arms into Cherokee country and a decades-long Cherokee-British alliance. Carolina promptly sent the Cherokees 200 muskets and ammunition to keep up the fight, followed in July 1716 by a present of 300 guns, 900 pounds of powder, and 750 pounds of shot. It also redressed long-standing Indian complaints about trader abuses and high prices by forming an oversight body called the Commissioners of the Indian Trade and establishing a tariff of thirty-five deerskins for a musket, twenty skins for a pistol, and one skin for thirty bullets. It is telling of Carolina's newfound concern for its Native trade partners that within ten years those prices had dropped considerably in response to Cherokee demands. Both sides appear to have expected the colony to supply the Cherokees with free gunpowder just as it sponsored a gunsmith "for the public" at the Cherokee town of Tugaloo. The Cherokees might be counted among the winners of the Yamasee War, given that these measures rectified their most important grievances against Carolina while also fortifying their defenses against Native rivals.[36]

The Creeks' pressing need for munitions to defend against the Cherokees led the Coweta chief, Brims, to step up diplomacy with the

77

Spanish, French, and, eventually, the Carolinians. Throughout the early stages of the war, Brims had sent out relatives as ambassadors to the Spanish at Pensacola and St. Augustine, and then Havana and Mexico City. Brims's Lower Creeks even returned to the Chattahoochee River from Ochese Creek to prove their good intentions to the Spanish (and, most importantly, to give themselves a buffer against the Cherokees). Meanwhile the Alabama Creeks reached out to the French at Mobile and Biloxi, extracting presents and promises that they would find "the same advantages with us that they had with the English." Finally, in 1717 Brims opened negotiations with Charles Town and won a restoration of the arms trade, set prices, and gunsmithing services. At the same time his niece, known to the English as Mary and to the Creeks as Coosapona-keesa, married the mixed English-Creek trader Johnny Musgrove and set herself up as a key merchant, translator, and diplomat between the peoples. The pinnacle of this multilateral diplomacy came on a single day in 1718, when Brims's town of Coweta hosted simultaneous Spanish, French, and English delegations.[37]

Each colonial power wooed the Creeks as if they carried a royal dowry. The Spanish and French in particular, knowing that they could never compete with English trade, bent over backward to conform to Indian protocol and showered the Creeks with gifts to the best of their ability. South Carolina countered with a pledge not to settle south of the Savannah River, though that promise was broken in spirit with the founding of Georgia in 1733. Yet even as the Creeks prohibited the English from their territory, they permitted the French to build Fort Toulouse on their western boundary at the headwaters of the Alabama River, and the Spanish to open Fort San Marcos on Apalachee Bay. Through this arrangement the Creeks were assured that no single European nation could dictate to them by threatening to sever the trade. As one Frenchman wrote of Brims, "No one has ever been able to make him take sides with one of the three European nations who know him, he alleging that he wishes to see every one, to be neutral, and not to espouse any of the quarrels which the French, English, and Spaniards have with one another." Not to be overlooked, each colonial power "made great presents to [Brims] to regain his friendship . . . which makes him very rich." It made his people rich too, and effectively brought an end to Creek involvement in the Yamasee War, leaving the Yamasees isolated and forced to seek refuge with the Spanish at St. Augustine, an area their own slave raids had cleared of indigenous people.[38]

———

Even as far west as the Mississippi River Valley, Indians' decisions about whether and how to resist colonial expansion had become deeply influenced by the strength of their military stockpiles and supply lines and those of their indigenous enemies. The Natchez of the lower Mississippi River Valley had endured a decade of French encroachment and violence when, on November 29, 1729, they launched a surprise attack on Fort Rosalie and its surrounding settlement, killing at least 238 French and capturing some 300 African slaves and fifty colonists. They were prepared for a drawn-out conflict, having amassed a "great deal" of powder and shot through their trade with the English via the Chickasaws, to which they added plunder from Fort Rosalie and a convoy of four French pirogues (supply boats) they had ambushed along the Mississippi River. The Chickasaw-English connection promised to keep the Natchez armed throughout this conflict. Additionally, the Natchez boasted two palisaded forts along St. Catherine Creek near their Grand Village, replete with bastions and loopholes. Atop they mounted cannons seized from Fort Rosalie, which might have been manned by captive African slaves who had joined their resistance. The Natchez armament and these structures were capable of meeting all the force the French and their Indian allies could muster.[39]

The question was whether the people's will could hold out as long as their martial supplies. In January 1730 a force of 200 French soldiers and a hundred Choctaw and *petites nations* warriors marched into Natchez country to lay siege to the main Natchez fort. They dug hundreds of feet of trenches to bring their artillery to within eighty yards of the walls, but Natchez gunfire repeatedly drove them back before they could coordinate a barrage. "When they get someone in their sights, they do not miss the target," marveled one French lieutenant. A soldier named Brinville learned this lesson the hard way after he dropped his pants and "mooned" the Natchez, shouting, "Here's my white flag," only to have his white flag absorb a direct volley that killed him. The Natchez tried to break the assault with a charge by 200 warriors who had wrapped their muskets in wool to protect them from a driving rain, but after four hours of close combat they had to retreat to the safety of their walls. Ultimately the two exhausted forces agreed that in exchange for the Natchez releasing their prisoners, the French and Choctaws would withdraw. The Natchez, after complying with the prisoner release, then disappeared under the cover of darkness.[40]

Despite losing this fort and then another stronghold the following year, Natchez survivors were determined to keep up the fight, but in the country of their well-armed allies the Chickasaws, to whom they fled. The French were all too willing to oblige them, seeing an opportunity to promote hostilities that would keep the Choctaws away from the Chickasaws' English gunrunners. Yet the Natchez knew better than the French that the Chickasaws were the strongest power in the neighborhood. A two-pronged French invasion of Chickasaw country in the spring and summer of 1736 failed miserably. The northern division from Illinois, consisting of 130 French soldiers and 300 to 400 mostly Great Lakes Indian warriors, arrived well ahead of its southern counterpart from Louisiana, then fell into an ambush in which the Chickasaws killed or captured almost all the French (most of the allied Indians escaped) along with 450 pounds of gunpowder and 1,200 pounds of bullets. The southern prong, consisting of more than 600 professional soldiers, volunteers, and slaves, reinforced by 600 Choctaws, fared no better when it reached Chickasaw country two months later. Louisiana governor Bienville was shocked to find the Chickasaws had built three fortified villages on high ground in such close proximity that their gunmen could form a crossfire. The strongest of these forts, named Ackia, was surrounded by a thick log palisade reinforced by earthen walls capable of absorbing artillery bombs, interspersed with loopholes for defensive gunfire, with corner bastions and mounted cannon. The houses inside were constructed as solidly as blockhouses and aligned to give defenders clear shots throughout the fort's interior. Chickasaw warriors were armed to the teeth, having received sixty horse-loads of goods from Carolina just before the battle, including, reportedly, a stash of grenades. Other munitions came from the plunder of the first French army and ambushes of French pirogues along the Mississippi and Ohio Rivers. The Chickasaws even flew a Union Jack to taunt their French enemies.

The attackers never got the chance to lower the flag. After the French fought through a "shower of balls" to breach the interior of Ackia, the Chickasaws greeted them with a withering barrage that cut them down in their tracks. One soldier recalled, "It was like a slaughterhouse." In the course of less than four hours of fighting, French forces lost thirty-two men to death and seventy to wounds. Bienville exclaimed that "the Chickasaws have the advantage of shooting more accurately than perhaps any other nation," his surprise probably coming in response to their gunmen redirecting fire at the invaders' legs after discovering that they were wearing bullet-resistant wool packs on their chests. It took the Choctaws (who had thus far kept their distance) dragging wounded Frenchmen to safety to prevent an outright bloodbath. Afterward Bienville had little choice but to retreat. Once again the Chickasaws had outgunned and outstrategized a French invading force. It was yet another example of Indians using European firearms better than Europeans.[41]

Collectively these wars taught people throughout the Southeast broad lessons about the balance of power and politics in the age of guns. Indians had become so well armed that they were capable of inflicting incredible damage with surprise attacks on colonial settler societies. Most of them were so resourceful in preparing for war and cultivating multiple supply lines that colonial authorities could not disarm them simply by declaring bans on the weapons trade. Yet if arms embargos could not starve Indians of supplies, they could induce hunger for them. These boycotts gave colonial authorities, particularly the English, an influential, albeit not a decisive, weapon to use, but only if they could manage to control their own traders. The problem, of course, was that colony governments exercised weak authority over their own people and none at all over those of neighboring colonies. Given these conditions, the colonists' most powerful weapon, aside from their artillery, was the lure of arms to recruit Indian warriors to fight for their side. Overall, long-term Indian success in war against colonial states required stockpiles of arms, dependable avenues of supply, regional alliances of tribes to prevent the colonial strategy of divide and conquer, and forts at remote locations where colonial forces could not haul their artillery guns. These conditions were enormously difficult to meet but, as the Chickasaws had demonstrated, far from impossible.

Politics and the Gun Culture

After the carnage of the slave wars and the wars of resistance, most Native people in the Southeast tried to avoid conflict with colonial powers in favor of a play-off political system and the deerskin trade. The idea was to avoid entangling alliances with any one colonial power while extracting presents and favorable trade from all of them. It was an approach to international affairs that, although constantly improvised and subject to the vagaries of imperial, intertribal, and domestic rivalries, brought a level of stability to the region compared to the chaos of the slaving era.

A thriving deerskin trade partially filled the gap caused by the decline in Indian slaving after the Yamasee War. These developments might very well have been connected, as the elimination of so many thousands of Indian people through slaving, warfare, and related diseases opened up new habitat for deer, which likely produced an explosion of deer population. The number of deerskins exported out of the southeastern English and French colonies climbed from 53,000 per year between 1698 and 1715, to 177,500 a year between 1758 and 1759, to 400,000 a year in 1764. These skins had less purchasing power than slaves, but they could make ends meet. Guns from English traders cost ten skins in 1735 and sixteen skins in 1767, and three-fourths of a pint of gunpowder cost one skin in 1767. By comparison, the price of French goods in 1721 was set at twenty deerskins for a gun and two-thirds of a pound of powder or forty bullets for one skin. An Indian hunter trading thirty to sixty skins a year (as appears to have been typical) had more than enough to cover the costs of his arms while leaving extra for other goods.[42]

Indians also addressed the decline in slaving by extracting gifts of munitions and gunsmithing from colonies courting their allegiance, in what amounted to the second phase of the gun frontier. South Carolina's public expenditure on Indian gifts climbed from 4 percent of the colony budget in 1716 to 7 percent in 1732. Carolina also rewarded Indians with arms for capturing runaway slaves and servants, paying out a gun and three blankets for every fugitive in the 1770s. The newly founded colony of Georgia, which occupied the territorial void created by slave raiding and the Yamasee War, gave the Creeks another British colony to play. Georgia's presents to Indians included 600 guns in 1735 and eight barrels of gunpowder, 1,400 pounds of musket balls, and 400 pounds of swan shot in 1739. Additionally, it stationed gunsmiths at Savannah and Augusta for the repair of Indian arms. The alternative was for Georgia to risk Indians taking their trade to South Carolina and putting their warriors in the service of Florida or Louisiana.[43]

The French used gifts of smithing, gunpowder, and shot, and a "judicious application" of other presents, to compensate for their inability to match the English supplies and low prices of military hardware. The French sent subsidized gunsmiths to live in key Creek and Choctaw communities, which, the English fumed, then led Indians to expect the same of them. Initially the French refused to repair English arms, much to the irritation of Choctaw leader Alibamon Mingo, "because almost all the warriors of his village are armed with these guns." However, Louisiana's inability to meet the demands of its Indian allies for arms eventually produced a relaxation of this policy, to great effect. Writing in 1755 about the imperial rivalry, Carolina trader Edmond Atkin stressed that free gunsmithing gave the French influence with the Indians well beyond the monetary value of the service. "We furnish the Indians with guns enough in exchange for their deer skins and furs," he recognized, "but the French mend them and keep them in repair *gratis*." Smithing was doubly important because when an Indian saw his damaged gun "suddenly restored to its former state, and as useful as before, it gladdens his heart more than a present of a new gun would," probably because the fix doubled as a gesture of friendship. The French also cultivated Indian alliances through gifts of munitions, particularly gunpowder. French gunpowder set the European standard, and Indians were eager to obtain it, even when they acquired their muskets from the English. Moreover, French powder and shot were available in high volume because the French were able to ferry their goods to Louisiana and its inland posts by water, whereas English traders were reluctant to burden their pack trains with heavy ammunition on journeys that ran hundreds of miles. One scholar has gone so far as to call powder and ball the "currency" of Fort Toulouse, much of which the Indians also received for free.[44]

Gifts of arms accompanied free blacksmithing and ammunition. Unable to compete with the dynamic English market, the French curried favor with Native leaders by presenting them with fancy "chiefs'

Military Commission Granted to Chief Okana-Stoté of the Cherokee by Governor Louis Billouart, Chevalier de Kerlérec, February 27, 1761. The French used lavishly illustrated commissions, like this one, to seal trade and political partnerships with Native individuals and groups. Sometimes these partnerships bypassed traditional Indian elites, which created civil strife within Native society. The French subsidized the trade in firearms, and routinely gave diplomatic gifts of munitions (such as the gun depicted here) as basic parts of their relations with indigenous people. Courtesy National Archives and Records Administration, Washington, DC.

guns" characterized by polished barrels, brass and silver plates, and elaborate engravings. The roster of chiefs, head warriors, and other important figures receiving such gifts stood at 111 men among the Choctaws alone in 1733. Initially France's common Indian-trade muskets *(fusils de chasse)* were less durable than the chiefs' guns, but eventually French authorities began to insist on higher-quality muskets manufactured to Indian specifications. Native customers wanted weapons of lightweight but with strong barrels of sufficient caliber "to receive balls of the various types that they normally use," referring to the Indians' practice of loading their arms with small shot and of reducing the gauge of single-shot loads as the barrel became coated with black powder residue in between cleanings. By the mid-eighteenth century, trade guns produced at the royal armory at Tulle had gained a reputation among Indians as "the best," to the point that French authorities complained "they will not have any others."[45]

Gulf Coast and Mississippi River Valley Indians extracted enormous amounts of free munitions from the French and Spanish by the mere possibility that they would throw in their lot with the British. In 1732 Mobile's commander put in an order for Indian gifts in the amount of 80,000 pounds of gunpowder, 14,000 pounds of lead, 25,000 gunflints, and 600 trade guns with brass mountings. The post already owed 120 muskets to Indians who "ask for them daily." The French showed even greater generosity in wartime, as in 1759 amid the Seven Years' War when Louisiana earmarked 900 guns for presents and 600 guns for trade. Spanish Florida was unable to keep pace, but episodically it too provided Indians with munitions as presents, as in 1736 when it hosted over a hundred unidentified Indians in St. Augustine and gave each one a gun, powder, and shot. All this was enough to make South Carolina merchant Sam Everleigh fume that "the Indians have been so used of late years to receive presents that they now expect it as a right belonging to them, and the English, French, and Spanish are in some measure become tributary to them."[46]

———

The uninterrupted flow of arms even after the decline of the slave trade enabled Indians in the Southeast to develop a gun culture much like the one that had taken shape in the Northeast in previous decades.

Indian [Chickasaw] Going Hunting, by Philip Georg Friedrich von Reck (1736). This drawing of a Chickasaw man heading out for the hunt illustrates the growing importance of firearms to southeastern Indians during the late seventeenth and early eighteenth centuries, the Chicka-saws foremost among them. Many Indian men preferred the gun over the bow and arrow for hunting because the power of its shot could drop a large game animal in its tracks. Courtesy Royal Library, Copenhagen.

Southeastern Indians preferred the gun over the bow and arrow for hunting deer because they could drop their kill with one shot. It was the opinion of John Stewart, a Scottish trader from Charles Town, that Indian hunters with firearms could "get more hides and furs in one moon than formerly with bow and arrow in 12 moons." Carolinian John Lawson agreed, recalling his travels with an Indian hunter who "always shot with a single ball, missing but two shots in above forty." If the hunter intended to trade the skin from his hunt, he would have to aim his shot at the head so as not to damage the hide, which attests to both the accuracy of smoothbore muskets when fired at close range and the skill of Native gunmen. Lawson's impression was that North Carolina Indians used the bow and arrow only for hunting small game like turkey and ducks, "thinking it not worth throwing powder and shot after them," probably because a single arrow could easily bring them down. By the mid-eighteenth century some colonial observers went so far as to claim that young Indian men were incapable of hunting without firearms, for they had never performed that duty with the bow and arrow. Exagger-ated or not, it is clear that Indians had turned firearms into essential tools for men to pursue their masculine roles as warriors and hunters.[47]

Southeastern Indians used guns in their rituals in a similar manner to Natives in the Northeast. They included guns and ammunition in the burials of adult men, alongside other gender-specific tools for use in travel to the afterworld. Ceremonial occasions such as making and renewing peace typically closed with Indian men "firing off their guns and whooping." The same was true of funerals because the Indians "imagine the report of guns will send off the ghosts of their kindred that died at home, to their quiet place." During thunder and lightning storms, southeastern Indians fired their guns toward the sky to show the Thunderbird "that they were warriors, and not afraid to die in any shape; much less afraid of that threatening noise." They were also demonstrating that they wielded the power of the elements no less than the spirits of the upper world.[48]

Likewise the southeastern Indians, no less than indigenous people in the North, developed expertise in firearms repair, bullet casting, and flint knapping. Lawson characterized southeastern Indian men as "curious artists in managing a gun." He elaborated, "When they have bought a piece, and find it shoots any ways crooked, they take the barrel out of the stock, cutting a notch in a tree, where in they set it straight, sometimes shooting away above 100 loads of ammunition before they bring the gun to shoot according to their mind." They were equally masterful at carving gun stocks "only with a small hatchet and knife." Not surprisingly, given these observations, spare gun parts, bullet molds, and knapped flints are found in plentiful amounts at Creek archaeological sites from this period. Women must have had their own part to play in the artisanal life of guns by sewing and decorating shot bags and gun cases for their male relatives, though no examples from this period have survived in the archaeological record or found their way into museum collections. In these ways, and doubtless numerous others that have eluded documentation, firearms had become a fundamental part of the southeastern Indians' material culture and community rituals.[49]

––––––––

The same deerskin trade and play-off politics that underwrote this gun culture carried the danger of civil strife as young men on the make circumvented established chiefs to open their own trade lines and drum up foreign recognition of their claims to leadership. There was a built-in tension in many Indian societies between established leaders and young aspirants. The former's leadership rested on their age, maturity, elite lineages, and accomplishments. Such men tended to favor peace and stability. Young men pursuing their own leadership credentials often provoked conflict with foreign peoples in order to prove themselves as warriors. With the onset of European trade, they obtained an additional route to influence, for if a young man managed to bring outside trade into the community, or convince a colonial government that he was a person worthy of receiving chiefly honors, he might actually acquire that status. This dynamic might help explain why one Upper Creek chief in the mid-eighteenth century went by the name of Gun Merchant. The problem was that making a power play by becoming a gun merchant usually involved the young man promising his people's allegiance to one colonial state exclusively, regardless of the will of the chiefs and the re-actions of the other colonial powers.[50]

The Choctaws suffered just this sort of strife after the Natchez War as a result of the ambitions of a warrior named Red Shoes and the draw of English trade. Red Shoes had developed a warrior following by virtue of his exploits against Chickasaws, but he aspired to even greater heights. Throughout the 1730s Red Shoes pursued English trade over the Franco-centric foreign policies of the established leadership, including his hometown's Mingo Tchito, the so-called "French Great Chief." One source of discontent for Red Shoes and his men appears to have been the lack of guns provided by the French and the chiefs' control over this meager stockpile. Generally the chiefs kept firearms given to them as presents by Louisiana and then loaned them out to hunters and war-riors, thus strengthening their influence. Red Shoes contended that this system not only put too much power in the chiefs' hands, but gave the French too much leverage over the chiefs and the people. The chiefs' response was the English were so far away that if Red Shoes prevailed, the people "would see themselves forced to take up their old arms, the bow and arrow, again," that is, "unless they wanted to load their guns with [English] limbourg [cloth]." Red Shoes would not be swayed, and thrice during the mid- to late 1730s he arranged for Carolina pack trains laden with trade guns to enter Choctaw country. In return Charles Town awarded him a medallion and proclamation naming him "King of the Choctaws." Red Shoes also tried to broker peace with the Chickasaws,

Carolina's main indigenous trade partner in the region, first in 1739, then again in 1745.[51]

It was time for the Francophile chiefs and Louisiana to intervene, for Red Shoes was on the verge of achieving a political and commercial realignment that would rob them of power and perhaps threaten the very existence of the French colony. The chiefs tried to limit the internecine violence by killing a visiting Chickasaw diplomat and his wife, but there seemed to be no other choice after Red Shoes retaliated by killing three Frenchman. With Lousiana governor Pierre de Rigaud de Vaudreuil threatening to institute a trade embargo and throw French support to the Choctaws' longtime enemy, the Alabamas, the Francophile chiefs assassinated Red Shoes in June 1747, just as he was leading another trade caravan from Charles Town into his community of Conchitto. It was the beginning of two years of bloody civil war in the nation. This dark chapter in Choctaw history came to an end only after the French-leaning eastern Choctaws, outfitted with French guns, powder, shot, and even cannons, managed to subdue the English-leaning western towns, which found their Carolina supply lines less reliable in wartime than they had hoped. Eight hundred of Red Shoes's followers lost their lives in this struggle, their scalps sold to the French for bounties double that offered for Chickasaw trophies. The expense to the French was some 62,000 livres in presents per year to a roster that by 1763 counted over 600 men. Play-off politics, like the adoption of guns, was full of opportunities to accumulate wealth and power, but also loaded with danger.[52]

In 1701 trader John Lawson met with a shaman of the Santee tribe of the Carolinian Piedmont, who used a parable to account for why so many Indians like himself had become disfigured by smallpox. He told that they had urged the Great Spirit "to make their capacities equal with the white people in making guns, ammunition, etc." The Great Spirit, however, discouraged their curiosity, and counseled that they should be satisfied with the way of life he had taught their ancestors. He would teach them if they insisted, but at a price. Now they had guns and no noses.[53]

Of course, the southeastern Indians' adoption of guns carried even greater costs, which was one of the underlying morals of the story. There is no way to calculate the exact number of Indians killed and captured during the gun violence of the late seventeenth and early eighteenth centuries, but the figure certainly ran into the high tens and even hundreds of thousands of people. To make matters worse, smallpox stalked the routes of slave raiding and gunrunning, preying on populations that were malnourished and traumatized by the predatory violence and clustered into defensive fortifications, which rendered them more vulnerable to communicable diseases. The overall effect was a population decline of some two-thirds between 1685 and 1730, from an estimated 199,000 people to some 67,000.[54]

To be sure, gun violence created even as it destroyed. Survivors formed new coalitions like the Yamasees, Creeks, and Catawbas, in part to protect themselves from slave raiders and organize their warriors into militant slavers. The Indians' quest for firearms led to political relations with a host of new colonies and empires, and trade lines that connected them to a burgeoning global commerce. Consequently their material life was richer than ever before, marked not only by munitions but brightly colored cloth, tailored clothing, exotic pigments, metal tools, and much more. It is apt to call this change in Indian life a consumer revolution, but it was one in which there were far fewer people to enjoy the goods.[55]

The relative calm—relative, that is, to the maelstrom of the slave trade—after the Tuscarora, Yamasee, and Natchez Wars, should not be romanticized. In all likelihood the reason the Indians stopped going slaving for Carolina was not that they saw the inhumanity in it or that they feared the slave merchants would double-cross them like the Westos, Shawnees, or Yamasees. Instead, the spread of firearms throughout Indian country had made this enterprise too dangerous.

There was yet another factor in the decline of the Indian slave trade, reflecting the sinister forces of colonialism at work. Colonial buyers shifted their preference in slaves from Indians to Africans. In 1716 only sixty-seven Africans entered South Carolina. Within a decade Carolina was importing 1,700 Africans a year and in 1736 that figure climbed to over 3,000. Efficiencies in the transatlantic African slave trade were making those unfortunate souls cheaper and more available than ever before in the North American market. These captives also came without the risk that their people an ocean away would rise against the colonies in which they toiled. In western Africa, the havoc unleashed by this trade became almost a mirror image of what had been wrought in the Indian Southeast for two generations. By the late seventeenth and early eighteenth centuries, the slave trade in western Africa often was an exchange of humans for guns in which some indigenous polities faced the choice of either slaving for the market or becoming slaves sold in the market. This devil's bargain had become a basic feature of colonialism throughout the Atlantic World.[56]

3. RECOIL

THE FATAL QUEST FOR ARMS DURING KING PHILIP'S WAR

Bad poetry should rank among the things for which seventeenth-century New England is known. As one might expect from Puritans, much of this tortured verse focuses on the stern judgment of God and the wondrous, if sometimes terrifying, features of the so-called howling wilderness in America. The surprise is how often Puritan poets addressed the topic of Indians and firearms. For all the colonists' anxieties about salvation and wolves preying on their sheep, they were also haunted by the fact of being surrounded by indigenous people with superior armaments. Equally unnerving was the danger of the Natives using these weapons to redress their grievances against the colonial order.

William Bradford, the longtime governor of Plymouth colony, devoted more space to this issue than any of his literary peers, beginning with his "Descriptive and Historical Account of New England," written around 1650. For him the problem was not only that gun-toting Indians were a threat, but that colonial New Englanders themselves had contributed to the dilemma through a black-market trade in violation of law and morality. He wrote:

> Base covetousness hath got such a sway,
> As, our own safety, we ourselves betray;
> For these fierce natives, they are now so fill'd,
> With guns and muskets, and in them so skill'd,
> As that they may keep the English in awe,
> And when they please to give them the law;

And of powder and shot, they have such store,
  As sometimes they refuse to buy more;
Flints, screw-plates, and molds for all sorts of shot,
  They have, and skill how to use them, have got;
And mend and new stock their pieces they can,
  As well in most things, as an Englishman.
Thus, like madmen, we put them in a way,
  With our own weapons, to kill and slay.

The blame for this situation rested not on the colonies' magistrates, like Bradford himself, for they did their Christian duty to legislate against the arms trade. Nor did the fault lie, in Bradford's estimation, primarily with the Dutch or French, whose arms dealers were just a fraction of the whole. No, the everyday sort of English—"Merchants, shopkeepers, traders, and planters too"—were the main source of their own trouble and an affront to God.[1]

The disaster Bradford portended finally materialized in King Philip's War of 1675–1676. For the better part of nine months, Indian gunmen lured colonial militia into devastating ambushes, sacked outlying English towns, and terrorized the roadways. It seemed within their grasp to push the line of English settlement back to the outskirts of Boston and even into the sea. What made the Natives' guerilla strikes so effective was that the warriors seemed to blend into the thick New England woods until the very moment they opened fire. As schoolteacher and poet Benjamin Thompson described it, "The trees stood like sentinels and bullets flew, From every bush (a shelter for their crew)/Hence came our wounds and deaths from every side, While skulking enemies squat undescried." Throughout King Philip's War, the English possessed the advantage of being able to import large quantities of firearms, gunpowder, and lead from the mother country. Yet they were the ones who felt under siege by Native enemies, who were often better armed and more adept at using guns in forest warfare.[2]

Nevertheless, the Indians who fought against the English lost King Philip's War, and a significant reason was that their military supplies waned as the conflict wore on, thus revealing the danger of their dependence on foreign munitions. If militant Indians had penned their own verse to explain their reversal of fortune, they might have started

93

with how the region's sachems had long debated whether a victory over the English was possible, given that their warriors relied on European munitions. Certainly they would have told of how the Mohawks, at the urging of the young English colony of New York, drove them away from the French and Dutch gun markets during the war, thus leaving them short of supplies, and how an English strike on one of their camps on the Connecticut River handicapped their ability to maintain their weapons and produce their own shot. They would have recalled bitterly how other New England Indians, equally skilled as they were at the "skulking way of war," chose to throw their support to the English. Of all the morals King Philip's War had to teach, among the most significant was this: It was dangerous, even suicidal, for Indians surrounded by the expanding English colonies and dependent on English munitions to go to war against them unless they had reliable trade alternatives among other European powers. Whereas interior groups like the Iroquois, Creeks, and Chickasaws were encircled by a gun frontier giving them relatively dependable access to multiple colonial markets, by the 1670s east-coast nations like the Wampanoags, Narragansetts, and Nipmucs had only tentative lines beyond the English. In peacetime that condition might not have seemed overly dangerous, given weak governmental control over gunrunners and the factious rivalries between neighboring English colonies. However, during King Philip's War the English closed ranks and showed unprecedented respect for laws banning the trade of guns and ammunition to Indians. Once the Mohawks cut off the French and Dutch arms markets, the warring Indians had to rely on plunder to restock their munitions. It was not enough.

The Indians of southern New England never put these events to verse or committed them to oral histories. The warring Indians in King Philip's War suffered the loss of thousands of their people to violent deaths and disease. The English captured hundreds and perhaps even thousands of others and sent them into the hell of Caribbean slavery. Most of those lucky enough to survive and escape captivity fled the region for good to take refuge in the Saint Lawrence or Hudson River Valley or places beyond. Even those who sided with the English wound up suffering, for after the war the colonies immediately seized hundreds of square miles of Indian land and began the long but indelible process of acquiring most of the rest, largely through underhanded means. It would be a wonder if anyone who had gone through these ordeals wanted to reflect on it. Nevertheless, it is time to remember that the war had sprung a trap set by the New England Indians' dependence on firearms.[3]

Arming Native New England

New England in the mid-seventeenth century was as favorable an arms market as Indians could hope to find, because of numerous divisions within the colonial ranks. Though all of the English colonies in the region were established by reformed Protestants (or Puritans) opposed to Catholic elements in the Anglican Church, several rifts emerged when it came to building their own ecclesiastical order in America. The subsequent hiving off of dissidents and fortune seekers from Plymouth and Massachusetts produced the colonies of Rhode Island, Connecticut, and New Haven, the independent plantations of Martha's Vineyard and Nantucket, and several semiautonomous English towns on eastern Long Island. Massachusetts, Plymouth, Connecticut, and New Haven tried to coordinate their foreign affairs, including Indian relations, by creating the United Colonies of New England in 1643. They excluded Rhode Island because of its religious heterodoxy. Until 1664 the Dutch of New Netherland were also a player. Their shipboard trade from their Hudson River base extended eastward throughout the full range of Long Island Sound. They also ran temporary trading stations on Buzzard's Bay, Narragansett Bay, and Block Island, and a long-term trade factory on the Connecticut River at the site of modern Hartford. Inland, the Dutch post of Fort Orange, just west of the modern Massachusetts/New York border, attracted Native customers from as far east as the Connecticut River Valley. Competition among the English colonies and between the English and Dutch allowed Indians to choose among multiple traders from the two most commercially minded and important arms-producing nations of Europe. The French of the Saint Lawrence River Valley were more remote, but still accessible through the Abenakis of the upper Connecticut River Valley. Southern New England rivaled the lower Delaware River Valley and Chesapeake Bay as a gun mart for Native people.[4]

Rivalries between Indian polities for tribute, people, and territory promoted the gun market. Southern New England was densely populated with indigenous people because it offered a rich combination of marine and freshwater resources, weather and soil conditions compatible with corn–beans–squash horticulture, and estuarine and forest environments for hunting and gathering. The large Algonquian-speaking population sustained by this bounty was organized into dozens of town-sized polities called sachemships, each headed by a sachem (or chief). Episodically, autonomous sachemships, affiliated by kinship and language, would co-operate in the interests of foreign policy, war, and trade, usually under the leadership of a great sachem. For the sake of convenience and the lack of a better term, we call these groups tribes. By the 1630s the tribes of southeast New England included the Wampanoags of what is now south-eastern Massachusetts, the Narragansetts of Rhode Island, and the Pequots and Mohegans of southeastern Connecticut (the Mohegans were distinct from the Mohicans of the Hudson and Housatonic River Valleys). More loosely organized peoples included the Nipmucs of central Massachusetts and the Woronocos, Pocumtucks, Norridgewoks, and Sokokis of the upper Connecticut River Valley. These polities competed with each other constantly for followers and to establish or escape hierarchical, tribute-paying relationships in which weaker parties paid wampum (shell beads), furs, and corn to stronger ones. Violence was part and parcel of these contests. The opening of colonial trade meant that guns and ammunition became essential to Indian politics too.[5]

The Indian demand for munitions, and the eagerness of colonists to sell them, was evident from the outset of New England colonization in the 1620s and early 1630s, when only matchlocks were available. The many struggles that Plymouth colony confronted during its first years included a rogue English trading post, on the south shore of Massachusetts Bay under the leadership of Thomas Morton that supplied muskets, powder, and shot to nearby Indians after discovering they "would give any price they could attain to for them." Plymouth found Morton's gunrunning so threatening that it arrested and transported him back to England even though his operation took place outside its jurisdiction. Yet no sooner was Morton gone than the arms trade revived through shipboard traders and fishermen, which, Bradford complained, "no laws can restrain, by the reason of the baseness of sundry unworthy persons, both English, Dutch, and French, which may turn to the ruin of many." Shortly these sea dogs were joined by a bevy of inland traders operating out of Plymouth and the newly founded Massachusetts Bay Colony, which attracted more than 13,000 migrants in the short span of 1629 to 1640. During the 1620s and 1630s Plymouth opened a string of trade posts in Maine and others closer to home on Buzzard's Bay, Cape Cod, and the Connecticut River. Massachusetts answered by expanding its commercial reach up the Concord and Merrimac Rivers west and north of Boston and eventually to the Connecticut River Valley. The Dutch dominated trade on Narragansett Bay for fifteen years until the founding of Rhode Island in 1636, and even then they maintained a presence there. The surrounding Narragansett and Wampanoag Indians, like increasing numbers of Native people throughout southern New England, reaped the benefit of having rival Europeans vie for their business.[6]

Such a competitive environment all but assured an expansive black market in arms, despite Charles I having issued two royal proclamations against trading munitions to Indians. It took only until 1631 for Massachusetts governor Thomas Dudley to begin complaining about Englishmen furnishing Indians with weaponry. Even common farmers, artisans, and servants participated in this traffic. In September 1632 Massachusetts ordered Richard Hopkins, who otherwise left no trace in the historical record, to be whipped and branded on the cheek for selling guns, powder, and shot to Indians on the Bay. One of the first governmental acts of the colony of Connecticut, in April 1636, was to bring charges against the carpenter Henry Stiles for trading a gun to an Indian in exchange for corn, followed quickly by passage of an official ban on such transactions upon "heavy penalty" (coincidentally—providentially, some Puritans might say—Stiles would die fifteen years later in a gun accident). When war broke out between the English and the Pequots in 1636, the Pequots already had a stockpile of sixteen muskets, though they lacked powder.[7]

Policing the arms trade to Indians had emerged as one of the colonies' most tenacious challenges. During the late 1630s and the 1640s, every colonial legislature passed sanctions to punish illegal arms sales and the repair of Indian weapons, with one fine running twenty times the value of the illicit goods. Massachusetts went so far as to have its ban printed and posted on the door of every meetinghouse in the colony. Nevertheless, year after year frustrated authorities railed that the trade continued through "indirect means." As Bradford put it, "And of the English, so many are guilty/ And deal under-handed, in such secrecy."[8]

Part of the difficulty in regulating the gun frontier was that it operated either in or on the edges of Indian country, far from watchful colonial eyes, and often on the small inlets of New England's craggy coastline where it was easy to land smuggled cargo undetected. Additionally, much of this trade probably flowed through men whom the colonies needed as interpreters and ambassadors to Indians, therefore encouraging magistrates to turn a blind eye to their indiscretions. Take, for example, the cluster of interpreters/traders active around Stonington, Connecticut, just west of the modern Rhode Island/Connecticut border during the late 1640s and 1650s. Stonington was located in territory contested by the Mohegans, Narragansetts, and Pequots, as well as between Rhode Island, Connecticut, and Massachusetts. English colonists began moving into the region by the late 1640s with the founding of New London, but still the overwhelming majority of people in the area were Indians. Stonington's shoreline on the north side of Long Island Sound was a labyrinth of bays, coves, river inlets, and islands perfect for discreet participation in the English and Dutch coastwise trades. This location also provided easy access by water and overland paths to the Narragansetts, Eastern Niantics, Western Niantics, Mohegans, Pequots, Montauketts, and Shinnecocks, each of whom lived less than a half day's journey away.

Though there is no clear evidence of this trade, given its clandestine nature, consider the following: Thomas Stanton, who worked as the United Colonies' primary interpreter-ambassador to the Pequots, Mohegans, and Narragansetts, appears to have started his career alongside the coastwise trader John Oldham, whose death in 1636 at the hands of the Manisse Indians of Block Island was one of the precipitating events of the Pequot War. A decade later, in 1646, Connecticut fined Stanton "for selling lead out of this jurisdiction"—to whom and where the official record does not say, but the implication was that Indians were involved. Many years later, in 1669, Stanton told Connecticut deputy John Mason that the Narragansetts had been pressuring him to sell powder and lead even though they were already "exceedingly furnished of ammunition." None of these details add up to "probable cause," never mind "beyond a reasonable doubt," but they suggest that Stanton was involved in the arms trade in some capacity.[9]

Also reflect on the career of Stanton's neighbor, William Cheese-brough, who, like Stanton, conducted Indian diplomacy on behalf of Connecticut and the towns of New London and Stonington. Cheese-brough, a gunsmith, was on the move shortly after his arrival in Massachusetts in 1630, first settling down in Seekonk on the border between the Wampanoags and Narragansetts and in between the jurisdictions of Plymouth and Rhode Island. Next he relocated to Long Island, where he fell into trouble with Connecticut for unspecified trade with the Indians. In 1650/1651 he asked for permission to relocate to Stonington, after apologizing to the magistrates for having previously lived in a "solitary" way among the Natives. To bolster his case, he claimed to have sold away all his smithing tools so indigenous people would not ask for his services and the English would not suspect him of proffering them. The court agreed, but only if he posted a £100 bond to ensure he would not "prosecute any unlawful trade with the Indians." Whether Cheesebrough remained true to his bond is uncertain, but the fact that he emerged as a go-between in English–Indian relations suggests that something about him impressed Native people besides his linguistic skills and diplomatic personality.[10]

The shadowy operations of Stanton and Cheesebrough were the norm in the Indian trade. Rhode Islanders Roger Williams and Richard Smith operated out of Coscumscussoc in Narragansett country, not in colonial towns. Whether they dealt in arms and ammunition is unknown, but Smith also maintained a house in New Amsterdam from which he could easily import Dutch goods, including, perhaps, munitions. Traders John Picket and John Wilcox, who had close ties to Williams and Smith, worked among the Narragansetts as subcontractors for the Dutch governor Willem Kieft. John Pynchon's Indian trade on the Connecticut River involved sending out agents from his base in Springfield to the Pocumtucks and Sokokis upriver and the Mohicans to the west. Were Pynchon's men running guns? The archaeological and historical records are unequivocal that the Indians with whom these men dealt were well armed by the 1650s, but somehow no one managed to see any contraband passing through the traders' hands. As the commissioners of the United Colonies lamented in 1649, "the trad[e] of guns, powder, and shot with the Indians [is] so mischievous to us all and yet so hard to be discovered and proved."[11]

One has to wonder how committed the commissioners were to cracking down on such men, given the colonies' dependence on them to handle Indian relations. The traders' knowledge of Indian languages, protocols, and politics, and the welcome they received in Native communities, extended from their commercial activities. Turning a blind eye to a certain amount of arms dealing by these figures might have been a pragmatic compromise on the part of authorities. Everyone also knew that Indians would turn to the Dutch if the English refused to sell them munitions. In any case, Indians were no more willing than English colonists to inform on their suppliers. "The Indians are nurtured so well," Bradford mused, "as, by no means, you get them to tell, of whom they had their guns, or such supply/ Or, if they do, they will feign some false lie." It was simply impossible to prosecute this deadly business without forthcoming witnesses.[12]

Another challenge in monitoring the arms trade was that the English colonies permitted licensed merchants to sell munitions to certain "friend Indians" but not to others. Those "friend Indians" included Christians such as the Massachusett Indians near Boston, the Wampanoags on Cape Cod, Martha's Vineyard, and Nantucket, and the Nipmucs some forty miles inland from Boston. The collective number of these "praying Indians" stood at over 4,800 by 1671. "Friend Indians" who served as military allies and sources of intelligence for the colonies also included the Montauketts of Long Island and the Mohegans and Pequots of eastern Connecticut, with the Pequots having resigned themselves to cooperating with the English after their bloody losses in the Pequot War. Weapons for the friend Indians came with instructions to keep them out of the hands of other indigenous people, but probably some of them honored this rule more in the breach than in the observance.[13]

If New England governments struggled to control their own arms dealers, they found it doubly challenging to police the French and especially the Dutch. In 1642 Massachusetts Bay Colony authorities searched the homes of nearby Indians amid a war scare and found numerous guns of French and Dutch manufacture, though some of these weapons might have come from English traders. The following year Roger Williams noted that Indians often acquired muskets from the French only to sell them to the English when they became damaged. Williams did not specify whether these weapons arrived overland from the Saint Lawrence River Valley or Maine, from shipboard traders, or from all of these sources. Judging from the number of Jesuit rings and other Catholic paraphernalia found in the archaeological sites of southern New England Indians, such exchanges took place fairly often, if sporadically, during this period.[14]

Indian trade with the Dutch was much more common because of New Netherland's proximity and the Dutch commitment to manufacturing and transatlantic commerce. New Haven caught Dutch merchant David Provoost trying to smuggle gun barrels, gun locks, and gunpowder hidden in wine casks into the colony in 1653. That same year Connecticut foiled an attempt by Captain Kempo Sybada, an Italian working for the Dutch West India Company, to begin trading arms from his fishing station on Block Island. The colony was able to catch wind of the scheme probably because Sybada owned a house lot in New London and had hired the English couple William and Mary Baker to manage his Block Island outfit. The Dutch gun trade was so widespread on eastern Long Island that English colonists there complained of Indians being "at least plentifully furnished as they themselves, as apt to give volleys of shot in their entertainments and compliments, and by exercise have become good marksmen." More to the point, the Indians had "grown insolent and injurious against the English." Roger Williams agreed that the Dutch arms trade had grown so out of control that "the barbarians all the land over are filled with artillery and ammunition" and their "insolency is grown so high that they daily consult and threaten to render us slaves." Yet New England authorities could do little about it because the overseas and coastwise merchant communities of New England and New Netherland were hopelessly intertwined and the maze of waterways they traversed was nearly impossible to monitor. Furthermore, Dutch military wares were in high demand among Native people, most of whom remained economically influential and fully autonomous even amid English expansion. They intended to stay that way by acquiring firearms from the English, Dutch, and French alike along New England's multifront gun frontier.[15]

Like their contemporaries elsewhere in the eastern woodlands, Indians in southern New England were keen to acquire smoothbore flintlocks, with the initial purpose of employing them against indigenous rivals. By 1645 the Narragansetts had built up enough of an arsenal to send out thirty gunmen against the Mohegans, with whom they competed to absorb Pequot survivors and territory following the Pequot War. English doctors tending to the Mohegans in the wake of this attack found thirty men in need of medical attention, "most of which were wounded with bullets." Uncas, the Mohegan sachem, stated the obvious when he complained that it was the Narragansetts' guns "which won them the day." Predictably, his people followed the Narragansett example. Just two years after this battle, John Winthrop Jr. complained about Uncas's brother, Nowequa, "with 40 or 50 men, many of them armed with guns," stalking New London to intimidate Pequots who had taken shelter with the English there.[16]

The use of firearms in intertribal battles had become so common by 1658 that the Connecticut town of Farmington ordered the nearby Tunxis Indians to move farther away, citing "bullets shot into the [English] Town in their skirmishes" with "strang[e] Indians." Yet this measure did not prevent terrified Farmington residents from receiving a surprise visit by Pocumtuck warriors on the march, "many" of whom were "armed with guns," an event that led Hartford to pass a ban against armed Indians passing through English towns. There was reason for worry. In 1659 Narragansett and Pocumtuck gunmen shot up the house of the trader Jonathan Brewster after he ignored their people's repeated warnings to stop selling munitions to the Mohegans. No one was killed in this incident, but the Narragansetts did hatchet a Mohegan, one of Brewster's servants, as he held on to Brewster's wife's waist, and afterward they boasted (incorrectly, it turned out) that their attack had killed John Mason, Connecticut's liaison to Uncas. The Narragansetts, like other Indians throughout the East, would not tolerate colonists supplying arms to their enemies if they had any say about it.[17]

In tandem with this arms buildup, New England Indians also began to develop the ability to repair their weapons and cast their own shot. They probably obtained these skills more quickly and efficiently than other indigenous people east of the Mississippi because of the particular intensity of Indian–colonial relations in New England. Numerous Indians labored in English homes and workshops in the years leading up to King Philip's War, some as slaves after their capture in the Pequot

War, and many others as hired hands. At least one Christian Indian from Nonantum (located on the border of modern Brighton and Newton, Massachusetts), apprenticed with an English blacksmith in Roxbury, just outside of Boston, with whom he learned to repair arms. Doubtless other Indians living among the English picked up such skills as well. Smithing tools appear as grave goods in the interment of at least one Narragansett man buried at midcentury. These examples, combined with the number of spare gun parts found at numerous Indian archaeological sites from the period, indicate that Native people had widespread access to smithing services, sometimes within their own communities. They also cast their own musket balls from bar lead, using metal molds purchased from colonists and stone molds they had carved themselves. The growing self-sufficiency of Indian gunmen spelled trouble for the English, given the rising tensions between their communities.[18]

By the mid- to late seventeenth century, southern New England Indians stockpiled arms to fend off English aggression as well as to battle one another. The English colonies, domineering from their very start, became even more so as their population swelled due to a high birth-rate and good health while the Indians' plummeted from epidemic diseases. The New England colonies were rare among their early seventeenth-century counterparts in starting with a relatively equal balance of men and women and managing to avoid large-scale famine and scourges. The women tended to marry young and bore, on average, eight children, most of whom reached adulthood and survived to old age (even by today's standard). Thus, even though English migration to the region virtually ceased after 1640, the colonies' population had climbed to over 30,000 people by 1660, with no end in sight. Meanwhile Indians were still trying to recover from a vicious epidemic in 1616–1619, which eviscerated numerous coastal communities, and then a smallpox outbreak in 1633, which killed an estimated one-third or more of indigenous people on Long Island Sound and up the Connecticut River Valley. The precise extent of Indian losses will never be known, but the best estimates are that the Native population of southern New England plunged from a range of 126,000 to 144,000 people before 1616 to approximately 30,000 in 1670. The survivors could not mistake that there was some sort of direct relationship between the English increase and their decline.[19]

Colonists took advantage of their growing power to appropriate more and more Indian land by means sometimes fair but too often foul. Even when Indians legitimately agreed to permit colonists to live and plant in a certain area, they were rarely prepared for how the colonists' livestock and timbering spoiled resources well beyond the bounds of English settlements. Disputes over trespass and damage mounted in turn. The English also interfered in Indian politics and community life. The United Colonies repeatedly asserted the right to arbitrate intertribal disputes between the Narragansetts and Mohegans, and offered protection to Indian communities at risk of Narragansett subjugation. A number of Indian peoples welcomed this support, but often it came with pressure to host Christian missionaries, who encouraged the Indians not only to adopt Christian beliefs and English behaviors but to halt their tribute payments to regional sachems. By the early 1670s the missions had cleaved off tribute payers on Cape Cod and the islands from the Wampanoag sachem, Philip, which accounted for about a third of his total. Missionaries had also begun making serious inroads among Nipmuc communities that paid tribute to the Mohegans and Narragansetts. With every passing year the Indians were reminded of a sage warning by the Pequot sachem Sassacus that the English would pursue a strategy of divide and conquer until they controlled everything. Firearms were one of the Indians' answers to that danger.[20]

The Indians' arms buildup combined with these political tensions to spark a series of colonial panics in the years leading up to King Philip's War. At first these alarms centered on Ninigret, sachem of the Niantic-Narragansetts, because he actively recruited the Mohawks and Dutch as allies to offset the United Colonies' support of the Mohegans. In 1653 numerous informants, headed by Ninigret's archenemy Uncas, testified that Ninigret had spent the winter visiting Indian communities across Long Island Sound, calling on them to unite against the English and Mohegans, followed by a secret meeting in New Amsterdam with Dutch governor Peter Stuyvesant. Reportedly Ninigret had returned home in a Dutch sloop carrying a gift of "twenty guns with powder and shot answerable" as evidence that New Netherland would provide the arms for a multitribal campaign against New England. "They [the Dutch] are furnished with [gun]powder as plentifully as if it were sand," Ninigret allegedly trumpeted. The fact that the Dutch and English were in the middle of a naval war for control of Atlantic trade added credence to these rumors. So did the sudden visibility of Ninigret's armament. In September 1653 the United Colonies sent an expedition to question Ninigret about his machinations, only to be met at the edge of his territory by "about forty or fifty Indians all in arms," the captain of whom brandished "a gun in his hand on the cock . . . as if he would have cocked it." The meeting with Ninigret went no better for the colonial ambassadors. Ninigret surrounded himself with "many armed men . . . and himself a pistol in his hand," and together they "charged their guns with powder and bullets and some primed their guns." The English read this display as a provocation, but it also served as a warning that the Narragansetts were ready to defend themselves. It was no coincidence that the United Colonies decided not to war against the Narragansetts over this crisis, if only by a hair's breadth.[21]

As the focus of English war scares in the 1660s and 1670s shifted to the Wampanoag sachems Alexander (or Wamsutta) and his brother Philip (or Metacom), Plymouth tried to subdue these leaders, practically and symbolically, by confiscating their firearms. In 1662 horsemen from Plymouth tracked down Alexander at one of his hunting camps and took him into custody to answer charges of plotting. The only way this expedition managed to accomplish its mission without bloodshed was by seizing the muskets of Alexander and his men, which they had left unattended outside while they were indoors eating breakfast. Later accounts described Alexander as "appalled" and in a "raging passion" at Plymouth's insult "to send for him in such a way." A worse injury occurred when Alexander fell ill while under English arrest and died shortly thereafter, which left the Wampanoags suspecting he had been poisoned.[22]

Plymouth's treatment of Philip was equally disrespectful. In 1671 there were fresh rumors of the Wampanoags fomenting war and stockpiling "many guns," some of which were being maintained by visiting gunsmiths from the Narragansetts, despite the historic enmity between those peoples. Fearing the worse, Plymouth ordered Philip and the sachems of the neighboring communities of Pocasset, Saconnet, and Assawompset to appear in court and forfeit their arms, as if they were subordinates rather than co-equals. When the Wampanoags delivered only a token number of weapons, Plymouth threatened to send dragoons to collect the rest. The crisis came to an end only after commissioners from Massachusetts and Connecticut intervened and convinced the sachem to sign a treaty in which he submitted himself to Charles II and Plymouth and promised to pay a fine of £100. Though this "agreement" has often been interpreted as a humiliation for Philip, it is conspicuous that the sachem managed to strike the requirement to turn over his followers' guns. Given how important firearms had become to the Wampanoags and their indigenous neighbors, both as practical tools and as symbols of the people's sovereignty, talks probably would have failed if Plymouth had insisted on such a provision.[23]

Remarkably, a spike in the New England colonies' own gun trade was partially responsible for the Wampanoag arms buildup that had put Plymouth on edge. In 1668, Massachusetts relaxed earlier restrictions by permitting licensed traders to sell arms and ammunition to Indians at peace with the colony, even though Philip had been accused the year before of conspiring with the French. Unwilling to abandon the lucrative Indian arms market to the Bay Colony, the following year Plymouth and Connecticut opened their trade too, mere months after a regional panic that the Narragansetts, Mohegans, Pequots, Montauketts, and Wampanoags were holding war councils. The irony was that the heavy Indian demand for firearms, which the profit-minded colonies struggled to resist, stemmed partly from colonies' heavy-handed reactions to Indian war scares, including the confiscation of Indian weapons.[24]

The Wampanoags had plenty of legitimate reasons to take up arms against Plymouth. The colonies' repeated seizures of their guns, by which Indians defended and fed their people, encapsulated them all. The colonies seemed determined to neuter them and drive them off their land. Plymouth took its aggression a step further in the late spring and early summer of 1675 by arresting, trying, and executing three of Philip's men for the murder of John Sassamon, a Christian, formally educated Wampanoag who had been passing intelligence about Philip to colonial authorities. To the Wampanoags this unprecedented breach of their sovereignty flowed naturally from Plymouth's repeated attempts to weaken them by impounding their weapons. If Plymouth could so boldly extend English jurisprudence over Wampanoag people in Wampanoag country, even to the point of capitally punishing them, then the Wampanoags had truly become a subject people. Neither Philip nor his followers would stand for that. It was time to go to war.

King Philip's War

Nothing drove Indians to take up arms against the English more than English attempts to disarm them on suspicion of supporting Philip. Initially only a portion of the Wampanoags rose against the English, including those living in and immediately around Philip's seat of Mount Hope on the modern border of Massachusetts and Rhode Island. After some running battles with Plymouth militia, Philip and his followers headed north, where they were joined by a portion (but only a portion) of warriors from the Nipmucs. Well into the fall of 1675 this was Philip's only base of support. The Mohegans and Pequots of Connecticut, a number of praying Indians near Boston, and even some Nipmucs, immediately volunteered to help the English hunt him down. Most other Indians wanted nothing to do with the fighting. Yet colonists often made Indian neutrality and even friendship impossible. When 160 mainland Wampanoags turned themselves in to Plymouth hoping to avoid hostilities, English authorities clasped them in chains and transported them out of the colony, probably to slavery in the West Indies. A short time later fifty-seven more Wampanoags entered the town of Sandwich "in a submissive way," yet the magistrates judged them to be "in the same condition of rebellion as those formerly condemned to servitude" and thus sentenced them to the same fate. Understandably, after these outrages, other Indians were unwilling to trust their fates to the English, even if they also had no desire to join Philip in arms. Wabanakis from the Androscoggin, Saco, and Penobscot bands entered the fray after colonists in Maine, unnerved by events to the south, halted the arms trade and ordered the Indians to surrender whatever weapons they had in store. When Wabanaki leaders protested that they needed their guns for the hunt, colonial spokesmen threatened to kill them all if they did not comply. As trader Thomas Gardiner came to regret, "Indians in those parts did never appear dissatisfied until their arms were taken away." Soon that dissatisfaction turned into outright hostility and Maine degenerated into bloodshed, with the fighting there outlasting that in southern New England by nearly two full years.[25]

The English did not trust even some of their staunchest Indian allies. They accused warriors serving alongside the colonial militia with shooting over the heads of the enemy, conspiring to ambush English soldiers from behind, and celebrating Philip's victories and hosting his ambassadors. With the English "so jealous and filled with animosity against all Indians without exception," colonists in the upper Connecticut River Valley ordered the disarmament of the "River Indians" or "Friend Indians," as they referred to the Agawams, Woronocos, Norridgewoks, and Pocumtucks. Yet these communities were unwilling to comply in light of the fury of the colonial population and the ongoing threat of the Mohawks. Fearing that the English aimed "to destroy them," River Indian warriors ambushed the expedition sent to seize their weapons, then launched devastating attacks against the unsuspecting towns of Hadley and Springfield. Puritan historian William Hubbard contended that these strikes "did more than any other to discover the said actors to be the children of the devil," but he and most of his fellow colonists failed to acknowledge that they were creating a self-fulfilling prophecy. By winter the English had also driven the powerful Narragansetts into Philip's camp by massacring hundreds of their people after they refused to turn over Wampanoags who had fled to them for refuge.[26]

Tellingly, the peace held in jurisdictions that not only refused to disarm local Indians but actually armed them if they joined the English war effort. Connecticut, lacking the vast population majority over local Indians enjoyed by Massachusetts, knew that it would suffer enormously if it drove its indigenous neighbors into Philip's camp. At least some clearheaded magistrates had learned the lesson of the Springfield debacle: confiscating an Indian people's weapons was a surefire way to make enemies of them. Fortunately the Mohegans and Pequots had accumulated a strong track record of service to the colony and engendered enough trust in governmental circles to offset popular suspicions of them. Thus, Connecticut took a gamble and arranged with the Mohegans and Pequots to fight alongside colonial forces in exchange for arms and ammunition, captives, and scalp bounties. Soon the ranks of Indians defending Connecticut also included warriors from smaller communities like the Tunxis, Western Niantics, and Wangunks. The colony's restraint paid off. Without the Connecticut Indians' invaluable service as scouts and fighters, it is questionable whether the English would have won King Philip's War and Connecticut would have escaped with as little damage as it did. A greater certainty is that if the Connecticut Indians had taken up arms against the English, much of Connecticut and more of the other colonies would have been destroyed.[27]

The same principle certainly applies to the island of Martha's Vineyard, where some forty English households shared a hundred square miles of land with approximately 1,500 Wampanoags. Despite the Christian status of the island Wampanoags and their vast population advantage, some Englishmen advocated impounding their weapons. They even organized an expedition to present this demand to the westside sachemship of Aquinnah, whose people "were mostly to be doubted." The sachem, Mittark, refused, contending that the island Wampanoags "had never given occasion of the distrust intimated" and "that the delivering their Arms would expose them to the will of the Indians engaged in the present War, who were not less theirs than the Enemies of the English." Instead, he made a bold counterproposal that the English should not only abandon any thought of disarming the Wampanoags, but actually outfit their warriors for use as a guard against hostile forces from the mainland. English debate over this matter must have been heated, as reflected in a protest by neighboring colonists on Nantucket that "an ill consequence may arrive upon the Indians training in arms on Martins [Martha's] Vineyard." Nevertheless, Vineyard authorities ultimately decided to place their fate in the island Wampanoags rather than watch their homes go up in flames like the towns of the upper Connecticut River Valley. Because of their moderation, the peace not only held, but late in the war the local Wampanoag scouts captured Indians from the mainland who tried to escape to the Vineyard or nearby Elizabeth Islands. Massachusetts and Plymouth could only have wished they had shown the wisdom of their counterparts in Connecticut and Martha's Vineyard to respect the sanctity of Indian arms and the authority of Indian sachems. By the spring of 1676 much of these colonies had been laid to waste and the wails of mourners filled the air.[28]

———

In the first eight months of King Philip's War, the Indians who fought against the colonies racked up victories through the same kinds of ambushes that had served the Iroquois so well in their wars against New France and its Indian allies. The war began with Plymouth and Massachusetts forces trying to rout the Wampanoags before they could escape from their coastal homeland into the interior, only to discover the impossibility of drawing them into an open-field battle. A party of 250 Englishmen searched futilely for the main body of Wampanoags on Philip's Mount Hope Peninsula and in the thickets of the Pocasset and Saconnet sachemships to the east, but the warriors appeared only to give fire and retreat. As bloody ambush gave way to long periods of quiet and then another ambush, English troopers began to lose their composure, leaving them "ready to fire upon every bush they see (supposing Indians were there)" because when the Indians did appear, they "possessed themselves of every Rock, Stump, Tree or Fence that was in sight, firing . . . without ceasing." The effectiveness of Wampanoag gunmen enabled most of their people to slip through Plymouth's cordon and join up with the Nipmucs in central Massachusetts, where they laid down plans for a broader campaign.[29]

Indian ambushes, showcasing the strength of the warriors' armament and their gun skills, devastated English troops repeatedly throughout the fall of 1675. On September 12, for instance, seventy-nine English soldiers guided a wagon train with provisions from the recently abandoned Connecticut River town of Deerfield, astonishingly unaware that Englishmen could no longer travel the paths of southern New England in safety. The expedition's leader, Captain Thomas Lathrop, neglected to employ flankers to scout the woods, and a number of his men set aside their muskets in a wagon to free their hands for gathering grapes. As this party crossed a stream (since known as Bloody Brook), hundreds of Nipmucs under the sachem Muttaump suddenly opened fire from a nearby swamp, then rushed forward with knives and hatchets, killing all but seven or eight of the colonists and seizing their store of guns, powder, shot, and other supplies. A relief force of colonists, Mohegans, and Pequots under Captain Samuel Mosely arrived quickly after hearing the shots, only to fall into another ambush by Nipmuc gunmen "skulking behind Trees, and taking their Aim at Single Persons, which is the usual Manner of the Indians fighting one with another." This was the single highest death toll the English and their indigenous allies suffered in a battle during the war, but it was hardly the only event of its kind.[30]

Massachusetts Bay Indian commissioner Daniel Gookin lambasted the colonial military for its initial overconfidence. "It was found another manner of thing than was expected," Gookin explained, "for our men would see no enemy to shoot at, but yet felt their bullets out of the thick bushes where they lay in ambushments; camouflaged with green boughs tied to the waists." To some English troops, it seemed as if "every stump shot like a musketeer," as Benjamin Thompson characterized it. Unfortunately for colonial troops, those stumps were remarkably good shots. Connecticut deputy governor William Leete was stunned to find that the Indians were "so accurate marks men above our own men, to do execution, rather than of theirs, whereby more of ours are like to fall, rather than of theirs, unless the Lord by special Providence, do deliver them into our hands." That special providence was difficult to discern well into the spring of 1676.[31]

Indian attacks on colonial towns relied on ambush by gunmen, albeit with several twists. The general pattern was for warriors to lie in wait overnight in haystacks, outbuildings, or fields, and then waylay colonists as they emerged from their homes in the morning, a tactic common in intertribal wars. After terrified English survivors rushed to the shelter of garrison houses, Indian gunmen would pin them down while other warriors burned houses and outbuildings and slaughtered cattle. The Nipmuc assault on the town of Medfield, twenty-two miles southwest of Boston, on February 20, 1676, is a case in point. During the evening of February 19, Native men took position "under the Sides of Barns and Fences of their [the colonists'] Orchards, as is supposed, where they lay hid under that Cover, till break of Day, when they suddenly set upon sundry Houses, shooting them that first came out of their doors . . . some were killed as they attempted to fly to their Neighbors for Shelter: some were only wounded, and some taken alive and carried Captive." The Indians' sharpshooting was evident throughout the attack as they picked off colonists who peeked out of windows or doors, until eighteen of them lay dead. The rest were so terrified that they stayed shut up within the protection of their blockhouses while Indians roamed freely outside, putting "near one Half of the Town" to the torch, amounting to forty or fifty houses and barns and two mills. It was a strategy that Indians followed over and over again until, by war's end, they had killed some 800 colonists and torched nearly two dozen colonial towns.[32]

Indians divined the fate of these battles through rituals in which they gave firearms a central role. During Englishwoman Mary Rowlandson's captivity among the warring Indians, she witnessed a ceremony preceding the Battle of Sudbury (April 1676) in which warriors formed a circle surrounding a kneeling powwow, or shaman, joined by a man with a musket. As the warriors drummed on the ground and sang or hummed, the gunman went out of the ring, then "made a stand," in Rowlandson's words, returned to the middle, picked up a second gun, and then exited again to assume a battle posture. The warriors called on the gunman in earnest to return to the circle, probably representing the safety of the group or the camp. According to Rowlandson, "he stood reeling and wavering as if he knew not whither he should stand or fall," at which the warriors raised their noise to a pitch. Eventually the gunman staggered his way back into the circle, to an eruption of shouts and applause. Rowlandson's impression was that the participants in this ritual thought it told them "that they should prosper, and gain the victory," which they did.[33]

Though some English dismissed the Indian mode of fighting as cowardice because it did not involve open-field engagements between formal armies, others perceived an effective strategy. The Indians' approach drew on their superior knowledge of the terrain, their warriors' readiness to travel quick and light, and their skill at precision shooting from cover developed in the course of hunting. Their unpredictable ambushes minimized the English strengths of being able to ferry large amounts of supplies and men by boat and horse-drawn cart, while strikes against outlying agricultural villages put stress on English food supplies and created a refugee crisis that taxed the resources of better-defended eastern towns. That is why, as Roger Williams learned, Philip's strategy was to move inland away from where the English population was densest and the roads were most developed in order to draw colonial forces into "such places as are full of long grass, flags, sedge, etc., and then environ them round with fire, smoke, and bullets."[34]

The warring Indians could have continued to press these advantages if they had maintained a steady supply of munitions, but in the late spring of 1676 the tide began to turn in the English favor in part because the warring Indians lacked gunpowder and shot and their guns needed repairing. In the war's early days, Philip had boasted (with good reason) that he was on the verge of opening up supply lines to the French on the Saint Lawrence. A full year earlier, Woronoco and Pojassick Indians had left the Connecticut River Valley to found a new settlement (later to be known as Schagticoke) at the confluence of Hoosick and Hudson Rivers, with access to the Saint Lawrence via the Hudson and Lake Champlain, and to the Dutch in Albany a short distance to the south. It is unclear whether they chose this location in anticipation of the war, with the intent of establishing a base of retreat for Indian combatants and a marketplace for French and Dutch arms. Regardless, that is precisely what the Hoosick confluence became. Two unidentified Englishmen, formerly prisoners of the warring Indians, reported that their captors had gone into winter quarters near Hoosick, where there was a rendezvous with 500 "French Indians" who had straw piercings through their noses. These pierced-nose Indians might have been Ottawas, who were known for such ornaments and for their close ties with the local Mohicans. A stronger possibility is that these Indians were nearby Missisquoi Abenakis from the upper end of Lake Champlain.

By all appearances the "French Indians" came to Hoosick carrying ample munitions to trade. The English informants told that after the rendezvous the warring Indians could marshal 2,100 young men "most of them armed with good firelocks, and full of ammunition." These warriors declared that they would soon carry the fight to the very streets of Boston, for "the French were their brothers and did furnish them with ammunition." Some of the Indians reportedly also hoped to destroy Albany before too long. If this account was correct (which is questionable, given that there is no way to know if the former captives spoke Algonquian or if their Algonquin captors spoke English to them), these sentiments probably came from Connecticut River Indians, who would have resented the Dutch for their history of arming the Mohawks, the River Indians' archenemy. Other testimony, taken from Indian prisoners of the English and from former English captives of the warring Indians, agreed that French-allied Indians and French traders alike brought supplies to warring Indians camped at Hoosick on the Hudson and Pocumtuck on the Connecticut River. They also encouraged them to keep up the resistance.[35]

Traders in Albany played a role in provisioning the warring Indians, though the details of this traffic are equally vague. A number of Indians contended, and even more Englishmen charged, that this trade was direct, but whether it was common is doubtful. In 1675 Albany was still overwhelmingly a Dutch colonial town, but it was no longer under Dutch jurisdiction following the English conquest of New Netherland in 1664 and repossession of the colony after a Dutch fleet retook it briefly in 1673–1674. The short-lived Dutch reconquest might have been a factor in the creation of Schaghticoke, as Indians planning to rise against the English would have seen an advantage in the return of Dutch rule over Albany. Yet by the start of King Philip's War, New Netherland had once again become English New York, and from his headquarters on Manhattan Island, Governor Edmund Andros forcefully prohibited dealing with Indians at war in New England. So instead Dutch arms dealers operated through Native middlemen. At least one Indian who spied on Philip's forces for the English judged that the hostile Indians were able to acquire Dutch gunpowder from Mohicans, Wappingers, and Paugussetts, who apparently had obtained these stores with no questions asked.[36]

By the winter of 1676, however, even that supply was no longer available. In February hundreds of Mohawk warriors fell on Philip's winter camp a short distance outside of Albany, driving the warring Indians eastward away from the Hudson. They kept up the pressure into the spring and summer with raids against the warring Indians in the upper Connecticut River Valley and even farther east. Andros had certainly encouraged the Mohawks to this action, providing them with "a free market for powder, etc." and "ammunition, arms, and all they wanted." He viewed them as his shock troops for New York's eastern front. Yet the Mohawks would also have been motivated by the fact that the ranks of the warring Indians included so many of their recent enemies from the Connecticut River tribes, such as the Pocumtucks and Sokokis. Philip might even have provoked them. Boston minister Increase Mather, in his history of the war, contended that Philip had some Mohawks murdered and tried to pin it on the English in the hope of drawing the Mohawks over to his side, only for his treachery to be discovered. Fact or fiction, the Mohawks cut off the warring Indians from the Albany market and the Hoosick rendezvous for the duration of the war, thereby forcing them to rely on plunder for fresh powder and shot. This setback should rank as the most decisive turning point of King Philip's War.[37]

The Mohawks' action reflected that their decades-long dependence on firearms was giving New York critical influence over their decision making. The Five Nations' ongoing conflicts with surrounding peoples, particularly New France and its many Indian allies, required steady supplies of munitions and blacksmithing services. Before the English conquest of New Netherland, the Mohawks might have considered taking up arms in support of Philip, particularly once their longtime allies, the Narragansetts, became involved in the war. Such a move would not have imperiled their access to guns from Albany as long as it was under Dutch rule. That was no longer the case. James, Duke of York, the proprietor of New York, was no friend of the New England Puritans, but he would not and could not countenance Indians to war against the royal family's colonial subjects. With the English takeover still in its early stages, there was no way for the Mohawks to know whether the new governor, Andros, had the power to shut them out of the Albany gun market, and they were not going to use the occasion of King Philip's War to find out. A more prudent approach was to cultivate an alliance with the new authority in the hope that it would maintain the flow of munitions established by the Dutch. Attacking Philip's winter camp, and then harassing the warring Indians as far east as the Connecticut River for the next two years, was the Mohawks' way of securing friendship with New York, while also dealing a fresh blow against the River tribes. Gratifying Andros, keeping the door open to Albany, diminishing longstanding enemies, and acquiring captives was a quadruple win from a Mohawk perspective.

The Mohawks also benefited when New England Indian refugees resettled Schaghticoke after the war. This time, however, they did so under Mohawk authority with the acknowledgment of New York. From this moment forward, if the English wanted to speak to the Schaghticokes or if the Schaghticokes wanted to speak to the English, they did so through Mohawk spokesmen, which was part of a broader Iroquois strategy of taking in Native people displaced by colonial or intertribal wars, settling them on the League's periphery as a defensive wall, and claiming the right to represent them in colonial diplomacy. The Mohawks' compliance with Andros's request to attack the New England Indians might be read as a sign that their dependence on firearms was leading toward a political dependence on New York; indeed, in the future the Mohawks would be the strongest pro-English voice in Five Nations' councils, a regular (if sometimes unenthusiastic) contributor of warriors to British military campaigns against the French, and the hosts of Anglican missionaries. At the same time, their intervention in King Philip's War must also be acknowledged as the pursuit of Mohawk interests that ultimately strengthened Mohawk power in Indian country, which was their primary concern.[38]

A few months after the Mohawks cut them off from the Albany gun market and the Hoosick rendezvous, the warring Indians suffered a severe blow to their capacity to repair arms and cast shot. During the winter of 1675–1676, spies reported that the warring Indians "have store of arms; and have [a] gunsmith among them, a lame man that is a good workman and keeps their guns well fixed." There was certainly plenty for him to do. On any given day he would have replaced the springs, hammers, and triggers of damaged firing mechanisms. There were dented gun barrels to be straightened and muzzles clogged with black powder that needed to be cleaned, lest they burst. Without someone to perform these services, the warriors would lack the resources to fight. Fortunately for the warring Indians, this artisan, or someone with similar skills, remained with them after they retreated from Hoosick to Peskompscut, a popular fishing site on the falls of the upper Connecticut River. There he established a full-fledged blacksmith shop with two forges, other smithing tools, and large amounts of raw lead. The Peskompscut camp was thriving when an English prisoner managed to escape from it to the English town of Hadley, some fifteen miles south, where he told authorities about the Indians' location and lack of sentries. Seeing a rare opportunity to catch the enemy off guard, Captain William Turner quickly raised 150 militiamen, had them ride on horseback to within a half mile of the Indian encampment, and then staged a dawn attack on foot. With the sound of their approach inaudible over the roar of the falls, the soldiers completely surprised the sleeping camp, killing dozens, perhaps even hundreds, of Native people, including the blacksmith. Equally devastating, they captured the Indians' forges and lead.[39]

The warring Indians' loss of the French and Dutch arms markets and their Peskompscut camp would have hurt a great deal less if they had been able to obtain supplies from rogue Englishmen, but such figures, who were so plentiful in peacetime, proved less reckless in this moment of crisis. Plymouth and Massachusetts threatened death to anyone caught selling munitions to Indians, while Connecticut put the penalty at twelve months in jail with quarterly severe whippings. The deterrent effect of these measures is evident in the utter lack, not only of prosecutions for selling guns to Indians during the war, but even of accusations in an environment otherwise rife with suspicion. It took until 1677 for someone to be charged and convicted with violating the ban, by which time the fighting was over everywhere but in Maine. The treasonous trader, a mariner named John Watts, managed to escape with his life, but only after running the gauntlet through the Boston militia and paying a £100 bond for good behavior. A year earlier he probably would not have been so fortunate.[40]

Throughout the late spring and summer, a pattern developed of the English and their Indian allies emerging virtually unscathed from engagements in which they killed or captured dozens of the enemy, which suggests that the warring Indians lacked the means to shoot back. In early April a force of Connecticut militia under George Denison and James Avery and warriors from the Mohegans, Pequots, and Niantics tracked down a "considerable" force of Narragansetts on the Blackstone River and managed to kill or capture forty-five of them, including the great war leader, Canonchet, "without the loss of one of their own men." A vast two-prong campaign in late May and June achieved even greater success. By the time English troops under Captain Daniel Henchman had finished sweeping through Nipmuc country, and another force of colonial militia and Mohegan and Pequot warriors had probed up the Connecticut River, they had dispatched 84 of the enemy while losing none of their own men. Barely a month later Major John Talcott of Connecticut, at the head of 300 colonial soldiers and 100 Mohegans and Pequots, fought another body of Narragansetts at Nipsachuck in the northern portion of Narragansett territory, killing or capturing 171 of the enemy in less than three hours while suffering casualties to just one or two allied Indians. Two days later, this same army killed 67 Narragansetts (just 18 of whom were men) and captured 27 on Warwick Neck, also with no losses. If the warring Indians had lost the will to fight, it was an extension of their meager stores of gunpowder and the disrepair of their firearms. What they had truly lost was their ability to fight.[41]

The warring Indians' sinking fortunes also stemmed from the growing numbers of Indians joining the English ranks in exchange for clemency and arms. By the spring of 1676 Plymouth and Massachusetts could no longer ignore that they had made a costly mistake in treating their Indian allies, even Christians, like wolves in sheep's clothing. Duly humbled by the examples of Connecticut and Martha's Vineyard, in mid-April Massachusetts organized and outfitted a company of praying Indians; by summer's end these warriors had killed an estimated 400 of the enemy. "I think it was observed by impartial men," judged Gookin, "that after our Indians went out, the balance turned on the English side."[42]

Plymouth followed suit in mid-May, first by enlisting Christian Wampanoags from Cape Cod who had previously stayed out of the fighting, then by extending amnesty to any mainland Wampanoags who agreed to abandon Philip and take up arms for the English. This change of policy brought into the English ranks dozens, perhaps even hundreds, of warriors who offered not only tracking and sharpshooting skills but advice on woodland warfare. When Captain Benjamin Church of Plymouth asked the Wampanoags how they had managed to best colonial troops so many times over the course of the war, they responded, "That the Indians gain'd great advantage of the English by two things; The Indians always took care in their marches and fights, not to come too thick together. But the English always kept in a heap together, that it was easy to hit them as to hit a house. The other was, that if at any time they discovered a company of English soldiers in the woods, they knew . . . the English never scattered" whereas "the Indians always divided and scattered." Doubtless the fear of being captured and killed by the English and their growing number of Indian allies motivated these Wampanoags to switch sides, but there was another factor as well. The main issue, according to Rhode Island's William Harris, was "want of powder," which put them "in great danger of their lives by reason of the Indians they called Mohawks their enemies that meet with them and that used to kill and eat their enemies." These Indians judged the English offer of mercy and arms to be a better gamble than taking their chances without ammunition against the Mohawks.[43]

Plymouth troops, backed by allied Wampanoags, relentlessly hunted down Philip and his warriors throughout July and August 1676, inflicting harsh punishment but absorbing little. By summer's end the war in southern New England was effectively over. Most of the English thanked Providence for their change of fortune, overlooking the warring Indians' struggles with starvation, disease, and especially the Indians who aided English forces. Colonist William Harris identified yet another factor. Crediting the Mohawks for their attack on Philip's forces, he observed, "Had all the Indians been our enemyes: and could have gotten powder: they might have forced us to Islands for safety." The "occasion of their coming in [to surrender]," he emphasized, was partly "want of powder."[44]

———

For all of their very real differences, both Indians and colonists in New England entered King Philip's War with some reassurance that the spirits had already divined what was going to pass. Some Englishmen in the Connecticut River Valley believed they had received portents of the war the previous fall when they experienced "a shaking of the earth, and a considerable Echo" resembling the firing of cannon, though none had been discharged nearby. During a lunar eclipse early in the war, some Englishman thought they spied on the moon a mark in the shape of a bow and arrow, which the historian William Hubbard found strange given that "the Mischief following was done by Guns, not by Bows." No English sources bothered to note what local Indians thought of the eclipse, though Indians elsewhere in the eastern woodlands tended to view eclipses as omens. An oral tradition recorded in the eighteenth century in the town of Swansea, Massachusetts, contended that one of Philip's powwows (or shamans) promised the Wampanoags victory in the war if they could get a colonist to fire the first shot, only to have one of their trigger-happy warriors gun down an Englishman before the prophecy could be fulfilled. Afterward some Indians believed that the Wampanoag sachem Tispaquin of Assawompset could not be pierced by a bullet, "for, said they, he was shot twice but the bullets glanced by him and could not hurt him." The English took satisfaction in executing him by firing squad in September 1676.[45]

As these signs predicted, guns were critical to the conduct and outcome of King Philip's War, but for reasons that are easy to mistake. Indian warriors had become dependent on guns after thirty years of steady access to a dynamic gun frontier supplied by multiple colonies and imperial powers. When the war began, they were at least as well supplied with firearms as their English counterparts, and by all counts better skilled with them. Colonists felt the deadly effects throughout the first nine months of the conflict. The New England colonies tried to cut off the warring Indians' access to munitions by threatening gun-runners with heavy fines, imprisonment, and even death if they dared to supply the Indian enemy. Certainly these measures diminished the Indians' stockpiles, but not enough to seriously inhibit the war effort—as long as the warring Indians had access to Dutch traders in Albany and the French on the Saint Lawrence, whether directly or through Indian brokers. The warring Indians were dependent on guns, powder, and shot, but not on the English.

What ultimately turned the warring Indians' reliance on firearms from a source of strength into a liability had little to do with the New England colonies. Rather, the critical factor was the Mohawks, whose interest in protecting their trade and political relations with the English authority of New York drove the New England Indians away from the Hudson River arms markets. It was doubly unfortunate for the warring Indians that there awaited them a reinforced enemy composed of English militia, Mohegans, Pequots, praying Indians, and increasing numbers of Wampanoags who switched sides in return for their lives and munitions. With rare exceptions the Indians who managed to guide their communities through King Philip's War to a future in English-dominated New England were the ones who swallowed hard and defended the colonies. The outcome of New England's great Indian-colonial war, like the great clashes of the Southeast, rested less on brute colonial strength than on colonial influence in Indian country tied indelibly to the Indian demand for guns and ammunition.

4. INDIAN GUNMEN AGAINST THE BRITISH EMPIRE

Nearly a century after King Philip's War, colonial administrators remained preoccupied with turning Indians' reliance on firearms into subservience, even as the British Empire was on the cusp of the greatest triumph in its history. By 1761 Great Britain had defeated France in the North American theater of the Seven Years' War, ending a long history of failed English invasions of Canada stretching back to 1690. Yet this was a global conflict as well as an American one, fought on every inhabited continent other than Australia and throughout the high seas. Even after the fall of Quebec in late 1759, the war raged on in other sectors at crippling expense until 1763's Treaty of Paris. In the interim it fell to General Sir Jeffery Amherst to govern occupied New France, including its network of posts in Indian country, in a manner that simultaneously projected British dominance and reduced outlays. Whereas others might have seen Britain's ambition and austerity as working at cross purposes, Amherst imagined them as complementary, at least when it came to Indian affairs. By his thinking, slashing the amount of munitions Indians received through gifts and trade would at once save London thousands of pounds sterling per year while demonstrating Britain's power to reduce the Indians to a Stone Age existence. Little did he anticipate how the high the actual costs of this policy would be.

One of Amherst's purposes was to disabuse the Indians of their contention that Britain had defeated only France, not them, and that therefore the eastern interior remained under Native control. He wanted them to realize that Britain now had the power to choke off their supply of arms and that therefore it was futile for them to resist the British take-over of French forts in the Ohio country and Great Lakes and colonial expansion into the trans-Allegheny region. "I am fully convinced the only true method of treating those Savages is to keep them in a proper subjection," he wrote to Colonel Henry Bouquet. Keeping them short of ammunition would teach them that "it is certainly not in their power to affect anything of consequence against us." In Amherst's view the age of play-off politics, in which Indians extorted presents from the British and French in exchange for unreliable pledges of support, had finally come to an end, and thus so had the Indians' leverage. The gun frontier was no longer a multinational circle around Indian country but a line of posts under strict British administration. It was time for the Natives to learn that they fell under British rule as well.[1]

Indians had their own lessons to teach, including that their need for munitions did not make them British lackeys but instead the strength of their arms required them to be treated with respect. Beginning in May 1763 warriors from a dozen peoples across the Great Lakes and Ohio country began sacking British forts and raiding farmsteads in a campaign since known as Pontiac's War, after the Ottawa war chief who led the resistance around Detroit. The warring Indian nations captured eight forts within a matter of weeks. These included Fort Michilimackinac at the straits between Lake Huron and Lake Michigan; Fort St. Joseph, along the overland trail from Detroit to the south end of Lake Michigan; Forts Miami and Ouiatenaon, on the river route from Lake Erie to the Mississippi River; Fort Sandusky, tucked along the north shore of Lake Erie between Forts Detroit and Niagara; and Forts Venango, Le Boeuf, and Presque Isle, in what is now northwest Pennsylvania. The garrison at Fort Edward Augustus, or La Baye, on Green Bay in Wisconsin, abandoned its post in haste rather than join this list. Three other stations, the stout Forts Detroit and Pitt, and Pitt's satellite, Fort Ligonier, remained under siege for six months. Fort Niagara never came under direct attack, but Seneca warriors disrupted its shipments of supplies and reinforcements to Detroit with several sharp blows against boatmen working a portage around the famous waterfalls. The easternmost theater of this war involved Delaware and Shawnee raids up and down the Allegheny and Shenandoah Mountains of what is now western Pennsylvania, Maryland, and Virginia, sometimes extending as far east as the Susquehanna River and even the Lehigh River Valley, a mere sixty miles north of Philadelphia. Clearly Amherst's policies, rather than cowing Indians into submission, had inspired them to unite on a scale that eclipsed even such storied intertribal uprisings as King Philip's War and the Yamasee War. It appeared that Indians had reversed the roles, taking up their guns to instruct the British that they remained independent in the postwar order.

Yet by 1764 the warring Indians had lifted their sieges, restored the captured forts to the British, and begun returning some of their colonial captives, which raises the question of whether Amherst had been right in the end. In other words, Pontiac's War was an opportunity to test whether Indians in 1763 had the material capacity to fight a lengthy war against the lone imperial power left in eastern North America. Throughout the conflict Amherst and his subordinate officers were certain that it was merely a matter of time before Indians ran out of ammunition, and some historians have agreed that Native supply shortages were an important factor in ending the war. A closer look reveals that scarcities of powder and shot were rare and quite temporary because the gun frontier remained international, competitive, and nearly ungovernable. Native warriors were able to keep up the fight in most quarters because they drew on deep stockpiles of munitions and could acquire additional stores through plunder, black-market trade with British colonists, and especially gifts and trade from the numerous French who remained in North America. The allied nations ended Pontiac's War not because they lacked the ability to fight and certainly not because the British defeated them. Instead, it was a combination of many other factors, including the inability of indigenous warriors to reduce Forts Detroit and Pitt without French assistance, the imminent threat of British scorched-earth campaigns against their villages, and pressure on Indian fighting men to return to the needs of their families. Perhaps most importantly, in the short term they had achieved one of their primary war aims—compelling the British to conform to French standards of generosity and respect for Indian protocols. Restoring the Union Jack to the interior posts had meant far less than the British liked. These places remained surrounded by autonomous Indian communities as capable as ever of rising in arms.[2]

Amherst's Fantasy

Amherst's rollback of gifts to Indians was a matter both of prudence and principle, as he defined these things. He understood that the French, though vastly outnumbered by the British in North America, had managed to fend off conquest for the better part of eighty years by cultivating Indian allies through the liberal circulation of presents, subsidization of trade goods, and respect for Indian protocols. The result was that the French had influence with Indians throughout the Ohio country, Great Lakes region, and Mississippi River Valley, to the envy of British colonists who eyed these places for commercial and territorial expansion. Yet this approach had also cost the French treasury enormously, compounded, as some French officers charged, by corruption among nearly everyone involved in the shipping, accounting, and distribution of these gifts. Furthermore, the service of Indian warriors lasted only as long as the French had presents to give. Warriors showed up in smaller numbers and with less enthusiasm as soon as French goods began to run short, as toward the end of the Seven Years' War due to a British blockade of the Saint Lawrence River. The unmistakable disdain for Indians exhibited by General Louis-Joseph, Marquis de Montcalm, the commander of French forces in North America, only exacerbated these problems. Amherst, who shared Montcalm's bias, certainly had no interest in replicating such an expensive and ultimately failed system.[3]

Whereas France had bent to Indian expectations from a position of weakness, including the Indian threat of withholding their support or throwing it to the British, Britain's victory in the Seven Years' War left the Indians in the North without rival suitors. Believing that Britain now held the upper hand, Amherst designed an Indian policy in accordance with his country's values instead of Indian ones. The gifts, which Indians saw as tokens of friendship by a wealthy nation grateful for permission to operate in Indian country, were nothing more than bribes in Amherst's opinion. The general had no objection to handing out charity in moments of dire need, or of paying for services rendered. The problem was doling out presents at the Indians' command without putting them under any duty to British authority. He explained, "Purchasing the good behavior, either of Indians or any others is what I do not understand; when men of what race soever behave ill, they must be punished, and not bribed." In British society, particularly within the military and political bureaucracy, gifts traveled up the social hierarchy as part of the obsequiousness that produced favor. Amherst viewed the Indians' demands for gifts as an inversion of this hierarchy by making the civilized and thus superior party grovel before the savage and thus inferior one. Amherst was not going to degrade himself or his flag by honoring people he considered to be savages. The British might distribute goods occasionally, but always sparingly. They were not to be offered in spirit of gratitude for the Natives' hospitality and alliance, but out of condescension and even pity.[4]

Amherst's objective of reducing Indians to dependence hinged on the strict regulation of trade, particularly of munitions. He imagined that requiring British traders to obtain licenses and operate out of just three forts, Detroit, Niagara, and Pitt, rather than within Native villages, would make Indians vulnerable to British embargos and thus easier to control. John Stuart, Britain's superintendent of Indian affairs for the southern district, echoed this vision back to the general. He agreed that the Creek Indians' "ideas of their own importance has been raised to a very great height" over the years because of imperial competition. Yet the French defeat put the Creeks in "absolute dependence on His Majesty's subjects for arms, ammunition, and such other European commodities as they cannot now subsist without." This condition meant that Britain had the power to humble the Indians whenever it wanted to, at least once trade and gift giving were "so regulated as to be restrained or withheld when necessary for purposes of government." To figure out what those regulations should be, Amherst consulted with Sir William Johnson, Britain's superintendent of Indian affairs for the northern district, who had dealt closely with the Mohawks for more than twenty years. Johnson advised that each Indian hunter annually required eight pounds of powder and eight pounds of lead, though he hedged that Indians were, in his estimation, "remarkably the very worst managers of powder on every occasion." Amherst used this statement to conclude that Indians should be limited to the purchase of just five pounds of powder and shot per individual per transaction. The idea was that if the Natives had to use all their ammunition for subsistence, and prudently at that, they would be in no position to threaten British interests. "Nothing can be so impolitic,"

Amherst reasoned, "as to furnish them with the means of accomplishing the evil which is so dreaded."[5]

Recent history offered some support for Amherst's projections. When the Cherokees rose up in arms against encroaching Anglo-Americans in 1759, South Carolina responded by shutting down sales of ammunition to the tribe, run primarily out of two British forts. This policy was more effective than arms embargos in previous colonial–Indian wars because the French at Fort Toulouse, feeling the effects of British naval blockades as part of the Seven Years' War, were unable to make up the difference. As hostilities dragged on, the ability of the Cherokees to fight back waned, providing the wedge for redcoats and colonial militia to march deep into tribal territory in 1761 and put half of the towns and much of the food supply to the torch. The subsequent Cherokee surrender, including the cession of a large portion of their hunting grounds, was a model for how future British–Indian wars would be conducted if Amherst had his way. He expected it to require only a few examples before Indians abandoned military resistance against British policy.[6]

Amherst conceived of the British as the Indians' stern patriarch, barking out orders and exacting strict discipline, but Native people envisioned a softer paternal role in which the king's officers provided for their material needs and mediated their intertribal disputes. In this they wanted the British to act like Indian fathers, not European ones, and to fulfill the long-standing French role in the diplomacy of Indian country. The Indians especially looked forward to enjoying improved access to the British weapons market. When veteran Pennsylvania trader George Croghan met up with a band of Ottawas in eastern Ohio, they "expressed their satisfaction of exchanging their fathers the French for their brethren the English, as they were well assured the English were better able to supply them with all manner of necessaries than the French." The lure of British trade had been one of the main reasons that parts of the Ottawas and several other Indian nations historically allied with the French had moved into the Ohio country in the early to mid-eighteenth century. France had responded by asserting its sovereignty in the region through a fort-building campaign, which basically precipitated the Seven Years' War. Now that the French were defeated, Indians assumed their trade with the British would flourish. As the Iroquois instructed William Johnson, "We [the British] were a wealthy people [so] we should be able to supply them with goods at a very reasonable rate." They also wanted this trade to be accompanied by generous gift giving, commensurate with Britain's riches and the status of its troops as guests in Indian country. When the British took possession of Detroit, Indian leaders explained that "while the French lived here they employed a smith to mend our guns and hatchets . . . we expect you will do the same."[7]

Imperial agents who understood how Indian country worked, including the power Indians still wielded, repeatedly warned that Amherst's policies invited dire consequences, but to no avail. Johnson urged Amherst that providing Indians with powder and shot "is considered by them as the only proof of friendship," and that "arms and ammunition will be expected by whatever nation enters into an alliance with us." It followed that denying them "will increase their jealousy and make them all very uneasy. I am certain." When Croghan told Six Nations warriors that he was under orders not to dole out presents of powder, lead, or clothing, they "signified that they had a right, as being the proprietors of the land," and demanded him to write Amherst and instruct him how things were supposed to run. In the meantime, Croghan reported, the austerity policy made the Indians "appear very sulky and ill-tempered" and heightened "the Indians' jealousies of us." Similar encounters led Colonel Hugh Mercer, Fort Pitt's commander, to conclude that "a blacksmith with a set of tools to work entirely for the Indians is absolutely necessary," which was to say, a requirement for the safety of him and his men. As Kickapoo, Wabash, Mascouten, and Piankashaw chiefs around Fort St. Joseph in Michigan stressed in the summer of 1762, "What we think hardest of, is that the British have never so much given us the least present, or even allowed a smith to be at this post to mend our guns." Yet these complaints ricocheted off Amherst's tin ears.[8]

Britons on the front lines of Indian diplomacy did what they could to limit the damage. Johnson contrived the lame excuse that it was the Indians' long-standing preference for French gunpowder that had prompted British traders to reduce the amount of ammunition they carried. Croghan advised officers at Fort Pitt to ignore their orders and provision warriors traveling the north–south path running near the post, warning of severe consequences otherwise. "I don't know on which foot to dance," protested Captain Simeon Ecuyer to his superiors. Ultimately a thoroughly frustrated Croghan distributed presents on his own account in the interest of saving his colleagues' necks and ingratiating himself with his customer base. Officers in charge of the small, isolated Great Lakes forts also violated Amherst's policy once they realized the danger of compliance. Just a week after taking command of Michilimackinac, Captain George Etherington began making daily gifts of gunpowder to visiting Indians. Lieutenant James Gorrell followed a similar course at La Baye, Britain's westernmost fort. Commanding a garrison of fewer than twenty men, surrounded by persistent Menominees, Ho-Chunks, Sauks, and Ojibwas, Gorrell wisely drew 910 pounds of powder and 605 pounds of shot from the military store to distribute as gifts in the months leading up to Pontiac's War. The efforts of Etherington and Gorrell to establish reciprocal relationships with local Indians helps account for the Natives' sparing of these officers and most of their men when the war began by helping them leave their posts under escort. To be sure, unauthorized gift giving did not fully compensate for the damage done by Amherst's policies, particularly the tone. The amounts of such presents were less than the Indians expected, and officers' reluctance to give them indicated that the British "did not look at them as brothers and friends," contrary to the familial spirit and language so central to Indian diplomacy. At the same time these breaches of Amherst's orders reflected the apprehension of Britons deep in Indian country that they were not the conquerors their superiors imagined.[9]

Some Indians interpreted British austerity, however unevenly implemented, as designed to weaken them in preparation for a war to seize their territory and force them into servitude. Such fears were particularly acute among the Shawnees and Delawares, generations of whom had suffered displacement and, in the case of the Shawnees, enslavement at colonial hands stretching back to the seventeenth century. The Senecas shared their worries because the British had been encroaching up the Mohawk and Susquehanna Rivers into Iroquoia. What other reason could the British have for curtailing Native armaments other than to quicken the pace? "These steps," an Iroquois delegation told Croghan, "appears to them as if the English have a mind to cut them off the face of the earth." In a foreshadowing of how Anglo-American colonists would respond to parliamentary taxes a few years later, some Indians charged that the British were trying to reduce them to a state of slavery, by which they meant abject dependence and subservience, even to the point of subjection to the master's will regarding whether they would live or die. As early as 1761, belts of purple wampum painted red to symbolize war began to crisscross through the nations of the Ohio country and Great Lakes, accompanied by a message admonishing "that they had better attempt something now to recover their liberty than wait till we [the British] were better established."[10]

Amid this burgeoning war sentiment, a Delaware prophet named Neolin began preaching a message of Indian purification and self-sufficiency as a means toward restoring indigenous power. Neolin had experienced several visions in which the Great Spirit revealed that he had created Indians and whites separately for separate purposes and given them all they needed to fulfill their special destinies. The Great Spirit had provided the Indians' ancestors with ample game, the bow and arrow, and rituals to ensure their success in the chase. He intended America, the land on the turtle's back, to be the home of indigenous people alone. To whites a full ocean away, the Great Spirit had bestowed the book, Christianity, alcohol, and the gun. Yet Indians had repeatedly violated this sacred order by seeking the white people's gifts at the expense of their own. They killed too much game and even each other to acquire European goods they did not need, particularly alcohol, which led only to their degradation. They hosted missionaries, who taught them to shun the religious practices that had provided for their ancestors and bound them together as a people. They sold land intended just for them to the white people. The time for change had come. If Indians wanted to enjoy peace and plenty in this life and the next, they had to stop behaving as so many separate clans and instead to band together as one. Collectively, they needed to teach their young people how to return to the ways of the ancestors, sober up, and purge themselves of the pollution of colonial influences.[11]

Neolin's vision expressed Indians' anxiety and resentment over how the new British authority tried to exploit their reliance on firearms. The Great Spirit asked, "Did ye not [once] live by the bow and arrow? Ye had no need of gun or powder, or anything else, and nevertheless ye caught the animals to live upon and to dress yourselves with their skins." To that end Neolin advocated a seven-year course of bow-and-arrow training for boys. In the meantime the Great Spirit wanted Indian men to take up their guns and unite against the British as part of their collective purification. The Great Spirit loved the French, "but as to those who come to trouble your lands," meaning the British, "drive them out, make war upon them. I do not know them at all, they know me not, and are my enemies, and the enemies of your brothers. Send them back to the land which I have created for them and let them stay there." If the Indians adhered to this call, the Great Spirit would restore them to the kind of health and abundance the ancestors had once enjoyed. If they did not, they risked losing everything.[12]

Indian militants, Pontiac foremost among them, drew on Neolin's vision to add a compelling spiritual imperative to the calls for war. The campaign finally began in early May 1763 when Pontiac and his followers, after failing to spring a surprise attack on the Detroit garrison, put the fort under siege. By late June Indians throughout the region had sacked unsuspecting forts at Sandusky, Miami, St. Joseph, Ouiatenon, Michilimackinac, Venango, Le Boeuf, and Presque Isle, all of them small outposts with garrisons of fewer than thirty-five men, sometimes far less. The only holdouts west of Niagara were La Baye, which the troops soon vacated, and Detroit, Pitt, and Ligonier, which the warriors were determined to eliminate. Never had so many Indian groups across such a wide geographic expanse acted jointly against colonial forces. As to their reasons, when the Genesee Senecas struck Fort Venango, they spared one of the officers just long enough so he could write down their grievances, the first of which was "the scarcity and dearness of powder these two years past . . . and that when they complained they were ill treated and never redressed."[13]

Amherst resorted to racial paroxysms to explain this disaster instead of reflecting on his own role. He declared Indians to be "the Vilest Race of Beings that Ever Infested the Earth, and whose riddance from it, must be Esteemed a Meritorious Act, for the good of Mankind." To that end he ordered his officers to "Take no Prisoners, but put to Death all that Fall into your Hands." The problem with following these horrid demands, of course, was that most of the prisoners in the war zone were Britons who had fallen into Indian hands. Native people had taken back control of their country, at least for the meantime.[14]

Indian Munitions

At the start of Pontiac's War the stockpile of Native arms was larger than one might assume in light of Amherst's cutbacks to the gifting and trading of ammunition and occasional Indian complaints that powder shortages were making it difficult to feed their families. To understand why, one must turn back the clock to the start of the Seven Years' War. Throughout that conflict the French and British poured munitions into Indian country in the hope of securing allies, to which Indian warriors added substantial military plunder collected from enemy soldiers and civilian farmsteads. Hard figures are elusive due to the poor record keeping of gift giving and pillage, but Indians of the eastern woodlands probably obtained more firearms and ammunition during the 1750s than in any other decade of the colonial era. Those supplies put them in a better position to fight Pontiac's War than Amherst had guessed.[15]

During the Seven Years' War era, Indians in the Ohio country enjoyed a thriving arms trade. A century earlier a combination of epidemics, slave raids, and Iroquois attacks had largely depopulated the region, but throughout the early eighteenth century Native people returned to the area in droves, partially because of the opportunity to trade with both the French and British. Ottawas, Ojibwas, Miamis, Kickapoos, Weas, and Wyandots entered the region from the Michigan peninsula and Illinois country. The Mingos, a composite group with a Seneca majority, arrived from Iroquois territory. Shawnees and Delawares moved in from the east to escape the expansion of Pennsylvania and the oversight of the Six Nations. All of them valued the trade options their new location afforded them. At first the main benefit was easy access to French posts in the western Great Lakes, Illinois country, and Niagara, and the British fort of Oswego on Lake Ontario. Increasingly the Ohio Indians also hosted itinerant British fur traders, most of them Scots-Irish from Pennsylvania who had followed the Shawnees and Delawares west. Foremost among these traders was the Pennsylvania Irishman George Croghan. By the eve of the Seven Years' War, Croghan and his crew of dozens of subcontracted men had established six trading houses stocked with "a great quantity of arms" among the Miami Indian towns in what is now western Ohio. Unable to compete with the price or quality of British goods, terrified French officials foresaw their phalanx of Indian allies transforming into a gateway for Anglo-American westward expansion. It did not soothe French nerves that this trade was accompanied by official diplomacy between Ohio Indians and the colony of Pennsylvania, including diplomatic gifts from Philadelphia, which in 1748 included forty muskets, eighteen barrels of powder (totaling 1,800 pounds weight), 6,500 gunflints, and twenty bars of lead. The combination of British and French sources left the Delawares so well supplied that when Pennsylvania militia attacked and torched their Allegheny River town of Kittanning in 1756, there followed "the vast explosion of sundry bags and large kegs of gunpowder wherewith almost every house abounded." Colonial prisoners freed during this attack related that "the Indians had frequently said they had a sufficient stock of ammunition for ten years."[16]

Throughout the Seven Years' War the French distributed unprecedented amounts of munitions to Indian allies and neutrals alike in the hope of enlisting their support against the British colonies. At the beginning of the war, militia officer Francois-Marc-Antoine Le Mercier informed Paris that French authorities would have to supply arms to Indians "on a daily basis" in order to meet the need for diplomatic gifts and to outfit warriors for battle. The French would even have to accommodate Indians who wanted to exchange their old guns, however serviceable, for new. "It is certain my Lord," Le Mercier explained, "that if the war carries on in this colony, one may expect an extensive consumption of guns. If we were, however, unable to provide them [Indians] with guns, we would soon see them abandoning the French and throwing themselves on the side of the English. This article [firearms] and our gunpowder are what keeps them, to a greater extent, bound to us." To that end France sent 2,000 guns to Canada in 1759 alone, a year in which it expected New France and Louisiana combined to provide Indians with 500 muskets as presents, 4,000 guns through trade, and 1,400 tons of powder through a combination of diplomacy and commerce. The British blockade of the Saint Lawrence River, which began midway through the war, probably interfered with the arrival of some of these goods, but it was not airtight. French officers also gave Indians whatever supplies their men could not carry when they evacuated their remaining posts at the end of the Seven Years' War.[17]

The pillaging of British troops and colonial civilians was another source of munitions for Indians in the run-up to 1763. After French and Indian forces shot down nearly a thousand British troops at the Battle of the Monongahela in 1755, Native warriors gathered "considerable plunder" from the dead and the abandoned baggage train. The infamous behavior of French-allied Indians at 1757's Battle of Fort William Henry, in which they attacked and looted unsuspecting Britons who had been given quarter by General Montcalm, can be explained partially by the fact that the terms of surrender allowed the British to return home with their arms. Native warriors were not going to allow that to happen when they were the victors and had need for these weapons. Delaware and Shawnee raids against outlying settlements in Pennsylvania, Maryland, and Virginia netted additional martial supplies, especially given that colonial householders had purchased ammunition and put their guns in good repair because of the Indian threat. There is no data with which to generate an estimate of Indian plunder during the war, but the cumulative anecdotal evidence suggests it was substantial.[18]

British diplomatic gifts during the Seven Years' War added to the arsenals of Indians who fought in Pontiac's War, particularly the Senecas. Besides the British-allied Mohawks, most of the Six Nations staked out a neutral position at the beginning of the conflict. Yet as French fortunes dimmed, and as the Six Nations began to fear losing their influence over the increasingly assertive Shawnees and Delawares in the Ohio country, they threw in their lot with the British, with a strong assist in the form of gifts from Sir William Johnson. Johnson's presents for the Iroquois included 400 "good light arms," which he considered to be "an article indispensably necessary," in addition to "good powder, small ball, or small bar lead." He also requested £3,000 from the army to reimburse Iroquois who used their own guns in the campaign to retake Oswego and conquer French Fort Niagara. Little did Johnson know that some of the same Senecas he provisioned in 1759 would join the multitribal uprising against the British just four years later.[19]

Not the least of all, the Indians who rose in Pontiac's War stockpiled munitions through trade that continued to thrive after the fall of New France despite Amherst's orders. The defeat of the French military did not give the British control over French colonists, particularly traders, who had a long history of navigating around official obstacles. Though

Delaware Indian Powder Charge. This Delaware Indian powder charge, which held a single shot's measure of gunpowder for easy loading, was carved out of deer antler and depicts the face of the hunting god, Misinghali'kun, with a rattlesnake tail. It might have seen action in Pontiac's War. Courtesy University of Pennsylvania Museum of Archaeology and Anthropology. Object No. NA3881B.

only twenty-four canoes in Montreal were licensed to trade among the Great Lakes Indians in 1762 (just a quarter of the average between 1760 and 1774), some accounts put the number of renegade *coureurs de bois* at several hundred. Their Anglo-American counterparts were no more law-abiding. A surge in Indian demand during the summer of 1762 prompted Detroit trader James Sterling to urge his eastern suppliers to "send me as soon as possible three thousand weight of the best and hardest corned [large-grained, glazed] powder you can find." He explained that "the Indians don't like small glazed powder, nor the large [grind] that molders down to dust when rubbed between the fingers; they are very curious in the choice of their ammunition, for which reason we should be as particular in buying it." By appearances Sterling's customers were stockpiling in anticipation of trouble. That certainly was the case when the Delaware Turtle Heart and a band of warriors appeared at the Pennsylvania colony provisions store at Fort Pitt just a day before Indian attacks began in the area. According to trader, James Kenny, "they had sold £300 worth of peltry very hastily with which they bought as much powder as they could get."[20]

For the same reason, plundering munitions was clearly a focus of the Indian strategy in the opening stages of Pontiac's War, just as Johnson had predicted it would be a year earlier. Indians killed a reported sixty-four Anglo-American traders and their servants in the first few weeks of Pontiac's War, which must have produced fresh supplies of arms and of deerskins that could be used to trade for munitions from the French. The Wyandots' and Ottawas' raid on Fort Sandusky included the killing of sixteen merchants and the pillage of a reported 2,000 pounds of gun-powder. It was followed by a series of attacks against unwitting mer-chants headed to Detroit in bateaux (flat-bottomed cargo boats) along Lake Erie and Grand River, leading to the capture of an additional six-teen half barrels (800 pounds) of gunpowder. In addition to their plunder of traders, Detroit-area Indians commandeered unspecified amounts of arms and ammunition from the 500 or so French inhabitants surrounding the fort, whom they otherwise generally left unmolested. And of course the Indians' capture of British posts netted them large amounts of military hardware and ammunition. Fort Michilimackinac, for instance, held 5,000 pounds of gunpowder and fifty pounds of lead when the Ojibwas took it, giving them "a sufficient supply of all manner of neces-saries to serve them three years at least," according to British sources. Croghan's best estimate was that the warring Indians had seized at least 10,000 pounds of gunpowder from the conquered posts. Amherst's no-tion of Britain holding Indians by the throat by virtue of their depen-dence on firearms was a fantasy. In the early stages of Pontiac's War, actual conditions on the ground amounted to a British nightmare.[21]

———

After the Indians' quick capture of the most vulnerable British posts, the war's western theater settled into a pattern in which Native war-riors tried to cut off the few remaining forts from outside supplies and reinforcements. There were few other options left because, in the cases of Detroit and Pitt, the opportunity to overrun these strongholds had been lost with the element of surprise. Each post boasted more than 200 armed men (soldiers and civilians combined), sophisticated fortifications, and powerful defensive guns, against which the Indians' light arms were no match. Thus, taking these places required either drawing the men out or starving them out. The only other hope was that sustaining the campaign would convince the French to rejoin the fight against the British, which some Indians thought to be a distinct possibility based on the historic pattern of on-again, off-again imperial warfare.[22]

The battle to control the traffic to and from Detroit centered on the Detroit River, the artery connecting the fort to Lake Erie some twenty-five miles away. To sever this lifeline to the east, the 850 or so warriors (Ojibwas, Ottawas, Potawatomis, and Wyandots) involved in the siege of

Fort Detroit stationed war parties in ambush along the lake and river approach and kept hundreds of canoes at the ready. As a last line of attack, they built a fortification of tree trunks, branches, and earthen ramparts on Turkey Island at the narrows of the river, so any approaching sloop would have to pass through a hot volley at a distance of just a hundred yards. These tactics were effective for months, but as the summer progressed British convoys began fighting their way through the Indians' cordon, largely by spraying enemy warriors with grapeshot from deck-mounted swivel guns. In late July twenty-two relief barges reached the fort with 280 troops and six cannons, albeit after Indian gunfire inflicted serious wounds on fifteen men, two of whom later died. If such deliveries continued, the siege was doomed.[23]

Another key to cutting off Detroit and replenishing Indian stockpiles lay more than 250 miles away at Fort Niagara, which served as the entrepôt for shipments to the Great Lakes. Indians did not dare a direct attack on this post, for it ranked with Pitt as the strongest of Britain's western bastions. However, the portage between the fort and Lake Ontario was vulnerable, for its operations involved British hands guiding ox-drawn carts with heavy loads along a steep, cliff-side path lined with woods, to reach boats and barges on the water below. On September 14, 1763, a party of several hundred Genesee Senecas took advantage of the opportunity. First a small party of warriors fell upon a convoy working along the river, less as an end to itself than to lure troops stationed atop the cliffs into the open. Just as the Senecas planned, two companies of soldiers came rushing down the escarpment road after hearing the shots and screams, whereupon dozens of gunmen ambushed them from the cover of trees. By the time the smoke cleared, the Senecas had killed seventy men, made off with unspecified amounts of munitions, and destroyed several teams of horses, oxen, and wagons needed to transfer supplies to boats headed for Detroit. This devastating attack, and ongoing Seneca harassment of the portage, prevented Detroit from receiving any relief from Niagara for over a month.[24]

Aside from choking it off, the Indians' best chance of taking Fort Detroit was to draw the defenders outside, where Native gunmen had the advantage. Their approach was to "annoy" the fort almost daily by sending small parties as close to the walls as possible, firing a few shots at whoever dared to peak above the parapets or venture outside to fetch firewood or water, and then withdrawing. Their perseverance finally paid off when Captain James Dayell, drunk with overconfidence after successfully leading the July convoy, managed to wrest permission from a reluctant Major Henry Gladwin to lead 250 men against Pontiac's village, two and a half miles north of the fort at a place called Cardinal's Point. Dayell's plan was to march in the dead of night up a road along the west bank of the river through two rows of French farmhouses and outbuildings and then surprise the sleeping Indian camp. Yet more than 200 Native warriors were ready in ambush when this mission set out in depths of a July 31 evening illuminated by a clear moon. At a bridge crossing a small stream, henceforth known as Bloody Run, Indian gunmen opened a "heavy fire" on the unsuspecting troops from as close as twenty yards. Additional warriors rushed to the scene over the course of fighting, which lasted about an hour, until the soldiers beat an orderly retreat under the cover of swivel guns from two row galleys in the river. It was a stirring Indian victory claiming some twenty British dead and about forty wounded. At the same time, British officers, at Fort Pitt as well as Detroit, had learned the valuable lesson that as long as Indian gunmen commanded the area outside the palisade, it was best to try to outlast the siege and not force a premature conclusion.[25]

The tiny garrison at Fort Ligonier, tucked amid the Allegheny Mountains fifty miles east of Pitt on the Forbes Road, did not have this luxury. With just fifteen men to defend a "very bad" inner stockade of 200 square feet, Ligonier would have seemed to be a prime candidate for abandonment, but it held a large cache of munitions, which the command did not want to risk falling into enemy hands. Additionally, any relief force hoping to reach Pitt from the east would have to bivouac there. Thus, the soldiers' orders were to defend the post. Improbably, the troops managed to repulse two major Indian assaults on their positions over the course of three weeks before almost throwing it all away. In late June the psychologically frayed and physically exhausted redcoats rushed out from behind their defenses to attack four Indian musketeers, only to be lured into an ambush set by an estimated hundred warriors at a creek 400 yards from the fort. "I dare say they fired upwards of 1,000 shot," imagined Lieutenant Archibald Blane, but remarkably, "nobody received any damage." Somehow all the men made it safely back inside the walls and then stayed there.[26]

Fort Ligonier, Sketched on the spot - 30th June 1762 - Lt. Archibald Blane Delint, Royal Americans

Fort Ligonier. This small outpost in western Pennsylvania remained under siege by Indian gunmen throughout Pontiac's War, along with its much larger counterpart, Fort Pitt, and distant Fort Detroit. Courtesy Fort Ligonier, Ligonier, Pennsylvania.

The unenviable job of breaking these sieges fell to Swiss-born Colonel Henry Bouquet, culminating in the bloodiest gunfight of the war, the Battle of Bushy Run. Leading 500 soldiers (most of them Pennsylvania Germans) and dozens of horses and wagons carrying military stores and provisions, Bouquet managed to reach Ligonier by early August 1763, despite Indian attempts to bog down his march by raiding civilian settlements all along the route. Recognizing the danger of ambush as he entered the mountainous, wooded terrain of the Alleghenies, Bouquet deposited his wagons, military stores, and a portion of his troops at Ligonier to create a lighter, more defensible force. It turned out to be the right decision. On August 5, roughly halfway to Fort Pitt, hundreds of Indian gunmen ambushed Bouquet's advance guard, then encircled the enemy force and unleashed a steady "heavy fire," before retreating the next day after Bouquet bluffed them into open battle. By the time the British survivors limped into Fort Pitt, they had suffered fifty men killed and sixty wounded. Indian losses are unknown. A grudging Bouquet conceded that his foes showed a "boldness" that was "hardly credible" and that "they are good marksmen." By every indication the British were going to have to continue to absorb more high-cost victories of this sort if they were going to achieve anything resembling a military triumph in Pontiac's War. In other words, they would have to rely on their superior numbers and resources to allow them to fight a losing war longer than the Indians could fight a winning one, as had been the case throughout the colonial past. It was a far cry from Amherst's vision of dominance.[27]

Holding Their Fire while Stocking Their Arsenals

By the fall of 1763 the sieges of Detroit and Pitt had begun to collapse as Indian fighters came to the demoralizing realization that the rumors of the Treaty of Paris were true. Even officers stationed at Fort de Chartres in Illinois, the lone French post remaining in Indian country, were ready to concede that the outcome of the Seven Years' War was final. Not only was there no chance of the French king renewing the fight, but in the treaty he had surrendered all his claims in North America, with territory east of the Mississippi (except New Orleans) going to the British, and western territory (Louisiana) going to Spain. The news struck several Indians dumb, and Pontiac refused to believe it, but it was not a lie, and many Natives knew it. Seeing little prospect of breaking the stalemate at Detroit without French assistance, and needing to redirect their attention to the late fall and winter hunt, scores of Pontiac's warriors left for their hunting grounds in October 1763. Some of them even sent out peace feelers to Major Gladwin, though Pontiac remained committed as ever to the resistance.[28]

The Delawares and Shawnees operating in Pennsylvania, and the Genesee Senecas around Niagara, suffered an additional setback in early 1764 when the eastern Iroquois nations agreed with William Johnson to throw their support to the British. Part of their rationale was that British resources could help them regain some control over warring groups like the Delawares and Shawnees, who over the previous decade had become increasingly dismissive of Six Nations authority, largely out of bitterness toward Iroquois sales of their territory. Another incentive was that Johnson courted them with presents, including guns, ammunition, and gunsmithing services. Iroquois warriors immediately put these weapons to use, twice striking Delawares in the Susquehanna Valley and destroying a number of their settlements. All of a sudden the Delawares and Shawnees found themselves on the defensive in the war's eastern theater.[29]

These raids, combined with news of the Treaty of Paris, created enough pressure on Indian militants that Johnson and the Iroquois were able to convene a July peace conference at Niagara attended by the representatives of nineteen tribes, including all the warring nations except the Potawatomis, Delawares, and Shawnees. The superintendent made their trip worth it, distributing gifts worth some £38,000, declaring an end to the ban on the liquor trade, and promising that a lasting peace would inspire the British to "fill their canoes with presents; with blankets, kettles, guns, gunpowder and shot, and large barrels of rum, such as the stoutest [man] will not be able to lift." For their part the warring Indians' delegates agreed to return their white captives, end their support for the resistance, compensate traders for their losses during hostilities, guarantee the safety of traders in Indian country, and submit their future grievances either to Johnson or to the commander at Detroit. Everyone knew this agreement was tentative: the Indians' emissaries still had to discuss the terms with their home communities, which were certain to oppose the condition about returning captives, given that many of those people had been adopted into Native families. Nevertheless, this preliminary step suggested that Pontiac's War, like so many earlier Indian–colonial wars, was being decided by Indians like the Iroquois intervening in the colonists' favor for their own purposes, including supplies of arms.[30]

British expectations of how to end the war once and for all were as illusory as the Indians' hope of rousing the French king to take up the hatchet. London recalled Amherst at the end of 1763, in part because Johnson had convinced enough ministers that the general himself was largely responsible for the crisis. Nevertheless, Amherst's replacement, Thomas Gage, was as insistent as his predecessor that Indians would have to turn over the instigators of the war to British justice and immediately release all of their colonial captives. Any person knowledgeable about Indians could have told Gage that they would never concede to the first point, and that the second issue would require patient resolve.

Regardless, the general intended to take the sword and torch into the very bowels of the Indian resistance if they would not comply.

Gage thought he could force the warring Indians to terms by invading the Ohio country with two large armies of British troops and Indian allies, but his officers immediately saw the folly of their mission. As soon as Colonel John Bradstreet arrived at Presque Isle at the head of 1,200 redcoats and 650 allied Native warriors, he began negotiating an unauthorized peace with a delegation of Delawares, Shawnees, Wyandots, and Mingos. By its terms Indians pledged to return captured forts, free captive colonists, provide hostages, surrender anyone who committed hostilities in the future, and affirm their status as subjects of the crown. In exchange Bradstreet suspended his campaign and sent his forces away to reinforce Detroit and repossess Michilimackinac. Bradstreet flattered himself that he had all but ended the war, a favorable assessment doubtlessly colored by the fact that he had stowed Indian trade goods amid the troops' baggage, which he and some business partners intended to sell for personal profit. Rogue colonialism was alive and well even in the ranks of the British military.[31]

Gage, lacking such a conflict of interest, denounced this peace and ordered Bouquet to march from Fort Pitt into the Ohio country and "extirpate" any Indian communities that failed to meet his original conditions. Yet Bouquet lost his will, too, as Indians began surrendering some of their captives before his troops had even reached their villages, and especially as he realized that there was no way to force additional demands without a bloody fight he might not win. Rather than force the issue, he returned to Fort Pitt from eastern Ohio's Muskingum River with some 200 former captives in tow and promises of more to come. As in the case of the Battle of Bushy Run, he had to wonder just what kind of victory he had won against an enemy that constantly gave way only in order to reappear when conditions were more favorable.[32]

If the question had been settled of whether the British would retain Detroit and Pitt and reoccupy the Ohio country and Great Lakes forts, it remained uncertain whether and when they could gain possession of the Illinois country, an issue that, in the short term, rested on the warring Indians' supply of munitions. The resistance and the 1763–1764 winter hunt had consumed significant amounts of powder and shot at the same time that returns in plunder were falling fast. By the spring of

1764, military supply convoys had adopted careful defenses against Indian attack and British traders were all but nonexistent in Indian country aside from a few rogues, so there were fewer opportunities to loot them. Delaware and Shawnee sorties had so successfully emptied western Pennsylvania, Maryland, and Virginia of colonial targets, and forced those few hearty souls who remained to take better defensive measures, that there were fewer easy targets left there as well. Fortunately for the warring Indians, they had other resources to exploit.[33]

Amherst had been convinced that the militants could sustain their resistance only "while we ourselves supply them with powder and lead," without which "their ammunition and supply must be soon greatly exhausted." To that end British authorities had done everything within their power to keep military stores out of Indian hands during hostilities. After the Indians' successful ambushes during the early stages of the war, British officers assigned extra soldiers to accompany shipments of supplies to the interior forts. Ecuyer had traders living near Fort Pitt stow their powder and shot in the post's warehouse, while Amherst ordered his subordinates at Oswego and Niagara not to let any traders pass west, judging it to be of the "utmost consequence" to keep arms from falling into Indian hands. These measures were never foolproof. For instance, Edward Cole, a trader operating out of Detroit, conspired with his business partners in Schenectady to smuggle ammunition to the fort for trade with surrounding Indians during the truce of early 1764. His plan was to ship this contraband by canoes instead of bulky bateaux to avoid drawing the attention of authorities. At the same time, the very fact that he had to take such measures reflects that the inspections regime disrupted such commerce. Even Pennsylvania's assembly, in a rare moment of attentiveness to military affairs, outlawed the sale of guns, powder, and shot to Indians on penalty of a fine of £500, thirty-nine lashes from the whip, and a year in jail. Out in the war zone, Gladwin periodically launched boats into the Detroit River "to draw out the Indians and make them expend some ammunition" in the hope that their stores would soon run dry.[34]

By early 1764 British officials had begun to insist that these measures were bearing fruit. Gladwin believed that the Detroit Indians' early peace feelers reflected that "the enemy have lost near 90 of their best warriors and have expended most of their ammunition, so that I imagine they will be miserable enough in spring." The acting governor of New York, Cadwallader Colden, agreed from his vantage point 600 miles away, citing the Detroit Indians' "want of ammunition" as the reason for their declining morale. "I am of the opinion that the Indians cannot be provided too cautiously with ammunition at this time," he emphasized to William Johnson, fearing that the superintendent would outfit the Six Nations with arms. "They should know and feel that they cannot live without us." Gage seized on intelligence that confirmed these assumptions. One freed captive, a fifteen-year-old boy from Virginia who had passed through several Shawnee settlements after Delawares seized him along the Potomac River, told in March 1764 "that they have hunted all this winter till spring with their guns, but that lately they have only made use of their bows and arrows, as the ammunition was very scarce, none of them having more than a pound of powder, some half a pound, and some none at all, and lead only in proportion." What British officials failed to appreciate was that these shortages appeared at the end of the hunting season while the men were away from their villages where ammunition would have been stored. Another piece of intelligence came from six men who described coming under attack by four Indians on February 22, 1764, while loading wood near Fort Pitt. Three of the four attackers, they noticed, were armed with just bows and arrows. The strength of this evidence, which Gage said arrived from "every quarter," could not support the weight of his conclusion "that the Indians are in want of ammunition and every other necessary" and therefore "it is in our power to become masters of their country."[35]

Gage and his officers soon found themselves eating their words. Gladwin cautioned in April 1764 that the Wyandots and Ottawas around Sandusky were still "much animated against us, that they have a good supply of ammunition, and plant abundance of corn, with which they supply the other nations." Weeks later the same Shawnees and Delawares who were supposedly reduced to using bows and arrows launched an attack against Virginia's Fort Dinwiddie in which they kept up musket fire for six hours, leading to fifteen British dead and sixteen captured. Gage had to acknowledge, grudgingly, that "they do not want powder and ball." A year later Croghan stated the obvious when he wrote to Johnson, "It does not appear to me that those nations have been so distressed by the war as has been thought, they having been well supplied by the French from the Illinois, and they tell me that if Colonel Bouquet had not solicited them for peace last fall, they would have fought with him."[36]

Illinois was indeed the Indians' primary source of munitions among several suppliers. Though Illinois was located east of the Mississippi in territory ceded to Britain, it remained under French control for the meantime. There were still nearly 200 French soldiers garrisoned at Fort de Chartres amid a hundred or so French *habitants*. Nearby the Mississippi River settlements of Cahokia, Kaskaskia, and Ste. Genevieve continued to receive supplies from French authorities in New Orleans. The Spanish would not take possession of that city until 1766. French provisions included large amounts of military wares sent without serious concern (other than lip service paid to British authorities) for whether the inhabitants would trade those materials to the warring Indians. Johnson had warned Amherst early in Pontiac's War not to assume that Illinois was too far from the Ohio country to serve as its supply depot, for "I well know that distance is little regarded by Indians." Under the straightened circumstances of wartime, he was right. Gershom Hicks, a colonist who initially appeared at Fort Pitt claiming to have escaped from Indian captivity, only later to be charged with serving as a spy for the Indians, testified to the same effect. With the threat of hanging to motivate him, he told that several Delaware chiefs, including the war leader White Eyes, had traveled to Fort de Chartres (which he called "the stone fort") in the winter of 1763–1764 seeking supplies. Though the French officer turned them away, nearby private traders stepped up to furnish them with nine horse loads of powder and lead. A French officer also revealed to Gage that upward of 4,000 Indians had visited Fort de Chartres every year, for reasons that required little explanation.[37]

French trade missions to the Indians' settlements also accounted for the warriors' arsenal during Pontiac's War. The captured Hicks recounted that the Delawares arranged to have a company of French traders ferry twelve barges full of goods up the Scioto River the spring or summer following the Indians' visit to Chartres. Given the context of his interrogation, Hicks's testimony can hardly be trusted on its own, but in its broad outlines it is confirmed by several other sources. During the fall of 1763, small parties of French traders out of Illinois reportedly traded munitions to the St. Joseph Potawatomis in Michigan. Thomas

Smallman, a cousin of George Croghan and an experienced trader in his own right, told that during his captivity among the Shawnees in the winter of 1763–1764, he had witnessed a French officer named Jonquiere excite the Indians to war and promise them that shipments of powder and ball were on their way from Illinois. Smallman also said that in May a trader named Ottina arrived with three canoe loads of ammunition, followed in September by a French trader from Miami who brought 800 pounds of gunpowder and answerable amounts of lead to exchange for black slaves the Indians had seized during the war. These French traders also escorted Delaware-Shawnee delegations back to Illinois for additional trade. Indian sources, including a former Cherokee captive among the warring Indians, and a Shawnee taken prisoner at Fort Pitt, made similar statements.[38]

The governor of Louisiana acknowledged this traffic to his superiors, but explained there was little he could do about it other than to order the voyagers not to provide Indians with munitions and hope they complied. Numerous French-Canadian traders worked the Ottawa River route between Montreal and Michilimackinac, drawn by the "exorbitant rates" Indians were paying for munitions. They were no more dutiful to British authorities than they had been over the previous century to French officials who railed against their illicit activity. The extent of this commerce is reflected in the fact that Canadian fur outfits managed to export 85,000 beaver pelts to London in 1764 despite the state of war in the Lakes region. A frustrated Gage demanded the identification and arrest of renegade traders and confiscation of their goods, but they were too slippery to grasp. His only solution was to solicit the Cherokees to ambush any of these traders they encountered in the Ohio country.[39]

Warring Indians enjoyed access to French gunsmiths, and not only at Fort de Chartres and New Orleans but even in their own villages. Hicks, during his interrogation, recalled the French sending two gunsmiths to live among the Shawnees during the war. At Detroit the warring Indians held two gunsmiths prisoner, including the fort's armorer, Frenchman Pierre Bart. Even the Virginia boy who escaped captivity among the Shawnees and testified about their supposed shortage of ammunition remarked that "the arms of those families he was amongst were in pretty good order," though they operated far from French Illinois.[40]

There is a great deal of circumstantial evidence to suggest that French officers provided warring Indians with substantial gifts throughout Pontiac's War. Louisiana's governor Jean-Jacques-Blaise d'Abbadie wrote to Paris that cutting off Indians from powder and shot, in addition to being inhumane, would put French colonists at risk of Indian attack. D'Abbadie's successor, Charles-Philippe Aubry, complained to his superiors in February 1765 that he was "continually visited by a multitude of barbarians who come to demand of him arms and ammunition to make war on the English" because "they do not wish another father than the French and they will never have another." Clearly they had not been discouraged by their earlier interactions with D'Abbadie. Captain William Howard, in command of Michilimackinac after the British reoccupied the fort in September 1764, heard that Frenchmen, including military officers, were at St. Joseph giving away powder and ball to Indians as late as April 1765. Mohawk sources shared intelligence with William Johnson in the summer of 1763 and winter of 1764 that warring Indians were getting arms and ammunition from the French governor in New Orleans, and that he promised them ample support throughout the conflict. The rumor around Detroit in the summer of 1764 was that Pontiac had a French-language letter telling him to be patient, for in French Illinois "powder and ball was in a great plenty as water." It is possible that such reports were a design by the warring Indians and their French partisans to intimidate the British and buoy the spirit of resistance. They did, however, raise Gage's suspicion that his French counterparts had been playing a double game. Clearly the gun frontier remained far more international than the British liked to think.[41]

As late as spring and summer of 1765 some Native militants continued to insist that they enjoyed enough French support to carry on the war. Shawnee chiefs conferencing with Croghan in Illinois claimed that Aubry said he "desired them to continue the war against the English, and that they should from time to time receive abundance of presents, and traders among them to supply them with arms and ammunition." This was more than wishful thinking or propaganda, though it served those purposes too. In late March 1765 the British agent in Illinois, Alexander Fraser, met a band of Shawnees from the Scioto River who claimed that during the winter they had received visits from three French traders carrying martial stores. A month later, when Fraser was in the midst of negotiations with Pontiac at Kaskaskia, a party of excited Shaw-nees arrived from New Orleans declaring that Aubry had promised them powder and shot, followed three days later by Fraser witnessing the arrival of "vast quantities of goods." Johnson's conclusion was that, regardless of whether French officers were provisioning Indians, "the lower order are perhaps to a man doing all in their power to alienate the Indians' affections and possess themselves of the trade," the effect of which was that the Indians remained "plentifully supplied with ammu-nition." The Indians reached quite a different conclusion. "They almost universally believe that the French are coming with a large force," Johnson complained, to which Lieutenant Colonel John Campbell of Detroit added, "They will never listen to any message sent to them from the English so long as they have got a Father at the Illinois that supplies them with everything they stand in need of." These warriors had not been defeated. They were merely waiting for the right time to strike again.[42]

General Gage probably had it half right when he concluded that "without the assistance of the French, no league of this nature can exist long," which was a far cry from the days of the British insisting that they had a stranglehold on Indian country. Where Gage had it half wrong is that no authority could control the arms trade. Long after the British sta-tioned troops in Illinois and the Spanish assumed possession of Loui-siana, Frenchmen continued to deliver munitions to the Indians who rose up in Pontiac's War. In December 1765, months after the British had taken possession of Fort de Chartres, Gage bristled that unlicensed French traders still dominated Indian commerce throughout the western Great Lakes and Ohio country as far east as the neighborhood of Fort Pitt, a condition that lasted for years. It was as if the British victory in the Seven Years' War had merely freed the French state from the ex-pense of trying to govern this region while allowing French people to retain the profits of it. Gage sounded like the Gallic officials he once criticized when he protested that "it is no easy matter to obtain proofs sufficient to convict them, though endeavors shall be used towards it." Bradstreet brought the long-standing debate about British–Indian affairs full circle when he opined that it was foolhardy to make policies based on the assumption that Indians were dependent on British goods as long as French traders operated so freely along the Mississippi. The only way to achieve peace was through "strict justice, moderation, fair trade," and, not the least of all, presents, the cost of which was far less than waging war. He also suggested that Britain should tax the trade in munitions rather than trying to prevent it, and apply the revenue toward the costs of administering Indian country. His latter proposal never received serious attention, but the fact that he felt comfortable at all presenting it to Gage reflects the growing British realization of how difficult it was to translate the Indians' dependence on firearms into political dependence on empire.[43]

British authorities were no more effective at controlling Anglo-American traders than French ones. By 1766 Britons trading in the Ohio country and Great Lakes were exporting more of their deerskins through New Orleans than through British posts because of the ease of shipping goods down the Mississippi and probably also to avoid governmental scrutiny. Yet the most startling aspect of this commerce was the appearance of rifled guns in trader inventories. The grooves on the interior of a rifle barrel sent a bullet into a spiral rotation that made the shot accurate at a distance as great as 300 yards, more than three times the effective range of a smoothbore musket. Over the long term many Indians continued to prefer smoothbores because they were cheaper and lighter than rifles, quicker and easier to load, and could accommodate musket balls of various sizes, including small lead, whereas rifle grooves became damaged by firing improperly sized shot. In the short term, however, Indians were becoming "very fond of them [rifles], and use them with such dexterity, that they are capable of doing infinite damage."[44]

The Shawnees and Delawares took a particular liking to rifles. During the period of the Seven Years' War and Pontiac's War, Pennsylvania gunsmiths, especially German craftsmen in Lancaster County, began to produce small numbers of high-quality rifles, some of which reached Indians as diplomatic gifts from the Pennsylvania government and as trade goods. As portions of the Shawnees and Delawares moved into the Mississippi River Valley country after Pontiac's War, they continued to obtain rifles from Illinois traders supplied by merchants in Pennsylvania, as the two areas were now part of a single British commercial empire. Bradstreet's concern was not only that "all the Shawnee and Delaware Indians are furnished with rifled barrel guns, of an excellent kind," but also "that the upper Nations [or Great Lakes Indians] are getting them fast," even as these same nations continued to talk about reviving the war. At least formally, Johnson agreed with Bradstreet that "all white persons should be restricted on a very severe penalty from selling them to any Indians." Yet just a few years later Johnson was distributing rifles as presents to the Iroquois and recruiting Lancaster gunsmiths to relocate to sites in and around Mohawk country. The British takeover not only failed to stem the arms trade to Indians, but witnessed Indians obtaining improved firearms technology, sometimes with the encouragement of high-ranking officials.[45]

Faced with their imperial and colonial governments' inability to keep munitions out of Indian hands, and sometimes even their complicity in arming them, some colonists in western Pennsylvania began forming vigilante bands to prevent war materials from reaching the interior tribes. Calling themselves the "Black Boys" (in reference to the blackface they wore to hide their identities) and the "Brave Fellows," some 200 of them intercepted a pack train of eighty-one horses heading west on Forbes' Road for Fort Pitt on March 6, 1765. They were outraged, but not surprised, to find a full stock of Indian goods among the bundles, some of which was earmarked for official diplomacy, but still more of which was contraband belonging to George Croghan and his business partners in Philadelphia, who wanted to be first to reach the Ohio Indians once restrictions on the trade ended. Instead the Black Boys destroyed sixty-three pack loads of merchandise with an estimated value of £20,000 to £30,000, saving the guns and ammunition to protect themselves from Indian raids or official retribution. Three days later they broke into the storehouse of a local justice of the peace, James Maxwell, whom they accused of being in league with Croghan, and seized eight barrels of gunpowder he had hidden there. Attempts by British troops to restore order only added fuel to the Black Boys' ire. When soldiers tried to recover the stolen goods and arrest the perpetrators, there began a series of confrontations, including firefights, that lasted until November when Fort Loudon's commander returned what few guns his men had confiscated from the crowd. Ultimately authorities let the matter drop rather than precipitate an armed rebellion. Yet even as late as 1769 the

Black Boys were a problem for anyone, including the army, trying to ship munitions to Indians through western Pennsylvania. The government found itself in quite a quandary. Arming Indians might keep them at peace, but that also meant fighting colonial vigilantes, whereas giving in to the vigilantes' demands risked inciting the Natives to war. As had always been the case, colonial and imperial authority never appeared weaker than within the context of a gun frontier.[46]

───────

Pontiac's War did not so much end as ebb, and its consequences were full of contradictions for the future of Indians, arms, and empire. When the Ohio and Great Lakes nations withdrew from Pontiac's War, it was not because their arms were in disrepair or they were out of ammunition. Rather, they saw the impossibility of dislodging the British from Detroit, Pitt, and Niagara without French troops and artillery. Additionally, continuing to resist the British reoccupation of the western posts would put Native families through serious privation by requiring their able-bodied men to fight instead of hunt and exposing their villages to British attack. The cost was just not worth it, not when the British seemed to have learned their lesson, at least temporarily, when it came to doling out presents and treating Indian leaders with a measure of respect.

That change was evident at a series of peace conferences held over the course of 1764 and 1765, which were marked by copious gift giving by the British sponsors and a diplomatic tone void of the condescension and disdain of Amherst's tenure. At a meeting hosted by Johnson Hall on May 30, 1765, Sir William approached the Delaware leaders Killbuck and Captain Bull, ritually removed an axe from their hands, and replaced it with a musket, symbolizing that he "desired they would apply themselves closely to hunting and trade in the future." It was also his way of acknowledging how British restrictions on the flow of arms had caused the war, and Johnson was hardly alone. By early 1765 Gage had authorized reopening the trade wherever Johnson saw fit, out of recognition that the Indians took it "as proof of sincerity on our part." That same year Johnson put the annual Indian trade for the region north of the Ohio River (including Pennsylvania and New York) at 3,000 guns, 80,000 pounds of gunpowder, and 160,000 pounds of lead. In other words, the flow of arms had returned to levels that marked the period of British-French rivalry, even though the British were the lone imperial power left in the region.[47]

Officers stationed deep in Indian country were out ahead of their superiors in conforming to the Indians' expectations of gift and gun diplomacy. It took only until the autumn of 1764 for Detroit's commander Campbell to begin repairing Indian arms again, "which I thought necessary to comply with, as I have hope it may be means of keeping them quiet and in good temper." He asked his superiors for advice on how to go about distributing powder and shot to Indians, because his subordinate officer was "very well convinced there is no living at this post without it [unless] he has it in his power to make some presents to Indians." As the British took possession of former French and Spanish stations along the Gulf Coast, the officers found the Indians' demand for presents "inconceivable," though they too had come to realize that without these gifts "a war with them would have been unavoidable." Thus, between December 28, 1763, and July 13, 1764, alone, the commander at Pensacola distributed gifts that included 352 muskets, 612 pounds of gunpowder, and 606 pounds of shot. To meet these expenses, London began allocating £20,000 a year for Indian presents and related expenses like transportation, having joined several earlier colonial regimes in discovering that it was cheaper to give gifts to Indians than to fight Indian wars.[48]

The Indians' greater goals of eliminating British forts and colonial settlements from Indian country fell far short of the mark, though they managed to achieve some marginal victories. British garrisons remained at Detroit, Michilimackinac, Fort de Chartres, Niagara, and Pitt, but Gage decided not to reoccupy the smaller posts in the interest of economy. By 1772 he had ordered Pitt to be evacuated too. The end of the war also coincided with Parliament's Proclamation Line of 1763, which offered at least some hope of slowing Anglo-American encroachment and ending the free-for-all competition for Indian territory by unscrupulous land speculation companies. The Proclamation was not a direct response to Pontiac's War per se, for it was in the works before the war even took place. Nevertheless, it did reflect London's concern that expensive Indian wars were going to become a constant drain on the imperial budget unless something was done to reduce the Indians' grievances. The Proclamation declared North America west of the Appalachians to be a royal domain reserved for Indians. Title to any of that land could not be legally transferred to British subjects unless by a treaty negotiated between Indians and commissioners of the crown. The point of these measures was not to evict all squatters from Indian land or prevent them by force from entering it in the first place. Such people were "too numerous, too lawless and licentious ever to be restrained," as Gage put it. Nor did the Proclamation envision a permanent freeze of Anglo-American expansion. Instead, the point was to put royal agents alone in charge of the diplomatic process. Henceforth, London would not recognize the titles of the colonial elites' land speculation companies; this in turn would destroy the point of those companies' trying to sell portions of those claims to would-be "settlers." Thus, Indians would be spared the corrupt practices of those companies and the chaotic encroachment they promoted. The Proclamation, in short, was not an answer to the Indians' question of how to prevent Anglo-Americans from seizing their territory, but at least it showed something of the brotherly spirit so lacking in the run-up to 1763.[49]

Such measures, combined with outright war weariness, were enough to end Pontiac's War, but the catalogue of problems plaguing Indian–colonial relations meant that it was only a matter of time before hostilities flared up again. Indeed, a long-term view indicates that Pontiac's War was just one spike in what amounted to a sixty years' war for the Ohio country and Great Lakes stretching between 1755 and 1815. With the French threat removed, migrants, free and slave, began thronging into the colonies as never before, with some 221,500 arriving between 1760 and 1775. They included over 55,000 Irish Protestants (2.3 percent of the total population of Ireland), 40,000 Scots (3 percent of the total population of Scotland), 30,000 English, and 12,000 Germans and Swiss. By comparison, the total number of Indians east of the Mississippi River was only about 150,000. A disproportionate number of these newcomers from Europe, joined by other struggling colonists seeking to improve their lot, streamed into territory belonging to some of the most powerful Indian nations in the East, including the Mohawk River Valley of the Iroquois, the Susquehanna River Valley and Allegheny country of the Delawares and Shawnees, and the Appalachian foothills and Smoky Mountains of the Cherokees. By the time of the American Revolution, 10,000 Euro-American families had moved into the Allegheny region the Delawares and Shawnees had fought to retain during Pontiac's War, with the town of Pittsburgh, the spawn of Fort Pitt, as their hub. Joining them, and usually ahead of them, were liquor traders and deer hunters from Pennsylvania and Virginia, and even land speculators who expected the Proclamation Line to fall in due course. Royal Indian agents like William Johnson tried to control this chaos, all the while lining their own pockets, by negotiating land cessions that hopped the line and cut deep into Cherokee, Shawnee, and Delaware country, but these measures served only to antagonize Native warriors already furious about colonial encroachment and their chiefs' passivity and even complicity in the face of it. These tensions resulted in back-and-forth raids and retributive murders throughout the trans-Appalachian region in the late 1760s and early 1770s, building into Lord Dunmore's War in 1774 between Virginia, on the one hand, and Shawnees, Delawares, and Mingos, on the other. From the Indian perspective, it was difficult to tell where these conflicts ended and the American Revolution began, except for the critical difference that in the Revolution most of the nations that rose up in Pontiac's War generally threw in their lot with the British as the obvious source of manufactured goods and the better of two bad options when it came to protecting their territory. In a sense the French king had returned, but this time he was wearing a red coat.[50]

Indians remained armed throughout this sixty years of war because of their sophisticated multilateral diplomacy and economic influence, the ongoing state of imperial competition, and the weakness of the state in the face of rogue traders. Indians had options even after the American Revolution. In the face of white American aggression, they turned to British Canada for munitions and diplomatic backing. Canadian fur traders of French, Scots, and Scots-Irish backgrounds continued to ply their wares to Indians throughout the Great Lakes, Mississippi River Valley, and beyond, sometimes deep within territory claimed by the United States. Well into the nineteenth century the Creeks armed themselves through Scottish-American and British traders operating out of Spanish Florida, and even sent political delegations to Spanish Cuba to secure military supplies. As portions of the Ohio tribes withdrew toward the confluence of the Missouri and the Mississippi Rivers to escape the Anglo-American threat, they continued to trade for guns and ammunition with Frenchmen who had moved west of the Mississippi, and thus into Spanish Louisiana, to found St. Louis and reinforce Ste. Genevieve after the Seven Years' War. Indians who relocated to Missouri also promised to protect Spanish interests against the United States in exchange for secure land title and arms. Such measures enabled the Ohio and Great Lakes Indians to carry on the fight against United States expansion into the 1810s under the leadership of the Shawnee Tecumseh, Pontiac's nineteenth-century counterpart. After the War of 1812, Indians would again lose their ability to extract guns, powder, and shot through the imperial play-off system. Yet even then the United States would struggle to use the Indians' dependence on guns to render them dependent on the federal government, for some of the same reasons that the British had proven unable to dominate Indians during the period of Pontiac's War. Indians battling the United States, even without the support of a Britain, France, or Spain, could still exploit suppliers hailing from the very society against which they warred, for the young republic was no more capable of controlling the gun trade than were its imperial predecessors.[51]

5. OTTERS FOR ARMS

Between the 1780s and early 1800s, Natives of the Pacific Northwest coast of North America went from being some of the most isolated people in the world to hosting merchant ships from a half dozen nations and participating in a global commerce linking Europe, the United States, and China. During the previous three centuries Western merchants had been on a quest to find goods to trade to the Chinese for their coveted tea, porcelain, and silk. Other than bullion, most of what Westerners had to offer—British woolens, India cottons, and ginseng—had limited purchasing power in China. Yet all that changed following Captain James Cook's famous exploration of the Pacific from 1776 to 1779. Cook discovered that indigenous people living along 2,000 miles of coast stretching between modern Oregon on the south and the Alaskan panhandle on the north possessed rich stores of lustrous sea otter pelts and surrendered them easily in trade. More importantly, those pelts fetched astonishingly high prices in Canton. The Natives who hunted the otter, by contrast, had little interest in Chinese products. What they wanted were metal tools, cloth, and, above all eventually, guns, powder, and shot, for the same basic reasons those items had commanded a market among Atlantic coast Indians for the previous century and a half. Such goods, particularly munitions, promised to become the new key to the balance of power in a densely settled region where chiefs and communities contended with one another for slaves, tributaries, territory, and prestige.

This era spawned a vibrant gun frontier in the Pacific Northwest with a transformative power that rivaled any indigenous arms market elsewhere in the continent. Native leaders whose communities controlled deep, sheltered harbors for merchant vessels, and indigenous trade and tributary networks capable of funneling otter pelts to their shores, had the means to claim a dominant position in the arms-for-otters traffic and in regional politics. Two such figures could be found among the Nuu-chah-nulth (or Nootka) people of the outer (or western) coast of Vancouver Island, the earliest and most intensive site of the trade. The chief Maquinna of the community of Yuquot at the mouth of Nootka Sound, and the chief Wickaninnish of Clayoquot Sound, used their favorable geography and already impressive clout to control the otter for arms trade and then expand their influence until it extended over a coastal range of some 300 miles. They grew so formidable that in two separate incidents they even managed to capture foreign merchant ships of over 250 tons with crews of twenty-five or more men. To the north, along the Alexander Archipelago of the Alaska panhandle, the Tlingits of Sitka Harbor wielded British and American arms to contest the expansion of Russian fur traders into their territory, most vividly in pitched battles in 1802 and 1804 that should rank among the most dramatic clashes between colonists and indigenous people in North American history. The strength of Tlingit weaponry placed serious limits on Russian activity and profitability, and ultimately provided an opening for the British Hudson's Bay Company along the Pacific coast. No less than in the Atlantic colonies, indigenous gunmen in the Pacific Northwest played a key role in how European colonialism unfolded.

The collapse of the gun frontier along the Pacific Northwest coast was almost as sudden as its rise. The arms trade rested on the exploitation of a fragile sea otter population that could not withstand the strain of indigenous hunting for the international market. As otter catches dwindled in the 1820s and 1830s, most gun merchants sailed off in pursuit of other opportunities, while others merely shifted their operations from the outer coast to mainland river mouths and river valleys to trade for beaver from interior peoples. In turn the regional balance of power tilted away from outer-coast communities like Yuquot and Sitka toward their previously isolated rivals, setting the conditions for payback. The subsequent violence, combined with losses from a succession of devastating epidemic diseases, meant that some residents of the outer coast had witnessed their people's strength peak and plummet within their lifetime. It was a sign that they had entered the gun age.

Guns and the Big Man of Nootka

The Pacific Northwest coast had been isolated from most of the rest of the world well into the eighteenth century, experiencing little contact with overseas people aside from the occasional visit by a ship blown off course, but it was a densely populated and dynamic region all the same. The coast's damp, mild weather, even along its northern reaches, played out against a magnificent backdrop of towering mountains, thick green forests, rushing rivers, deep fjords, and long inlets. Strong winds and the mighty Pacific, temperamental even on its best days, pounded the shore relentlessly, producing a jigsaw of curiously formed rocky islands and outcroppings, long crescent-shaped beaches, pebble-filled coves, and steep beachside cliffs. Though the region was too cool and overcast for corn-bean-squash horticulture, wild and semidomesticated foods were plentiful enough to sustain some 200,000 people on the coastal strip from northern California to the northern tip of the Alaska panhandle. Salmon was their most important staple, to which they added wide varieties of fish and shellfish, sea mammals, water fowl, game, and untamed plants. This natural bounty, which the people enhanced through such means as making productive improvements to herring runs and shellfish beds, gave local populations leisure time to develop what was arguably the richest material life of any North American indigenous culture area. It was marked by exquisite woodworking, weaving, and painting in the form of cedar masks, totem poles, canoes, boxes, rain hats, baskets, robes, shell ornaments, and decorated weapons and tools. The people also developed steeply graded social hierarchies, which, with several local variations, involved a chiefly nobility, commoners, and slaves, the latter of which were more numerous than in other Native North American societies. Warfare focused on capturing enemy women and children as slaves and controlling economic resources like prime fishing spots. This violent competition also meant that gun merchants would find plenty of demand for their wares in the Pacific Northwest.[1]

The Russians were the first fur traders in the region as a capstone to their expansion across Siberia in search of fox and sable furs for the European and Chinese markets. Vitus Bering's 1741 exploration of the Gulf of Alaska not only introduced Europe to the geography of the Gulf but drew the attention of Russian fur traders *(promyshlenniki)* to the otters of the Aleutian Island chain, whose volcanic outcroppings crest across 1,200 miles of ocean from the Alaskan mainland toward Russia's Kamchatka Peninsula. With the Chinese willing to pay about nine times more for otter than for beaver, which itself was one of the more lucrative furs, it took only a decade before the *promyshlenniki* had organized several private companies to exploit the islands' hunting grounds. By 1797, forty-two Russian companies had made over 101 voyages to the region. Along the way they followed a ruthless pattern that had served them profitably with indigenous Siberians. Rather than trade for the skins or hunt for the otters themselves, the *promyshlenniki* raided the settlements of the indigenous Aleuts, took the women and children hostage, and then held them until the men paid a ransom in seal, fox, walrus, and especially otter. After several Aleut attempts at resistance met brutal Russian suppression, this exploitation became routinized in the form of an annual tribute calculated per man, eventually to be replaced by a labor draft applied to every adult Aleut male. Yet there was no stability for the Aleutian population, which nearly collapsed from a combination of deaths at Russian hands, male casualties in the dangerous work of hunting otter in seal-skin kayaks, and especially the introduction of foreign epidemic diseases. The otter population, which is slow to reproduce, suffered too under the strain of overhunting. By 1785 otter had become so scarce on the Aleutians that the Russians moved their operations eastward to Kodiak Island and then the Alaskan mainland. It was only a matter of time before they came face to face with the Tlingits of the panhandle.[2]

Captain James Cook's voyage to the Pacific in 1778, followed by the publication of two journals from the expedition in 1783 and 1784, was to the Anglophone world what Bering's voyage had been to the Russians: an announcement of a previously unknown corner of the globe teeming with sea otters from which riches were to be had on the Chinese market. Briton James Hanna, captaining the aptly named *Sea Otter,* leapt at the opportunity, procuring 560 otter pelts after just five weeks anchored in Nootka Sound in 1785, which he then sold for 20,000 Spanish dollars in Canton. Seven more British ships worked the coast the next season until there were twenty-two vessels in the otter trade by 1792, half of them British, six of them American (mostly from Boston), and the others flying the Spanish, Portuguese, or French flags, though usually captained by Britons. From that time forward the majority of craft sailed out of the United States, particularly Boston, partially because of disruptions to British shipping extending from the Napoleonic Wars, but also because New England merchants were desperate for new markets after being shut out of the British Caribbean following the American Revolution. By 1801 American ships outnumbered British ones twenty-two to two. With crews of twenty to twenty-five men and ships often larger than 250 tons, the costs of doing business were high, as were the risks of losing everything to storms, accidents, or hostile indigenous communities. Yet with investments commonly bringing a return of 300 to 500 percent, merchants clamored to place their bets.[3]

Guns, powder, and ammunition quickly moved to the head of the Natives' list of most desirable trade goods. The Yakutat Tlingits claim to have first obtained guns from a shipwreck. Not knowing what to do with them, they heated the barrels in a fire and then pounded them into spears, for "at that time an iron spear point was worth a slave." However, eventually foreign demonstrations of these weapons spurred demand. In 1786, for instance, a French exploring mission dazzled the Tlingits of Lituya Bay by firing a musket shot through a set of indigenous leather armor (made from the hide of sea lion, walrus, moose, or elk, placed within wooden slats), which was famous along the coast for its impermeability. That night some daring young Native men snuck past twelve French guards into a tent and made off with one of the weapons. The following year Englishmen trading among the Yakutat Tlingits showed off the utility of their guns for hunting waterfowl, after which the previously unruly Natives became "perfectly quiet and inoffensive." Soon the weapons were in high demand up and down the coast, with the people of Nootka and Clayoquot Sounds first declaring that they would "not sell a single skin but for copper or muskets or powder and shot" and then that they "would trade for nothing but ordnance stores."[4]

For Pacific Coast Natives, as for indigenous people elsewhere on the continent before them, only quality arms would do. In 1792, explorer George Vancouver encountered a Tlingit who "by means of signs and words too expressive to be mistaken, gave us clearly to understand, that they had reason to complain of one or more muskets they had purchased [from another merchant], which burst into pieces on being fired," a problem the captain judged to be all too common. Yet merchants

159

interested in dealing with these customers for more than one season quickly grasped the necessity of offering more durable wares. After working the coast for several years in the early phase of the trade, Sullivan Dorr advised his brother back in Boston that the "cunning savages . . . are great merchant traders" who would only accept "good trade powder muskets," adding for good measure, "the Indians won't have other than good." Indigenous people knew what they meant by this term. Boston merchant William Sturgis wrote of Native men subjecting his trade guns to "a very thorough examination, often even taking the lock to pieces to look at every screw." Thus, he counseled, "muskets need not be sent unless the best kind [of] King's [British] arms can be procured." Eventually most firms stocked better trade guns for the Natives than for the protection of their crews. In 1802 a German naturalist visiting the coast was surprised to find "that one can now buy the best English arms on this part of the Northwest Coast of America more cheaply than in England." Merchants also learned to respond promptly when indigenous people's tastes in guns shifted, as in 1808 when the demand arose for "French arms with Iron bands [and] brass pans." Traders who wanted to corner the otter market raced to get these goods to the coast ahead of the competition and before Native preferences changed again.[5]

Fortunately for the merchants, the relatively low cost of trade goods and high price of furs in China more than offset the inconvenience of pleasing discerning indigenous customers. In 1799 the Boston merchant Thomas Lamb filled the inventory for the ship *Alert* by purchasing muskets in bundles of fifty costing $416.66, or $8.33 per gun. His captain then traded the arms along the Northwest coast for six otter skins apiece at a time when those pelts were selling in Canton for $20 each. The profit margin per musket was thus $111.67, or $5,583.50 for each case, exclusive of overhead. Even selling at a price of just one otter skin per gun, as was the going rate a few years later, produced a healthy return. For one thing, owning a musket required the purchase of a host of other associated items, such as powder, shot, flints, and gun worms. The sale of other high-yield goods, like blankets, clothing, pots, axes, combs, mirrors, and tobacco, also depended on arms, because indigenous people were most willing—and often only willing—to trade for such items with merchants who first met their demand for guns, powder, and shot.

The upfront costs for this traffic were great, with the value of American exports to the Northwest climbing from $10,362 in 1789–1790 to reach a ten-year high of $746,153 in 1799–1800, then settling into an average of $197,359 a year between 1803 and 1811. Yet the earnings were enormous, with two-year voyages to the Northwest and China often reaping $200,000. If one had capital to invest, there were fortunes to be made in the Pacific trade.[6]

———

Sea otter pelts were available for trade practically everywhere along the Pacific Northwest coast, but safe harbors suitable for large, oceangoing sailing vessels were rare because of the area's mix of ship-eating shoals, unpredictable tides, windstorms, thick fogs, and heavy rains. Fewer still were places that combined good anchorage with local leadership capable of bringing some order to a trade full of suspicion and violence. One such setting was the village of Yuquot on Nootka Sound, about two-thirds up the western shore of Vancouver Island. In the late 1780s and the 1790s, this place emerged as the region's most active gun-trading center, with its residents becoming fearsome warriors and influential gunrunners in their own rights. Here as in so many other parts of North America, indigenous people were drawing on colonialism to rise within the ranks of their own social and political networks. They were also becoming threats to the very colonial interests that fueled their ascendency.

The village of Yuquot and its chief, Maquinna, were synonymous with the rise of the sea otter trade. Nootka Sound, on which Yuquot was located, was one of the safest harbors in the region for European craft. Several small forested islands protected its mouth from waves and wind, while its main artery led to three inlets extending deep into the interior of Vancouver Island, thereby providing vessels with easy access to wood and fresh water. The anchorage right off of Yuquot was especially favorable. Tucked within a peninsular hook on the west side of the sound, it possessed placid water, a broad flat beach suitable for landing ships and making repairs, and, not the least of all, people who seemed to welcome foreigners. After Cook dubbed the spot "Friendly Cove," seaboard merchants began arriving in crowds. Roughly 70 of the 107 foreign vessels that worked the Northwest coast between 1785 and 1795 paid a visit to Yuquot, with several voyages making it their primary stop.

The Launch of the North West America at Nootka Sound.
Being the first Vessel that was ever built in that part of the Globe.

Nootka. The harbor of Nootka, or Friendly Cove, on the west side of Vancouver Island, was the busiest site of the Pacific Northwest arms trade during its opening stages, hosting Spanish, British, American, French, and Portuguese ships. This image depicts the launching of a British vessel built in Nootka harbor. Native people appear in boats and on shore throughout the foreground. In the background is the village of Yuquot. From John Meares, *Voyages Made in the Years 1788 and 1789 from China to the North West Coast of America,* 2 vols. (London: J. Walter, 1791). Courtesy The Library Company of Philadelphia.

At one point in September 1792 there were ten ships at anchor in the tiny cove and two more coasters under construction on the beach. The extent of this traffic so alarmed the Spanish, whose imperial claims included the region, that in 1790 they sent seventy-five soldiers to establish a garrison at Yuquot, followed by their seizure of several British craft and arrest of the crews as an additional assertion of sovereignty. With Britain threatening war in retaliation, it took three conventions between 1790 and 1795 before the two sides agreed that Nootka Sound should be a free port, whereupon the Spanish withdrew from the region and the trade revived with a fury. The word "Nootka" comes from a Washakan term meaning "go around," but sea merchants so closely associated it with Friendly Cove that they thought it meant otter pelt.[7]

The Yuquot chief, Maquinna, expanded his influence by carving out a niche as a middleman between Native people and foreign vessels. Maquinna's prestigious family held exclusive hereditary rights to the most valuable resources at Yuquot, including the entrance to Nootka Sound and access to its visitors. Anyone else who wanted to fish, hunt, or trade at this site had to pay Maquinna for the privilege. For Maquinna's core supporters, this obligation took the form of ongoing loyalty, material tribute, and military service. Outsiders who wanted to deal with the merchant ships paid "port dues," as Europeans characterized it. Even then Maquinna's followers always acted as "agents or brokers" in this commerce and, according to Cook, "assumed the prerogative of introducing the new comers to us." Before the onset of the trade, Maquinna's band used the area only as a spring and summer site for the harvesting of outer-coast resources after having spent the winter months hunting game in the hilly, thickly forested interior. During the first twenty-five years of the otter trade, however, the population of Yuquot appears to have grown from 400 to some 1,500 people who stayed year-round to traffic with the ships and prevent rivals from doing the same. They had become, in a sense, full-time port managers.[8]

Maquinna also strengthened his base of friends and allies by distributing munitions and other trade goods through the potlatch ceremony, the famous give-away feast used by Northwest Natives to mark rites of passage, memorialize the dead, and, not incidentally, put attendees in the obligation of the host. There are few written accounts of these events by virtue of their very nature as indigenous ceremonies, closed by invitation. Nevertheless, Maquinna would have followed any successful trading season by redistributing large amounts of what he had collected. No Nuu-chah-nulth leader with a reputation for stinginess could expect to sustain his following, because the people would just leave him for a more generous leader. Rather than hoard wealth, Maquinna circulated it to deepen the people's loyalty to him and therefore strengthen his ability to call on their support when it was time to project his power outward.[9]

Control over the flow of exotic goods, particularly arms, also enabled Maquinna to broker multiple strategic marriages for himself and his kin. Nuu-chah-nulth leaders typically married several high-ranking wives over the course of their political careers as part of the process of building alliances between elite families and communities. At the same time, the custom of paying steep bride prices to the families of such women made these marriages part of the redistribution of wealth within political co-alitions. A male suitor who could outbid his competitors had the best chance of having his proposal accepted, though political considerations also came into play. It is certainly no coincidence that Maquinna in-creased the number of his wives from four in 1792 to nine by 1803. Male followers of Maquinna profited too by drawing on his largesse when it was time for them to compile wealth for the payment of bride price, which might include "a quantity of cloth, a number of muskets, sea-otters, skins, &c." Maquinna's growing profile, as reflected in the number of his wives, also meant that the women of his family fetched higher prices as part of the cost of connection to the great chief. In 1803 a neighboring chief seeking to marry Maquinna's niece paid Maquinna "thirteen fine skins, forty fathoms of cloth, twenty fathoms of ifraw [dentalia shells], twenty muskets, two blankets and two coats." The onset of European trade meant that the circulation of arms and women went hand in hand as part of the processes of forging political and military alliances and building chiefly stature.[10]

Maquinna prevented other, more distant groups from directly con-tacting the foreigners at Yuquot, forcing them instead to acquire mili-tary stores and other trade goods through him as part of the exercise of his hereditary rights and privileges. As best the Spanish could tell, in 1789 Maquinna's network included nine villages to the north of Yuquot and another nine to the south, running practically the entire length of Vancouver Island. The Nimpkish people of Queen Charlotte Strait on the north side of Vancouver Island were said to deliver the chief as many as 6,000 otter pelts a year; it was certainly no coincidence that in July 1792 George Vancouver found them in possession of a hundred Spanish muskets. Maquinna also acquired the pelts of the Kwakiutls from the Strait of Georgia on the east side of Vancouver Island "for a very trifling consideration in comparison to what they are afterwards sold to for-eigners," according to captain John Hoskins. In return Maquinna out-fitted them with munitions too, as a group of Kwakiutls told George Vancouver when he asked them how they had obtained their arms. At some level this exchange was but an extension of a long-standing re-gional trade in which the Yuquots exchanged shark's teeth and dentalia shells to the Kwakiutls for yellow cedar bark robes and wooden utensils. The difference was that Maquinna used the Kwakiutls' otter to purchase arms and ammunition, which he then sold to the Kwakiutls at a markup. The subsequent profits contributed toward Maquinna maintaining a superior arsenal through which he prevented groups like the Kwakiutls from making direct contact with the foreigners at Nootka Sound.[11]

Certainly warfare played a critical role in consolidating and extending Maquinna's network of allies and tributaries. The few times foreign merchants bothered to record the details of indigenous conflicts in the region, they plainly captured the growing importance of firearms. In August 1788, just a few years into the trade, Briton John Meares gave Maquinna and his subchief, Callicum, a present of guns, powder, and shot on the eve of a raid against people on the opposite side of the sound. This weaponry "animated them with a new vigor" and enabled them to raise a company of men from a variety of villages, even though the enemy was "more powerful, numerous, and savage than themselves," as Meares understood it. The expedition's canoes returned days later with the ammunition spent and thirty human heads in baskets. Such victories would have strengthened Maquinna's hand the next time he called on neighboring communities for support. They certainly emboldened him in political confrontations. When the Spanish dared to arrest and interrogate two Yuquot men for the murder of a Native boy, and then call in Maquinna himself for questioning, the chief threatened that he had the power to conjure up an angry storm of Nuu-chah-nulth gunmen from near and far to wipe out the foreigners' camp. "Know well," he warned, "that Wickaninnish has many muskets, has much powder, has many balls; know well that chief Hanna has no small store and that his men, like the Nuchimases are my relations and allies; all of us, joined together, would form a far more numerous army than that of the Spaniards, English, and Americans together." The better course, he added, was to give him a cannon as a sign of friendship.[12]

Maquinna's growing military and economic prowess enabled him to expand his slaveholdings and protect his people against slave raids, though this dynamic also attracted little interest from foreign record keepers. Slavery was fundamental to the social structure of the Nuu-chah-nulths and most Native people along the Pacific Northwest Coast. Slaves made up approximately a quarter of the Northwest indigenous population, with chiefs commonly holding a dozen slaves or more. The slaves' work at fishing, collecting wood and water, cooking, building, and military service was basically the same as the class of commoners, with the critical difference that slaves performed these tasks for someone else's benefit and always under the threat of corporal punishment, even murder. It was not only the Pacific Northwest's bounty but slave labor that freed elites for the specialized, high-prestige activities like politics, artistic endeavors, potlatching, and (in the south) whaling, for which the people of this region became so well known. The challenge in maintaining this system was that, though slavery was heritable, the slave population does not appear to have been self-sustaining because slaves so often lost their lives to military action, ceremonial sacrifice, and random abuse. Keeping up their numbers required raids and trades, both of which came to involve firearms in the late eighteenth century. Maquinna's arsenal and the alliances it facilitated would have at once enhanced his slave raiding, which mostly targeted people on what is now the British Columbian mainland and south as far as modern Oregon and even northern California. Additionally, the arms he distributed would have boosted his allies' ability to fend off raids, which usually came from northern peoples like the Tsimshians and Tlingits.[13]

Another benefit was that munitions and other foreign goods increased the chief's leverage in a regional slave trade that funneled captives from as far south as Puget Sound and sometimes the Columbia River northward to the peoples of Vancouver Island and the Queen Charlotte Islands. Slaves were "the principle article of traffic on the whole of this coast," a number of foreigners commented. Just what slaves cost during the heyday of the otter trade at the turn of the century is unknown, but by the 1830s a highly valued slave among the Bella Coolas north of Vancouver Island was worth "nine blankets, a gun, a quantity of powder and ball, a couple of dressed elk skins, tobacco, vermillion paint, a flat file, and other little articles." This traffic was so lucrative that shipboard merchants got in on the act, buying slaves from sources along what is now the Oregon and Washington coast and then selling them to northern peoples. Maquinna's enormous slave holdings, which in 1803 constituted "nearly fifty, male and female slaves, in his house," suggests that he used his martial stores to raid and trade for slaves, thus reinforcing another pillar of his rank.[14]

Maquinna. This Nuu-chah-nulth chief of Yuquot (also known as Nootka, or Friendly Cove) dominated the firearms for otter trade of the Pacific Northwest coast during the late 1780s and 1790s. His wealth and firepower enabled him to enlarge his political following, tributary network, and slaveholdings. Courtesy the Royal BC Museum and Archives.

Maquinna's military wares became equally critical to his ceremonial displays. By 1788 Maquinna greeted visitors wearing a genteel suit of European clothing and a brace of pistols that had been given to him as a gift by English merchants in exchange for allowing them to set up a temporary trade factory on his land. Four years later, when George Vancouver dined with the chief at his house, the meal ended with a dramatization of the exploits of Yuquot warriors, featuring a dozen men "armed with muskets." Maquinna welcomed Vancouver back to Friendly Cove in 1794 with an elaborate dance of men dressed for war carrying "muskets, others with pistols, swords, daggers, spears, bows, arrows, fishgigs, and hatchets, seemingly with the intent to display their wealth and power." In 1803 an English sailor saw firearms incorporated into a performance of the Shamans' or Wolf Dance initiation ceremony hosted by Maquinna. It began when "Maquinna discharged a pistol close to his son's ear, who immediately fell down as if killed, upon which all the women of the house set up a most lamentable cry, tearing handfuls of hair from their heads, and exclaiming that the prince was dead," only to have him revived days later after a staged captivity among a band of men dressed as wolves. The use of the gun in this ritual made sense at several levels. It represented the increasingly likelihood that Maquinna's son would wield and face guns in his role as a warrior, given that Native people throughout the Pacific Northwest coast were acquiring these weapons. It signaled that, as a man, he would need to know how to fire and maintain this tool to fulfill his duties as warrior and hunter. It reflected the wealth, political power, and military prowess of his father and his community by virtue of their stockpile of arms and control of the flow of munitions in and around Vancouver Island. Nootka ceremonies incorporated firearms because they were becoming an indelible part of the people's war, hunting, politics, gender roles, and material culture.[15]

The arms trade Maquinna used to enhance his authority also threatened to produce rivals on his very doorstep, a danger he managed by turning such figures into allies. His chiefly counterpart, Wickaninnish of Clayoquot Sound, forty miles to the south as the crow flies, was his main concern. Whereas Maquinna's career began with an inheritance of several subject communities on Nootka Sound and control of a primary trade route running across Vancouver Island, Wickaninnish started with a much slimmer political base that he then extended through wars of conquest. The otter trade made Wickaninnish an even greater threat by encouraging him to extort pelts from his tributaries and trading partners to exchange with foreign merchants for arms and ammunition. Indigenous communities along Barkley Sound, just south of Wickaninnish's base at Clayoquot, refused to deal with shipboard traders directly, explaining that they had to send their pelts to Wickaninnish and then wait for him to bestow trade goods on them. By 1792 such tactics had enabled Wickaninnish to build up an arsenal of some 200 guns and plenty of ammunition. He then used these weapons to wage a decade-long campaign to subjugate the Haachahts on the west side of Barkley Sound. Raids against the Haachahts netted Wickaninnish plunder in furs, which he used to purchase still more arms and ammunition. Soon he boasted 400 warriors armed with muskets. Maquinna must have been wary of Wickaninnish's growing strength, just as Wickaninnish would have been of his, but the two men managed to forge an alliance, sealed by Maquinna's marriage to Wickaninnish's daughter, in which they respected and defended each other's sphere of influence. Maquinna also granted Wickaninnish access to the trade at Yuquot. Wickaninnish does not appear to have extended Maquinna reciprocal privileges at Clayoquot, but he did take in the Yuquot chief for a brief period in 1789 when he feared for his life from the Spanish. Such measures appear to have kept the peace between the two men throughout Maquinna's lifetime.[16]

Foreign merchants were another hazard, because dealing with them required suffering their rough, even murderous, tactics. One of the very first contacts between the Nuu-chah-nulths and a trading vessel, the British *Sea Otter* in 1785, produced a "considerable slaughter" when Captain James Hanna fired on one of their canoes to punish them for stealing a chisel. More minor, if sometimes deadly, confrontations were the norm until 1797, when Captain Robert Gray of the ship *Columbia* had his crew torch 200 houses in Wickaninnish's community of Opitsatah, a "fine village, the work of ages," while its inhabitants were away for a potlatch. Gray's explanation was that he suspected "a conspiracy concocted by the Natives to take the ship and murder us all." His judgment was shaped, it would appear, by the people's insistence on receiving arms and ammunition for their otter whereas in previous seasons they had been content to trade for copper. The Nuu-chah-nulths saw things differently, telling some Spanish soldiers that "the natives had not wished to engage in bartering skins with the Europeans, and that they [the Europeans] had used force to make them do so," which included Gray holding up Wickaninnish at gunpoint. The following year there was yet another murderous exchange, when fifty crewmen from the ship *Jefferson* stormed into Wickaninnish's new village of Seshart to recover a stolen canoe and thirty feet of cable. The foreigners fired on the Natives, killing two or three and wounding two, then rampaged through the community, plundering, destroying houses, and staving canoes. The Nuu-chah-nulths, like other indigenous people across the continent, were coming to the realization that the costs of dealing with gunrunners could be very high.[17]

Maquinna himself accumulated a catalog of grievances against shipboard traders. Captain Hanna had humiliated and injured him in 1785 by inviting him onboard the *Sea Otter* and offering him a supposed seat of honor, only to light a charge of gunpowder that had been placed underneath, blowing the chief into the air and leaving him burnt and scarred. Another captain, whose name Maquinna remembered as "Tawnington," had capped off a winter spent at Friendly Cove by ordering his crew to loot forty otter pelts from Maquinna's own house. Maquinna charged that the Spanish Captain Estéban Martinez killed four of his subchiefs around the same time. Doubtless many other incidents went unrecorded. Maquinna had been willing to tolerate a certain amount of abuse as long as he occupied a dominant position in the trade, but by the mid- to late 1790s his control was beginning to ebb as local supplies of otter diminished and merchants gained a better familiarity with the geography and peoples of the region. This combination meant that Maquinna and his people were losing face, power, and lives at the same time. It was too much for them to bear.[18]

The breaking point came on March 22, 1803, after Maquinna suffered another set of injuries, this time at the hands of Captain John Salter of the *Boston,* a Massachusetts ship. The vessel had anchored five miles north of Friendly Cove a few weeks earlier to trade and collect wood and fresh water. At first nothing seemed amiss as the Natives brought in furs and food to exchange for metal tools and socialized with the crew over the ship's fare of rum, biscuit dipped in molasses, and sweetened tea and coffee. Yet the mood began to sour when Maquinna returned a fowling gun Salter had given him as a gift, after it broke while the chief was out hunting with it. Maquinna tried to soften his complaint that the weapon was "*peshank,* that is, bad," by offering the captain his own present of nine pairs of wild ducks, but it was no use. Salter flew into a rage, cursing high and low and throwing the fowler into the gunsmith's cabin and snapping at him to fix it. Maquinna understood enough English to follow Salter's rant, as it had not taken long for coastal people to pick up such English curses as "damned rascal" and "son of a bitch." He signaled the captain to calm down, "repeatedly" putting "his hand to his [own] throat and ru[bing] it upon his bosom," symbolizing the need "to keep down his heart, which was rising into his throat and choking him," but Salter either misunderstood or ignored the gestures. Maquinna, who later said that Salter's behavior rekindled his urge to revenge past insults, then resolved to send the message another way.[19]

Three days later Maquinna led his men on a dramatic raid to seize hold of the *Boston.* Accompanied by "a considerable number of chiefs and other men," he rowed out to the ship wearing a war helmet, described as "a very ugly [war] mask of wood, representing the head of some wild beast." To disperse the strength of Salter's crew, Maquinna offered to have some of his men escort a group of sailors to shore to go fishing for salmon, which the captain accepted without suspicion that it was a trap. Then Maquinna took out a whistle with which to direct his warriors to positions around the deck. Finally, when everything was in place, the men attacked, revealing hidden knives and daggers, breaking open the *Boston*'s arms chest, seizing the guns, and then overpowering and killing the sailors. The fishing party met a similar fate.

The Yuquot people's return on this raid was considerable. First and foremost they captured the ship's gunsmith, John Jewitt, deliberately sparing him among the entire crew. The only other sailor to make it out alive was John Thompson, and then only because Jewitt falsely claimed him as his father. It is possible that taking Jewitt captive had been one of the prime motivations for the Nuu-chah-nulths to sack the *Boston*. "They were always very attentive to me," Jewitt remembered of the days before the attack, "crowding around me at the forge, as if to see in what manner I did my work, and in this manner became quite familiar." Now they had his services on command. For twenty-eight months the Nuu-chah-nulths kept him busy, Jewitt recalled, "making for the king [Maquinna] and his wives, bracelets, and other small ornaments of copper or steel, and in repairing the arms, making use of a large square stone for the anvil, and heating my metal in a common wood fire." A great deal of Jewitt's work involved mending items looted from the *Boston,* for the Nuu-chah-nulths had stripped it of everything of value that was not nailed down, including "a great quantity of ammunition, cutlasses, pistols, and three thousand muskets and fowling pieces." Jewitt's account of what they did with these goods, recorded using a notebook, writing implements, and a desk he had recovered from the ship, are the clearest view into the role firearms had assumed in Northwest indigenous communities enmeshed in the otter trade.[20]

Maquinna's first response to his sack of the *Boston* was to announce a celebratory potlatch featuring his enhanced armament. It took only a few days before canoes began arriving from numerous other communities (twenty, as far as Jewitt could discern), "the most of whom were considered as tributary to Nootka." A spectacle of Maquinna's newfound treasure was waiting to greet them, perhaps as new expression of a long-standing potlatch custom (at least among the Tlingit people to the north) of greeting rivals and potential enemies with displays of weapons and barely veiled threats. The chief had his men assemble on the beach "with loaded muskets and blunderbusses . . . their necks hung round with numbers of power-horns, shot-bags, and cartouche [ammunition] boxes, some of them having no less than ten muskets a piece on their shoulders, and five or six daggers in their girdles." Right up the hill from the beach, directly in front of the village, Maquinna placed a cannon manned by Jewitt's would-be father, Thompson. Perched higher still was Maquinna atop his house, beating violently on a drum with his prize captive, Jewitt, at his side, for everyone to see. Jewitt found the entire affair "ludicrous . . . dressed as they were, with their ill-gotten finery, in the most fantastic manner, some in women's smocks, taken from our cargo, others in *Kotsacks* (or cloaks) of blue, red, or yellow broadcloth, with stockings drawn over their heads." Yet these costumes were not an attempt to mimic European processions, but an indigenous display of power and wealth for an indigenous audience. The participants fully understood the message. As the visitors' canoes drew close, Maquinna ordered his gunmen and Thompson to fire in unison, "immediately on which they threw themselves back, and began to roll and tumble over the sand as if they had been shot, when suddenly springing up, they began a song of triumph, and running backward and forward upon the shore, with the wildest gesticulations, boasted of their exploits, and exhibited as trophies what they had taken from us." It was a way of saying that they had seized the sources of strength from the foreigners who had insulted them one too many times.[21]

Afterward visitors crowded into Maquinna's house, a richly decorated cedar plank structure over a hundred feet long, for a feast and dance, following which "Maquinna began to give presents to the strangers [guests]," including "no less than one hundred muskets . . . and twenty casks of powder." Upon receiving these presents, the recipients would respond with shouts of *"Wocash! Wocash Tyee,"* or "That is good! Very good prince [chief]!" Visitors had their own gifts to offer in turn, including blubber, oil, and fish, which helped to feed Yuquot for months. In other words, the ceremony at once reasserted Maquinna's greatness as a chief capable of marshaling tactical savvy, warrior strength, and spiritual power to bring foreign wealth and glory to his people, even as it memorialized the prosaic exchanges of food that bound people together. It was a microcosm of Nuu-chah-nulth society.[22]

Maquinna's distribution of military wares in and out of the potlatch was part of his maintenance of hierarchical alliances he had spent decades constructing. Jewitt saw him treat subordinate chiefs "according to their respective ranks of degree or favor with him, giving to one[,] three hundred muskets, to another[,] one hundred and fifty." Maquinna soon tested the loyalty he expected these gifts to inculcate, calling out 600 men in forty canoes for a surprise dawn-light raid against the Haachahts of Barkley Sound, Wickaninnish's longtime enemies. The attack was a smashing success for Maquinna, and not only because his party returned having killed or captured nearly everyone in the targeted village. Maquinna also had confirmed the strength of his following and showed his followers the quality of his leadership. Perhaps not the least of all, he had simultaneously demonstrated his friendship for Wickaninnish while upstaging him.[23]

Maquinna's bonanza in trade goods enhanced his stature among people from far away, who for months flocked into Yuquot seeking trade. The Nimpkish of northeast Vancouver Island arrived at Yuquot with "with no furs for sale, excepting a few wolf skins; their merchandise consisting principally of the black shining mineral called pelpelth," which the Nuu-chah-nulths used as face paint on "extraordinary occasions," and a "fine red paint" that was also of ritual importance. Most other visitors brought commonplace merchandise, including "principally train oil, seal or whale's blubber, fish, fresh or dried, herring or salmon spawn, clams, and muscles, and the *yama,* a species of fruit which is pressed and dried, cloth, sea otter skins, and slaves." In return Maquinna provided his visitors with arms, ammunition, and other plunder from the ship, including Jewitt's smithing services, the rarest and most valuable of all these riches. From an outsider's perspective these exchanges might look like simple bartering, but Jewitt was learning to see them as more political in nature, based not simply on calculations of profit but on relationships of power and mutual obligation. Jewitt noticed that "many of the articles thus brought, particularly the provisions, were considered as presents, or tributary offerings" by the Natives involved. Yet the captive missed the point in his judgment that these were "little more than a nominal acknowledgment of superiority" because the givers "rarely failed to get the full amount of the value of their presents [in return]." After all, it was the visitors who came to Maquinna, not vice versa. The goods they delivered enabled him to demonstrate his diplomatic and commercial reach and, in the case of the pigments and other exotic goods, surround himself and his people with objects of spiritual power. There was nothing nominal about this acknowledgment.[24]

Maquinna's troubles with foreign merchants would continue long after the *Boston* affair, but they rarely ended with such favorable results. Jewitt managed to free himself after twenty-eight months through a remarkable series of events that ended in yet another degrading episode for the chief. In July 1805 the brig *Lydia* sailed into Nootka Sound, whereupon Maquinna asked Jewitt to write the captain a letter explaining that he was not responsible for the destruction of the *Boston*. Instead Jewitt's note pleaded for the captain, Samuel Hill, to take Maquinna hostage until the Yuquots set him and Thompson free. Once Maquinna was in custody, Hill raised the stakes to include the restoration of what little remained of the *Boston*'s cargo. Yuquot had little choice but to comply.[25]

Six years later the Nuu-chah-nulths nearly had another revenge as complete as the sacking of the *Boston,* only to be thwarted. The ship *Tonquin* sailed into Clayoquot Sound fresh off a mission to deliver a party of Americans to the mouth of the Columbia River to found the post of Astoria, part of fur trade magnate John Jacob Astor's ill-fated plan to create a cross-continental commercial empire linking New York, St. Louis, and the Pacific. Unfortunately the *Tonquin* had a bad sense of timing, for a year earlier the captain of the ship *Mercury* had hired twelve Nuu-chah-nulths from Clayoquot Sound to join a sea otter hunt along the California coast, only to abandon them there when the mission was complete. Remarkably, they managed to return home on their own. After they had stoked their people's anger with the story of their betrayal, the *Tonquin* was the next ship to sail into Clayoquot. It did not help that its captain, George Ayers, was said to have responded to the Nuu-chah-nulths' sharp dealing with a fit that included rubbing a peltry in the face of a chief and kicking about his people's furs. The next morning, warriors approached the ship under the color of trade and then swarmed its defenses, killing everyone but a man who jumped overboard and lived to tell the tale, and another who hid below deck. Seeing no avenue for escape, but seeking his own revenge, the remaining crewman waited for the raiders to begin pillaging the boat, then set fire to the powder magazine, blowing up the vessel, up to 200 Nuu-chah-nulths, and himself. It was, symbolically and practically, the end of Maquinna's and the Nuu-chah-nulths' remarkable ascension, for with the local otter depleted, few ships were willing to risk the fates of the *Boston* and *Tonquin* in order to tap into this meager trade. The wealth and influence of the chiefs dwindled in turn.[26]

Bloody Harbor

The Sitka Tlingits followed a similar trajectory as the Nuu-chah-nulths in terms of quickly accumulating wealth and power through the exchange of otters for arms, followed by a series of dramatic gun battles with Europeans and then the collapse of the trade. However, the ways in which their stories diverge also shed light on the differences between their social structures and the colonial contexts in which they operated. The Tlingits did not follow leaders akin to the great chiefs and subchiefs who were at the center of Nuu-chah-nulth society. Rather, Tlingit communities, or *kwáans,* were made up of several distinct, self-governing clans in which leadership was also decentralized. Thus, trade and diplomacy focused less on a single elite figure than on group interests and rivalries, which made coordinated action difficult but also enormously forceful once a consensus had been reached. Another critical distinction is that the Tlingits sought arms from British and American traders in order to use them not just against other Native people but against the Russians encroaching on their territory. The result was some of the most stunning examples of indigenous military resistance to European colonialism in the history of North America.

After furtive commercial contacts with Britons, Americans, Spaniards, and the French during the 1780s, the Tlingits of the Alaskan panhandle began to occupy a greater role in the maritime otter trade in the 1790s, just as the Nootkans' position was slipping. This was particularly true for the Tlingits of Sitka, comprised of the Kiks.ádi and L'uknax.ádi clans of the Raven moiety and the Kaagwaantaan and Chookaneidí clans of the Eagle moiety, though in later times (and perhaps earlier as well) the Kiks.ádi predominated. Their territory rested along a deep, sheltered harbor on the west side of Baranof Island, cast against a dramatic backdrop of densely forested mountains. Local waters were some

175

of the richest otter-hunting territory in the region. Sitka's outer-coast location not only made it easily accessible to merchant ships, but positioned its residents to obtain pelts from northern Athabascans, Haidas, Tsimshians, and other groups "farther back in sounds where water at entrance was not deep enough for a vessel," as one captain put it. This system was a new iteration of an old indigenous trade network that funneled shells, blankets, pigments, skins, leather armor, canoes, slaves, and high-value, specialized foods like herring oil and eulachon oil along the panhandle and between the coast and inland areas. In this version, however, the Sitka Tlingits' offerings included foreign manufactures, particularly military stores. The Tlingits sent an unequivocal message to shipboard merchants that "muskets, powder, etc. was their first demand." With the right cargo, a boat anchored at Sitka could net as many as 800 pelts in four days. The fur traders responded enthusiastically, outfitting the Sitka Tlingits with "plenty" of arms and ammunition by as early as 1792. A decade later some observers judged that the Tlingits' "former instruments of war, such as spears and arrows, are almost wholly out of use." By then Sitka Tlingit men even hunted otter with guns.[27]

Accounts of the Sitka Tlingits and the culturally and socially similar Haidas to the south indicate that women played a greater public role in this trade than in most other parts of North America. During his visit to Sitka, Samuel Curson was struck that "the wife has here great voice in all bargains made. She must know and approve of the husband's sale; and if not, she sometimes cancels the agreement." Likewise, merchant William Sturgis found it surprising that "among the tribes upon the Queen Charlotte Islands and the adjacent coast the management of trade was in a great measure entrusted to the women, and they proved themselves worthy of the trust, for keener traders I have never met with." Men would select the weapons they wanted, but leave it to the women to strike a price. "The reason given by the men for this practice was," Sturgis claimed, "'that the women could talk with the white men *better* than they could and were willing to talk *more*.'" Sturgis's attempt as misogynistic humor aside, he might have been witnessing a manifestation of the high public profile enjoyed by women belonging to the matrilineal, matrilocal clans of the outer coast. It is also likely that women took a special interest in trade goods destined as potlatch gifts because their clans had honor at stake in the quality of their presents.[28]

Potlatch. This photo from a Tlingit potlatch in the early twentieth century suggests the prominent role of women in this ceremony. Note the two women in front holding guns distributed as gifts at this event. Indigenous women along the Pacific Northwest coast also played a public role in the trade of otter for guns in the late eighteenth and early nineteenth centuries. One likely reason is that, in this matrilineal society, women knew that the honor of their family was at stake in the quality of goods, like guns, to be given away at potlatch. Courtesy Sitka National Historical Park.

Given the vibrancy of this arms trade, it was an inopportune time for the Russians to expand their fur enterprise south into Tlingit territory. The Russians turned toward the panhandle following the decimation of the otter population farther north and the tsarist government's 1799 charter of the joint-stock Russian American Company (RAC), which gave it a monopoly of the Alaskan fur trade after years of chaotic, sometimes violent competition among the *promyshlenniki*. Yet the Tlingits were not as easily dominated as the Aleuts and Alutiit (of Kodiak) had been. For one thing, they were much more numerous and more densely settled, with access to the resources of a vast continental interior. Equally important, their warriors were highly trained and well equipped with indigenous bows and arrows, knives, spears, clubs, armor, and firearms. Indeed, they were at least as well armed as the Russians. In 1799 the RAC witnessed five foreign ships trading in the vicinity of Sitka (the *Hancock, Dispatch, Ulysses,* and *Eliza* out of Boston and the *Caroline* from Britain), much to the outrage of Governor Alexander Baranov, whose job it was to assert the company's claims to the area. On February 15, 1799, he remonstrated that a Boston ship had bartered for some 2,000 sea otters right before Russian eyes, with no apparent concern for their breach of jurisdiction. Their going rate for a single pelt was a gun along with three or four pounds of powder and six to eight pounds of lead. The shipboard merchants even traded artillery to the Tlingits. A stunned Baranov recounted, "I myself saw in neighboring villages four cannons of one pound caliber and have heard that in other villages they have more of them of heavier caliber." The Bostonians were the most "shameless" of these arms dealers, utterly indifferent to how they were putting everyone in danger, namely the Russians.[29]

On its very face the RAC plan to build at Sitka was an affront to the Tlingits. Its purpose was not to trade with them for furs, but instead to employ the Aleuts and Alutiit to hunt otter in Sitka Tlingit territory that the Sitka Tlingits needed for their own trade with the Americans and British. The Teikweidí Tlingits of Yakutat, 235 miles north of Sitka, had already declared their opposition to Russian expansion with a 1792 raid that claimed eleven members of a Russian/Alutiiq/Chugach hunting party. The Russians merely absorbed the loss and pressed on, establishing a transshipment base at Yakutat in 1796 and continuing to extend their hunts even farther south. Three years later the RAC began constructing a palisaded fort, St. Michael's redoubt, at Starrigavan Bay in Sitka Harbor, seven miles north of the modern town of Sitka. Tensions mounted immediately. Within a year the RAC was receiving three-quarters of its otter from Sitka Sound, with overall yields of 2,000 pelts in the summer of 1800 and as many as 4,000 in the summer of 1801. All the while, the Russians refused to trade the Sitka Tlingits liquor or armaments. Worse yet, Kiks.ádi Tlingit traditions tell of the Russians, Aleuts, and Alutiit committing murders, rapes, kidnappings, imprisonments, grave desecrations, and an abominable joke in which they fed a Tlingit visitor human flesh. There was no mistaking Tlingit resentment. In the spring of 1800 a band of Tlingits beat and robbed the Russians' female interpreter, and when the Russians sent out twenty-two armed men to return the insult, they found themselves surrounded by 300 or more Tlingit warriors armed with guns. The Tlingit party scattered when one clear-headed Russian fired a cannon, but the warning had been sent, if not necessarily received.[30]

Subsequent efforts to unite a cross-section of Tlingits and Haidas in resistance involved sending arms to the most tactically important communities as a matter both of military strategy and political solidarity. Native informants would later tell the Russians that the plot had been months in the making, drawing together peoples located across some 46,000 square miles of the Alexander Archipelago and beyond. For instance, the Stikine Tlingits of Wrangell Island and the mouth of the Stikine River, as well as an unnamed leader from Prince of Wales Island, "provided much powder, lead, and other weapons, and delivered several large cannons, distributing munitions to each of the toions [community leaders]." The Tlingits of Xutsnoowú, located a short distance northeast of Sitka, received military stores from the Haida village of Deikeenaa, 170 miles away at the southern tip of Dall Island, which had recently become one of the most trafficked sites of the otter trade. A bird's-eye view of the Alaska panhandle during these months of preparation would have witnessed lines of canoes with shipments of arms busily crossing this way and that, like the pods of whales that descended on the Sitka coast each spring. Clan leaders waited until the very last minute to tell the young people just what these measures were for, lest they reveal the plot. By the time they were done, they had built a solid front among otherwise independent communities and ensured that the Russians would never be able to disarm the resistance.[31]

The militants' coordination was as effective in execution as it was impressive in scope. The first strike, on May 22, 1802, targeted a hunting party of 450 kayaks under the leadership of Ivan Aleksandrovich Kuskov at a place called Akoi (or Akwe) just south of Yakutat. Buoyed by the knowledge that other Native communities were ready to stand up to the Russians, the Akoi Tlingits used a small raid to draw Kuskov's party into an ambush, then opened a "heavy fire from a great number of guns and musketoons [blunderbusses]," which killed one and wounded four and ultimately drove the survivors back to Yakutat. Kuskov was surprised to find that the Tlingits "had plenty of firearms and ammunition. Though we saw that among them last summer [there were] no more than one-third of what they had now or at best half." This community's improved arsenal doubtlessly reflected the work of the anti-Russian alliance to supply key communities with weaponry.[32]

The largest and most tactically important Tlingit attacks took place in and around Sitka. By the spring of 1802 St. Michael's redoubt was still unfinished, but it already boasted a two-story barracks, two blockhouses, and a surrounding palisade. For most of the early spring its population stood at twenty-nine Russian men, 200 Aleut men, and a number of Alutiiq wives, but then in May its manpower fell sharply as ninety kayaks (some of them carrying two paddlers at a time) left for a hunt in Frederick Sound. Tlingits had been waiting for just this opportunity. At the site of Kake on Kupreanof Island, Tlingit gunmen sprung an ambush on the hunting party in which they killed all but twenty-four of the men and seized some 1,300 otter pelts for the purchase of more munitions. Meanwhile, on June 15, as many as a thousand Tlingit warriors armed "with guns, spears, and daggers," used a pincer movement to strike the Russians at Sitka, with one side rushing the fort from the wood's edge while another made an amphibious landing by war canoe. After silently taking up positions around the palisade, the warriors "opened strong gunfire through the windows [gun ports], all the while keeping up that horrible roar and noise, imitating the [clan] animals whose masks [helmets] they were wearing." The attackers utterly overwhelmed the sixteen armed defenders, killing most of them in short order and taking the rest into captivity along with several Aleut and Alu-tiiq women and their Russo-indigenous children. The victors then completed the assault by looting an estimated 3,700 otter pelts and torching the structure. Between the attacks at Kake and Sitka, the Tlingits had killed nearly 200 of the enemy, the vast majority of them Aleut hunters.[33]

The Russians, like many colonial powers in the face of indigenous or slave uprisings, refused to consider how their own aggression had created a backlash and instead pointed the finger at foreign gunrunners, especially the Americans. RAC officers fulminated that ten to fifteen American and British ships a year had supplied the Tlingits and their neighbors with "firearms such as cannon, falconets, guns, pistols, sabers, and other instruments of destruction; they also bring gunpowder; and they even teach the savages how to use these weapons." The Russian consul in Philadelphia had pleaded with the United States government to put a stop to this nefarious commerce, only to discover that the federal Constitution gave it no power to do so. The result, as far as the RAC was concerned, was the disaster at Sitka. Governor Baranov was convinced that shipboard merchants had incited the Tlingit with an eye toward selling them munitions for the campaign and then doubly profited by acquiring their plundered furs. The truth of the matter, however, was that the Tlingits hardly needed such encouragement, given the depth of their grievances against the Russians.[34]

It took almost two years for Baranov to organize a counterstrike, during which the Sitka Tlingits also had been preparing by stockpiling munitions and strengthening their defenses. Seeing the vulnerability of their hillside village at the site of modern Sitka town, they had abandoned the site and constructed a stout fort two miles away on a peninsula at the mouth of the Indian River. This location gave them easy access to fresh water and fish and offered a series of natural defenses. With the river running along one side of the fort, and dense tree cover blocking the approach from land, any attack would have to come from the harbor side, which was a daunting prospect. The ocean waters right off the peninsula were so shallow that Russian gunboats would have to anchor at a far distance, thereby reducing the danger their cannons posed to the fort. An amphibious landing would require soldiers to slog across lengthy, exposed mud flats strewn with gravel and broken shells, while under heavy Tlingit fire. Those who managed to fight their way to the fort would confront a palisade (constructed of spruce logs "about two arms' length around") 10 feet high and 245 feet long on the side facing the water. Stacked mast timbers reinforced the base of this wall inside and out and enabled the vertical posts to be positioned at a seventy-degree slant sloping inward so cannon balls would roll off toward the outside of the fort. Mounted atop the walls were at least two and perhaps three small artillery guns capable of firing one-pound balls, of which the defenders had more than a hundred at the ready. Inside were at least fourteen houses built within excavated pits to provide them with earthen insulation from Russian fire. By all accounts, it was an impressive structure.[35]

The Tlingits would need it against an invading force of six ships with cannon, 400 kayaks, and as many as a thousand Russian and Aleut men. The fleet included the forbidding naval ship the *Neva,* carrying fourteen guns capable of firing balls weighing as much as twelve pounds. Russian conditions were for the Tlingits to surrender their fort, release any remaining prisoners, and concede to the RAC rebuilding a post at the site. The Tlingits refused to budge unless the Russians provided hostages, and negotiations quickly gave way to battle. Yet the defenders suffered a serious blow before the fighting even began in earnest. They had stored a large quantity of ammunition on one of the harbor islands, and on September 29, as a canoe of young men returned from a mission to fetch it, a Russian longboat opened fire, igniting the store, blowing the canoe and most of its paddlers sky high, and leaving the people in the fort with a serious shortage of supplies. It was a critical loss.[36]

Nevertheless, the power of Tlingit guns almost drove the Russians to abandon the campaign. On October 1, a Russian/Aleut force tried to storm the fort with 150 men and four small cannons positioned on the flats, only to be met with an "awesome fire" directed "with an order and execution that surprised us." "In a very short while," Captain Iurii F. Lisianskii remembered, "every one of them [the attackers] was wounded" and ten lay dead. Tlingit warriors then poured out of the fort and toward the Russian flank for hand-to-hand combat, with their war captain, K̲'alyáan, leading the charge, formidably dressed in a fearsome helmet bearing his clan's raven crest and wielding a heavy blacksmith hammer captured from the Russians in the battle of 1802. Only protective fire

Battle of Sitka, 1804. The second Battle of Sitka featured an attempt by the Russians and their Native allies to storm the Tlingit fort, which was repulsed by Tlingit gunmen, followed by Tlingit warriors rushing out from behind the walls for hand-to-hand combat. That scene, featuring the war leader K̲'alyáan, is captured dramatically in this modern painting. Courtesy National Park Service, Sitka National Historical Park; SITK 9664.

from ships anchored out in the harbor prevented a complete rout and the loss of Russians' siege guns, which would have enabled the Tlingits to devastate the fleet. The next day the Tlingits shelled the Russian vessels from their small cannons but inflicted only minor damage to some rigging. Under heavy Russian bombardment, and facing the prospect of a long siege, the Sitka Tlingits sent to the community Xutnoowú (or Angoon) on Admiralty Island for reinforcements and supplies and tried to buy time, raising a white flag and handing over nine people as hostages. Yet even then the Russians "were compelled repeatedly to fire at the fortress, because many people were emerging toward the shore to collect our cannon balls," probably the ones left on the flats but perhaps including some of those that had bounced off the palisade, which the Tlingits now intended to fire back at the Russians. It appears that, under the dire circumstances, none of the participants saw the humor in it.[37]

Russian ultimatums and Tlingit promises to surrender passed back and forth for several days until the morning light of October 7, when the Russians awoke to find the fort completely abandoned, the inhabitants having decamped in the dead of night for Point Craven on the opposite side of the island. If they had possessed enough ammunition, the Tlingits could have held out far longer. The Russians found the fort so undamaged and well stocked with artillery guns and cannon shot that they judged "the chief cause of their flight was the want of powder and ball, and that, if these had not failed them, they would have defended themselves to the last extremity." Intelligence from Tlingit hostages of the Russians and later Tlingit oral histories reached the same conclusion.[38]

The Tlingit leader, K'alyáan, visited the new Russian fort at Sitka, New Archangel, to perform ceremonies of peace on July 25, 1805, but the level of consensus behind him appears to have been shallow. Everywhere the Tlingits seemed to be bracing for the war to continue. At Point Craven the Sitka Tlingits had constructed a double-palisaded stronghold atop a steep rock outcropping several hundred feet above the water, and visitors to the site reported the people to be well-armed, edgy, and ready for another battle. Intelligence from other parts of Tlingit territory also carried news of the people stockpiling arms and readying their forts, and not just for defensive purposes. Less than a month after Baranov thought a peace had been reached, a party of Tlingit warriors sacked the Russian fort at Yakutat, killing somewhere between twelve and twenty Russians and Aleuts, capturing several others, and permanently wiping out the post.[39]

Ongoing Tlingit hostility made Russian activity perilous almost anywhere beyond the range of New Archangel, and sometimes right alongside it. In 1806, barely a year after peace negotiations, RAC shareholder Nikokai Resanov admitted, "In truth, our fort is more like an island," because any activity beyond the walls required an armed guard. Small groups of Tlingits occasionally visited the fort, but largely, it seemed, to scout its defenses. In the winter of 1806–1807 a Tlingit attack on New Archangel seemed imminent, as hundreds of war canoes carrying thousands of warriors from at least five communities suddenly appeared in Sitka Harbor, with the men taking positions on islands all around the fort. It took desperate Russian diplomacy, marked by uncommonly generous gift giving, to break the coalition and avert disaster. Nevertheless, Tlingit ambushes of Russian-Aleut hunting parties remained a constant danger, punctuated by large strikes, as in 1818, when Tlingit gunmen killed twenty-three and wounded eighteen hunters off Prince of Wales Island. There was little the Russians could do. "The local peoples

Totem Pole, Sitka National Historical Park. The site of the Second Battle of Sitka is today a National Historical Park featuring a path lined with totem poles by Pacific Northwest Natives. One of them features this image of a European bearing a firearm, a written document, and a cross, symbolizing the forces of colonialism. Courtesy National Park Service, Sitka National Historical Park; SITK 5231.

have more firearms than we," the Russians were still grumbling as late as 1818. A Tlingit fort near Sitka was so bold as to present more than ten mounted cannon. And all of this, charged Captain N. M. Golovin, "I can state without hesitation" was "by means of the gunpowder and bullets supplied by the enlightened Americans."[40]

Blowback

Overhunting and the devastation of epidemic disease meant that the Nuu-chah-nulths and Sitka Tlingits could not sustain their ascendency built on the back of the otter-for-guns trade. The coastal otter population was already buckling in the early 1800s. By the 1830s it had nearly collapsed. In turn the volume of otter pelts shipped by Americans to Canton dropped precipitously from 18,000 in 1800, to 4,300 in 1815, to just 500 in 1828. To make up the difference, shipboard merchants extended their missions along the Northwest coast to as many as three years and diversified their trade to include ferrying indigenous goods, including slaves, between distant indigenous communities. Some vessels contracted with the Russians to provide New Archangel with food and supplies, and carried hunters and their kayaks south to hunt off the coast of California, with the Russians and merchant captains splitting the catch. The Russians even built a base in northern California, Fort Ross, to exploit these hunting grounds. Yet the otter trade was dying, and everyone knew it.[41]

By the 1830s foreign merchants had shifted their focus from sea otter to beaver, land otter, and other terrestrial furbearing animals, and the geography of their commerce had moved from the coastal islands to mainland river mouths and even inland to riverine trade posts. This was the wedge for America's preeminent beaver trading firm, the Hudson's Bay Company (HBC), to inaugurate its expansion along the coast. Anchored by the transshipment-trading center of Fort Vancouver, founded in 1824 on the Columbia River, and by more than a century of experience trading along the most remote Canadian waterways, it soon had a network of stations throughout the region and a fleet of coastal trading vessels. In the long term, this development was the first step toward integrating much of this region into Canada as the province of British Columbia. In the short term Native people in control of the mainland coast and river mouths, such as the Stikine and Chilkat Tlingits and Tsim-shians, experienced HBC expansion and the company's subsequent competition with the Russians as a boon. For the island otter hunters, however, this development was just another sign of their diminishing economic and military prominence. As one HBC employee explained of Nootka Sound in the 1840s, "the company's vessels seldom visit this place for traffic, as there is now scarcely any fur to be found there."[42]

Though accounts of the coastal Natives became as rare as their ship traffic, it is apparent that the decline of the trade was a severe blow to the regional authority and military fortunes of the Yuquot and Clay-oquot chiefs, tightly linked as they were. In 1818, fifteen years after the sacking of the *Boston*, Maquinna was said to be sending his pelts north to the Chicklisahts of Nasparti Bay (Cape Cook) for trade to the foreigners, whereas communities from that region used to send their furs to him. By the 1840s and 1850s the people of Barkley Sound, who had once been the scourge of the area by virtue of Wickaninnish's armament, had become the targets of slave raids by the neighboring Pach-keenahts and Ditidahts, the Challams to the north, and the Makahs to the south. Outer-coast Tlingits felt the decline of the otter trade less severely, though they also absorbed some harsh blows. The Tlingits, led by the Kiks.ádi clan, eventually returned to Sitka, with many of them settling right outside the walls of New Archangel. Their commodities for trade with the Russians and occasional ships from Britain and the United States now consisted of provisions (including a new crop, potatoes), what little otter they could find, and the sexual favors of their female slaves. They received arms in return, including, after 1847, a limited amount from the Russians, but the flow was a mere trickle compared to the early nineteenth century. The Sitka Tlingits began to suffer the consequences in the form of attacks from mainland communities armed through the profits of the beaver trade. In 1830 gunmen from the Stikine and Chilkat Tlingits, whose people occupied a lucrative middleman role between inland fur hunters and foreign traders, ambushed a flotilla of Sitka canoes, killing 110 of the 150 boatmen. Afterward the Sitka Tlingits fled to the protection of New Archangel and pleaded with the Russians to lift their long-standing ban on the sale of munitions, but to no avail, at least for the meantime.[43]

Gunrunning, the Russians concluded, was the very problem. The RAC governor, Ferdinand Petrovich von Wrangel complained that the British and American militarization of communities like the Stikines and Chilkats and even of the "northern tribes" up the river valleys had produced an endless series of wars in which "thousands" of indigenous people died, including a disproportionate number of outer-coast Natives. He was not going to add fuel to the fire. The Stikine Tlingits understood the dynamic too and the possibility that they could be next. In 1834, when the HBC attempted to build a trade post up the Stikine River, which would have eliminated the Stikine Tlingits' middleman role between the coast and the interior tribes, the Natives blocked them, complaining that "depriving us of our trade, you want to bring us into the position of slaves," which they appear to have meant literally as well as figuratively. The Chilkat Tlingits were equally unwilling to experience this fate. In 1852 they sent a party of warriors 300 miles inland to destroy the HBC's Fort Selkirk on the Yukon River, which was circumventing their long-standing trade with the Athapascans. One imagines that they saw the costs of losing this advantage in the recent declines of Nootka and Sitka.[44]

Outer-coast populations also absorbed staggering population losses from diseases like smallpox, tuberculosis, and malaria, introduced by foreign ships that increasingly visited their shores only to trade for provisions and sex and then sail off to arm their rivals. Already by 1803 the Yuquot population had dropped from an estimated 3,000 to 4,000 people in 1788 to as few as 1,500 in 1803. Overall numbers for the Nuu-chah-nulths plummeted from as high as 25,000 in the 1780s to one-fifth that number by the mid-nineteenth century. The Tlingits were hit hard too, suffering the deaths of some 6,000 people out of an overall population of 10,000 during a smallpox outbreak of 1835–1837; the Kiks.ádi alone lost between 300 and 400 people in that scourge.[45]

Like the tides and winds that lashed the Pacific Northwest coast, building up and eroding the land in cycles, the gun frontier had a way of elevating a people only to pummel them in the end. Certainly one reason was that some groups with an advantage in arms, such as the Nuu-chah-nulths, undertook predatory raiding to subject others to tributary or slave status and claim valor for their warriors, then received the same treatment in return once the locus of the gun trade shifted to new areas. Yet the main factor was the international capitalist market, which linked Pacific Northwest Natives to arms and ammunition manufacturers in Europe, oceanic and financial middlemen from Boston and Britain, fur customers in China, and consumers of Chinese wares in the American Northeast. These markets, which would absorb as many furs as indigenous people produced, and produce as many arms and as much ammunitions as they would buy, enticed Northwest Natives to kill off the otter just as eastern Indians had nearly put themselves out of business more than a century earlier by overexploiting the beaver and wiping out the groups from which they captured slaves. The unwillingness of indigenous communities to see political rivals claim the lion's share of this trade and gain the political and military rewards, created an arms race that ultimately became a race to the bottom as the people exhausted their natural resources and turned their weapons against each other. Foreign epidemic diseases, the fellow travelers of munitions on the ships of the gunrunners, were more than just insult to this injury, though they were insulting just the same. In an eerie parallel to coastal people overhunting the otter to the brink of extinction, these contagions reduced the human population of this region to its lowest ebb since ancient times, forcing the disbanding of several communities and the near breakup of several others. When such losses would stop, nobody knew. Predatory warfare, environmental degradation, and catastrophic population loss—all linked to guns—were of a piece in the cycles of colonialism in Native America.

6. THE SEMINOLES RESIST REMOVAL

On the surface there was no possibility of the Seminoles successfully resisting the United States policy to deport them from Florida to federal Indian Territory. By the time the Indian Removal Act went into effect in 1830, Florida, like eastern North America as a whole, was no longer the international battleground it had been for a 150 years. Though Spain had managed to recover Florida from Britain in 1783's Treaty of Paris, its inability to defend the colony against American incursions convinced Madrid to cede the territory to Washington in 1819. With France having sold Louisiana to the United States in 1803, and Britain having withdrawn its support to the Great Lakes Indians after the War of 1812, Indians living east of the Mississippi River seemed to have no European powers left to support them against white American hegemony.

The Seminoles faced particularly stark disadvantages in terms of population and resources. The Seminoles numbered only about 6,000 people, including at most 1,500 warriors, living in twenty-one towns throughout the Florida peninsula and panhandle. They also drew strength from several hundred semiautonomous Black Seminoles (or maroons), many of them fugitive slaves from the United States or the Creeks. By contrast the United States had a population of some thirteen million people in 1830, with almost 35,000 living within Florida Territory and another 826,355 residing in the adjacent states of Georgia and Alabama. The size of the U.S. Army alone, standing at 7,000 men, was greater than the entire Seminole population. Furthermore, the military had a commander in chief, President Andrew Jackson, who had banked his presidential legacy on clearing the eastern United States of indigenous people. Though this policy applied to the Northeast and

Midwest, it took on particular urgency in the South because states like Georgia and Alabama threatened to subjugate the Cherokees and Creeks and take their land forcibly if the federal government did not act quickly. Southern whites were especially insistent on the speedy removal of the Seminoles, not only because the northern part of their territory was suitable for cotton, which had emerged as America's most valuable cash crop, but because they provided freedom and arms to runaway slaves. For that reason, more than any other, Jackson was determined to expel the Seminoles from Florida.[1]

The result was the Second Seminole War, the nation's costliest Indian war in terms of lives, treasure, and time. Over 1,500 American troops died in fighting that stretched from 1835 to 1842. More of them took the field against the Seminoles than were involved in the conquest of Mexico City in 1847. And these soldiers did not come cheap. The United States spent $30 to $40 million battling the Seminoles, about twice the average annual federal budget during the first seven years of the Jackson administration. The financial and political strain of this war was so great that Washington eventually dropped its insistence on the return of fugitive Black Seminoles to slavery and permitted them to join their Indian compatriots in the west in the hope that this concession would weaken Seminole resistance. Later it even recognized the right of a few holdout Seminole bands to remain in Florida, unconquered and independent. The country was just too exhausted to pursue them any longer.[2]

How did the Seminoles manage to put up such a stiff fight and extract major concessions against an opponent with vastly superior resources? Certainly part of the answer lies in familiar explanations that the Seminoles were battling for their very homes using guerilla tactics conditioned to Florida's dense foliage and swamps. Yet without stockpiles of guns, powder, and shot, these factors would not have taken them very far. Sustaining the fight challenged the Seminoles to replenish their armament while surrounded on three sides by water and on another by land controlled by the enemy.

From the perspective of white Americans, the Seminoles were hemmed in by the U.S. national boundary. The Seminoles, however, did not see it this way. The water was not an obstacle, but a gateway to the overseas arms markets of Spanish Cuba and the British Bahamas. The U.S. Army generally cut off direct Seminole access to northern gun dealers, so instead the Seminoles waited for American troops to bring munitions south to them, which they plundered at every opportunity. Furthermore, they repeatedly pillaged Anglo-American plantations of war materials. The Seminoles' participation in international trade while they supposedly were enveloped by the United States, and their extraction of guns and ammunition from the very forces battling to subjugate them, offers poignant testimony that Indians' dependence on firearms did not render them impotent in the face of empire. Rather, the Seminoles met their need for arms with a level of resourcefulness that should count among their most significant transformations during the gun age. Their ingenuity, combined with the struggle of the United States (like previous American empires) to exercise coercive power on its periphery, made guns less a Trojan horse for colonialism than a means for Indians like the Seminoles to defend their independence.

Renegades, Arms, and Resistance

The Seminoles had a defiant streak from their very origins in the early to mid-eighteenth century. Their progenitors were Creeks who left their people's territory in what is now Georgia and Alabama and moved south into Florida to take advantage of the thronging deer populations, vacant agricultural fields, and unclaimed cattle herds remaining from the slavers' destruction of the missions decades earlier. Followers of the mico (or chief) Cowkeeper settled the Alachua Savannah (now Payne's Prairie) seventy miles west of St. Augustine and eventually created satellite communities in the St. John's River Valley. Another cluster of towns formed on the Apalachicola River fifty miles west of modern Tallahassee. Over the years additional settlements arose to the west in the panhandle, in northern Florida along the banks of Lake Miccosukee and the Suwannee River, in west-central Florida on the Withlacoochee River, and as far south as the Caloosahatchee River. By the late eighteenth century, outsiders called these Florida Indians "Seminoles" in acknowledgment of their independence from Creek politics even as they were related to the Creeks by culture, kinship, and history. This is not to say that the Seminoles had their own tribal council. Though their communities sometimes consulted with one another informally, each town and its dependencies had the freedom to go their own way under the leadership of its mico and his advisors. It is probably not a coincidence that the name "Seminole" bears close resemblance to the Muskogean (or Creek) word *simaló ni,* meaning "wild" or "nondomesticated."[3]

This association took on greater meaning after the American Revolution as the Seminoles became protectors of a growing number of semiautonomous "Black Seminole" towns made up of free African-Americans. Some of the Black Seminoles had formerly toiled for Seminole Indian masters who had either purchased them from white slave dealers or seized them on raids against Anglo-American plantations. These slaves eventually received their liberty after serving for greater or lesser periods of time, for most Seminoles do not appear to have expected bondage to last a person's entire life. Nor did they consider slavery to be hereditary. Among the Seminoles, the children of slaves were born free and, if belonging to a Seminole woman, were considered full members of the community. Other Black Seminoles had origins as runaways from white plantations, with a number of them having originally escaped to Florida to take advantage of British or Spanish offers of freedom for military service, after which they sought refuge among the Indians. Eventually these people gathered into separate Black Seminole or maroon communities that paid the mico of a nearby Seminole town tribute in agricultural produce and occasional military duty. Otherwise the Indians left the Black Seminoles alone to run their daily affairs. This population contributed mightily to troubled relations between the Seminoles and southern whites. A spike in slave rebelliousness following the American Revolution, including the Haitian Revolution of 1791–1804 and Gabriel Prosser's supposed plot to sack Richmond in 1800, already had southern whites on high alert. They viewed the Seminoles' practice of harboring fugitive and plundered slaves, arming them, and permitting them to live in semiautonomous towns as a recipe to turn Florida into a contagion for more unrest. Hardly anything the Seminoles did could have been more provocative to them.[4]

Except, that is, for taking in Native militants who saw it as a religious duty to fight white expansion and Indian accommodation to the end. In 1812 the Creeks descended into civil war as an anticolonial faction known as the Red Sticks rose up against fellow tribesmen, particularly those of Anglo-Creek descent, who had sold land to whites and adopted many of their behaviors—too many, the Red Sticks argued. The

Red Stick movement drew inspiration from several Creek prophets, most prominently Hillis Hadjo (or Josiah Francis), who preached cultural purity, religious revitalization, and defense of the Creek homeland. It was also a southern iteration of a broader anticolonial revolt including portions of several Great Lakes and Illinois country tribes under the leadership of the Shawnee, Tecumseh. To white Americans, the scale and tone of this Indian unrest was disturbing enough. The fact that it became part of the War of 1812 and drew British and Spanish support meant that it posed a significant threat to the nation's western expansion. It took barely a year before the United States intervened in the Creek civil war, culminating in March 1814's Battle of Horseshoe Bend, in which General Andrew Jackson at the head of 3,000 U.S. volunteers and allied warriors from the Cherokees, Choctaws, and Creeks, sent 800 Red Sticks to their deaths. Yet even after this staggering loss, the Red Sticks refused to abandon their resistance. As many as 2,000 of them retreated down the Apalachicola River to the Gulf, where they joined forces with the Seminoles and hundreds of fugitive slaves who had taken up arms in the British service. Together they resolved to keep white Americans and their slave catchers out of Seminole territory. An alliance of militant Indians and black maroons supported by European resources was the materialization of a nightmare that had haunted white southerners ever since the seventeenth century.

If the subversive makeup of the Seminoles and their location at the frontier of the expansionist plantation South all but guaranteed hostilities with the United States, then their access to foreign rivals of the Americans also gave them the means to fight. Indeed, securing arms from imperial powers had always been a source of Seminole strength. The Alachua Seminoles had received plentiful amounts of British arms and ammunition during the American Revolution, which contributed to their initial hostility to Spain's recovery of Florida. After a visit to Florida in the mid-1770s, Philadelphia naturalist William Bartram judged them to be "the most bitter and formidable enemies the Spaniards ever had." The Seminoles' mood lightened, however, as the new Spanish regime implemented the French model of trade and gift diplomacy in hopes of winning Indian allies and keeping them out of the U.S. orbit. Spain's recognition of the Indians' preference for British goods and lack of enthusiasm for Spanish ones led it to contract with a merchant firm of Scottish-American Loyalists known as Panton, Leslie, and Company (and later as John Forbes and Company) to handle the colony's Indian trade and to grant it the right to import goods from London. The company did a brisk business, exporting at least 124,000 deerskins a year out of Florida during the 1790s, with gunpowder as its best-selling item. The following decade the company expected annual sales to the Indians of three tons of gunpowder and six tons of lead shot. Indians received most of this ammunition on credit at the beginning of the fall hunting season, a practice that gave the company a widely recognized advantage over U.S. government trade factories, which offered subsidized prices but no advances on goods. In turn Spanish Florida enjoyed peace and alliance with Indians throughout the Gulf Coast region, including the Seminoles. This mutually profitable arrangement was a result not just of Panton and Leslie's entrepreneurialism or of Spain's newfound pragmatism in Indian relations. It was also an outgrowth of the Seminoles having convinced the Spanish regime that it had to cultivate their favor if Florida was going to survive.[5]

Spanish Florida's diplomatic gifts of arms to the Seminoles were another foundation of the relationship. Between 1784 and 1795, Florida's annual expenditures on Indian presents ranged between 9,000 and 14,000 pesos a year (with about 6,000 a year earmarked for the Seminoles), enough to leave the colony with a deficit. The typical list of presents for each chief included six pounds of gunpowder, eight pounds of shot, and eighteen flints, while a warrior normally received four pounds of powder, six pounds of shot, and nine flints. The governor distributed British-made rifles and smoothbore muskets at his discretion. Spanish authorities kept these gifts small enough to give them plausible denial to charges that they stoked Indian warfare against the United States—indeed, the Creeks complained endlessly that Spanish supplies were inadequate for them to roll back white encroachment from Georgia—but they were also large enough to cultivate good will between the Seminoles and St. Augustine.[6]

Seminole and maroon support was practically the only thing that kept Florida from falling into American hands before 1819. Early in 1812 a filibuster army made up of Georgians and Anglo-Floridians, with the backing of U.S. Navy gunboats provided by the Madison administration, invaded East Florida with the goal of annexing it to the United

States. Yet with the sturdy defenses of St. Augustine holding firm, Spanish authorities provisioned Seminole, Black Seminole, and other free black units to attack the self-declared "Patriot" army on more fronts than it was capable of defending. One ambush after another wore down the filibusters' morale and stretched their supplies thin at a time when the campaign was already reeling from President Madison's sudden withdrawal of support following the United States' declaration of war against Britain. Ultimately Seminole attacks contributed to the defeat of this invasion, but at the cost of retributive Anglo-American search-and-destroy raids that drove the mico Bowlegs and his followers from the Alachua Savannah forty miles west to the Suwannee River. It was a high price to pay for Spanish trade and diplomatic gifts.[7]

The Seminoles and their maroon allies also received military supplies from the British, who were interested in diverting U.S. resources south from the Canadian border and possibly asserting the empire's claims along the Gulf of Mexico, particularly at New Orleans. During the 1790s and early 1800s American Loyalist filibusterer William Augustus Bowles repeatedly tried to rally the Creeks and Seminoles behind him to create an indigenous state called Muskogee, which he promised would enjoy ample British material and political support and thus enable them to defend their lands against the United States. Despite some encouragement from John Murray, Earl of Dunmore, the royal governor of the British Bahamas and former governor of Virginia, Bowles never had enough resources, particularly arms and ammunition, to build a substantial indigenous following or to prevent Spanish authorities from twice arresting him and foiling his plans. The delivery of British arms had to wait until the War of 1812, when Britain opened a theater on the Gulf Coast from a base in Spanish territory at the mouth of the Apalachicola River. Though this operation culminated in the British loss at the Battle of New Orleans in the winter of 1814–1815, for the Seminoles and maroons it was a windfall in munitions. Over the course of two years British officers in the Gulf distributed some 5,500 firearms (muskets, carbines, pistols, and rifles), and tens of thousands of pounds of powder and shot to Creek and Seminole warriors in exchange for their military service. The British also outfitted the hundreds of fugitive slaves who escaped to the Union Jack to fight for their freedom. White planters saw this development as the terrifying revival of the British–Indian–

black slave alliance that rained chaos on the South throughout the American Revolution. It looked like Florida was on its way to becoming the source of infection for another Haitian Revolution, in which enslaved people threw off their chains, murdered their masters, and declared their own republic.[8]

The so-called First Seminole War of 1817–1818 was, from the Seminoles' perspective, less a distinct conflict than an extension of Florida's "Patriot War" and the War of 1812, fought for the same reasons and even with the same arms. Mutual raiding between Seminoles and white Americans had persisted between the conflicts as white American encroachment on Seminole territory reached new levels. In the Treaty of Fort Jackson following the Battle of Horseshoe Bend, the United States forced the Creeks, including those who had fought against the Red Sticks, to surrender a fifth of modern Georgia and roughly half of Alabama, with most of the cession concentrated on the Florida border. The ink was barely dry before a land rush of legendary proportions began, in which tens of thousands of white Americans and their slaves suddenly moved to the edges of Seminole country and sometimes right into it. American soldiers followed them, cutting roads and setting up a base at Camp Crawford (later renamed Fort Scott), just north of the modern Georgia/Florida boundary at the head of the Apalachicola River. It took little time for an environment of free-for-all violence to develop, marked by retributive murder, cattle rustling, horse stealing, and slave kidnapping committed by whites and Seminoles alike. The stakes grew even higher as hundreds of fugitive slaves and Indians took possession of a British stronghold sixteen miles up the Apalachicola River; the redcoats had abandoned it after the War of 1812, but left it stocked with cannon, shoulder arms, and ammunition. Known as "the Negro Fort," this place became a beacon of hope for the maroons and many of their Indian compatriots. Like Indians during Pontiac's War awaiting the return of the French, they took the donation of the fort and its arms as a sign that the British would soon renew both its fight against the United States and its support of their independence. As far as they could tell, 1815's Treaty of Ghent was merely a pause in the long-standing imperial contest for the Southeast, not an end to it.[9]

The First Seminole War involved American troops and allied Creek warriors invading Seminole and Spanish territory to eliminate the maroons and the remaining Red Sticks. In effect, if not always in written histories, the first major clash took place in July 1816, when 116 U.S. soldiers and some 500 Creek warriors laid siege to the so-called Negro Fort and managed to blow it up after a heated cannonball fired from a gunboat somehow ignited the bastion's well-stocked powder magazine. From the wreckage U.S. and Creek forces salvaged 2,500 muskets, 500 carbines (light guns), 400 pistols, and 1,062 kegs of powder, along with other martial stores, all of which went to the Creeks as payment for their service. Meanwhile black and Indian survivors of this explosion fled to Seminole towns for protection. Armed encounters between American troops stationed at Fort Scott and Seminoles living along the Apalachicola mounted in turn, underscored by General Edmund P. Gaines destroying the mico Neamathla's community of Fowltown on the Flint River in November 1817, followed by deadly Seminole ambushes against American boat convoys. In the spring of 1818, then, 3,000 U.S. troops and Tennessee and Georgia volunteers under Andrew Jackson and 1,400 Creeks under William McIntosh invaded Seminole country on a scorched-earth campaign. From March through May this force destroyed several Seminole and Black Seminole settlements along Lake Miccosukee and the Suwannee River, killed some forty Seminole and Black Seminole warriors, captured a hundred women and children, and occupied the Spanish fort at St. Marks and the town of Pensacola as punishment for their material support of the Indians and maroons. Additionally, Jackson seized, court-martialed, and executed two British traders, Alexander Arbuthnot and Robert Ambrister, on the charge of supplying the Seminoles and maroons with arms. One of the pieces of evidence used in their conviction was a letter in which Arbuthnot told the British minister in Washington that he intended to import a thousand muskets, 10,000 flints, fifty casks of gunpowder, and 2,000 pounds of lead to encourage the resistance. Though these men had acted independently of London, it would have been fair for the Seminoles and maroons to have interpreted their roles as evidence of ongoing support from Britain.[10]

The American public was divided on whether to laud or court-martial Jackson for this mission, because Washington had not authorized him to occupy Spanish territory or execute British traders and it did not want the international crisis he had provoked. Additionally, the value of his invasion was questionable, as the vast majority of Seminoles and Black Seminoles had withdrawn southward and allowed Jackson's troops to burn and plunder property that was fairly easily replaced. Yet when Spain ceded Florida to the United States in 1819 out of its embarrassing inability to defend it, the question of reprimanding Jackson was settled. Not only did Jackson go unpunished, he became the United States' first territorial governor of Florida in 1821, seven years before his election as president.

The Indian Removal Act of 1830 would have precipitated war with the Seminoles under any circumstances, for they were unwilling to be deported. Yet they were all the more determined because this legislation had been preceded by a negotiated settlement that created a reservation for them in Florida. In 1823 U.S. representatives and a Seminole delegation led by Neamathla signed the Treaty of Camp Moultrie (or Moultrie Creek), which established a four-million-acre Seminole reserve in central Florida guaranteed for twenty years, and granted the people a $5,000 annuity, also for twenty years, among other provisions. To be sure, this agreement had not been without controversy. Many Seminoles refused to move off the ceded lands. Some of the signatories were surprised to learn that the treaty made the entire Florida coast off-limits to the Seminoles to keep them away from Cuban and Bahamian arms dealers. Though the agreement required the Seminoles to return fugitive slaves, clearly they had no intent of abiding by that condition either. Most of all, the Seminoles wanted the reservation boundary moved northward to include better planting grounds, for even Florida's governor, William DuVal, admitted that "nineteen-twentieths of their whole country within the present boundary is by far the poorest and most miserable region I ever beheld." However, these were details to be negotiated. The Seminoles expected to stay in Florida for the indefinite future and certainly did not anticipate the Americans returning a mere seven years after the Moultrie treaty to insist that they uproot entirely.[11]

Yet that is precisely what happened. By 1832 American agents were threatening to cut off the Seminoles' annuities unless the micos signed the Treaty of Payne's Landing authorizing their deportation. Washington still hoped to achieve removal through political rather than military means. Even then the Seminoles interpreted this treaty as binding them only to send a delegation to scout land in Indian Territory and then report back so the chiefs in council could decide whether to relocate there. Washington, by contrast, argued that the exploratory party had the power to commit the rest of the people to move, then used bribes and threats to have its members sign another document pledging the Seminoles to vacate Florida within three years. Worse yet, the government wanted to compromise the Seminoles' sovereignty in Oklahoma by forcing them to live among, and basically subject to, the Creeks, against whom many of them had been fighting for years and from whom a number of Black Seminoles had run away. It was obvious that federal authorities were going to cooperate with slave catchers, white and Creek alike, to return the Black Seminoles to slavery if the Seminoles consented to removal. The entire process was corrupt by any measure, but U.S. authorities were unwilling to have it any other way. Few Seminoles were budging either. Only 152 of them had left Florida by the time of the three-year deadline. The rest were not going without a fight.[12]

Waging a Guerilla War

The Seminoles had been preparing for this moment for years by building up their arsenals. Archaeological and eyewitness evidence agrees that after the First Seminole War the Seminoles ended the long-standing practice of burying adult males with guns and ammunition as grave goods, obviously in order to stockpile those materials in the expectation of ongoing hostilities with the United States. Under these urgent circumstances, the needs of the living took precedence over those of the dead. Furthermore, the Seminoles took advantage of the growing number of American arms dealers who appeared around the reservation agency near Fort King whenever it was time to distribute their annuities under the terms of the Treaty of Camp Moultrie. As early as 1828 white observers were alarmed by Seminoles "buying up all the powder they can get at unusually high prices." In October 1834, as tensions over the removal deadline built to a head, federal Indian agent Wiley Thompson learned that the Seminoles had spent their annuity on "an unusually large quantity of powder and lead . . . I am informed that several whole kegs [probably 25 pounds each] were purchased." That same season nearly all the ammunition on the St. Augustine market went to Seminole and Black Seminole buyers. Fearing the obvious, Thompson ordered an immediate ban on sales of martial stores to Indians, coupled with a toothless if insulting declaration that all micos opposed to removal would be considered by the United States to have forfeited their office. The rising Seminole war leader Osceola roused his followers with the retort that only slaves were denied the right to arm themselves. Fortunately for him, he could boast that he had already stockpiled 150 kegs of powder and that he would not leave Florida until it was used up.[13]

There was a broad consensus among Seminole leaders about war aims and tactics. Their first purpose was to maintain a united front against deportation. Osceola, a Red Stick who had arrived in Florida shortly after the Battle of Horseshoe Bend, was only the most vocal and visible of the militant leaders. Joining him were the hereditary Alachua Seminole mico, Micanopy, his spokesman, Jumper, his warrior and advisor Halpatter Tustenuggee (or Alligator), and his black interpreter, Abraham. From the St. Johns River bands came the young warrior-chief Coacoochee (or Wild Cat) and King Philip. Holata Mico (or Billy Bowlegs) and Tukose Emathla (or John Hicks) led the Tallahassee band into the resistance, while the Miccosukees followed the elderly shaman Arpeika, or Sam Jones. To announce the solidarity of this diverse collection of peoples, and more, on November 26, 1835, Osceola intercepted Chief Charley Amathla returning home from the sale of his cattle in preparation for removal, shot him dead on the spot, and scattered the money he had collected around his dead body. Any Seminoles who broke ranks and accepted the white people's lucre could expect similar treatment. The next steps were to ambush and plunder American military forces at their most vulnerable points, loot and destroy civilian plantations south of St. Augustine, and then retreat into the dense hammocks and swamps. The Seminoles' aim was not to defeat the U.S. Army, per se, or even to clear the Florida peninsula of whites, but to erode the American will for deportation. They almost reached their goal a number of times over the next several years.[14]

The Seminoles' opening strikes not only showcased the strength of their arsenal but netted them plunder that added to it. Their first attack took place on December 18, 1835, as Osceola and some eighty warriors ambushed a military baggage train crossing the Alachua Savannah, killing six, wounding eight, and seizing four barrels of gunpowder. Yet the most dramatic announcement of war came on December 28 with

Osceola. The great Seminole war leader, featured here with his rifle in a drawing made during peace negotiations, was a staunch opponent of the American policy of Indian removal. He developed a well-earned reputation as a skilled gunman during the fighting. Courtesy Library of Congress, Washington, DC.

two nearly simultaneous raids against U.S. troops in the heart of the Seminole territory. One targeted Fort King, the headquarters of federal Indian agent Wiley Thompson, who had managed to offend just about every important Seminole figure during his short tenure in Florida. Osceola was foremost among them. Back in June 1835 Thompson had placed Osceola in irons to silence his tirades against removal. Now, a year and a half later, Osceola had his revenge. He and a band of warriors took up positions just outside the gates of the fort, waited patiently for Thompson to step outside for his customary postdinner walk, and then riddled him with bullets and lifted his scalp. Immobilized by fire from enemy guns, the garrisoned troops looked on helplessly as Seminole warriors pillaged the storekeeper's house and then disappeared back into the tree line.[15]

Meanwhile, just twenty-five miles south of Fort King, another band of Seminoles led by Micanopy, Jumper, and Halpatter Tustenuggee ambushed a relief train of 110 troops under the command of Major Francis Dade. With its van stretched out over the space of a hundred yards, lacking flankers, and the soldiers permitted to keep their coats buttoned over their cartridge boxes of ammunition to ward off the chill, this force was an inviting target. The Americans' naiveté came to an abrupt end along the Withlacoochee River as 180 warriors camouflaged in a "perfect ambuscade" of dense palmetto "poured in a sheet of fire" that instantly killed Dade and seven other men, followed by a three- to four-hour firefight that left just thirty-five of the soldiers alive, most of them wounded, several mortally. Seminole gunfire then paused for a few hours, apparently to permit runners to fetch more ammunition, while the remaining Americans hastily stacked up pine rails into a triangular breastwork in hopes of mounting a defense. However, once the soldiers ran out of powder for their cannon, there was nothing more they could do to prevent the Seminoles from penetrating their lines. The four Americans who managed to survive did so only by playing dead, while the Seminoles made off with massive amounts of plundered arms and food. Skeletons left on the field of battle long after this so-called Dade Massacre would warn future expeditions to leave the Seminoles at peace in their homes.[16]

It took only until New Year's Eve for federal officials to realize that subjugating the Seminoles was going to require more men and material than anyone in Washington had anticipated. Three days after the December 28 attacks, Native gunmen ambushed yet another American force crossing the Withlacoochee, this one 750 men strong under the command of General Duncan L. Clinch. The soldiers' mission was to force their way into the Seminoles' natural fortress, the Withlacoochee Cove, a watery maze of lakes, swamp, and grassy wetlands interspersed with dense island hammocks of cedar, oak, and magnolia. In this impassable setting Seminole gunners merely had to wait for the troops to get bogged down and separated before springing an ambush. That chance came on December 31, with Clinch pushing his soldiers faster than they could reasonably go in order to get them into action before their enlistments ran out at midnight. Instead the Seminoles brought the battle to him, unleashing a volley from tree cover against 200 of the regulars who had crossed the river, while the rest of the U.S. force remained stuck on the opposite bank incapable of providing help. Eventually the Seminoles retreated in the face of a bayonet charge, but not before they had killed fifty-nine (including four officers) and wounded four others. Stunned by this succession of disasters, at the end of January Congress allocated $620,000 for the war effort and authorized the raising of volunteer companies from South Carolina, Georgia, and Alabama. Indian removal was already costing far more than the frugal Jackson administration had planned.[17]

Despite all of the resources the United States expended, Seminole gunmen continued to accumulate victories through surgically executed ambushes and quick retreats. On February 27, 1836, as many as a thousand warriors waylaid three columns under General Edmund Gaines at another Withlacoochee River crossing, near the site of their ambush of Clinch two months earlier. Seminole fire was so punishing that the troops were forced to jerry-rig a defensive breastwork, subsequently known as "Fort Izard" after a mortally wounded lieutenant. Soon the place resembled a charnel house. For eight days the Seminoles peppered Gaines's command with shot until five U.S. soldiers lay dead and forty-six were wounded. Finally, on March 5, the Seminoles agreed to cease fire to discuss terms, only to retreat in alarm at the surprise appearance of American reinforcements from Fort Drane. Where they fled, no one in the U.S. ranks could tell, a pattern that was already building American frustration to a pitch.[18]

The Seminoles were waging a psychological as well as a tactical war. No one captured this point more vividly than Brevet Second Lieutenant Henry Prince, who arrived in Florida at age twenty-five, just six months after completing his studies at West Point. During the first couple of weeks on the march, Prince and his fellow troops coursed with nervous adrenaline, for they had already heard the stories of deadly Seminole ambushes leaving the bodies of U.S. soldiers strewn and desecrated along the banks of the Withlacoochee. In the dead of night the clamor of a bear lumbering through the bush or even a barking dog was enough to throw the camp into a panic. Jumpy sentinels repeatedly shot blind toward the sound of rustling leaves or breaking branches, producing a friendly fire incident on January 23 that broke a sergeant's leg. Yet there was a good reason for these loose triggers. In late February while on patrol with General Gaines, Prince passed by "the scene of a massacre" littered with the remains of Dade's command, followed shortly by "a deserted Indian and Negro town," a "burial ground," fresh Indian tracks, and then "two bodies or rather skeletons on the right side of the road—one had soldiers' brogans on." As the men paused to reflect on the macabre scene, Seminole gunfire erupted on the left side of their column and then lasted half an hour, killing one and wounding six, until the Indians retreated with celebratory whoops and *feu de joie*. The next day as the soldiers tried to cross the river, there was another assault, this one lasting from 9:30 a.m. until late afternoon. Prince managed to escape without injury that day, but the terror he had experienced was seared into his memory as a sonic event. As he recalled, the air was filled with nature's chorus and the rhythm of the march when all of a sudden, "the guns went spitter spatter spitter spitter spitter spatter spatter spatter, then whang!—whang!—the big gun roaring and making the trees tremble." Soldiers like Prince trembled too.[19]

The only thing more stressful for the infantry than waiting to be ambushed was the ordeal of besiegement at flimsy Fort Izard. On March 3, after the troops had spent nearly a week ducking enemy gunfire from behind their makeshift palisade, a group of Seminole warriors disguised in plundered blue army coats, trousers, and caps casually approached an American work party. They behaved as if they were scouting for Indians, and then simultaneously opened fire from point blank range. "We were completely deceived for some moments," Prince exclaimed, with some soldiers shouting "They are our men!" and others "They are all Indians!" Two days later a thick late-morning mist permitted a handful of warriors to approach the American lines and pick off soldiers huddled around an illuminating fire. "They fired two rounds each, howled, and drew off a hundred yards." Later that afternoon the Seminoles unleashed five to seven shots a minute; a volunteer named Butler was pierced through the head and another was wounded in the arm. The siege ended at 1:30 p.m., then commenced again two hours later "as if the enemy had finished his dinner and picked his teeth." The troops felt like the Seminoles were toying with them in a deadly game.[20]

The saving grace for the blue coats was that Seminole gunmen were far less effective at pitched warfare than at ambush. One reason was their military organization and culture, with the Seminoles, like most other North American Indians, fighting in decentralized, kin-based units in which leaders issued directions rather than orders and for whom any loss of life was too much. Thus, Seminole warriors were reluctant to move within close range to fire and almost totally unwilling to attempt or defend a charge. Another critical factor was the Seminoles' often haphazard loading of their guns during the heat of running battles. First Lieutenant John T. Sprague's judgment was that although "the first discharge of an Indian rifle is generally fatal; afterwards they load carelessly and hurriedly. The weapons, to be efficient, must be charged with care; but the Indian fills his mouth with bullets, pours the powder from his horn into the barrel, then spits the ball down the muzzle, causing it to roll down without patch or ramrod, then, between whoops or frantic gestures, seeks an opportunity to fire." The point in all this was that Seminole warriors placed a higher premium on preserving their own lives than on taking American lives. They knew as well as Lieutenant Sprague that quick loading on the move compromised the quality of their shots, but their first priority was making themselves into difficult targets. Thus, though most Seminoles had high-quality rifles as compared to the rudimentary smoothbore flintlocks issued to American infantry at the beginning of the war, their volleys often lacked the accuracy and power this superior technology afforded. During the Battle of the Withlacoochee, Prince was twice hit in the head by spent balls, neither of which broke his skin. Another solider in Prince's company was merely knocked out by a blast to his skull. Likewise, at the Battle of Pilaklikaha in March 1836, U.S. troops faced Seminole gunmen at a distance of just seventy yards, but emerged from the fray unscathed. Myer Cohen of the South Carolina volunteers, like Sprague, attributed this pattern to "imperfect loading, without patches, after the first fire."[21]

With pressure mounting in Washington for a quick end to what was becoming a public relations nightmare, General Winfield Scott, a veteran of the War of 1812 and the recent Blackhawk War, designed a campaign in which 1,200 troops would march in three synchronized columns to drive the Seminoles northward out of the coves and onto firmer ground. Yet U.S. forces plodding through unfamiliar, sometimes unmapped, water-logged terrain just multiplied the targets for camouflaged Seminole gunners. Even the army's deployment of 750 allied Creeks with experience in forest warfare was of limited use in Florida's swampy haunts. Instead of the army flushing out the Seminoles, during the spring and summer of 1836 Seminole warriors besieged Camp Cooper in the Withlacoochee Cove, Fort Alabama on the Hillsborough River near Tampa Bay, Fort Defiance in the central peninsula, and even the formidable Fort Drane south of the Alachua Savannah. Soldiers found that even abandoning the forts was perilous. In July the U.S. command decided to close disease-ridden Fort Drane, only to have eight men transporting baggage fall into an ambush by some 200 warriors. By the end of 1836 the army had managed to deport only 400 Seminoles as compared to 16,900 Creeks, prompting questions in the national press, government, and even the army about whether this war was worth fighting or even winnable. This reaction was precisely what the Seminoles intended.[22]

Any American victory was going to take more time and resources than the public or politicians had anticipated, and more than some of them would stomach. Cohen, after three months of service in Florida, characterized the army's dilemma this way: "We are not inaptly compared to a prize-ox stung by hornets, unable to avoid, or catch, his annoyers; or we are justly likened to men harpooning minnows, and shooting sand pipers with artillery." Army surgeon Jacob Rhett Motte agreed, complaining:

> That the enemy had an espionage over the whole country, and knowing all our movements was met or not at his own

convenience; that they always fought from their own positions, and never took any form from which they could not secure a safe retreat; that his position was always right on the edge of some hammock whence every Indian posted behind some covert, made his deliberate shot;—the fact of his being near not known until the crack of his rifle and savage yells were heard; and our men were seen falling; and when charged upon he precipitately retreated. Thus it was in every engagement with these Indians; nothing but a succession of running fights from hammock to hammock, and swamp to swamp.

It took repeated losses before the men directing this war grasped the enormity of their challenge. General Dade captured their initial over-confidence when he boasted "that he could march, with impunity, through the [Seminole] nation with 100 men." A year later Dade was dead at Seminole hands, as were many of his troops, with hardly any American gains to show for it. In November 1836 even Andrew Jackson finally had to admit, "It is true, that the whole Florida war from the first to the present time had been a succession of blunders and misfortune."[23]

For all of the Seminoles' many disadvantages, they were getting the better of this contest in part because of their success at maintaining their stocks of arms and ammunition and using them effectively in first strikes against the much larger and wealthier American force. At the Battle of the Withlacoochee on December 31, 1835, Osceola was said to have threatened General Clinch, "You have guns and so have we—you have powder and lead, and so have we." As if to accentuate the point, at the Battle of Thonotosassa on April 27, 1836, the Seminoles mockingly answered a shot from an American six-pound artillery gun with their own blast from a blunderbuss, a large-caliber shoulder arm. A fifty-year-old Seminole man named Nethlockemathlar, captured by the army in spring of 1842, put it another way. He remembered how at the beginning of the war he had favored relocating to Indian Territory, but "as the young men had obtained sufficient powder and lead, they disregarded my solicitations to peace." As long as that remained the case, and as long as the Seminoles were capable of keeping their women, children,

Seminoles Attack. Sudden attacks by camouflaged Seminole gunmen on exposed American positions, military trains, and forts, like the one pictured here, character-ized the Second Seminole War. The Seminoles' skillful use of the swampy Florida terrain to launch hit-and-run raids, and their cultivation of multiple international sources of supply for military stores, enabled them to drag out the war far longer than most Americans expected and to extract important concessions from Washington. Courtesy Library of Congress, Washington, DC.

crops, and cattle hidden away from American troops, they were deter-mined to keep up the fight.[24]

A stinging irony for the Americans was that the Seminoles' resistance partially depended on arms seized from the very forces trying to subju-gate them. Seminole prisoners told in January 1837 that Osceola "had taken six kegs from white men" in just one fight that winter in which "the white men . . . were so scared that they left these kegs in the bushes—threw them away." The pattern continued throughout the war. On Jan-uary 15, 1838, for instance, three divisions under Lieutenant Levi Power mistakenly abandoned a keg of powder along with a boat when retreating from a clash near the head of the Jupiter River. And, of course, the Semi-noles were able to plunder arms and ammunition on a smaller scale from the bodies of dead soldiers left behind at the scene of battle, a situation that was all too common during the first couple years of the war.[25]

The Seminoles' pillage of American plantations and coastal stations was another critical source of their munitions. After war's opening

strikes, these raids took on a seasonal quality, spiking in the summer-
time when U.S. troop levels dropped and soldiers on duty generally went
into quarters to escape the heat and humidity. This lull in military activity allowed plundering parties to go about their business deliberately.
For instance, they often looted in stages to maximize their haul and
avoid detection, stripping a property of its most important items but
leaving it standing while they moved on to other nearby sites. Later they
would return to grab less essential materials and put the place to the
torch. Military stores were among the most desired pickings, as when a
band of Seminoles sacked Junior Cooley's New River plantation in
southeast Florida in January 1835 and carried off a keg of powder and 200
pounds of lead. Sugar works were inviting targets because the lead lining
from the inside of industrial boiling pots could be stripped and cast into
bullets. Late in the war, when most of the remaining Seminoles had been
driven into southern Florida, far from the plantations, they still managed to seize large amounts of arms and ammunition from American
interests. Indeed, their most daring plundering raid of the war was not
until August 6, 1840, when the mico Chekaika led twenty-eight canoes
of warriors across thirty miles of open water to attack a naval hospital
on the island of Indian Key. This force, crossing in the middle of the
night and then striking at 2 a.m., took the station completely by surprise,
killing thirteen people and then retreating with enough booty, including
at least four kegs of powder and answerable amounts of lead, to fill all of
the twenty-eight canoes plus six captured boats. American officials cor-
rectly anticipated that this ammunition would fuel a surge in Seminole
military activity.[26]

Ongoing trade with Cuban fishermen was probably the steadiest
source of arms and ammunition for the Seminoles during the war; it
was certainly a great cause of frustration for American officials trying
to assert U.S. sovereignty over the Florida peninsula. Cuban fishermen
had been working Florida's Gulf Coast since the mid-eighteenth century,
including the construction of seasonal fishing camps on the inlets and
keys of Tampa Bay, Charlotte Harbor, and San Carlos Bay. A number
of these places evolved into permanent "ranchos" with a character not
unlike that of continental fur trade posts. In such places one could find
Indians working for the Spanish as deckhands, day laborers, and hunters.
Fishing boats sailing to Havana often carried Indian passengers with

their own trade cargo of deer, alligator, and bear hides, jerked beef, and honey. Predictably, relationships between Spanish fishermen and Indian women produced a population of Indian–Cubano children, some of whom went to Havana for school and then returned to Florida to become cultural, political, and certainly commercial go-betweens. It took little time before the ranchos spawned trading houses, such as one at Sarasota operated by Captain Frederick Tresca and another run by William Bunce at Shaw's Point on Tampa Bay. This way of life was so was distinct that the Natives living in and around the fishing stations became known to outsiders as "Spanish Indians."[27]

Cuban–Indian arms traffic took place up and down the Florida coast throughout the war. In 1840 a prisoner in U.S. custody "who says he is a half breed, his mother being an Indian and his father a negro, and that he belonged originally to the Creek Tribe," confessed that he had traveled to Havana to purchase gunpowder for the Seminoles. Another Seminole warrior taken by the Americans admitted that his band had received some of its ammunition from the Tampa Bay trader Bunce, who himself did business with Cuba. This gunpowder included a high-quality "mixture of fine rifle and musket" grains. It might have been Bunce to whom a Black Seminole referred when he bragged that his people did not worry about running out of ammunition because "they could get a supply from a white man 'down the country.'" The mother of the war leader Coacoochee told American captors that her band had acquired military stores from a trading station on the St. John's River "supplied by the fishing boats along the keys." Other Seminole women taken by U.S. forces said that their people had obtained supplies from "small Spanish turtle-hunting boats" and that "there were three Spaniards in the Everglades, who supplied the Indians with salt and ammunition." It is also possible that some Seminoles made their own trading visits to Cuba in dugout canoes, something they had been known to do on occasion before the war. The combination of the remoteness of the ranchos and provisional trade houses, the difficulty for the United States of monitoring boat traffic along Florida's extensive coast, and the Spanish Indians' consanguinity with the Seminoles, ensured that the Seminoles remained armed throughout the war.[28]

The Seminoles probably obtained ammunition from the Bahamas as well, which was just a full day's sail away. Arms traders with ties to the

Bahamas, including William Augustus Bowles, Alexander Arbuthnot, and Robert C. Ambrister, had been active among the Seminoles throughout the second Spanish period in Florida. Additionally, up to sixty Bahamian boats specializing in salvaging coastal wrecks also could be found regularly in Florida waters, particularly on its dangerous, reef-ridden, southern shores. As in the case of the Cuban ranchos, Bahamian salvaging and fishing gave rise to a number of small beachside settlements and a trade post along the New River at the entrance to the Everglades, the site of modern Fort Lauderdale. The war made little difference. In 1837 Seminole chiefs boasted to General Thomas Jesup that they had a "constant communication" with the Bahamas. Furthermore, some of the fugitive slaves who had taken refuge among them had since fled to the Bahamas in British vessels via Key Biscayne, joining a previous exodus to the Bahamas' Andros Island after the First Seminole War. Given such ties, it is all but certain that the Seminoles obtained some of their munitions from the Bahamas during the Second Seminole War.[29]

Anyone with a basic familiarity with Florida's geography knew how to stem this flow of munitions. As Florida's territorial governor Robert Reid urged the secretary of war, "There should be a competent naval force upon the coast to second the efforts of the army on shore and to intercept the fishermen who are trading with the Indians and providing them with ammunition." Competent was the operative word here. Though the Second Seminole War marked the first and only significant time the United States employed its navy against an Indian foe, it did not commit anywhere near enough ships to disrupt the Seminoles' international commerce. During the first three years of the war, there were at most a few naval vessels at a time in the Florida theater, with predictably poor results. "Nothing was intercepted" in the winter of 1836–1837, which the commander of the Pensacola squadron, Alexander J. Dallas, tried to justify by questioning whether "any [ammunition] was obtained by the Indians in the manner supposed." Yet Indian intelligence said otherwise, prompting the navy to step up its effort by creating a Mosquito Fleet of seven ships manned by 622 crewmen, supplemented by a number of small, shallow-draft vessels to search coastal inlets and swamps. Any boat found in Florida was to be stopped and searched, "particularly examining fishing smacks, and other small craft, as it is by this means that it is supposed powder and lead are introduced among the Indians." If these measures managed to disrupt the trade, however, it was not due to the arrest of any arms traffickers. Not once during the war did the navy discover a foreign boat trading arms to the Seminoles, even as military officials were sure that this practice continued under their noses. Washington's maps and policies might imagine cutting off the Seminoles from the international world, but the Seminoles created a different reality.[30]

Even inside American lines, the army could not stop the clandestine trade. St. Augustine, which contained a number of free blacks by virtue of the old Spanish policy of granting refuge to runaway slaves from the British colonies, discovered that some freemen were smuggling out ammunition to the Seminoles and Black Seminoles in casks disguised as flour. In all likelihood the point man in this trade was the Black Seminole interpreter, Abraham, whom the American leadership suspected of keeping hidden stores of powder. On the other side of the peninsula U.S. troops discovered "two miscreants" trafficking powder and shot to Indians and liquor to soldiers. That operation was broken up, but nonetheless it appears that traders and civilians around U.S. military installations continued to deal munitions to the Seminoles whenever they came in for negotiations. The sources documenting this commerce are suspect because they were generated by officers trying to justify several cases late in the war in which they took Seminoles captive under the color of parlay. At the same time, the evidence rings true with the long history of rogue arms dealing and of Seminole resourcefulness in securing military wares. For example, during peace talks in 1839 at Fort Andrews, U.S. military repeatedly noticed Seminoles disappearing into the bush and returning with fresh supplies of powder, lead, clothing, and tobacco. Likewise, in March 1841 war leader Thlocklo Tustenuggee, or Tiger Tail, entered discussions for his surrender only long enough "to obtain ammunition, whiskey, and subsistence" for his band, after which he returned to fighting. Later in the war a black informant reportedly warned General Jesup that Osceola and Coe Hadjo were negotiating in bad faith, merely angling to acquire powder and clothing and then return to fighting. Even Seminoles seized by the army under a flag of truce supposedly "declared openly, after capture, that it was not their intention to emigrate or surrender; they came for powder, whiskey, and bread." There is no way to know whether these accounts

213

were truthful and based on good intelligence. Military contingencies and black-market trade had a way of eluding verification.[31]

No one bothered to record precisely how the Seminoles protected their arms and ammunition from Florida's humidity and the wear and tear of combat, but anecdotal evidence suggests that underground caching was the norm. In February 1837 Lieutenant Prince's command discovered an abandoned Seminole town along the Withlacoochee containing a house "in which powder & lead had been buried. There was the powder keg—the green hide it was done up in—the bullet box and the hole in the ground lined with bark." The following year U.S. troops under Lieutenant Colonel James Bankhead stumbled upon a Seminole camp in the Everglades in which the people had also put canisters of lead and powder in underground storage. The mico Halleck Tustenuggee and his warriors revealed where they had stored their arms after U.S. forces captured them in April 1842 under the ruse of parlay. "Some had placed them in hollow trees," wrote Lieutenant John T. Sprague, "some under logs, others wrapped in moss and buried, others secreted among the palmettoes. Twenty-five excellent rifles were found, well charged." Halleck also directed the Americans to "five canisters of powder, which the chief said he buried two years previous to the war, and from that time improved the opportunity to obtain powder and lead." In this, he appears to have been in good company.[32]

Among some bands, at least, stored powder fell under the control of the micos, as had been the case with the Choctaws in the early eighteenth century during their wars with the Chickasaws. The black interpreter Sampson, who escaped from the Seminoles in the Big Cypress Swamp after two years of captivity, said that when the Indians plundered ammunition, "it was deposited with the chiefs," who thereafter distributed it free to members of war parties a powder horn at a time, but required hunters to purchase it at a rate of a hog for five charges. He added that several micos in the Everglades held a council in April 1841 at which they decided to conserve their remaining powder, and to guard against the report of their guns revealing their locations, by prohibiting anyone from firing a shot except in combat. All hunting was to be done by bow and arrow. Whether the exercise of such authority had the sanction of custom or was an innovative response to the stresses of war, Sampson did not say.[33]

Despite the American public's criticism of the war and the country suffering a severe three-year recession, Martin Van Buren began his presidency in 1837 by doubling down on Jackson's policy to remove any and all Seminoles from Florida. He knew that eliminating the Seminole resistance, and with it the haven for runaway slaves, was critical to keeping southern planters in his Democratic Party coalition. To that end Congress, still controlled by Democrats, appropriated $1.6 million for the war in 1837, enough to bring October troop levels to 8,993 men, more than half of whom were regulars. Throughout the winter and spring of 1837 and then again in the fall, U.S. soldiers invaded Seminole sanctuaries in such overwhelming numbers that they could press on even after absorbing devastating ambushes or some of the troops being waylaid by illness. Seminole casualties and property losses mounted in turn, as in January's Battle of Hatchee-Lustee near modern Orlando, when U.S. Colonel Archibald Henderson captured upward of forty Indian and Black Seminoles, one hundred ponies with packs, 1,400 head of cattle, and large stores of gunpowder. By March, Micanopy and several lesser chiefs had signed a capitulation, and by June some 700 Seminoles were camped at Fort Brooke on Tampa Bay awaiting their deportation. It seemed like the war was all but over until Osceola and Sam Jones arrived under cover of darkness and led most of the detainees away to keep up the fight. Given how apprehensive most Seminoles were about surrendering in the first place, there is no way of knowing whether they went along voluntarily or under duress. The certainty is that after this debacle, enraged U.S. officers were unwilling to extend diplomatic immunity to Seminole dignitaries if taking them into custody served military ends.[34]

That fall the United States lost another chance to end the war. In October, General Joseph Hernandez followed up his capture of the war leaders King Philip and Yuchi Billy by seizing Osceola and mico Coe Hadjo under a flag of truce, willingly enduring the charge of dishonor in favor of dealing the Seminoles a possibly fatal blow. Captain George McCall explained that the army command had decided "the ends must justify the means. They have made fools of us too often." Yet such double-crossing also became a Seminole rallying cry. In one of those truth-is-stranger-than-fiction moments, sixteen of twenty-five Seminole leaders imprisoned deep within the walls of Fort Marion at St. Augustine managed to escape on November 29, 1837. They had removed the iron bars from a single eight-inch-wide porthole fifteen feet above their cell's floor, squeezed through one by one, climbed down a twenty-foot wall on a rope made of strips of canvas bedding, and eluded the sentries outside. Their numbers did not include King Philip, who was too old for such exertions, or Osceola, who was sick with a fatal bout of malaria. A mere two weeks later, one of the escapees, Coacoochee, the so-called Napoleon of the Seminoles, was 200 miles to the south at the Battle of Okeechobee, the bloodiest exchange of the war, at which Seminole gunmen stationed in a dense hammock killed or wounded 138 U.S. troops slogging through a marsh while losing only about a dozen warriors themselves. For Coacoochee and doubtless others too, the United States' repeated violations of white flag diplomacy had made this war about even more than removal or the fate of the Black Seminoles.[35]

For the majority of Seminoles, however, the fight was no longer worth it. Unable to pause anywhere long enough to tend crops or graze cattle, and with the American leadership finally conceding the right of the Black Seminoles to join them in Indian Territory, the people began surrendering. During May and June 1837 the United States deported nearly 1,600 Seminoles from Florida. Another 2,000 capitulated or were captured between September 4, 1837, and May 1838 in the face of the largest army the United States had employed since the War of 1812. By the spring of 1838 Sam Jones and Coacoochee were the only major leaders still in arms and more Seminoles were out west than remained in Florida. The war seemed to be shifting in the United States' favor enough to warrant a reduction of troop levels from 9,000 to about 2,300 and for General Jesup to sign over to Zachary Taylor the command he had held since late 1836. The army's focus now turned to building a network of roads and posts to solidify American control over north Florida. It seemed to be just a matter of time before the rest of the peninsula was cleared of Indians too.[36]

Never-Ending War

Yet the war would drag on until 1842 and even beyond because of the resourcefulness of the Seminole holdouts in restocking their munitions and surviving on the run in the harshest, most remote environments of Florida. Though the bulk of the militants would eventually concentrate in the Everglades, as late as 1841 there were still bands ensconced in the hammocks near Lake Okeechobee, the Okefenokee Swamp on the Florida/Georgia border, and along Choctawhatchee Bay in the panhandle. Their resistance remained so intransigent that on May 18, 1839, Major General Alexander Macomb made an offer to chiefs Chitto Tustenuggee and Halleck Tustenuggee granting the remaining Seminoles a reservation in southwestern Florida on which they could live in peace for the next twenty years. All they would have to do in return was stay their warriors. Put another way, he told them that they had won. Macomb had not been authorized to make such an offer, and outraged white Floridians proclaimed they would never honor it, but the issue became moot that summer when warriors who had not subscribed to the agreement attacked a military detachment led by Colonel William S. Harvey on the Caloosahatchee River south of Charlotte Harbor, killing twenty-two soldiers and two traders. With this action negotiations collapsed, and the war ground on between a Florida Seminole population that now stood at probably fewer than 400 people against an American army that had climbed back up to 6,500 regular troops and militia by 1840.[37]

Tiring of the expense and futility of trying to track down every last Seminole, on December 6, 1842, President John Tyler declared in his second annual message that the war "has happily been terminated." He did not say "won," because the United States, despite deporting or killing the vast majority of Florida Seminoles, had given up trying to track down the remainder. Instead the administration accepted Colonel William Jenkins Worth's recommendation to create a Seminole reservation in Florida out of the same 6,700-square-mile tract at the Big Cypress Swamp in southwestern Florida that General Macomb had proposed in 1839. The costs of this war for the United States had been enormous, but the gains were also, at least over the long term. Whereas there had been fewer than 35,000 Americans in Florida in 1830, by 1850 there were 90,000, attracted by cheap land and a booming economy of cotton production, lumbering, and cattle raising. Such growth enabled Florida to become a full-fledged state of the Union in 1845. It also became, culturally and politically, part of the militantly expansionist slave South that was already casting a shadow on the very Seminoles whom the nation had deported from Florida to Indian Territory.[38]

The Seminoles who persevered in Florida had little more than a moral victory to celebrate. The United States had shipped off 4,420 of their people, slayed innumerous others, robbed them of the vast majority of their territory, and forced them to live hidden in unforgiving swamps in which they had to invent almost an entirely new way of life. Periodically they also had to continue to fight. Despite the peaceful counsel of the aged Sam Jones and Billy Bowlegs, in July 1849 five renegade Seminole warriors killed a number of whites and plundered their settlements along Pease Creek and the Indian River. The chiefs handed over of three of the five culprits and executed another, hoping to avoid a renewal of war, but it was not enough to satisfy white Floridians calling for the remaining Seminoles' removal or extermination. For the next seven years federal and state forces fruitlessly probed the Everglades hoping to capture the holdouts and destroy their settlements, interspersed by Seminole guerilla strikes on troops, surveying teams, and isolated farmsteads. It took until the summer of 1857 for a party of Florida militia and volunteers to locate and destroy the village of Billy Bowlegs's band and bring the chief to the negotiating table. Finally, after years of resistance, the mico relented to the deportation of his band to Indian Territory, pushed by the loss of his settlement and pulled both by Congress's offer of lucrative payouts to him and his 164 followers and its concession in 1855 to mark out a western Seminole reservation distinct from the Creeks'. The intrepid Sam Jones, said to be more than a century old, remained in hiding with just a reported seventeen warriors and perhaps a hundred followers. Unconquered, his people gave rise to today's Florida Seminole and Miccosukee tribes.[39]

———

Coacoochee wanted to remain in Florida too, but after the capture of his mother and daughter he surrendered in March 1841. Yet he found life in Indian Territory intolerable for so many reasons. The federal government had relocated the Seminoles to the reservation of the Creeks (this was prior to Congress agreeing to a separate Seminole reservation), whom Coacoochee despised for the support they had given the United States during the Red Stick War and the First and Second Seminole

Wars. Wealthy slaveholders dominated the Creeks' laws and courts, which meant that free Black Seminoles were subject to constant harassment, including the threat of re-enslavement. There was even reason to doubt the territorial integrity of the Seminoles' supposedly permanent new western home. Equestrian tribes like the Comanches and Kiowas rustled the Seminoles' horse herds, sometimes taking human lives in the process. An equally serious long-term threat was the expansion of Texas following its secession from Mexico in 1836, its annexation by the United States in 1845, and the war between the United States and Mexico from 1846 and 1848 in which the United States seized the northern third of Mexican territory. Texas had proven unwilling to respect Indian land claims, regardless of whether they had been guaranteed by Texas itself or the federal government, the result of which was an almost constant state of war between the Lone Star State and the Indians of the southern Plains. Under such circumstances the federal government's promise to preserve Indian Territory forever appeared to be no more than a temporary expedient, as it was. Not least of all, there was hardly any room for Coacoochee to fulfill his ambitions for leadership in a reservation setting where he had to compete with the full roster of Seminole micos and aspirants for the few roles afforded to them by the Creeks.

Rather than brook these conditions, Coacoochee laid the foundations for another Seminole refuge in the west, though not in Indian Territory where the U.S. government wanted it to be. Instead he had in mind a place where Washington had no say, on the south side of the Rio Grande. His lengthy preparations included stockpiling provisions and cultivating political relationships with powerful tribes like the Comanches by buying up manufactured goods in the east, including vast quantities of munitions, transporting these goods to the Plains tribes to exchange for their bison robes, horses, and mules, and then selling this stock on the American market for more arms. He pursued this commerce not only despite the Plains tribes' hostilities with the people of Texas, but partially because of it, for Texans were cut from the same cloth as the southern whites who had forced the Seminoles from Florida. Everything was ready by 1850, whereupon Coacoochee and a band of a few hundred Seminoles, Black Seminoles, and fugitive slaves from the Creeks struck out for the border. With Mexico City welcoming as settlers anyone willing to help shore up its northern margin against the United States, on June 27, 1850, Coacoochee negotiated an agreement granting him and his followers 70,000 acres (or 109 square miles) along the Rio Grande between the headwaters of Rio San Rodrigo in the north and Rio San Antonio on the south. And no sooner was this done than the settlement became a destination for another north-to-south Underground Railroad paralleling the one that had once brought fugitive slaves from Georgia, Alabama, and Creek country to Seminole havens in Florida. This time, however, the runaway slaves came from Indian Territory and Texas assisted by a network of Black and Indian Seminoles. They knew better than anyone that freedom for people of color in the United States was a never-ending fight requiring arms, ammunition, international support, and iron-willed determination.[40]

7. INDIAN GUNRUNNERS IN A WILD WEST

Gun frontiers developed not only in regions with Euro-American settlements, but often several hundred miles away, where Indians had little or even no contact with those communities. Sometimes munitions from remote places arrived through maverick Euro-American fur traders traveling deep into Indian country by canoe or horse train, as was the case among the Chickasaws and the Ohio country tribes in the early to mid-eighteenth century. In other times and places, large corporations took the lead. The late eighteenth and early nineteenth centuries saw London's Hudson's Bay Company and Montreal's North West Company extend their lines of trade posts to the Canadian subarctic and Plains and even west of the Rocky Mountains. To their south, a number of St. Louis firms led by the American Fur Company expanded their commerce up the entire length of the Missouri River to its sources. These enterprises were premised on connections between distant places and people. Goods manufactured in the cities of Europe and eastern America arrived at landing points on Hudson Bay, the Saint Lawrence River, and the Mississippi, then traveled by dog-sled teams, horse-drawn carts, bateaux, keel boats, and eventually steamboats, to reach the hands of indigenous people in the remote interior. Yet well into the nineteenth century, small groups of traders from these outfits were practically the only interactions Indians of the Plains and tramontane west had with people from the United States, Canada, and Europe.

Traditionally accounts of the gun trade in the continental interior have focused on Euro-American initiatives because they generated the kind of paper trails on which historians rely. Furthermore, these histories lend themselves to classic heroic American themes of (white) rugged individualism, entrepreneurialism, and Western civilization's supposedly inevitable penetration and taming the so-called savage wilderness. It is often overlooked that a key factor in the spread of gun frontiers far away from the centers of colonial population and power was Indians themselves, who were not only the buyers but often the purveyors of arms and ammunition.[1]

Some of the most visible and important areas where this occurred were the Arkansas and Red River Valleys of what is now Arkansas, Oklahoma, Kansas, Texas, and Colorado. These waterways, flowing from sources deep in the Rocky Mountains and then snaking across the Prairie-Plains to empty into the Mississippi River, linked the gun suppliers of the East (French, British, Spanish, and then American) to the rising equestrian peoples of the southwestern Plains, especially the Comanches. Drawing the two sides together were the equestrians' desire for arms and other manufactured goods, and the colonial powers' demand for horses, mules, bison robes, bison meat, and indigenous slaves. Yet the distance between these markets—and sometimes the military barrier erected between them by other Native groups—meant that east–west commerce had to run through Native intermediaries on the Prairie-Plains. From the mid-eighteenth to the early nineteenth century, these economies found their point of connection on the middle to lower reaches of the Arkansas and Red Rivers, in the villages and trade caravans of the Wichitas and later the "removed Indians" from the Southeast, like the Cherokees and Seminoles. Eventually the nomadic Cheyennes and earth-lodge Pawnees of the central Plains joined this roster, too, as part of their own efforts to manage changes sweeping across the continental interior.

For these middlemen, as with all Native people operating within a gun frontier, controlling the flow of arms became a key aspect of their politics. All of the middlemen came from relatively small groups surrounded by larger, militant peoples. Initially their main concern was the well-armed Osages to the northeast, who maintained a near stranglehold on the lucrative colonial trade at the confluence of the Missouri and Mississippi Rivers and threatened to become gatekeepers of westward traffic along the Arkansas. To the southwest loomed the Apaches of what is now the Texas–New Mexico–Mexico border region, sometimes in alliance with the tiny Spanish colony of Texas. Additionally the stunning expansion of the populous, horse-rich Comanches on the southwestern Plains was a development no one in this region could over-look. As the nineteenth century wore on, new threats emerged in the form of the Lakota Sioux on the northern Plains, Anglo-American Texas, and eventually the United States. Carving out a niche in the arms trade was one way vulnerable people avoided being crushed by these forces. When a weak group funneled arms and ammunition to an indigenous power like the Comanches, it became a means to achieve peace and even alliance with them, which could then be used to offset threats like the Osages. Middlemen used this business to build up their own armaments, which became more essential to self-defense with every passing year.

The gun frontier of the Arkansas and Red Rivers was a creation of Indian savvy and power, not white American Manifest Destiny. For Indians in this region, colonization was something remote, even as it influenced them through the long-distance effects of the arms trade, slaving, and the spread of epidemic disease. To the extent that Indians in this region experienced direct relations with Euro-Americans before the nineteenth century, it was largely with small fur trade outfits and underwhelming Spanish missions and presidios, which Indians tolerated as it suited them. Given this background, it would have come as a great surprise to most of the region's Indians that the United States would seize their country by the late nineteenth century. Well supplied with military hardware and organized into strong military confederacies by virtue of their middlemen status in the trade, they had every reason to expect to remain in control of their destiny.

Midcontinent Middlemen

The development of a gun frontier on the southern Prairie-Plains, as elsewhere in North America, had as much to do with indigenous demand for munitions to fend off foreign Indian gunmen as it did with Euro-American supply. Two key groups appear to have arrived in the region in the seventeenth century as part of the diaspora of Ohio Valley peoples fleeing the Iroquois. They were the Quapaws of the Arkansas and Mississippi Rivers confluence, and the Osages of the Osage River, near the intersection of the Missouri and Mississippi Rivers. Yet there was no escape from gun violence even this far west. In the mid- to late seventeenth century, Iroquois marauders had reached the Mississippi River Valley too, followed by the emergence of a host of other gun-toting threats. In the late seventeenth century, Chickasaw slavers terrorized the area as part of that group's trade with South Carolina, while Miami, Potawatomi, Ottawa, and Fox raiders bearing French muskets struck from the northeast. Soon, however, the Quapaws and Osages caught up in the arms race. They began by trading periodically with Illinois Indian middlemen and itinerant *coureurs de bois,* and sometimes traveled all the way to Detroit to deal directly with the French. French expansion down the Mississippi into Illinois country and Louisiana then brought arms trafficking to the Quapaws' threshold. In the spring of 1686 Henri de Tonti established the first French trade post west of the Mississippi, at the Quapaw town of Osotouy, which became a way station for voyageurs and *coureurs de bois* working the Arkansas River. Contributing a mere 1,000 deerskins to Louisiana's annual average export total of 50,000, this was a marginal enterprise of a marginal colony. Yet it took only until 1714 before French travelers described the Quapaws as "almost all armed with guns," which they used "very skill-fully." A portion of this stockpile also came from English traders probing beyond their regional customer base among the Chickasaws. As early as 1700 the Quapaws reported receiving a present of thirty muskets, powder, shot, and other goods from a party of English traders guided to their country by a French defector named Jean Coutre. Though such contacts were rare, they reminded the French that the Quapaws had alternatives for arms.[2]

The Osages' militarization was even more dramatic, to the point that they themselves became the scourge of the region. By the 1720s the Osages also had the benefit of French trade posts in their own country, beginning with Fort Orleans at the confluence of the Missouri and Grand Rivers, followed by Fort Cavagnolle at the meeting of the Kansas and the Missouri. At the same time the Osages began to adopt horses, giving their warriors and hunters greater range and speed than ever before. The Osages' embrace of these colonial technologies, combined with their geographic position at the transition zone between the eastern woodlands and the western Prairie-Plains, allowed them to trade, raid, and hunt westward for slaves, bison robes, deer hides, bear furs, and horses, which they then sold to the French for arms and ammunition that supported those very activities. Soon the Osages boasted control of the Mississippi-Missouri artery, while their ambushes south along the Arkansas River prevented rivals from reaching the French posts and French *coureurs de bois* from heading west. Thus, throughout much of the mid- to late eighteenth century, Osage power was self-generating. The Osage superiority in military hardware permitted raids against western people who were poorly armed because of the Osage blockade, which in turn produced slaves and horses that the Osages could exchange for more guns. The groups who suffered these Osage attacks, particularly Taovayas, Tawakonis, Iscanis, Guichitas, and Panis Noirs, up the Arkansas and Red Rivers, known collectively as the Wichitas, were desperate for weapons to offset this menace.[3]

Spaniards in the region were too few and undersupplied to fulfill the local Indians' needs. They began building missions in east Texas in the 1690s, and then promoting secular migration to the area in the 1710s as a bulwark against potential threats posed by the Apaches of the southwestern plains and the French of the Mississippi River Valley to the silver mines of northern Mexico. By 1721, Spain had established three missions among the Caddo Indians of the Texas/Louisiana border, and the fort of Neustra Señora del Pilar de Los Adaes (or Los Adaes for short), just twelve miles from the French settlement of Natchitoches. Farther west was the presidio (or military post) and municipality of San Antonio de Béjar and another five missions, anchored by San Antonio de Valero. Yet this growth was more impressive on the map than in person. The Spanish population of missionaries, soldiers, and ranchers stood at just 500 in 1731 and 1,190 in 1760. Indians came and went from the missions as they pleased, based largely on whether they needed relief from famine or military protection from the Comanches or other raiders. Usually they left just as soon as the emergency had passed. The missions found the task of retaining Indians to be next to impossible, in part because Texas refused to provide them with arms in the form of trade or gifts. Imperial regulations choked Texas commerce by closing the colony's Gulf Coast harbors to shipping and requiring all imports and exports to arrive by lengthy, expensive, overland routes through Mexico. In any case, Spanish policy placed serious limits on the distribution of guns to Indians. The remoteness and poverty of the colony provided few opportunities or incentives for Spanish smugglers to evade these laws.[4]

French supplies also were meager throughout the late seventeenth and early eighteenth centuries, particularly as one moved up the Arkansas from its confluence with the Mississippi and into Wichita territory, but there were periodic bursts of commerce. In 1719 Frenchman Jean-Baptiste Bénard de La Harpe led twenty-two horses loaded with goods to Tawakonis villages on the Red River, where one of the chiefs urged him "to carry to them some arms in order to defend against their enemies," the Osages and Apaches. La Harpe sensed an opportunity. Noting that the Wichitas "have no fire arms, there being an inviolable law among the Spaniards not to furnish them to the savages," he imagined that "if one could control the trade . . . one could become master of this region." The Spanish feared the same thing. Though La Harpe's expedition was the first trading expedition on record to have reached the Wichitas, French and English guns had already appeared among Apaches in New Mexico, who raided and traded with Indians from the Arkansas and Red Rivers. Startled Spanish officials panicked that their imperial rivals might be on the verge of penetrating into Texas and New Mexico and setting the stage for an invasion of the Mexican silver mine region. To preempt such a disaster, in the summer of 1720 New Mexico sent out Pedro de Villasur at the head of a small party of Spanish and Pueblo Indian soldiers onto the central Plains in search of the arms traffickers, only to have them fall into a deadly ambush of gunfire, probably set by Pawnees and Otos wielding French arms, at the intersection of the Platte and Loup Rivers in what is now Nebraska. It was already too late to hold back the spread of the gun frontier.[5]

In the mid-eighteenth century the Wichitas seized the opportunity to become intermediaries between French gunrunners from Louisiana and the Comanches of the southwestern Plains; this enriched them materially and empowered them politically and militarily. One factor in this transformation was the increased pace of French trade along the Arkansas to meet the demands of the growing colony of Louisiana. Despite ongoing conflict with the Chickasaws and supply shortages due to imperial warfare, Louisiana's population was on the rise, expanding from 6,872 in 1732 to 8,860 in 1746; more than half of the new population were African slaves. The actual number of immigrants to the colony would have been even higher than these figures suggest, given high death rates among new arrivals. This growing population needed more food than the colony's agriculture, hunting, and local Indian trade could provide. Louisiana's plantation economy was expanding too, with corresponding demand for human labor and horsepower. The Prairie-Plains along the Arkansas and Red Rivers was an attractive place for the French to seek these resources, because the Indians had livestock, Indian slaves, bison robes, and jerked meat that they were eager to exchange for European manufactures.[6]

The French market opened at a time when the Plains tribes' wealth was expanding due to their adoption of the horse, a technological watershed rivaling previous paradigmatic moments such as the invention of the bow and arrow and the development of maize horticulture. Historically Indians had stalked bison on foot, thus limiting large kills to periodic communal drives, but even then the amount of meat the people could haul was limited by the carrying capacities of their dogs and travois and the strength of their own backs. There was always the risk of a failed hunt, thus requiring several economic safety nets, including some combination of corn-beans-squash horticulture, the hunting of smaller game animals, the gathering of wild plant foods, and trade. Economic diversification had always been essential to life on the Great Plains.[7]

The horse upended this calculus. The horse began spreading from the Rio Grande to the southwestern Plains and lower Rocky Mountains following the onset of Spanish colonization in New Mexico during early seventeenth century, and especially after the Pueblo Revolt of 1680, in which the colony's Indians temporarily drove out their oppressors and seized their mounts. By the mid-eighteenth century the Indian-to-Indian exchange in horses had expanded to encompass nearly half of the present-day United States and beyond, stretching to modern-day Oregon and Washington, north to the Canadian Plains, and as far east as the Mississippi River. The results were momentous. With perhaps eight million bison on the southern Plains and as many as thirty million on the Great Plains overall, hunting on horseback gave the people unprecedented access to a seemingly limitless supply of meat and other bison by-products, such as skins for clothing and tents, bones for tools, bladders for jugs, and far more. Not only could hunters on horseback keep up with stampeding bison and use the horse's speed and height to leverage their javelins, but entire communities on horseback could follow the bison herds wherever they migrated. This was an opportunity for the people to live more richly than at any time in their memory.

Taking to horseback also allowed men to fulfill their masculine roles as hunters, warriors, and husbands like never before, albeit in ways that made everyone's lives more perilous. Warriors could strike their enemies more quickly and ferociously than ever, and they had new incentives to do so. The economic necessity to replace mounts lost to enemies or drought meant that horse raiding became a basic feature of equestrian life, with many human casualties along the way. The warriors of nomadic equestrians also had to fight for their people's claims to hunting territory, grazing lands, and river bottoms, the latter of which provided water, wood, and winter shelter to humans and horses alike. There were new motivations to raid enemies for women and children as laborers to tend to the horse herds and process the growing number of bison robes needed for teepees, clothing, and trade. Plains groups valued captive women for reproduction during an era in which the stresses of warfare and epidemic disease were taking a heavy toll, particularly among men, which made polygamy more common. In so many ways the lives of men were becoming more dangerous, but equestrian peoples encouraged them to risk themselves for the group by lauding them for their martial and hunting achievements, while also shaming them for failures. Those same male exploits created a world of constant back-and-forth violence encompassing the growing ranks of horse people and everyone within their reach.[8]

Many Natives decided the trade-off was worth it. Pulled by the material and masculine rewards, and pushed by the recognition that sedentary life invited raids by other mounted peoples, over the course of the eighteenth century groups such as the Comanches, Utes, Cheyennes, Arapahos, Crows, Kiowas, and Lakotas, became equestrian nomads focused almost entirely on chasing bison and raiding enemies for horses, captives, and food. To round out their protein-rich diet of bison flesh, they traded meat, hides, and slaves to farming tribes on the edges of the Plains in exchange for their corn, beans, squash, and other produce. Some peoples, including the Apaches and Wichitas of the southern Plains, the Pawnees of the Platte and Loup Rivers, and the Osages, Mandans, Hidatsas, and Arikaras of the Missouri River Valley, responded more conservatively to the horse insofar as they continued their horticultural activities and village-based settlements even as their men went hunting and warring on horseback. Yet for them as well as their fully nomadic neighbors, the adoption of the horse meant both newfound wealth and peril. That would become even truer with the arrival of firearms.[9]

The Comanches, as an expanding equestrian power, sought out the Wichitas for French guns, powder, shot, and metal-edge tools, as well as agricultural produce. The Comanches had enjoyed explosive growth since the late seventeenth century, when they abandoned their former lives as pedestrian hunters and gatherers in the Rocky Mountains to become mounted nomads on the southern Plains. By 1780 their population had more than doubled from its size just a few decades earlier, to reach as many as 40,000 people, while the number of their horses was many times that figure. Yet expanding their hunting and grazing range from their base in the upper Arkansas River Valley required them to fight a growing roster of other equestrian groups, beginning with the Apaches to their south, then including tribes to the north and east such as the Arapahos and Pawnees and sometimes even the Osages. Metal wares and agricultural produce from the Spanish and Pueblo Indians of New Mexico helped the Comanches address these threats and their basic nutritional needs, but the colony's supply of manufactured goods was just too small to satisfy the Comanche demand. By the 1740s the Comanches were seizing in raids against New Mexico what they could not obtain in trade. As these hostilities degenerated into outright war, some Comanches looked eastward to the Wichitas as a new source of European merchandise.[10]

The Wichitas' retreat from the Arkansas to the Red River to escape horse-mounted Osage gunmen carried the silver lining of positioning them to become middlemen in the region's arms traffic. This migration, beginning in the early 1700s, had by 1757 put the Wichitas in control of the head of navigation of the Red River, a key way station in east–west travel to and from Comanche territory and between New Mexico and Louisiana. The Red River location was also more accessible to French *coureurs de bois* canoeing out of New Orleans or Illinois to trade among the Wichitas' linguistic kin, the Caddos and Hasinais. The Wichitas took advantage of this position by ferrying French goods and sometimes guiding French traders to the Comanches, and delivering

Pawnee-Pict (Wichita) Village, by George Caitlin. During the late eighteenth century, the Wichitas developed a middleman trade in which they ferried munitions and other European wares from the French, British, and then Americans, westward to the Comanches, in exchange for Comanche horses, mules, buffalo robes, and slaves, which they then ferried back east. Much of this business took place in the distinctive beehive house villages of the Wichitas along the Arkansas and Red Rivers, like the one depicted here. Courtesy Gilcrease Museum, Tulsa, Oklahoma.

Comanche products to the French in turn. The long-distance travel and hauling facilitated by horses allowed the Comanches, Wichitas, and French to conduct their commerce wherever it was most convenient, sometimes in the Wichitas' fortified villages on the Red River, and at other times in the Comanches' seasonal camps high up the Arkansas, in what amounted to giant trade fairs.[11]

One such event early in the history of this arrangement, witnessed by Spaniard Felipe de Sandoval in 1749, took place at a camp of more than 400 tipis pitched by the Big Timbers of the Arkansas, along the modern Kansas-Colorado border. Even at this remote location, a thousand miles from New Orleans, the Comanches were joined by a collection of Wichita, French, and German (probably from Louisiana) traders who engaged in "the barter of rifles, gunpowder, bullets, pistols, sabers, coarse cloth of all colors and other inexpensive merchandise, for skins of deer and other animals, horses, mules, burros, and a few Indian captives whom the Comanches have taken as prisoners." One transaction involved a young Comanche man exchanging three horses with a Wichita for a musket and a hatchet. Clearly there were few places left in the continental interior still cut off from arms traffic, slaving, and fur trading connected to the colonies. In addition to the spread of epidemic diseases, these were the manifestations of colonialism long before colonial settlement was a threat of any sort.[12]

The Wichita-Comanche partnership was military as well as commercial in nature. These groups shared a mutual hostility for the Apaches, with whom they warred for horses and captives. They also had a common enemy in the Osages, who battled the Comanches for access to the Arkansas River Valley bison herds and raided the Wichitas for horses and slaves and to drive them away from the French. Now the Apaches and Osages would have to face the combined might of Comanche-Wichita warriors armed with French guns, the shockwaves of which were soon felt across a broad swath of the middle continent. In or around 1750 a Wichita-Comanche war party struck the Great Osage Town and killed a reported twenty-two chiefs to revenge an earlier attack on a disease-ridden Wichita village. As such victories began to accumulate, other groups clamored to join the alliance. They included the Pawnees of what is today Nebraska, close kin of the Wichitas, seeking to prevent Osage incursions into their own hunting territory. The Hasinai confederacy, made up of the Tonkawas and Caddos of east Texas, added its strength to the coalition in the interest of striking a blow against the Apaches. The Comanches viewed these developments so favorably that a branch of them joined the Wichitas on the Red River, where they became known as a distinct eastern division. This new location provided them with enhanced opportunities to trade with the Wichitas and to raid the horse herds of the Apaches and Spanish, who increasingly clustered together near the Texas missions to protect themselves from the mounting threat.[13]

Yet the missions offered little refuge from the Norteños [northerners], as the Spanish called the allied Indians to reflect the direction from which they struck. The Norteños' largest attack came on March 16, 1758, when an estimated 2,000 mounted warriors from the Comanches, Wichitas, and ten other nations fell upon the recently founded mission of San Sabá. With a small post of Spanish soldiers located three miles off, and the next source of assistance another 135 miles away at San Antonio, the mission did not stand a chance. There was also the matter of the raiders' armament. One Spanish source claimed that they carried "at least 1,000 French muskets"; another contended that "most of the enemy carried firearms, ammunition in large powder horns and pouches, swords, lances, and cutlasses." Only the Norteño "youths" used "bows and arrows." The raiders' overwhelming advantage permitted them to spend a full three days burning buildings, plundering property, and herding livestock to drive back to their country, leaving behind a scorched shell of a mission and eight people dead. To Spanish Texans it seemed only a matter of time before other similar attacks plagued the rest of the vulnerable colony. One official panicked that the Norteños boasted such superiority "in arms as well as in numbers . . . that our destruction seems probable."[14]

That probability seemed even higher after Norteño gunmen punctuated their victory at San Sabá by repulsing a counterstrike by the Spanish and Apaches. In August 1759 an expedition of 380 presidio soldiers, 90 mission Indians, and 134 Apaches marched against the Wichitas along the Red River, only to be confronted with a moated, palisaded village flying a French flag and possessing enough weaponry to provide each warrior with two muskets, thereby allowing a woman or child to load one while a man fired the other. Additionally, Spanish scouts counted fourteen French inside the walls assisting in the defense. The attempt to breach this stronghold was a disaster for Spanish and Apache forces, which suffered fifty-two men dead or wounded and the loss of two swivel guns during the retreat. Unrelenting Norteño warriors drove the invaders all the way back to the ruins of San Sabá.[15]

The commercial chain of the French-Wichita-Comanche gun trade extended as far west as New Mexico, where the Comanches had long alternated roles between traders and raiders. Commerce between the western division of the Comanches, on the one hand, and the eastern division and the Wichitas, on the other, meant that it was only a matter of time before Comanches appeared in New Mexico bearing French guns. In November 1750, for instance, a Comanche force that included sixteen gunmen attacked the Pueblo of Pecos. Twelve years later Comanche delegates arrived at a Spanish-hosted peace conference sporting muskets to demonstrate that they were bargaining from a position of strength. Such conspicuous displays made Governor Tomás Vélez Cach-upín fear for the survival of the colony, "since this kingdom is so lim-ited in armaments and its settlers too poor to equip themselves and too few to sustain the burden of continuous warfare." He did not know that, in general, the western Comanches' stockpile of guns was small, poorly maintained, and subject to chronic shortages of ammunition. How could he, when by the 1770s sometimes it was the Comanches who supplied guns to New Mexico colonists rather than vice versa?[16]

The flow of arms through Wichita hands reached its peak in the af-termath of the Seven Years' War, as British and American traders began competing with French *coureurs de bois* far west of the Mississippi. The Peace of Paris ending the war extended British claims all the way to the east bank of the Mississippi River, but Anglo-American gunrunners were unwilling to restrict their activities even to these expansive borders. Their commerce on the Red River probably accounts for a Spanish in-telligence in 1768 that the Wichitas had delivered seventeen horse loads of munitions to the western Comanches, who in turn circulated some of the guns at New Mexican trade fairs. Spanish authorities in Texas grew so alarmed by this news, and by growing evidence of the British trade in the form of Wichita and Comanche weapons stockpiles, that they agreed to raise the prices they would pay for Wichita goods. In exchange they secured Wichita pledges to halt their trade with the British and en-courage the Comanches to end their plundering of Spanish horse herds. Yet the Wichitas' words were empty. By at least May 1775 there were fresh reports of several Britons trading arms and ammunition to Indian communities in east Texas. It was probably not coincidental that the Co-manches had a striking amount of wealth to trade at a fair in Taos, New Mexico, in 1776. Fray Francisco Atanasio Domínguez marveled that "they sell buffalo hides, white elk skins, horses, mules, buffalo meat, pagan Indians . . . good guns, pistols, powder, balls, tobacco, hatchets, and some vessels of yellow tin" and that "they acquire these articles, from the guns to the vessels, from the Jumanos [Wichita] Indians."[17]

The Wichitas continued to acquire munitions from Louisiana too, despite Texas's ongoing attempts to halt the arms trade from that sector. Though the transfer of Louisiana from France to Spain after the Seven Years' War meant that Louisiana joined Texas within the viceroyalty of New Spain, it remained a separate colony with its own policies, some of which worked at cross-purposes with those of its neighbor. In particular, whereas Spanish Louisiana eventually adopted French-style trade and gift diplomacy to enlist Indian support against Anglo-American encroachment, Texas adhered to more restrictive policies. Louisiana traders had never respected Texas's laws before the war and were not about to do so afterward, regardless of which imperial power claimed jurisdiction over them and the Indians. The Wichitas were even less willing to cooperate. According to Spaniard Antonio Treviño, who lived as a captive of the Taovayas for six months in 1764–1765, the Wichitas' favorite trader in French arms was a middle-aged man, also named Antonio, "who has been established on the bank of the above-mentioned [Red] river about forty leagues from them for a long time. They like and love him very much, not only because of the above-mentioned [arms trade] but also because he is the first one [trader] they have come to know." Less love emanated from the French-born, Spanish-employed Natchitoches commander Athanase de Mézières, who in 1770 denounced the Arkansas River as a "concourse of malefactors" and a "pitiful theater of outrageous robberies and bloody encounters" because of French gun-running and Osage piracy. Illegal arms trading was so common that an exasperated Texas governor Domingo Cabello exclaimed that "a million men would be needed" to police it "[and] the Indians would not tell who furnished them [illegal weapons] even if they were killed." By and large, he was right. Just months later he received a report of nine *coureurs de bois* among the Wichitas, encouraging them to raid Spanish horse and mule herds to trade for arms. Spanish authorities could not sever such relationships with mere strokes of the pen or with the skeleton crews of soldiers dispersed throughout the empire's northern borderlands.[18]

Texas governors did what little they could to funnel at least some guns to the Wichitas, out of recognition that the arms traffic was the most important consideration in the Wichitas' colonial diplomacy and that the Indians harbored a "great resentment" toward the Spanish for their stinginess. During the 1750s Governor Jacinto de Barrios y Jáuregui addressed the shortage of Spanish supplies by buying arms from French merchants at Natchitoches to provide to Indians. Twenty years later Governor Juan María Ripperdá took this practice a step further by employing French arms dealers as government interpreters so they could carry out their illegal commerce under official guise. Ripperdá's excuse was that "if [the Indians] are not provided with such prejudicial equipment, they will embrace their friendship with the English and [this] will make their sudden attacks more deplorable." Certainly the colony's official gifts to Indians were miniscule. In 1786, for example, these presents amounted to just thirty-four rifles, 142 pounds of powder, and 284 pounds of bullets for the Comanches, and sixty-nine rifles, 233 pounds of powder, and 466 pounds of bullets for a variety of "friendly nations." Nevertheless, the colony's attempts generated some goodwill among the Norteños even if it did not prevent them from dealing with foreign traders or plundering Spanish horses and mules. As long as the Spanish failed to meet the Indians' needs and police the colonies, Indians were determined to do business with equally determined gunrunners and to take what they wanted from Texas.[19]

Yet the Wichitas eventually lost control of the forces that had given rise to their role as middlemen. The burgeoning flow of arms from the Mississippi Valley worked more to the Osages' advantage than to theirs. By 1758 the Osages had seized control of 500 miles of the Arkansas Valley, forcing the remaining Wichita bands south to the Red River. The Osages' advantage in arms only increased in subsequent years with the 1764 founding of the fur trade headquarters of St. Louis, right on their doorstep, followed in the mid-1790s by the opening of a trade and military post, Fort Carondelet, on the Osage River, run by the St. Louis fur trade clan, the Chouteaus. The amount of furs traded by the Osages increased from a reported 8,000 pounds in 1757 to 22,200 pounds in 1775. The strength of their arsenal and the boldness of their warriors rose concomitantly. From the late 1760s through the 1780s, the Osages struck south of the Arkansas against the Red River settlements, which, combined with losses from a smallpox outbreak in 1777, drove the Wichitas southwestward toward the Neches, Trinity, and Brazos Rivers of Texas and farther up the Red. Tepid Spanish responses to Wichita pleas for arms did little to reverse the tide. Another wave of Osage attacks led to the death of Chief Eriascoe in 1808 and of Chief Awahakei in 1811 in addition to the loss of several hundred horses, prompting the Wichitas to quit the Red River for good.[20]

The Wichitas' dimming fortunes included the Comanches' establishment of direct ties with a variety of gunrunners from the east, north, and even west. The Comanches were expanding so fast, in terms of both population and geography, that the Wichitas could no longer control their access to arms. Some Comanche bands grew dismissive of the Wichitas to the point that they raided the Tawakonis and Iscanis on the Brazos River, well east of Comanche territory, in the late 1770s. Their trade, diplomacy, and conquests had enlarged their range to encompass the entire southern Plains. They rustled horses, mules, and cattle from Texas and New Mexico with such impunity that it is reasonable to conclude that these colonies existed more for the profit of the Comanches than of Spain; in the 1770s, for instance, Comanche raiders struck New Mexico over a hundred times, seizing most of its horse herds. With the Comanches pressing in from the west, and Euro-Americans encroaching from the east, the Wichitas lost control of the east–west trade. Increasingly, itinerant Euro-American arms merchants and the eastern Comanches dealt with each other directly until they had almost entirely bypassed the Wichita middlemen by the early 1800s.[21]

The Comanches also cultivated new indigenous sources for arms. The spread of the British-Canadian and Franco-American fur trade up the Missouri River and onto the northern Plains allowed the Cheyennes, Kiowas, and Pawnees of the central Plains to develop a middleman role in which they ferried Comanche horses and mules to the earth lodge trade centers of the Mandans and Hidatsas to exchange for manufactured goods, including arms, which they then funneled south to the Comanches. Like the Wichitas, who had been galvanized by the Osage threat to seek arms and alliances through the trade, these groups operated in the shadow of the equestrian, gun-toting Lakotas (or western Sioux) sweeping south from the Missouri River Valley. They continued this commerce well into the 1830s, largely because the Pawnees had better access than white American traders to the British-made muskets favored by the Comanches, and they delivered these goods directly to Comanche camps. Small numbers of weapons also arrived from St. Louis through the eastern Comanches' trade with the Kansa, Ponca, and Iowa peoples of the eastern Prairie-Plains. Meanwhile the western Comanches enjoyed the business of New Mexican itinerant traders, aptly called "Comancheros," whom the Spanish government had freed from earlier restrictions in the hope of encouraging the Comanches to redirect their attacks away from the colony and toward the Apaches. Occasionally, too, Comanches acquired ammunition directly from New Mexican villages,

Comanches, by Lino Sanchez y Tapia. Until the mid-nineteenth century, most Comanche firearms came from other Indians, beginning with the Wichitas and then from a vast array of suppliers, including the various removed Indians in Indian Territory, Pawnees, and Cheyennes. Courtesy Gilcrease Museum, Tulsa, Oklahoma.

as in 1831, when a band of Comanches, Kiowas, and Pawnees paid a visit to Cuesta in the Pecos Valley to trade horses to the villagers for small charges of powder and serapes. The flow of arms and ammunition onto the Plains no longer ran east to west along one or two rivers. The expansion of horse-mounted nomads and Euro-American states had created a multinational, multitribal, and multidirectional arms trade, all to the detriment of the Wichitas.[22]

The Wichitas tried to direct the Comanche arms trade through their villages for as long as they could, even as their grip was slipping. In 1794 the Taovayas hosted a blacksmith from Philadelphia, John Calvert,

237

doubtlessly with one eye toward him repairing the arms of visitors from other tribes. That same year they also conducted a "great commerce" with a French trader from Natchitoches. Several times during the 1790s they welcomed American Philip Nolan of Mississippi as he explored the Red River, trading arms and other manufactured goods for horses and mules. In 1801 Spanish forces killed Nolan in the process of trying to arrest him, but it was not enough to stem the flow of foreign arms, which found new holes as soon as officials plugged old ones. The Tawakonis Wichitas, no less than the Comanches, obtained American weapons through Skidi Pawnees on the Kansas River. Yet for all the Wichitas' adjustments, there was no reversing their declining position in the arms market. One portent of the changing times came in 1799 when the Wichitas hosted a motley band of traders that included not only white Americans but Cherokees and Chickasaws, who had recently moved to the eastern Arkansas River and then the southern Plains to escape Anglo-American expansion. News of this trade party prompted Spanish officials at Nacogdoches to dispatch twenty-two men with orders to arrest them, but the Taovayas blocked the way, threatening a fight if the soldiers forced the issue. The expedition returned empty-handed. Little did the Wichitas know that the very people they had defended would shortly take their place as the primary gunrunners of the southwestern Plains.[23]

"Civilized" Tribes and a Wild Gun Market

From the Wichitas' perspective, Andrew Jackson's removal of the southeastern Indians in the 1830s was just one stage in a long-running invasion of the Prairie-Plains by eastern Indians with strong ties to the American weapons market. The movement had begun shortly after the Seven Years' War, as the Spanish invited Native people frustrated by Anglo-American encroachment and the loss of their French allies to relocate along the eastern boundary of its newly acquired colony of Louisiana, promising them land and trade in exchange for their loyalty and defense. Thousands of Shawnees, Delawares, Sauks, Foxes, Potawatomis, and Kickapoos took up the offer and migrated into what is now eastern Missouri, heightening the competition for Osage hunting grounds. Following them were hundreds of Choctaws, who settled on the Ouachita and Red Rivers, soon to be joined by portions of the Creeks, Chicka-saws, and Cherokees. The pace picked up considerably after the United States acquired Louisiana, whereupon the Jefferson and Madison admin-istrations began pressuring Indians to relocate west of the Mississippi River, particularly after Indian losses in the War of 1812. Already by 1817 there were some 6,000 Cherokees on the St. Francis and Arkansas Rivers, and by mid-1827 villages containing hundreds of Cherokees, Shawnees, Kickapoos, and members of other tribes could be found on the Red and Trinity Rivers. All this activity took place even before Jack-son's forced relocation of tens of thousands of eastern Indians to Indian Territory in what is now Oklahoma and Kansas during the 1830s. The conditions were ripe for conflict, with the new arrivals determined not to be forced from their homes again, the old residents resolved not to lose their homes to the newcomers, and both sides eager to raid each other for horses.[24]

The newcomers possessed a distinct military advantage, for whereas the Wichitas and other southern Plains tribes tended to be armed with smoothbore, flintlock muskets that had hardly changed since the mid-seventeenth century, the migrants had flintlock rifles accurate at three times the distance, which was a critical advantage in the wide vistas of the Prairie-Plains landscape. For instance, in 1829 fifty-five rifle-bearing Cherokees revenged a horse raid by marching against the Waco Indian village on the Brazos River, killing dozens of the enemy before with-drawing in the face of 200 reinforcements from the Tawakonis. The next spring a band of Texas Cherokees, led by Chief Bowles, struck a Tawa-koni Wichita fort at the head of the Navasota River, using their long rifles to pick off the defenders until more than thirty-six lay dead. This threat multiplied severalfold with the arrival of Cherokee emigrants under Jackson's removal policy, bearing thousands of new rifles furnished by the federal government. Unwilling to absorb such losses amid on-going bouts of epidemic disease, many of the Wichitas withdrew back north of the Red River, while others relocated to the Brazos and joined the Comanches for lengthy bison hunts out on the Plains where there was less of a chance of encountering their enemies. In a marked reversal of the Wichitas' earlier status as co-equal partners of the Comanches in the Plains trading system, they began to acknowledge their subordina-tion to the Comanches in trade and diplomacy with foreigners.[25]

The Wichitas were hardly alone, as indigenous people throughout the Prairie-Plains found themselves in a constant struggle with eastern Indian riflemen for control of hunting grounds and horse herds. The once-formidable Osages fared especially poorly against the invaders. Little Rock's *Arkansas Gazette* reported in 1820, the Osages "have a few muskets and shotguns, but make little use of the rifle," whereas the Cherokees, who were "determined to drive [the Osages] from their country," were "well supplied with everything necessary for a vigorous prosecution of the war." And not just Cherokees, but also Delawares and Shawnees, with whom the Osages were also at odds. Indian trader George Bent characterized these migrants as "perhaps the most dreaded Indians in the whole West" because "they were armed with good rifles and were fine shots," which meant "they usually had little difficulty in getting the upper hand of poor armed Plains warriors." By 1825 the Osages had ceded ninety-seven million acres of land to the United States and relocated to Kansas, partly out of their desperation to escape these riflemen and to receive arms, ammunition, and blacksmithing services as compensation from Washington. Yet their retreat, by providing a clearer path for immigrant Indians to extend their hunts onto the Plains, also heightened the conditions for the newcomers to clash with equestrian peoples. In 1832 a small band of twenty-nine Upper Creeks repulsed an attack by 150 Comanches, killing or wounding upward of half. That same year U.S. officials heard that a Delaware party had destroyed a Pawnee village and that a band of forty-eight Shawnees out hunting had fought off 300 Comanches, killing seventy-two while losing only seven men themselves. More than any other factor, it was the size and quality of the eastern Indians' armament that produced such lopsided outcomes.[26]

Even amid this violence, the migrant tribes established themselves as middlemen between the nomadic hunters of the southern Plains and the Anglo-American weapons market. As with the Wichitas, the newcomers occupied a geographically favorable position to take up such a role. Their settlements could be traced in a broad "S" shape across the interior of the continent, beginning in the north at the confluence of the Missouri and the Mississippi, then arcing in a west-southwest direction through Kansas and Oklahoma, before curving east and then back southwest through Arkansas and Texas. In effect this course charted the boundary,

permeable as it was, between Plains Indian territory and the rapidly expanding United States. By 1830 the young state of Missouri had 140,455
white and black residents, the lower Arkansas River Valley contained
some 30,000, and another 30,000 Americans had moved into eastern
Texas. Though ultimately this trend would prove to be a disaster to
Indians on the Plains, in the meantime proximity to U.S. merchants
allowed the migrants to use proceeds from the annuities the U.S. government paid them for their ceded lands in order to buy munitions for
resale to the Plains tribes, and then to carry horses, mules, and bison
robes from the Plains back east. In this they were aided by a U.S.-brokered
peace agreement in 1834–1835, in which the Comanches and their allies
agreed to open their hunting territory west of the Cross Timbers, in
what is now central Oklahoma and Texas, to the immigrant Indians in
exchange for trade. It proved to be a mutually beneficial arrangement.[27]

For twenty years, beginning in the late 1830s, the immigrant Indians
served as the primary gunrunners to the Comanches and their allies.
Already by 1837 the Texas Cherokees, Shawnees, Delawares, Kickapoos,
and other immigrant Indians were said to "trade with" and be "in
continual communication with the Prairie Indians." During the mid-
1840s, the most active middlemen were Kickapoos, Shawnees, and
Delawares who had moved to the Canadian River of the Texas Panhandle and Oklahoma after Anglo-Americans drove them out of east
Texas. They traded for firearms and ammunition from the so-called
Five Civilized Tribes—the Cherokees, Creeks, Chickasaws, Choctaws,
and Seminoles of Indian Territory—who acquired military wares as part
of their annuities and through purchases from white traders. The middlemen then carried the manufactured goods to the camps of the allied
Comanches, Kiowas, and Cheyennes to their south and west, with whom
they traded for buffalo robes, horses, mules, and cattle rustled from
Mexico, Texas, and even other immigrant Indians. For example, Cherokee Jesse Chisholm was active among the Comanches in 1857, supplying them with seventy-five rifles and answerable ammunition, which,
Indian Agent Robert S. Neighbors complained, "they have since used
in depredating on our frontier." Ultimately the middlemen sold the buffalo robes to fur companies from St. Louis and the livestock to a variety
of markets, including the farming Indians of Indian Territory, Americans along the Mississippi and Arkansas Rivers, and white migrants

traveling the Santa Fe and Oregon Trails. In exchange they received more manufactured goods to begin the cycle anew.[28]

Though indigenous traders on the Canadian River were small in number, amounting to just a few hundred people, the effects of their activities were wide-ranging. Take, for instance, a trio of immigrant Indian traders who operated among the Comanches and Kiowas in 1846–1847. Consisting of a Delaware named Jim Ned, a Seminole named Lilin, and a Shawnee named Black Cat, this outfit used the lure of military wares and other merchandise to encourage the nomads to raid Texas for horses and cattle. It was an easy pitch to make, given the fury of ongoing hostilities between Plains Indians and the Lone Star State. The next summer the Comanches announced that they had accumulated a great surplus of mules and buffalo robes, prompting a trade fair along the Salt Fork of the Arkansas River in what today is Oklahoma, attended by Comanches, Kiowas, Osages, Seminoles, Creeks, Cherokees, Delawares, Shawnees, and others. According to one report the immigrant Indians traded guns worth $20 each for one or two mules worth $60. That same September U.S. Army Captain Randolph Barnes Marcy encountered Kickapoos hunting with the Comanches along the Brazos, carrying "good rifles, upon which we saw the familiar names of 'Derringer' and 'Tyron,' Philadelphia makers." These guns were for more than personal use. Marcy further observed that these Kickapoos "form a commercial communicating medium between the white traders and the wild Indians, and drive a profitable trade."[29]

The Osages' involvement in this trade reflected the weakened state into which they had fallen. Throughout the mid- to late eighteenth and the early nineteenth century, the Osages had warred with the Comanches and Wichitas for hunting territory and intimidated foreign gunrunners to keep them from supplying those tribes. But that was when the Osages were strong, numerous, and in control of the Missouri-Mississippi confluence and lower Arkansas River. With the United States having forced them from their territory, and war and disease having reduced their population to a mere fraction of its previous size, the Osages turned to commerce to build wealth and political allies. The Osages were well positioned to become middlemen in the southern Plains arms market. Their new location on what is now the Kansas-Oklahoma border provided them with easy access to the equestrian tribes and to manufactured goods at the nearby military trade post of Fort Scott and Westport Landing (now Kansas City, Kansas), a way station for commercial traffic with St. Louis. Furthermore, their sales of land back east to the United States had earned them an annual payment in cash and arms. They took full advantage of the opportunity. The Osages were said to have arrived at the Comanches' 1847 trade fair with guns, ammunition, and other manufactured goods worth $24,000, and to have returned home with 1,500 head of horses worth $60,000. Yet there was more to this business than the search for profits. As U.S. Indian Agent John M. Richardson realized, the Osage-Comanche trade also "has had the tendency to cement them in the bonds of friendship," at a time when the Osages needed Comanche protection and the Comanches needed Osage arms. By 1854 U.S. officials viewed the Osages as Comanche "allies," valued not only for their merchandise but for the fact that they used their own "fine rifles" to defend Comanche hunters on the Plains from rifle-toting immigrant Indians.[30]

With white commercial networks and settlements pressing onto the southern Plains, it was only a matter of time before white gunrunners began to compete with the chain of Indian arms traders. The Mexican declaration of independence from Spain in 1821 was followed by a wave of illegal white immigration to Texas, which Mexico City tried to control by offering free land to those who pledged to uphold the authority of the government and adopt Catholicism. What Mexico got instead was a rebellion, ultimately leading to Texas's independence in 1836, its annexation by the United States in 1845, and a war in 1846–1848 in which Washington seized an additional northern third of Mexico's territory. By the late 1840s the number of white Texans and their African-American slaves had vaulted to 160,000 people. Indian access to white traders grew apace, alongside militant calls from white settlers to drive the Indians from their midst and even from the face of the earth.[31]

The spread of American trade posts and itinerant arms traffickers were among the few positive results of these developments for Indians. Beginning with Thomas James's fort (founded in 1823) on the North Canadian River, trading establishments proliferated throughout the region to include Holland Coffee's "Station" (founded 1834) on the upper Red River, Auguste Chouteau's Camp Holmes (1835) on the South Canadian River of Oklahoma, and the Bent brothers' posts on the upper

Arkansas and South Canadian. Mobile traders also fanned out through Comanche country from these forts as well as bases in Natchitoches, Vicksburg, Natchez, and New Orleans. Other arms dealers operated out of Pueblo, Colorado, carting buffalo robes, tongues, deerskins, and beaver pelts to Westport Landing for shipment by steamboat to St. Louis and to pick up trade goods for the return trip through Indian territory. The southern Plains had been a site of long-distance trading for countless generations, and of firearms traffic for a century, but the bustle of this commerce was utterly unprecedented.[32]

The southern Plains Indians used the expanding weapons trade to develop the most formidable, wide-ranging warriors the region had ever seen. Already by 1820 a U.S. expedition to explore the Arkansas Valley noted that the Comanches "are becoming quite expert in fire-arms . . . having been furnished by traders from the United States by way of exchange, for horses and mules, which these Indians would, from time to time, plunder the Spanish settlements of." Indeed, this swelling market encouraged the Comanches to extend their horse and mule raids ever deeper into Mexico, particularly after a peace agreement in the 1840s with the Cheyennes and Arapahos freed Comanche warriors from the need to defend their home fronts so closely. The growing power of Texas and the United States on the southern Plains was another incentive to redirect raids away from American-claimed territory into Mexico. These attacks, which often involved hundreds of warriors, utterly devastated northern Mexico as far south as a few days' ride from Mexico City, leaving that nation ill-prepared to defend itself against the U.S. invasion in 1847. Mexican authorities howled in protest that the United States was using the arms trade with the Comanches to wage war by proxy, but in fact Washington had little control over the matter. Guns, powder, and shot reached the southern Plains from too many sources for any government to control it, even if it wanted to do so.[33]

Tellingly, Texas and the U.S. military found it impossible to cut off the flow of arms to southern Plains Indians even during times of war. A large portion of those munitions and blacksmithing repairs came from the U.S. government itself in the form of annuities to compensate Indians for land cessions and other treaty provisions, much to the frustration of the Indians' American opponents. Amid fighting with the Comanches and Kiowas in 1857, the federal officer stationed at Brazos

Agency chastised civilian authorities in Washington, "At the same time those bands . . . are depredating on our citizens, waylaying our roads, destroying our mails to El Paso, etc., an agent of your department is distributing to them a large annuity of goods, arms and ammunition on the Arkansas River." He even claimed to have heard the Indians boast that "they are prepared to use the arms and ammunition received from the government agent on our troops." Secretary of War Edwin Stanton and General William Tecumseh Sherman considered it an "absurdity" to expect the army to subdue Indians on the Plains even as the government issued them arms. They contended that if Indians knew they could acquire weapons by signing treaties, they would wage war in order to produce peace treaties they had no intention of honoring just to acquire additional means to renew the fight. General George Armstrong Custer joked dryly that the government's distribution of arms to Indians extended from a "strong love of fair play which prevails in the Indian Department." Incidents in which American forces found U.S.-issued guns in the hands of enemy Comanches did nothing to soften this outrage. Yet federal Indian agents felt they had no choice but to distribute munitions to their charges. Annuities of guns and ammunition and provision of blacksmithing services were essential to the agreements that had produced Indian land cessions and continued to keep violence contained. There were already too many examples of Indians stepping up their raids when Washington broke these promises. From the agents' perspective, arms annuities were a way to wage peace, if admittedly an imperfect one.[34]

The result was that the Indians who resisted Anglo-American expansion and attempts to herd them onto reservations often went into battle as well armed as their opponents, even as weapons technology advanced dramatically at midcentury. Initially the Comanches preferred short-barrel, smoothbore muskets because they were lighter than rifles and more easily loaded on horseback by pouring in powder and spitting in bullets, but losses in battle to immigrant Indians and Anglo-Americans alike forced them and other Indians to accept the new weaponry. By 1852 the Wichitas and Wacos were said to be "provided with rifles, and are good shots." The same statement held true for practically all Plains Indians after the Civil War, as military surplus sales flooded the arms market with guns of every type. These included percussion guns in which the flintlock mechanism was replaced with a more dependable aluminum ignition cap that fit snuggly on a nipple where the hammer struck. There were quick-action breechloaders in which the shooter inserted ammunition from the rear of the barrel, superseding the cumbersome muzzle loaders of the previous 200 years. This period also saw the arrival of Colt and Remington six-shooter pistols, ideal for easy handling and close-range fighting on horseback. Yet the most dramatic development was the appearance of Henry, Spencer, Winchester, and Springfield repeating rifles, capable of firing seven to fourteen rounds between loading, and taking ammunition cartridges that combined the propellant powder and bullet in a single small metal casing. Colonel Richard Henry Dodge judged that breechloading, repeating rifles turned the Plains Indian "into as magnificent a soldier as the world can show. Already a perfect horseman, and accustomed all his life to the use of arms on horseback, all he needed was an accurate weapon, which could be easily and rapidly loaded while at full speed."[35]

Indians throughout the Plains obtained these arms in large quantities, much to the chagrin of the blue coats attempting to subdue them. Dodge, from the perspective of his station in Kansas in 1867, exclaimed that "the issue and sale of arms and ammunition—such as breechloading carbines and revolvers, powder and lead (loose and in cartridges) and percussion caps—continues without intermission . . . Between the authorized issue of [federal Indian] agents and sales of the traders, the Indians were never better armed than they are at the present moment. Several Indians have visited this post, all of whom had revolvers in their possession. A large majority had two revolvers, and many of them three." Dodge considered Plains Indians to be "connoisseurs in these articles, and have the very best that their means or opportunities permit." Those opportunities were numerous. In addition to their annuities, Natives had nearly free access to traders who operated with little oversight near federal Indian agencies. Furthermore, Dodge believed that there were too many rogue agents who turned a blind eye to illegal arms sales in exchange for a cut of the profits. He understood the temptation, explaining that "for a revolver an Indian will give ten, even twenty times in value, in horses and mules; powder and lead are sold to them at almost the same rate, and as the bulk is small, large quantities can be transported at comparatively little expense." Barely a generation

before the beginning of the reservation era, Indian economic and political power, black-market trade, and the weakness of state authority in
the hinterlands were still facilitating indigenous resistance to empire.[36]

These superior weapons gave southern Plains Indians at least some
fighting chance throughout the war for Texas, despite being vastly outnumbered. Cooke County's W. H. Whaley was startled that in several
battles during the fall of 1866, it appeared that the Indian "raiders are as
well armed as we are, each man bearing from one to two six-shooters."
The following February a party of seventy or eighty Kickapoos ambushed
a Texas patrol in which they "opened with revolvers, [and] afterwards,
when in close quarters, used lances, and finally long range guns from a
mountain nearby." Similar reports of Indians bearing six-shooters proliferated during these years. Texas could not even cut off this flow of
weapons by controlling its own backyard. One Comanche chief reported
that his weaponry came from "a depot of trade, established with Kansas."[37]

The new mix of firearms made it difficult for Indian gunmen to acquire properly calibrated ammunition cartridges and slugs, but they
made do with the kinds of innovations that had long characterized Indian gun culture. Dodge marveled at the Indian practice of collecting
spent shells of proper caliber for their guns and then refilling them with
powder and lead, sometimes from other dismantled casings. "Indians say
that the shells thus reloaded are nearly as good as the original cartridges,"
Dodge wrote, "and that the shells are frequently reloaded forty or fifty
times." This practice freed Indian gunmen from reliance on the decisions of traders and federal agents over which ammunition to stock. At
the same time, one of the attractive features of six-shooter pistols was
that their calibers were more uniform across different models and manufacturers, thus making it easier to purchase cartridges for them.[38]

Like the Seminoles of Florida, who forced the United States into the
longest, most expensive Indian war in its history, southern Plains Indians were able to battle Anglo-American encroachment for a full fifty
years, from the 1820s through the 1870s, because of their success at obtaining firearms and ammunition. That achievement was part of a long
history in which they constantly adjusted their trading and diplomatic
partners and their enemies to direct the flow of arms in their favor. To
no small degree that cast of characters included the shifting array of
empires—Spanish, French, British, and American—that competed for

authority in the midcontinent. Yet the most dynamic, innovative actors of all were the Indian middlemen in the trade—Wichitas, Caddos, Pawnees, Cherokees, Shawnees, Delawares, Seminoles, Osages, and others—who took advantage of their position between the eastern arms markets of Euro-Americans and ascendant Comanches of the west, to carve out critical economic and political roles for themselves. Without their shrewdness, they likely would have been crushed by the Comanches or other equestrian powers, and white Americans would have dominated the southern Plains much sooner.

Indians did not lose the fight for the southern Plains to the United States because they lost an arms race. Their ingenious acquisition and application of guns, powder, and shot helped ensure that their warriors were more than a match for American soldiers right up to the last moment before the people's subjugation. Instead, they fell short in a numbers game. The population of Texas alone had climbed to 600,000 by 1860. Meanwhile the combination of recurrent outbreaks of epidemic disease and warfare with whites and indigenous people alike had sent the number of Indians into a freefall. The Wichitas plummeted from some 20,000 people in 1719 to no more than 3,700 in 1821. By 1896 they stood at just 365. The Comanches suffered an equally dramatic decline, with their population tumbling from a peak of some 40,000 people in the late 1770s to half that number in the 1830s then to 4,000 or 5,000 in 1870 before reaching the nadir of 1,500 in 1875. There was no way for Native people to continue their resistance under such circumstances, particularly not when their primary source of food, the bison, was also teetering on extinction amid the slaughter that accompanied white expansion onto the Plains and the discovery in 1871 that bison hides could be sold for use as belts for industrial machinery. Indian men could not feed their families in the absence of game. Nor could they defend their families when blue-coated soldiers and civilian rangers many times their number repeatedly tracked down Indian civilian camps and killed whomever they found there. The fact that southern Plains Indians like the Comanches and Kiowas fought against these odds for as long as they did is evidence that their arms were a means to mount a heroic defense of what was theirs, not a Trojan horse for their colonization.[39]

8. THE RISE AND FALL OF THE CENTAUR GUNMEN

The Blackfeet of the northern Plains and Rocky Mountain West had a way of drawing sharp characterizations from white outsiders. British and Canadian fur traders denounced them as "notorious thieves" and "among the greatest thieves now on the face of the earth" on account of their horse rustling from trade posts and neighboring tribes. Others concluded that the Blackfeet had "an infernal itching for telling lies" and that "no faith can be put in their words or promises," because the chiefs seemed to exercise so little control over the young men. The commander of the Hudson's Bay Company fort at Edmonton, infuriated by the Blackfeet playing his firm off against Americans far to the south on the Missouri River, denounced them as "d[amne]d fellows . . . not worth an hundredth part of the trouble we take with them."[1]

The Blackfeet fared no better in American opinion. Trader William Gordon dreaded the Blackfeet as "the most dangerous, warlike, and formidable [of the Indians]," because "they go in larger bodies than other Indians, and are well armed with guns, chiefly obtained from the British." These advantages made them "a terror to all the tribes . . . a wild, roving, restless people, committing murder, and stealing everything that falls in their way." U.S. Indian Agent Edwin Hatch went so far as to charge them with being "the most warlike and, heretofore, the most hostile tribe on the continent." It was telling that a Rocky Mountain pass at the edge of their territory went by the name of "Hell Gate" to warn travelers that supposedly demonic Blackfeet raiders lurked inside.[2]

The fear, loathing, and respect the Blackfeet evoked reflected that they were the major power of the northwestern Plains from the late eighteenth through the late nineteenth century, an achievement that depended on their forceful management of the evolving gun frontier. During the mid-1700s they offset the advantage of horses enjoyed by their western enemies, the Shoshones, by acquiring guns, powder, shot, and metal-edged weapons through Native middlemen, the Crees and Assiniboines, supplied by Hudson's Bay Company stations in the Canadian subarctic. Toward the end of the eighteenth century, the Blackfeet permitted the Hudson's Bay Company and North West Company to operate trade posts in their country as long as they limited their commerce to Blackfeet customers and offered free blacksmithing services and gifts of powder and shot. Whenever company men fell short of these expectations, the Blackfeet punished them by driving away other indigenous people from the forts and sometimes attacking the traders themselves. The Blackfeet were determined that the arms trade in their region was going to operate for their benefit or not at all.

This principle underlay the decades-long Blackfeet campaign to control the Rocky Mountain passes. The purposes of the Blackfeet blockade were to prevent gunrunners from supplying their enemies in the mountain valleys and plateaus west of the range, to keep those Indians from traveling east to the trade posts, and to protect the mountain beaver and Plains bison the Blackfeet depended on for furs to trade for guns and other manufactures. When white American mountain men began to appear in the Rockies in the early 1800s, trapping beaver themselves instead of trading for it from the Blackfeet, Blackfeet warriors ambushed and robbed them at every opportunity. Eventually these attacks became another source of Blackfeet wealth, as warriors often took furs and horses they had plundered from the mountain men to the Hudson's Bay Company and North West Company posts on the Saskatchewan River to trade for munitions.

By the early to mid-nineteenth century, Blackfeet management of the gun frontier had become inextricable from their politics, war, economy, and society, which is to say that they had developed a full-fledged political economy of firearms. Decades earlier Blackfeet expansion had been premised on their differential access to arms, but eventually the defense of their gains also demanded guns because so many of their rivals had acquired them too. The job of processing bison robes for trade belonged to women, and thus the Blackfeet had a new incentive to enter into polygamous marriages. Whereas a first or second wife typically came from within the group and held high status, additional wives often were captives from other tribes. Warriors needed guns to seize those captives and, for that matter, to protect Blackfeet women and children from falling into enemy hands. The Blackfeet also needed firearms to raid enemies for the horses they used in warfare, hunting, seasonal migrations, and the rounds of gifting that structured Blackfeet society. Alongside horses, guns had become deeply interwoven into the fabric of Blackfeet life.

Eventually the Blackfeet used products of the bison not only to feed, clothe, and house themselves but also to trade for European goods, including arms. The appearance of American fur traders in the early nineteenth century was a boon to the Blackfeet because the Americans, unlike their British counterparts, accepted payment in buffalo robes. The reason was that the Americans had a long, navigable river, the Missouri, down which they could float the heavy, bulky robes by keelboat to St. Louis, whereas the British had to transport furs by sled and canoe to distant Hudson Bay or Montreal. The appearance of the steamboat on the upper Missouri in the early 1830s made shipping even easier for the Americans, much to the advantage of the Blackfeet. The Blackfeet supply of manufactured goods no longer required them to make specialized hunts for lightweight furs such as beaver, wolf, and fox. The robe trade with the Americans meant they could fulfill their consumer needs by simple extension of their primary subsistence activity, the buffalo hunt. Trade with Americans was additionally appealing because these partners offered high-quality, low-cost munitions from an increasingly robust U.S. arms manufacturing sector. Seizing the opportunity, the Blackfeet permitted Americans to set up trade posts along the upper Missouri River and its tributaries, thus giving Blackfeet people the option of trading either with American firms or the Hudson's Bay Company on the Saskatchewan. They also continued to raid both their Indian enemies and occasional mountain men to stem the flow of guns to their rivals and to plunder furs and horses, which they then traded at the posts for guns. The terrified victims of these attacks often denounced the Blackfeet as lying, bloody, warlike savages, but there was a clear logic

251

to what they did, aimed at remaining the best-armed people commanding the region's best hunting grounds and grazing places.

The Blackfeet Ascendency

Like so many Indian groups who rose to power in the gun age, the Blackfeet were a coalition of neighboring peoples whose friendship gave them a stronger measure of security at home and an ability to project their strength outward. There were three core groups—the Siksikas (or Blackfoot proper), the Kainais (or Bloods), and the Piikanis (or Peigans/Piegans/Pikunis). Ranging between the Saskatchewan River on the north (in modern-day Alberta and Saskatchewan) and the Missouri River on the south (in contemporary Montana), Blackfeet peoples hunted the bison on foot until the advent of the horse in the mid- to late eighteenth century. They all spoke a variant of the Blackfeet language, one of the westernmost iterations of the broad Algonquian language family. At their height in the early 1830s the collective population of the core Blackfeet groups and their allies was perhaps 45,000 people. They were not in any sense a formal political confederacy. General nonaggression between the tribes (subject to occasional breakdowns) and between the various bands constituting the tribes was maintained by frequent councils, ceremonies, gift giving, trade, intermarriage, and communal hunts. Agreement on foreign policy sometimes emerged in the course of these interactions, but dissidents were free to go their own way. Mutual consultation and imperfect consensus, not central authority, were the bases of shared Blackfeet approaches to foreign tribes and traders.[3]

Blackfeet territory, among the most beautiful in North America by any measure, was a land of geographic contrasts. Most of it was vast, short-grass Plains, but not tabletop flat like much of the southern high Plains. Ancient glacial activity and river runs had created a landscape interspersed with pockets of rolling hills, surreal hoodoo-filled badlands, rimrocks, ravines, and wind-chiseled buttes. The eye-catching frame for the western portion of Blackfeet country was the towering, snow-topped peaks of the Rockies, while sister ranges like the Sweet Grass Hills, Bears Paw Mountains, and Bighorn Mountains, cropped up at intervals across the south. Though the setting was generally arid, several river systems originating in the Rockies trenched across the grasslands on their way to Lake Winnipeg or the Missouri-Mississippi drainage, attracting the flows of innumerable coulees and minor streams. River channels and mountain bases contained enough moisture and protection from the Plains' harsh winter winds to support stands of cypress, aspen, poplar, cottonwood, and birch. These were places of refuge and resources for humans and grazing animals alike, particularly during the coldest months of the year.[4]

Early signs of the colonial technologies that would transform Blackfeet life began to appear in the early to mid-eighteenth century. Indigenous trade networks took horses originating with the Spanish in the Rio Grande and transferred them up the Rocky Mountains until they had reached the northern Plains. Simultaneously European manufactured goods, including arms, arrived from the northeast and east, some from Hudson's Bay Company posts in the Canadian subarctic, others from the French on the Great Lakes. Eventually the horse would become a basis of Blackfeet strength, but before it reached them it fell into the hands of their enemies, the Shoshones (or Snakes), via the Comanches and Utes, giving the Shoshones a marked advantage in the competition for the eastern foothills of the Rockies.[5]

The best account of these times was told by an elderly Cree man named Saukamappee, aged about seventy-five or eighty years, to the Welsh-Canadian fur trader David Thompson during a visit by Thompson to the Blackfeet in 1787–1788. Saukamappee had married a Piikani woman in his youth and still resided with her people, giving him a long vantage on the history of the group. Thompson spoke Cree, so the two were able to talk freely during the long winter that Thompson lodged in the elder man's tent. Saukamappee recalled with trepidation that when he was young, "the Snake Indians and their allies had Misstutim (Big Dogs, that is Horses) on which they rode, swift as the Deer, on which they dashed at the Piegans, and with their stone Pukamoggan [or war hammers] knocked them on the head, and they [the Piikanis] had lost several of their best men. This news we did not well comprehend and it alarmed us, for we had no idea of Horses and could not make out what they were." The Shoshones used this advantage to take control of rich Plains hunting territory stretching from the North Platte River in the south to the Saskatchewan River in the north, thereby forcing the

Blackfeet to retreat east toward the Eagle Hills of modern Saskatchewan. The Shoshones might also have seized Blackfeet people as captives for eventual sale into Spanish slave markets in New Mexico, the southern terminus of the same chain that funneled horses up to the Shoshones.[6]

Saukamappee remembered with pride how the Blackfeet answered the Shoshones by acquiring firearms through Cree and Assiniboine middlemen. The Crees had been trading for munitions from the Hudson's Bay Company (HBC) ever since the late seventeenth century, when the firm opened York Factory at the mouth of the Hayes River in the Canadian subarctic. By 1700 the volume of this trade averaged about 400 guns a year. In the 1730s and 1740s, guns also arrived from the east through the Assiniboines' trade with the French on Lake Winnipeg and as far west as the confluence of the North and South Saskatchewan Rivers. Initially the Crees and Assiniboines used these weapons to raid people to their south and west, including the Blackfeet. In time, however, they also visited the Plains to exchange munitions and worn metal tools, at a steep markup, for Blackfeet beaver pelts and wolf furs, which they then sold to the posts for new European manufactures. Saukamappee's father had been one of these long-distance traders. The Crees' upper hand in this exchange was reflected in their use of the sobriquet "Slaves" to refer to the Blackfeet. Whereas the HBC charged the Crees fourteen beaver pelts or wolf skins for a single gun, the Cree price for the Blackfeet was fifty beaver. This commerce was so profitable that some Cree bands appear to have given up trapping beaver themselves. In this they occupied a middleman role between colonists to the east and equestrian Plains bison hunters to the west, much like their contemporaries, the Wichitas, at the eastern edge of the southern Plains.[7]

"Slaves" or not, the Blackfeet managed to use this arms trade and the Cree alliance to turn back the Shoshones. One imagines Saukamappee leaning forward excitedly as he recounted the first time the Blackfeet, Crees, and Assiniboines brought as many as ten muskets and thirty shots' worth of lead balls and powder into battle, back in the 1730s when he was youthful enough to join the fight. Facing a war party of Shoshones on foot at the opposite end of an open range, the allied forces adopted a line formation and stationed the gunners behind the bowmen, out of sight, with their muskets covered in leather cases. Once the Shoshones closed to within firing range in preparation for making a charge, the allied gunmen stepped to the fore, "and each of us [had] two balls in his mouth, and a load of powder in his left hand to reload." Then just as the Shoshones rose up from behind their shields to string their arrows, the musketeers unleashed a volley, killing and wounding several of the enemy, and filling the rest with "consternation and dismay." In their retreat the Shoshones acknowledged that their rivals had obtained a technological advantage just as formidable as the horse.[8]

The Blackfeet arms buildup, followed by their own acquisition of the horse, shifted the balance of power in the region to their favor. As Saukamappee put it: "The terror of that battle and of our guns has prevented any more general battles, and our wars have since been carried by ambuscade and surprise of small camps, in which we have greatly the advantage, from the guns, arrow shards of iron, long knives, flat bayonets and axes from the Traders. While we have these weapons, the Snake Indians have none, but what few they sometimes take from one of our small camps which they have destroyed, and they have no traders among them." This change in war tactics was not a swap of open-field battles for ambushes, but instead the abandonment of one old tactic in favor of another old one. Saukamappee clarified, "The mischief of war then, was as now, by attacking and destroying small camps of ten to thirty tents which are obliged to separate for hunting." The Blackfeet became even more deadly as they acquired horses from the Nez Perces, Flatheads, and Pend d'Oreilles (who had obtained some of them from the Shoshones) west of the Rockies, probably in exchange for the very manufactured goods supplied by the Crees and Assiniboines. By 1754, when the Blackfeet were visited by HBC employee Anthony Henday traveling in the company of some Crees and Assiniboines, they not only possessed horses but had become traders of them. Eighteen years later, HBC factor Matthew Cocking characterized them as the best equestrians he had ever seen.[9]

Combining guns and horses with the manpower of the Piikanis, Kainais, and Siksikas, transformed the Blackfeet into an expansionist force. Saukamappee's memory of this period was of the Blackfeet forcing the Shoshones southwest of the junction of the Red Deer River and the south branch of the Saskatchewan to retake control of the "fine Plains." They also drove the Kootenais and Flatheads from the bison hunting grounds back west into the mountains. A Flathead named Faro remembered of these times, "Our people were in continual fear of the

Blackfeet, who were already in possession of firearms, of which we knew nothing, save by their murderous effects. During our excursions for buffalo, we were frequently attacked by them, and many of our bravest warriors fell victims to the thunder and lightning they wielded." Within a matter of years the Piikanis dominated the Bow River (in present-day southern Alberta) south to the Rocky Mountain foothills, the Kainais controlled the Red Deer River Valley to the north of the Piikanis, and the Siksikas claimed the upper Battle River south of modern Edmonton.[10]

Furthermore, the ranks of their allies were growing. Not only did they continue to enjoy the trade and occasional military assistance of the Crees and Assiniboines, but they had established a fragile peace with the Sarcees, a small Athapaskan-speaking group of the North Saskatchewan, and the Gros Ventres, a tribe of Algonquian-speaking equestrians who had moved north onto the Saskatchewan plains by the mid-eighteenth century. The Blackfeet relationship with the Gros Ventres was particularly important because that nation possessed trade and kin connections to horse-rich Arapahos of the central and southern Plains, thereby giving the Blackfeet the means to replenish mounts lost to raiding or the harsh northern Plains winters. The Blackfeet now dominated the entire region east of the Rockies and north of the Yellowstone River.[11]

The Blackfeet ascendency, fueled by guns and horses brought to them by other Indians from faraway colonial sources, nearly burned out because of colonialism's most vicious long-distance curse: smallpox. The fateful day came in 1781 when a Blackfeet war party launched an attack on a suspiciously quiet Shoshone camp that, unknown to them, had already been devastated by the disease. Despite fearing a trap, the warriors rushed in and slashed through the Shoshones' tents, whereupon, according to Saukamappee, "our eyes were appalled with terror . . . there was no one to fight with but the dead and dying, each a mass of corruption." Though foreign epidemic diseases had been crisscrossing the Plains since the late seventeenth century, the Blackfeet had no previous knowledge of smallpox and could only surmise that "the Bad Spirit had made himself master of the camp and destroyed them." Little did they know that the Bad Spirit was angry at more than just the Shoshone camp. This outbreak had begun in Mexico City and then spread the length of co-

Blackfeet Indian on Horseback, by Karl Bodmer During the late eighteenth century the Blackfeet combined guns obtained from the East with horses obtained from the Southwest to become the dominant power of the northern Plains and Rocky Mountain West. They jealously guarded this position by attempting to force their indigenous rivals and gun merchants to stay apart. Courtesy Joslyn Art Museum, Omaha, Nebraska.

lonial and indigenous trade networks to afflict people throughout North America, ultimately as far away as Alaska and Hudson Bay.[12]

Sadly, the Blackfeet joined those ranks. Their warriors proceeded to loot the Shoshones' camp without any fear of contagion—"we had no belief that one Man could give it to another any more than a wounded Man could give his wound to another." Within two days of returning home, the pox was in their camp as well, careening "from one tent to another as if the Bad Spirit carried it." Many of the sick, burning with fever and covered with sores, leaped into a nearby river and drowned. Others, their skin breaking open, mattering, then breaking open again, lay gasping for breath with no one to bring them water and food, or to light the fire when it went out. Saukamappee's tent was comparatively lucky. When the disease lifted, "only" about a third of his family had perished, whereas "in some of the camps there were tents in which everyone had died." "Death came over us all," Saukamappee remembered, doubtlessly with a lump in his throat and his words cracking, "and swept away more than half of us by the smallpox, of which we knew nothing until it brought death among us." The smallpox scars left on his face were a daily reminder of those horrible times.[13]

With his people "low and dejected" and the air filled with the "tears, shrieks, and howlings," Saukamappee had feared "we shall never be again the same people," but that nightmare never materialized. For every Indian nation destroyed by epidemic disease, there was another that persisted, rebuilt its strength through natural growth or banding together with neighboring peoples, and reconstituted some semblance of normalcy. Some groups, including the Blackfeet, not only recovered but eventually reached unprecedented heights. They restored order to their spiritual and social lives by swearing off war, at least for the meantime. Some of them had made sense of this disaster by concluding that the Great Spirit allowed the Bad Spirit to smite them with smallpox as punishment for their being "fond of War" and "making the ground red with blood." Conveniently, this idea arose at a time when they could hardly afford to lose any more of their young men in battle. Yet the Shoshones would not let them wait in peace for their population to begin rising again. Two or three winters later, the Shoshones wiped out a Blackfeet hunting party along the Bow River, leaving as their mark "snakes' heads painted black on sticks they had set up." Predictably, the people began calling for revenge, but their elders channeled this rage toward a greater goal. They instructed the warriors that "the young [Shoshone] women must all be saved, and if any has a babe at the breast it must not be taken from her, nor hurt; all the Boys and Lads that have no weapons must not be killed, but brought to our camps, and be adopted amongst us, to be our people, and make us more numerous and stronger than we are."[14]

The incorporation of captive women and children would become a means for the Blackfeet to recover from the decimation of smallpox. By the time Thompson visited the Blackfeet in the late 1780s, their warriors would "carry on their predatory excursions to a distance scarcely credible in search of their enemies." Their raids struck the Shoshones, Kootenais, and Flatheads deep in the Rockies, the Crows south along the Yellowstone River, and, in one case in 1787, even a Spanish party based out of New Mexico. Guns gave them a significant advantage, as evident in a 1795 attack in which Kainais and Siksikas reportedly killed twenty-five Shoshones, who, the Blackfeet said, were "unacquainted with the productions of Europe, and strangers to those who convey them to this country." The HBC's Alexander Henry noticed the results during his visit to the Blackfeet in 1811. His understanding was that "about 20 years ago the Piegans amounted to only 150 tents, so much had smallpox reduced that once numerous tribe; but their numbers are now increasing fast."[15]

———

One of the most significant sources of this expansion was a vibrant gun trade by rival fur trade interests within Blackfeet country. Initially this competition pitted French traders based in Montreal against London's Hudson's Bay Company. During the 1730s and early 1740s, French explorer Pierre de La Vérendrye's search for "the Great Western Sea" not only took him and his sons as far west as the foothills of the Rockies and as far south as the Mandan towns of the Missouri River Valley in what is now North Dakota, but initiated a trade-post building campaign through Assiniboine country into the eastern edges of Blackfeet territory. French stations gradually spread west from Lake Superior to Rainy Lake, Lake of the Woods, and then Lake Winnipeg and Cedar Lake, until by the early 1750s there were three posts on the Saskatchewan River just east of the forks: Fort Paskoya (built in 1750), Fort La Jonquiere (1751), and Fort de la Corne (1753), all of which lasted until the fall of New France in 1759. Their purpose and effect was to intercept furs that otherwise would go to HBC posts to the north.[16]

The initial HBC response was to send Anthony Henday to convince the Blackfeet to take their trade directly to York Factory on Hudson Bay instead of relying on Cree middlemen. He might have been the first European who had ever visited them in person and the first of many to discover that they insisted on having trade on their terms. A Blackfeet chief explained that his people were unwilling to make such a journey across unfamiliar territory because York Factory "was far off, and they could not live without buffalo flesh" ("real food," they called it), which was unavailable in the Canadian subarctic; eating fish along the way was not an option because the Blackfeet considered it taboo. The Blackfeet were equally unwilling to abandon their horses and travel by canoe through the dense boreal forest between their country and Hudson Bay. No, if the HBC wanted their trade, its agents would have to come to them.[17]

Sure enough, by the late eighteenth century the Blackfeet had two firms with posts in their country vying for their business, the HBC and the Montreal-based North West Company (NWC). During the 1780s and 1790s these rivals opened shop at every strategic point along the North Saskatchewan River, often within a literal stone's throw of each other. The Blackfeet took advantage by dealing with both companies and making sure that each side knew it. By 1821 the competition between the two companies had become so financially and politically crippling that they decided to merge into a greater HBC. In the meantime, however, their contest translated into options and lower prices for the Blackfeet, particularly when it came to the arms trade.[18]

The search for competitive advantage also meant that the arms suppliers carefully tailored their guns to the Indian market. Like many other American Indians, the Blackfeet wanted light, durable, smoothbore muskets for which they could mold their own bullets for use with whatever type and quantity of powder was at hand, often for the purpose of employing the weapon as a shotgun. Trigger guards were wide enough to permit use with mittens during the frigid winters of the northern Plains. Decorative elements were also important. During this period the HBC and NWC made the serpent side plate a standard feature of their trade guns, which for the Blackfeet carried the same cosmological associations of the Horned Water Serpent as it did for their Algonquian-speaking cousins of the Atlantic coast. Both companies also stamped their barrels with the image of a sitting fox looking sideways, outlined by a tombstone shape or circle. This symbol first appeared on HBC trade guns (or Northwest guns) in the early eighteenth century as the mark of a particular inspector. The NWC then adopted the stamp as part of its policy to copy HBC guns as closely as possible, knowing that Indians had come to associate the stamp with a trade gun's quality. American firms followed suit in the nineteenth century. Yet the Blackfeet might also have wanted the stamp because of its social and cosmological symbolism. One of the leading Blackfeet warrior societies was known as the Kit Fox. The Blackfeet also associated the red fox with the sun, likening the color of its fur to fire. It would not be surprising, therefore, if

Fox-in-Circle Punchmark. The Fox-in-circle or Fox-in-tombstone mark was first used in Hudson's Bay Company guns. Indians' association of the mark with quality led other trade firms to include this feature on their trade guns as well. The Blackfeet might have liked this feature because they associated the fox, and guns, with the fire of the sun. Courtesy Museum of the Fur Trade.

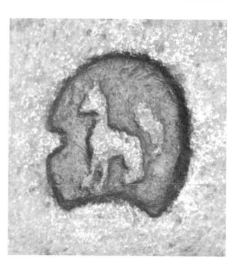

they also liked having the fox depicted on a weapon that belched fire. Regardless of the various reasons Indians wanted the fox stamp on their muskets, the point is they got it because they controlled economically valuable resources and traders had to compete for their business.[19]

The fur companies were more careful to document the number of furs obtained from the Blackfeet than the amount of guns, powder, and shot sold to them, but their records leave the clear impression of a brisk commerce. Thompson emphasized that the goods in greatest demand among the Blackfeet were "above all, guns and ammunition." William Tomison of Edmonton House agreed, telling his superiors that "guns, powder, tobacco, and hatchets" were "the only articles wanted during the winter." Camps of Indians typically bought up a trade post's entire (admittedly small) inventory of guns within a matter of weeks or even days, as in March 1787 when a group of Kainais purchased eighteen guns and four pistols from Manchester House in preparation for an expedition against the Shoshones. Though the trade factors complained endlessly that their supplies of munitions, particularly guns, fell far short of the demand, still they often managed handsome returns. For instance, on just one day in 1799 the Piikanis brought in 1,511 tradable beaver pelts to Edmonton House, while on March 2, 1800, a Siksika camp delivered a thousand wolf and small fox furs to the post. Tellingly, by 1806–1807 the HBC judged a trading season at Edmonton netting 1,700 beaver pelts to have been poor.[20]

Blackfeet economic leverage meant that they received free black-smithing, powder, and shot from the companies as part of a larger set of ritualized transactions and ceremonies that structured their trading relations. Small parties came and went from the posts throughout the year, but most commerce took place during semiannual visits by camps of several hundred people marked by proceedings that the company traders generally found to be "tedious and often troublesome . . . as the whole performance is slow and serious," much like "a parade." The pattern was for the Blackfeet to send a messenger to inform the post commander that the people were on the way and to request tobacco for every principal man so he could smoke and clear his head for political talk and commerce. On the day of arrival the women and children would wait outside the stockade while the men filed in according to their status. The commander would then greet them in a large, central building known as the Indian hall for communal smoking, rounds of toasts, speeches, and a discussion of prices. Blackfeet leaders would offer the chief factor a present of furs loaded upon a horse, explaining that they had come a long way and that he should "take pity" on them by providing generous gifts and keeping the cost of trade goods low. In return they might receive a keg of liquor and some more tobacco, while every man in attendance would get four or five lead balls, tobacco, liquor, and gunsmithing services. The principle was that beginning with such noncommercial transactions renewed the good feelings and friendship that permitted mutually beneficial trade in the first place.[21]

At this point in their history the Blackfeet sought out HBC and NWC guns more for warfare than for hunting. Fur trader Peter Fidler complained that while on the trail with a camp of Piikanis during the fall of 1792, his hosts pestered him daily with requests to borrow his gun so they could experiment with shooting bison from horseback. Eventually he decided just to sell it, "as it was of no use to me while they had it and I could not refuse lending it to them with any propriety." Yet most of the Piikanis and other Blackfeet ultimately concluded that the gun was inferior to the bow and arrow for hunting bison from horseback. First and foremost, it was heavy and difficult to handle while riding, particularly if one had to reload. Second, the noise of a premature shot could set a bison herd into stampede before other hunters were in position. Not least of all, whereas arrows had decorations identifying the shooter so he could claim the honor and prime cuts from the kill, bullets did not carry such marks. In a Blackfeet culture that emphasized the recognition of masculine achievements, this would have been a considerable sacrifice.[22]

The only time Fidler saw the Piikanis kill a bison with a gun was when they drove a number of the beasts into a corral. In that case the chief (whom Fidler called the "Pound Master") made the first kill with a musket shot, after which "the Young Men kill the rest with arrows, bayonets tied upon the end of a Pole, &c." Yet whereas a Blackfeet hunter did not need a gun, a warrior did. Thompson noticed that among the Blackfeet, "a war party reckons a chance of victory to depend more on the number of guns they have than on the number of men." Their enemies agreed, attributing Blackfeet prowess to their "great advantage in the use of firearms." Consequently, by the 1810s guns, powder horns, and shot pouches had become "necessary appendages to the full dress of a young [Blackfeet]" man.[23]

Hell Gate

The Blackfeet judged guns to be a key to the intertribal balance of power and therefore began applying their newfound strength to keep the traders and other tribes apart. Strikingly, the Crees were among the first groups they targeted. By the late eighteenth century the Blackfeet no longer needed the Crees as middlemen in the arms trade because of the spread of HBC and NWC posts. Rather, the Crees had become competitors of the Blackfeet for horses and hunting ranges. As the HBC and NWC bypassed the Crees to reach the Blackfeet, the Crees carved out a new economic niche in which they supplied the posts with provisions, especially buffalo meat. This role required the Cree to spend more time on the Plains as equestrian bison hunters instead of tacking back and forth between the Saskatchewan River and Hudson Bay by canoe. Violent competition with the Plains tribes for horses, hunting grounds, and grazing territory mounted in turn. The bloodshed included a summer 1793 attack in which a mixed Cree-Assiniboine force of more than a thousand men reportedly massacred 150 lodges of Gros Ventres. The Blackfeet sided with the Gros Ventres in this contest, both out of solidarity with an important supplier of horses and out of their own resentment toward Cree incursions.[24]

Part of their strategy was to cut off the Crees from the Saskatchewan trade posts and force the traders to cooperate. From late 1793 until late 1794, Siksika and Gros Ventre bands raided HBC and NWC posts along the lower Saskatchewan, peppering the walls with shot, running off horses, burning outbuildings, and capturing or killing the unfortunate few who happened to be caught outside at the time of these attacks. NWC man Duncan McGillivray understood that the attackers meant to avenge some Cree killings of their people carried out with guns obtained from the post. Piikani chief White Buffalo Robe, the primary Blackfeet liaison with the fur traders, managed to broker a peace, but tensions continued to flare. Clashes pitting the Blackfeet and Gros Ventres, on the one hand, against the Crees and Assiniboines, on the other, claimed hundreds of lives from the 1790s through the 1820s and turned the area immediately south of the North Saskatchewan River into a dangerous no-man's land. In 1808 the Crees tried to set up their own blockade to prevent the trading companies from restocking the posts because they "had determined . . . to keep the Slave [Blackfeet] Indians from receiving any supplies from us in arms and ammunition." The Blackfeet responded in kind, as in 1815 when they stationed ambushes all around Edmonton after the Crees killed one of their people nearby. Well into the 1830s the Blackfeet subjected HBC forts Pitt and Carlton on the North Saskatchewan to constant horse raiding and intimidation because they considered the Crees to be the traders' "most intimate allies and always betray an inclination to make us participate in vengeance intended for them," which was to say, to make the traders pay for murders the Crees committed with trade guns.[25]

Soon the Blackfeet effort to corner the gun market involved an arms blockade of Indians in the Rockies and the adjacent plateau, partially as an extension of the war with the Crees. The Crees' fallout with the Blackfeet led them to seek mounts among the horse-rich western nations, including the Kootenais, Flatheads, Pend d'Oreilles, Spokanes, and Salish. In return those tramontane people wanted munitions to protect themselves from Blackfeet attacks and end their status as "easy prey . . . killed or driven away like sheep." Working the Rockies during this period, trader Ross Cox found that "the great object of every Indian was to obtain a gun," because in their "continual wars" with Blackfeet gunmen "they were generally the greater sufferer." HBC and NWC traders were also eager to deal with these people because they were more dedicated to beaver trapping than the Blackfeet. The problem was that the Blackfeet stationed armed men along the mountain passes to intercept any gunrunners heading west and any western Indians trying to make it to the eastern posts, and rejected repeated offers of payment to ease the blockade.[26]

At first the western Indians tried to break the cordon by using the Crows of the Yellowstone River Valley as middlemen in an exchange of horses for arms from the Hidatsas, Mandans, and Arikaras of the upper Missouri River Valley, who acquired their munitions from a variety of Cree-Assiniboine, Spanish, American, and Canadian sources. In one such trade the NWC's Charles McKenzie witnessed the Crows obtain "two hundred guns, with one hundred rounds of ammunition for each, a hundred bushels of Indian corn, [and] a quantity of merchandise articles as kettles, axes, clothes, etc.," in return for 250 horses, buffalo robes, and leather clothing. Yet this commerce was too undependable to meet the tramontane Indians' needs. The real opportunity came in the early 1800s when Cree and Anglo-Canadian traders opened a northern detour around the Blackfeet "warlands," following a route from the North Saskatchewan River to Yellowhead Lake and the Athabasca River and ultimately to the Columbia River. Despite the danger, the company men refused to miss out on the potential material rewards. According to Cox, the Flatheads were willing to pay twenty beaver pelts for a gun, "and some idea of the profit may be formed, when I state the wholesale price of the gun is about one pound seven shillings, while the average value of twenty beaver skins is about twenty-five pounds!"[27]

As the distribution of guns began to even out because of breaches of the mountain passes, the Blackfeet doubled down on their strategy of containment. In the summer of 1810 a Piikani war party lost upward of sixteen men in an engagement with Flathead gunmen, a change of fortune the Flatheads punctuated by having one of their chiefs end the torture of a Blackfeet captive by shooting him dead with a musket ball. The Blackfeet reaction was furious. NWC trader Alexander Henry wrote from Rocky Mountain House "that all the relations of the deceased were crying in the Plains; that no Crees should go there in the future, to take them arms and ammunition; and that, to crown all, four camps of Piegans [Piikanis] were camped on the river at the first ridge of the mountains, one day's ride hence, to prevent supplies from going across." Blackfeet sources told the HBC's Edmonton House that they knew the NWC trader John MacDonald was preparing to attempt a mountain crossing and that they would "intercept him, or any white man, who might attempt to convey goods to the Flat Heads." As for what they would do next, they threatened "if they again meet with a white man going to supply their Enemies, they would not only plunder & kill him, but that they would make dry meat of his body." Nobody doubted their word.[28]

True to their promise, Piikanis keeping a "strict watch" blocked the NWC's Columbia Brigade from crossing the mountains in October 1810, though they did not fix dry meat. By 1813 the Blackfeet were also raiding the horse herds of the trading posts to punctuate their resolve. The Edmonton commander believed "that the Blood Indians and Blackfeet are determined to steal every Horse belonging to White Men, in revenge for the death of their Relations, fifty of whom have been killed by the Flatheads since last Summer. White Men, they say, by supplying the Flatheads with fire Arms, are the principal cause of their great Loss."[29]

Though the NWC's Rocky Mountain House probably did more business with the Blackfeet than any other British or Canadian post, from this point on it always remained on high alert because of these tensions. Indeed, in 1807 it took every last effort of chief White Buffalo Robe to prevent Gros Ventre and Blackfeet warriors from destroying the site after they discovered that some of its men had managed to deliver guns to the Pend d'Oreilles. Thereafter, company men would allow visiting Blackfeet to enter into the interior of the fort only a few at a time, requiring them to pass through several heavy sliding doors that then closed behind them before they entered the company store. Once inside, the company factor handled the trade through a grated window only a yard square in size. The ceiling above contained loop holes through which company guards watching from upstairs could fire down on Blackfeet customers in the event of trouble. Extra thick walls prevented Blackfeet in the store area from communicating the contents to their tribesmen outside. No other party could come in until the previous one had left. These precautions reflected hard experience that "the wily Blackfeet seize every opportunity to overpower the garrison."[30]

The Blackfeet stemmed and redirected the flow of arms, but they did not have enough resources to wall off the Rockies, given the determination of the gunrunners and the tramontane Indians to reach each other. The number of traders operating west of Blackfeet country began to mount after the NWC's establishment of Kootenai House in 1807, followed two years later by Kullyspell House on Lake Pend d'Oreille and Saleesh House in Flathead country, and then by an influx of itinerant traders from the NWC, HBC, and American firms. This "opportunity of purchasing arms and ammunition" left the region's Indians "overjoyed," according to Ross Cox, because "from this moment affairs took a decided change in their favor; and in subsequent contests the number of killed, wounded, and prisoners were more equal."[31]

One reason was that they became better shots than the Blackfeet by hunting small antelope from as far away as a hundred and twenty yards. Another was that although the various western tribes "generally tent apart," they would "form one against the common enemies of their country, namely the Piegans [Piikanis] and Blackfeet [Siksikas]." In other words, it was not just the guns that gave them strength, but, as with the Blackfeet, political cooperation across tribal lines. To the extent that the Blackfeet saw an upside to these developments, it was that the growing number of western Indians hunting in their territory also increased the chances to plunder their horses. Young Blackfeet men leaped at the opportunity, but overall this was weak compensation for the mounting number of Blackfeet who lost their lives to enemy gunfire each and every year.[32]

The Blackfeet effort to control the mountain passes became even more challenging as Americans began to appear in the northern Rockies intent on trapping beaver themselves rather than trading with Indians for it. St. Louis's Manuel Lisa, of Spanish birth, was the trailblazer of this activity beginning in 1806, when he established a base, Fort Raymond, at the junction of the Yellowstone and Big Horn Rivers, just south of the Piikani range. His expectation was that his own men could harvest more beaver pelts than part-time Blackfeet trappers, while freeing his operation from the innumerable diplomatic challenges of dealing with Indians. When early returns seemed to prove him right,

Lisa formed the Missouri Fur Company (MFC) with several other St. Louis merchants, including future fur trade magnates Jean Pierre Chouteau and his son Auguste Pierre. Their capital sponsored several additional expeditions, only to have the enterprise wrecked by Blackfeet attacks on the trappers and their posts. In 1808 Piikani, Kainai, and Gros Ventre warriors were said to have killed and plundered two parties of Americans on the southern branch of the Missouri River, leaving only a handful of survivors. Two years later the Blackfeet chastised the MFC again, particularly in April 1810 when in three separate incidents they killed twenty to thirty members of one of its outfits. Unable to sustain these losses, Lisa's company dissolved and organized attempts to send trappers into the Rockies abated until the 1820s.[33]

Blackfeet attacks have too often been attributed to a general hostility toward Americans stemming from the deaths of three Gros Ventres and/or Piikanis at the hands of the Lewis and Clark expedition in 1806 (after one of the Indians tried to steal a gun), but likelier explanations can be found by examining Blackfeet actions through the lens of the gun frontier. For one thing, the trappers were harvesting resources that the Blackfeet, especially the Piikanis, used to purchase munitions—the Piikanis annually traded some 800 pelts total to the HBC and NWC posts at Edmonton—and were doing so without paying for the right. Worse still, the trappers typically had Indians in their company recruited from the ranks of Blackfeet enemies, including the Crows, Flatheads, and Pend d'Oreilles. What the trappers got out of the deal were guides and protection. The tramontane Indians profited by using the trappers as armed escorts while they, too, harvested beaver pelts for the purchase of arms and ammunition. The Blackfeet had every reason to want to end this activity. Attacking the trespassers netted Blackfeet raiders ample amounts of plunder in the form of furs, horses, weapons, and other supplies, much of which they then ferried to HBC and NWC posts to trade. In October 1808, for example, a party of Kainais showed up at Edmonton House with 300 beaver pelts and a rifle captured from the Americans. The men then returned home with a full stock of trade goods and stories of achievements their communities would honor.[34]

Nothing had changed in the Blackfeet position when foreign trappers (including a sizable number of Iroquois) began to appear in the Rockies again in the 1820s and 1830s in the employ of several St. Louis firms like the Rocky Mountain Fur Company, a reorganized Missouri Fur Company, and the American Fur Company (AFC). This time, however, the business had adapted to the Blackfeet threat. A new system, the rendezvous, would spare the trappers the peril of traversing between the mountains and trade posts. They would gather annually at predetermined campsites within beaver country (such as the Green River of Wyoming) to unload their catches, resupply with goods sent by the companies along a safer southern route, and engage in commerce and entertainment with Indian allies. They then stayed in the mountains for another year or more. Though the rendezvous system is often viewed nostalgically as a time when rough-and-tumble white entrepreneurialism and Indian life were complementary, it was very much a product of the Blackfeet's violent insistence that they should be the ones to profit as long as outsiders insisted on hunting beaver in their country.[35]

With this the Rockies became the site of a ruthless contest of men hunting beaver to near extinction and of men hunting other men. HBC expeditions arrived on the heels of the Americans, charged with exhausting the region's beaver supply as quickly as possible to delay U.S. expansion into the broadly defined Oregon territory contested by Washington and London. Not far behind were Blackfeet war parties, often numbering in the hundreds, who emerged out of the steep-sloped, thickly forested hills of the stream beds to lay ambush to the trappers. For the period 1820 to 1831, conservative estimates put the loss of American life at fifteen to twenty men a year and the value of lost property at $100,000. Adding HBC losses to these calculations might raise them by a fifth to a quarter, for its men were also "tormented" by the Blackfeet, who seemed to be "everywhere." Trapping in Blackfeet country was, according to the HBC's George Simpson, "perhaps the most dangerous service connected with the Indian trade."[36]

Warren Angus Ferris, a keen young adventurer from Glens Falls, New York, captured the anxiety of trapping under the constant threat of Blackfeet gunmen in his colorful account of six years working for the AFC during the late 1820s and early 1830s. On any given day AFC men out checking their traps disappeared without a trace, while others turned up dead, "having been shot in the thigh and neck and twice stabbed." Larger attacks were rare, but they were still an ever-present danger. In October 1831, for instance, the trappers' river-bottom camp came under assault by an estimated 133 Blackfeet, who, "finding they could not dislodge us, they fired upon and killed our restless horses, who were fastened a few paces from us." A year later, history seemed to repeat itself. Ferris's party was working a quiet stream bed enclosed by steep, forested hills when "suddenly the lightning and thunder of at least twenty fusils [muskets] burst upon our astonished senses from the gully, and awoke us to a startling consciousness of imminent danger, magnified beyond conception, by the almost magical appearance of more than one hundred warriors . . . both before and on either side of us, at the terrifying distance of thirty steps." Two trappers fell to Blackfeet fire as the rest of the men scattered. The ambush was the Blackfeet way of saying that they were determined to control the beaver supply as long as it could be used to purchase guns, and to keep foreign trappers from carrying munitions to their rivals.[37]

Blackfeet attacks on trapping parties earned them plunder in beaver and weaponry, which contributed to the strength of the arsenals that made their strikes so effective in the first place. Looted trade beaver might have constituted the majority of the Blackfeet catch during the 1820s and 1830s. For instance, an 1823 Kainai raid against MFC trappers near Pryor's Fork of the Yellowstone netted them as much as $16,000 worth of beaver pelts, plus fifty horses and twenty-eight mules. The following trading season, Kainai fur packs contained stamps reading "W.G.C.K.R.I.J.M," which HBC authorities knew to be the initials of Missouri traders. "There is no end to their stories about the Americans," the officer of Edmonton House wrote of the Blackfeet in December 1833. "They told us of a war party having taken some beavers from a few American trappers and having made the owners run for their lives." These beaver pelts then went toward the purchase of weapons for future raids, many of which produced plunder in guns and ammunition. One Kainai party showed up at Edmonton boasting of a victory over the Americans and sporting trophies "such as rifles, the first volume of the Arabian Knights, [and] Lewis and Clark's travels in two volumes." Elsewhere, at the site of a Blackfeet ambush of AFC trappers, Ferris discovered that the raiders had removed the lock and mountings from two heavy guns, wanting the hardware but not the stocks.[38]

In the 1830s a combination of Blackfeet raids and overtrapping brought an end to the rendezvous system, only to be replaced by permanent American trade posts along the Missouri River from central Montana to the present-day border with North Dakota, which provided the Blackfeet with seemingly all the munitions they could desire. The Blackfeet had always insisted that their hostility was limited to outsiders harvesting their beaver and arming their enemies. As U.S. Indian sub-agent John F. A. Sanford explained, Blackfeet chiefs had told him, " 'If you send traders in our country, we will protect them, treat them well; but for your trappers, never.' " The AFC, founded by John Jacob Astor and later absorbed and directed by Pierre Chouteau, decided to test this pledge. In 1828 it built a post named Fort Union at the confluence of the Missouri and Yellowstone, right in the heart of Crow country. It then hired a veteran HBC man, named Jacob Berger, who knew the Blackfeet language, to broker a peace conference at which Piikani spokesmen reiterated that they welcomed trade but not trespass. The result was the 1831 construction of Fort Piegan on the Marias River in the southern portion of Piikani territory. After its abandonment in 1832, it was followed in 1833 by Fort MacKenzie on the Missouri River near the mouth of the Marias, and by Fort Cass on the Yellowstone River near the mouth of the Bighorn. With this, the Blackfeet gained the benefit of another series of trading posts in a new part of their country. More importantly, they also gained a commercial outlet for buffalo robes, because the AFC, unlike the HBC, could profitably ship these heavy loads by keelboat and, eventually, steamboat downriver to its warehouses in St. Louis. It also offered attractive prices, with a single robe fetching sixty loads of ball and powder. The result was a frenzy of fur trading. In its first ten days of business, Fort Piegan brought in 2,400 beaver pelts, and in 1832 the AFC operations on the upper Missouri netted 25,000 beaver pelts and 40,000 to 50,000 buffalo robes. Between 1833 and 1843, the AFC traded for an estimated 70,000 robes annually. And in exchange the company armed the Blackfeet as never before.[39]

The Blackfeet, especially the Piikanis, reveled in regaining the upper hand in the intertribal arms race. In December 1831, during a military standoff with the Pend d'Oreilles on the Jefferson River, one of the Blackfeet party boasted that "the white chief [the AFC's Kenneth Mc-Kenzie] had built a trading house at the mouth of the Marias; and had already supplied the Blackfeet with one hundred and sixty guns and plenty of ammunition," with which they would "commence a general war of extermination of all the whites [trappers], Flatheads, and others in this part of the country." A few years later, in 1835, the Blackfeet sent the Flatheads a pictograph communicating a similar message. A Flathead chief took it to mean that the American forts were supplying the Blackfeet with all their needs, and that "if, therefore, you consult your own interests and safety, you will not venture on our hunting grounds, but keep out of our vicinity."[40]

It was sound advice. During the 1830s the AFC's annual inventory of Indian trade goods included some 2,000 guns, including 1,200 to 1,500 smoothbore, flintlocks known as "Northwest guns," and 300 to 600 rifles, commissioned from a variety of American and British manufacturers. It also stocked 30,000 to 45,000 pounds of gunpowder, purchased largely from the DuPont family's operations in Delaware's Brandywine River Valley. It shipped more than 5,000 guns to the upper Missouri posts between 1834 and 1839, and equivalent amounts of ammunition. The profits for the company were enormous, with guns purchased for $7.50 in St. Louis selling for $25.00 in Blackfeet country and powder costing thirty cents a pound in St. Louis selling for $1.50 a pound upriver. Yet the Blackfeet do not appear to have considered this price gouging. Buying arms and ammunition with buffalo robes seemed to them an opportunity to expand their range and better protect their people, hunting grounds, and horse herds.[41]

———

Another benefit was that American competition increased Blackfeet economic and political leverage with the HBC. Blackfeet bands had always thought of themselves as "entitled to be treated and rewarded for having visited us with empty hand as well as if they had filled our stores with beaver skins," but the American option forced the HBC to fulfill those expectations as never before. The Blackfeet made sure that the company knew the costs of ignoring their wishes. "They talk much of the Americans," Edmonton's officer complained, "and have the face to tell us that they lose a great deal by coming here." One such case included a Kainai showing up "decorated in [an] American chief's Scarlet coat of no inferior quality and large green Blanket, Powder horn, and Blue bead wrought Shot Bag, thrown over his shoulder. The Indian told us that he gave four large Beaver for the coat and three for the latter. He left us to judge the price of them had they been disposed of by our-selves." Under such circumstances the HBC had little choice but to be generous with its presents and keep the price of its goods as low as possible, otherwise the Blackfeet would take their trade to the Missouri. An investigation by the HBC's Select Committee into company prac-tices found that Indians "never" had to trade for gunpowder at company posts, receiving it "gratuitously if they require it." The same went for gun repairs. The Company even maintained a barrel stamp on its muskets reading "London" after shifting to manufacturing firms in Birmingham, because it worried that the Blackfeet would not like any change.[42]

It was something of a stroke of luck for both the company and the Blackfeet that the HBC demand for pemmican—a Plains Indian con-coction of dried, pounded buffalo meat, melted fat, and dried fruit—was on the rise at the very moment that Americans on the Missouri began trading for bison robes, thereby giving the Blackfeet another market in which they could purchase arms with bison products. As the HBC ex-tended its operations northwestward beyond the Saskatchewan, deep into the Athabasca, Peace, and Mackenzie River drainages, it faced the challenge of feeding its traders in areas where large game animals were scarce and agriculture was impossible. Its answer was to trade with the Plains tribes for pemmican, which packed up to 3,500 calories a pound and kept even under extreme fluctuations in temperature, making it ideal for long transport into harsh subarctic conditions. By 1840 the volume of this trade had reached 91,000 pounds and by 1860 it had climbed to 202,680 pounds. The Blackfeet were among the HBC's main suppliers, thereby allowing them to maintain a northern source for arms and other manufactured goods even at a time when their commercial orbit had shifted south.[43]

Despite the Americans' trade advantages, they also had to meet the demands of their Blackfeet customers for free ammunition and guns manufactured to their specifications, or risk them returning to the HBC fold. James Kipp, the head of Fort MacKenzie, complained that during a visit by the Piikanis, "I was compelled to clothe fourteen chiefs besides all the liquor, tobacco, and ammunition which I presented them . . . I tried to impress upon them that they could not expect to continue to get things for nothing." Yet the expectation remained and the Blackfeet continued to have it met. At least one Blackfeet leader, the Piikani Ninoch-Kiaiu ("Chief of the Bears"), managed to wrest a gift of a fine suit of clothes and a double-barreled shotgun as gifts from Fort Mac-Kenzie as a reward for supposedly having never traded with the HBC.[44]

The Blackfeet also got what they wanted from the Americans in terms of the design of their firearms. The AFC had its agents contract with the same Northwest gun manufactures in Birmingham used by the HBC, emphasizing, "We want precisely the same gun as that company uses in their trade with the North American Indians." The AFC also wanted the barrels of these guns to carry a bright, clear blue finish, for "although the color of the barrels is not in reality essential in the use of guns, yet it pleases the Indians," perhaps because the color evoked the watery lair of the Horned Serpent depicted on the side plate of Indian trade guns. Rifles, as opposed to smoothbores, generally came from American manufacturers like Boulton Gun Works in Nazareth, Pennsylvania, Martin Smith of Greenfield, Massachusetts, and a variety of small workshops in Lancaster, Pennsylvania, and, later, St. Louis. The company, doubtlessly reflecting the will of its indigenous customers, de-manded that each rifle be accompanied by a ball mold fit to the gun's caliber, so that the Native buyer could cast his own bullets. Gun locks were to be constructed of uniform parts "so that a screw, a spring, or any other part of one lock may be used advantageously and without al-teration in the repairing [of] another." Stocks were to be carved from a single piece of wood, not two pieces combined, because otherwise "our Indians consider them not *new,* but old arms patched up, and in nu-merous instances, have returned them to our traders, accusing them of having practiced an imposition." Company inspectors rigorously tested commissioned guns for strength, wear, and accuracy, emphasizing, "Guns are so important an article" that "we spare no pains to provide them [the Indians] with the best we can procure." Yet Indians would not pay more than three or four robes for a gun, which put pressure on the AFC and its arms suppliers to maintain this quality at low cost. If it failed to meet these demands, the Blackfeet could simply take their busi-ness elsewhere, as the Piikanis did in March 1840, when they suddenly moved north and indicated that "for at least the season [they] will give all their furs to the Hudson's Bay Company." American traders were never under any misconception that the Blackfeet lacked options.[45]

F. W. Flight Flintlock, North-West Burnett, 1845 Trade Gun. Plains Indians often shortened the barrels of flintlock muskets to make them easier to handle on horseback. This one features that modification as well as a repair using rawhide to keep the barrel fastened to the stock. Native men across the continent learned to make such fixes themselves to keep their guns serviceable. Collection of Glenbow Museum, Calgary, Canada, AX 263.

The rich supply of weapons from Canada and the United States enabled the Blackfeet to incorporate firearms into the full range of the hunting, warfare, male honors, and material culture that defined their society. U.S. agent to the Blackfeet, Edwin Hatch, was struck that he rarely saw a Blackfeet man "out of his lodge without the gun in his hand and bow and quiver on his back." Oftentimes this gun had been modified, as "the Blackfeet commonly file off a piece of the barrel, leaving it but a little longer than a horse pistol," so it was easier to handle while riding and in close combat. Observers disagreed as to whether these sawed-off shotguns had become the weapon of choice for hunting, clearly indicating some variety in practice, perhaps having something to do with the age of the hunters. U.S. Colonel Richard Henry Dodge contended that a young Indian man on the Plains rarely had the opportunity to own a gun until he obtained the means to buy or capture one. It was almost "a rule, therefore, [that] the Indian warrior does not arrive at firearms before the average age of twenty-five; and though he sometimes becomes very expert with the new weapon, he is never as thoroughly at home with it as with his first love, the bow."[46]

This desire of young men to acquire their first guns contributed to making the capture of a musket or rifle from an enemy the highest of war honors among the Blackfeet, the only Plains group among whom this was the case. The very Blackfeet name for war honor, *namachkani,*

Blackfeet Image of Capturing an Enemy Gun. The Blackfeet warrior Wolf Carrier painted this image of himself capturing an enemy musket on a buffalo robe depicting a number of his wartime exploits. This deed represented the most prestigious Blackfeet war honor. Courtesy Royal Ontario Museum, Toronto.

means literally "a gun taken." Glorifying the plunder of guns reflected the importance of these weapons to the capture and protection of horses, women, and children, and the expansion and defense of the people's hunting grounds, which is to say, the issues at the heart of Blackfeet and Plains Indian economy and society. This esteem encouraged warriors to raid the horse-poor, gun-rich Crees, against whom the Blackfeet struggled for control over the Saskatchewan hunting grounds and access to its trade posts. Whereas war parties went south against the Crows when they wanted horses, they knew that battling the Crees would involve more hand-to-hand fighting and thus opportunities to capture enemy arms. Raiding for guns was a way to attribute credit to individual bravery and performance, something that became compromised during a period in which many enemies died from the wounds of anonymously fired bullets instead of arrows containing marks identifying the bowman. Only a man who captured an enemy gun could wear a shirt trimmed with enemy scalps. The shirt, in turn, might be painted to represent this exploit.[47]

Men depicted their feats on other canvasses too, including teepees, wearing robes, cliff faces, and even horses, capturing the often chaotic violence of gun battles in scenes with bullets flying in all directions while mounted warriors bear down on camps of teepees and enter into hand-to-hand combat with the enemy. Adopting a new personal name like "One Gun," "Many Guns," or "Night Gun" was another way for a man to call attention to his martial achievements. With young Blackfeet men typically going to war three times a year, and married men twice a year, there were many opportunities over the course of a lifetime to achieve the honor of capturing an enemy's firearm. But everyone knew it took a special kind of bravery to seize the chance.[48]

Warriors and hunters were not the only ones who participated in Blackfeet gun culture. The high likelihood of suffering a gun wound during this era gave rise to doctors who specialized in treating such injuries. During James Southesk's travels along the Saskatchewan and in the Rockies for the HBC in 1859–1860, he heard of two cases in which cures of serious gunshot wounds "were affected by the application of certain herbs known only to the medicine men . . . consisting of women as well as men." Such medical expertise probably accounts for how one veteran warrior, Big Nose, managed to absorb six gunshots over the course of thirty-six fights and live to tell the tale. The painted shirts and teepees that illustrated warrior exploits were the products of women's leatherwork, sewing, and beading, not only of men's brushstrokes. Women also fashioned the gun bags and shot pouches in which

Blackfeet Rifle Bag. Though Native women rarely handled firearms, they had their own part to play in the material culture of these revolutionary weapons, such as fashioning rifle bags like the one pictured here. Courtesy Buffalo Bill Center of the West, Cody, Wyoming, U.S.A.; Gift of Mrs. Hope Williams Read, NA.102.4.

men carried their arms and ammunition. Just as Blackfeet women processed the bison robes and cooked the meat their men brought back from the hunt, or tended to the horses and captives their men captured in raids, or profited as well as suffered from the exploits of Native gunmen, they were creative participants in their people's culture of guns.[49]

Hell

The very forces that allowed the Blackfeet to reach the peak of their power in the 1830s also carried some of the seeds of their downfall. The trade posts, particularly the American ones, were more than just sources of arms, ammunition, and other coveted manufactured goods. As links to a U.S. population numbering in the millions of people and to commercial networks stretching across the globe, they were also vectors for merciless epidemic diseases to enter Blackfeet society. They served as markets for more than just Blackfeet bison robes, but the robes of any indigenous nation, thereby contributing to the murderous competition for hunting territory and overkill of a bison population that once seemed inexhaustible. Perhaps worst of all, the forts, as the only stable American presence in Indian country, doubled as advance stations for the expansion of U.S. society, attracting a succession of American trappers, migrants, miners, ranchers, railroad workers, bureaucrats, soldiers, and storekeepers, until the Blackfeet found themselves a minority in their own territory. Amid all this the Blackfeet remained well armed, even better armed sometimes than American troops and civilians, but the forces arrayed against them were too formidable for even the surest shot to combat.[50]

Wave after wave of epidemic disease exposed new generations to horrors known only through the stories of elders. Measles and whooping cough struck in quick succession in 1818–1819, carrying off a reported third of those afflicted. According to one HBC man, "It is impossible to describe, or for any person (except those who were eye witnesses) to form any idea of the state of wretchedness [to] which these diseases reduced all the unfortunate natives." Wretchedness of this sort became all too common in step with the intensifying American presence along the Missouri. The most horrific outbreak came in 1837, when smallpox introduced by a ship that had docked at Fort Union whipsawed through the northern Plains, leaving places once teeming with people "literally depopulated" and resembling "one great graveyard." AFC officials estimated that this pestilence carried off four-fifths of the Arikaras and three-quarters of the Gros Ventres. Only thirty-one or so Mandans survived out of a population that once numbered in the thousands.[51]

Higher up the river, the Blackfeet also wallowed in misery. One band of a thousand tents was said to be completely wiped out. Other accounts put Blackfeet losses at 80 percent and claimed that "the Piegans, Blackfeet are reduced to less than four hundred lodges!!" The fallout was still evident even after years of population recovery. Whereas in 1834 U.S. officials had put the Blackfeet (Siksika, Kainai, and Piikani) population at 45,000 (consisting of just 9,000 men and 36,000 women and children), tallies from the 1850s ran between just 9,000 and 13,000. Even allowing for some error in counting, the smallpox of 1838 was a wrenching blow.[52]

One might imagine that such heavy losses would discourage warfare, as had happened back in the 1780s, but such was not the case. Tribes that escaped the disease or suffered the least saw an opportunity to seize horses, captives, war honors, and hunting territory at the expense of depopulated ones. Weakened tribes sought to replenish their numbers by raiding for captives, while young men sought to rise and fill the leadership vacuum by proving themselves in battle. To try to sit out this contest was to become a sitting duck.

Blackfeet country, particularly the area between the Missouri River and the headwaters of the Yellowstone, became a churning war zone contested by the Blackfeet, Crows, Shoshones, Flatheads, Kootenais, and Coeur d'Alenes. Trader Edward Thompson Denig estimated that in a given year, fighting between the Blackfeet and Crows claimed a hundred human lives on each side and the theft of several hundred horses. The cruel irony for the Blackfeet was that the Crows made up for the loss of horses by trading arms and blankets for mounts to the Flathead and Nez Perces, who also did battle with the Blackfeet. One particularly devastating Crow attack in 1846 nearly wiped out the Small Robes band of the Piikanis that had dominated the tribe's beaver trade since the late eighteenth century, killing all the men of forty-five lodges and capturing 150 women and children. The Crows also put Fort MacKenzie under assault in the wake of the 1838 smallpox, based on the rationale that "the Blackfeet were their enemies and that fort supplied them in

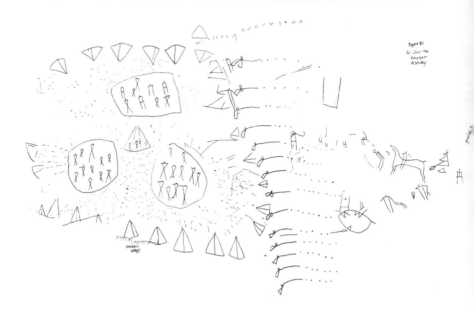

Blackfeet Petroglyph. This Blackfeet rock carving, from Writing-on-Stone Provincial Park in the badlands of southern Alberta, captures a chaotic gun battle with Crees in the mid-nineteenth century. The circles with men inside represent gun pits, the triangles represent tipis, and the dots represent bullets flying this way and that. Courtesy Alberta Parks.

guns, ammunition, knives, and other implements of war." It took the expansion of the Lakotas in the 1850s and 1860s to divert Crow attention away from the Blackfeet before a peace could finally be reached in 1864. Yet Blackfeet hostilities with the Crees and Assiniboines to the northeast and the tramontane Indians to the west raged on unabated.[53]

Little did the Blackfeet know at this point that their primary threat was the expansion of the United States. The Americans' overland migration to Oregon Territory had passed well south of Blackfeet territory, and American expansion up the Missouri had yet to reach Blackfeet territory in appreciable volume. By the mid–1850s the Blackfeet certainly were aware of growing hostilities to the east between the Lakotas and encroaching Americans, and of the wars in the Pacific Northwest in which white forces brutally suppressed Indians in arms. Such knowledge led chiefs like Little Dog and Seen-from-Afar to counsel

peace with the newcomers. A line of American forts had extended up the Missouri to its sources, just east of the Rockies, anchored by Fort Benton near the confluence of the Teton and Missouri Rivers, but these places had not yet become the wedge for an influx of newcomers. From today's perspective it should have been an ominous sign when Benton hosted a treaty conference in 1855 in which the Blackfeet conceded to American settlement and travel in Montana, agreed to a reservation, and promised to keep the peace with other tribes. Yet there were still so few whites in the region that the Blackfeet had little reason to believe they were giving up much or that the Americans could enforce the terms.[54]

In any case, the Blackfeet seemed to be getting value out of the deal in the form of annuities. The treaty obligated the federal government to deliver the Blackfeet goods worth $20,000 each year for twenty years. Soon it was clear just what that meant in practical terms, as the 1856 annuity goods included 1,007 pounds of gunpowder, 1,715 pounds of shot, and twenty-seven cases of guns, probably containing ten or twenty guns each. Two years later the Piikanis alone received 108 Northwest guns, 1,300 flints, sixteen kegs of gunpowder, twenty-nine bags of bullets, and seven dozen powder horns. Furthermore, the U.S. government was making every effort to deliver these goods to the heart of Blackfeet territory, thereby reducing the people's need to travel to faraway posts to collect their due. These developments coincided with the arrival of Colt revolvers on the Blackfeet market, with some gun-runners favoring chiefs "friendly with the whites," such as Little Dog, with the first pick of these weapons. "Their eyes sparked with pleasure," trader William T. Hamilton wrote of the Blackfeet after he first offered them these pistols in 1858, and "the young warriors' hearts bound[ed] with delight." By the 1860s, revolvers and breechloading repeating rifles had become part of the Blackfeet annuity. With so many arms flowing into Blackfeet country, the Blackfeet could have been excused if they believed a new era of dominance by their warriors was about to dawn, not despite but because of the American presence.[55]

Any such hopes came crashing down in a heap during the 1860s and early 1870s, particularly after white Americans discovered gold in Montana in 1862 at Grasshopper Creek, within hunting grounds of the Blackfeet and Gros Ventres. Though the United States was in the midst of the Civil War, which required the military service of more than two million men, the opportunity to strike it rich lured a motley crew of thousands of fortune seekers, outlaws, and transients, and, along with them, a culture of alcohol-fueled violence. Worse yet, they were accompanied by massive herds of horses and cattle, which competed with Indian mounts and bison for grazing range and enticed Native raiders as targets. Horse raiding and murders between the Blackfeet and Americans mounted with every passing year until it was impossible to differentiate between friend and foe. Compounding this chaos, an outbreak of disease reported variously as scarlet fever or measles struck the Blackfeet in the winter and spring of 1865, killing 280 Piikanis and, the Indians reported, 1,500 Siksikas and Kainais. It was indicative of the deteriorating state of affairs that some Blackfeet charged the whites with causing the disease by poisoning their annuity goods. It also speaks volumes of the Blackfeet need for such merchandise that Piikani representatives still showed up at Fort Benton in 1866 to collect their annuities and meet with U.S. agents, only to come under fire by a party of white residents and suffer one man killed and scalped and another wounded.[56]

The year 1870 was the worst of a terrible era, as once-distant forces of colonialism gathered into a raging storm that tore the people apart. Smallpox struck in the winter of 1869–1870, killing an estimated 1,400 Blackfeet, or a quarter to a third of the population, and laying the survivors low. The increasing difficulty of finding bison to hunt that winter, combined with bone-chilling temperatures, made recovery even more of an ordeal. And that was before the American soldiers came. By New Year's Day 1870, U.S. officials had reached the limits of their patience with Blackfeet horse rustling and raiding. Authorities gave a small group of Blackfeet chiefs two weeks to turn over the murderers of the white rancher Malcom Clarke (himself the husband of a Piikani woman) and return any stolen horses and cattle. After the deadline predictably came and went, four companies of the Second Cavalry under the command of Eugene M. Baker marched out to strike the Piikani band of Mountain Chief, with orders to pursue them across the international boundary into Canada if necessary. It was not necessary. In the early light of January 23, Baker's men attacked a smallpox-ridden camp of thirty-seven lodges on the Marias River, south of the border, killing at least 173 and capturing 140 women and children and 500 horses in less than an hour. Then, after putting the teepees to the torch, Baker released the diseased, traumatized captives into subzero weather to fend for themselves without mounts or supplies. But as it turned out, this was not the camp of Mountain Chief, which was several miles way. Instead Baker had slaughtered the followers of Chief Heavy Runner, who had a record of cooperation with the Americans.[57]

Despite this tragic, callous case of mistaken identity and a firestorm of criticism from the national press, federal officials celebrated that the Blackfeet were now "completely subdued." But that would have come as news to the Blackfeet—1870 was also the year they achieved one of their greatest military victories over their longtime Cree enemies, drawing on the technological superiority of their armament. The Crees had tried to take advantage of Blackfeet misfortune by following the buffalo herd as it wandered south into Blackfeet territory. The Crees did not realize that the Blackfeet, for all their suffering, were newly armed with an arsenal of revolvers and long-range repeating rifles, whereas the Crees and Assiniboines still carried mostly smoothbore Northwest guns as well as bows and arrows. On October 25, 1870, Piikani gunmen under the leadership of Big Leg, Black Eagle, and Heavy Shield came rushing to the relief of a Kainai camp at the junction of the Oldman and St. Mary's Rivers that was under attack by hundreds of Cree and Assiniboine warriors, and from there the rout was on. Driving their enemies into a ravine near the Belly River, just north of the modern Montana/Alberta border, Blackfeet sharpshooters picked them apart for four hours and then charged, letting up only after a handful of survivors managed to ford the stream and reach a defensible stand of trees. Most counts put the Cree and Assiniboine dead at 200 to 300, which avenged a similarly bloody Cree victory over the Blackfeet five years earlier. None of the participants appear to have reflected that as they slaughtered each other with ever greater efficiency afforded to them by their firearms, they were weakening their ability to fight white expansion and defend a way of life they both shared.[58]

In many ways the battles of 1870 had brought the Blackfeet full circle from the dark days of the smallpox of 1781. During the former cataclysm, the people, reeling from a disease for which they had no name, combined the speed of horses acquired from the western tribes with the power of guns obtained from the eastern Crees to transform themselves into the consummate warrior-hunters of the northern Plains. In this process they even became fierce enemies of the Crees. Now, ninety years later, they stood at another threshold, except this time there were no appealing paths to follow. Once again they held potent new guns in their hands, but with the U.S. Army and civilians bearing down on them, with their longtime indigenous enemies withdrawing onto reservations, and with the bison population weak-legged and about to collapse in 1877, there was little left to shoot at. The unscrupulous merchants who sold the people these military wares now also carried increasing amounts of whiskey, which took an enormous toll on people trying to black out the horror they were experiencing as their world collapsed; an estimated 25 percent of the Blackfeet died in alcohol-fueled fights and accidents and from overdrinking between 1867 and 1873.[59]

With their very existence hanging in the balance, the Blackfeet were in no position to expand or even defend their range, as they had in the wake of the 1781 smallpox. Instead, in 1877 they signed Canadian Treaty Number 7, recognizing Canadian authority and ceding 50,000 square miles in exchange for reservations and annuities. Subsequent treaties with Ottawa and Washington had by 1880 created four reservations, one for the southern Piikanis in Montana, and three others in Alberta for the northern Piikanis, Kainais, and Siksikas, respectively. The year 1877 was also when the Lakota warrior Sitting Bull, having retreated to the

Canadian Plains, tried to recruit the Blackfeet to join his resistance. He knew firsthand the terror of their mounted gunmen. Doubtless Sitting Bull also had the respect of the Blackfeet. After all, he was fighting for a dream that they and practically all Indians shared, whatever their differences. The parties might have shown their solidarity through a trade of arms, for in the collections of the Royal Alberta Museum is a Blackfeet pistol with a replacement cartridge bearing the serial number of one of Custer's troops who fell at the Battle of the Little Bighorn; in all likelihood the cartridge had been traded or gifted to the Blackfeet by Sitting Bull or one of his warriors. Despite such exchanges, and the empathy they symbolized, the Blackfeet had already lost so much in such short time that they could not bear to gamble what little they had left on Sitting Bull's risky venture. Swallowing hard, they left him to fight on his own.[60]

EPILOGUE

AIM RAISES THE RIFLE

Throughout the late winter and spring of 1973, Americans across the country opened their morning newspapers and turned on the television evening news to see images of a few hundred rifle-bearing Indians occupying the South Dakota village of Wounded Knee, surrounded by growing ranks of white federal marshals and FBI agents. By the Indians' design, this confrontation was rife with symbolism. Wounded Knee, of course, was the site of one of the most notorious massacres of indigenous people by the United States, for there, on December 29, 1890, the Seventh Cavalry (Custer's old unit) had slaughtered chief Big Foot's band of Minneconjòu Lakotas for nothing more than holding an unauthorized dance that they hoped would bring back their ancestors and the buffalo and make white people disappear. Worse yet, in the century that followed the United States had seized this hallowed place from the Lakotas and sold it to whites; like most of the reservation, it had been guaranteed to the people "forever" in the 1868 Treaty of Fort Laramie. Forever had lasted only nine years, until whites discovered gold in the Black Hills. The U.S. government, tireless in inventing new ways to subjugate and impoverish an already subjugated and impoverished people, continued the trend in the twentieth century by permitting mining and timber companies to strip profitable resources from Indian land it judged as "surplus," often leaving behind a poisonous, environmental wasteland. As if to add insult to injury, the U.S. had turned other parts of Lakota country into tourist attractions celebrating Manifest Destiny. Lakotas had to bear the likeness of presidents Washington, Jefferson, Lincoln, and Theodore Roosevelt glaring down triumphantly at them from a rock face in the Black Hills, as throngs of patriotic visitors marveled. At Wounded Knee, billboards called on tourists to "Visit the Mass Grave" and "See the Wounded Knee Massacre Site," while a nearby "trading post" sold postcards with historic black-and-white photographs of the frozen bodies of the Lakota dead. The demonstrators who took over Wounded Knee in 1973 were no longer willing to tolerate these insults and the myriad other ways white American society either degraded or ignored Native people. Instead, while occupying the site of their people's very worst days, they announced the formation of the sovereign Oglala Sioux Indian Nation with boundaries established by the Treaty of Fort Laramie of 1868, and declared its independence from the United States. Raising the rifle was a way of saying "Enough!"— Indians were ready again to fight back.[1]

The men who served as the public faces of the American Indian Movement (AIM), such as Russell Means and Dennis Banks, also raised the rifle to reclaim the masculine warrior role, which U.S. policy had sought to crush systematically for the better part of a century. These men had already cultivated a warrior affectation with their long braided hair, buckskin clothing, headbands, and jewelry popularly associated with classic Plains Indians. Wielding arms in front of the cameras filled out the picture, making them appear like modern-day Crazy Horses and Sitting Bulls resisting the American subjugation of their people. Their message was for indigenous audiences too. It called on Native men to reclaim the responsibility of protecting their families and communities and asserting their dignity, by force if necessary.

AIM was an outgrowth of mounting civil rights activism in Indian country and throughout the United States and Canada since World War II. Native leadership in this campaign tended to come from those whose off-reservation experiences in boarding schools, the military, universities, and urban neighborhoods put them in contact with a diverse set of indigenous people and gave them a broad perspective on the plights of Indian country and the operations of American and Canadian politics and society. Such figures formed new multitribal organizations, such as the National Congress of the American Indians (1944) and the National Indian Youth Council (1961) in which they could consult about their shared grievances and lobby the government and the public for reform. Direct confrontation was on the rise. Highlights included the Tuscaroras' 1958 obstruction of New York state surveyors who tried to map out a new reservoir on their territory, the Lumbees of North Carolina taking up arms to break up a Ku Klux Klan rally in their neighborhood, and Indians throughout the Pacific Northwest conducting "fish-ins" in which they asserted their treaty rights to salmon runs under threat from dams and other development. Of these sorts of protests, nothing captured the public's attention and influenced AIM so much as the 1969 takeover of Alcatraz Island in San Francisco Bay by a collection of Native college students and urbanites, who called attention to the plight of Indians in the cities as well as on the reservations. Additional inspiration came from the black civil rights movement, ranging from the nonviolent, media-savvy protests led by Martin Luther King to the Black Panthers' platform of armed resistance and Afro-separatism. AIM's pursuit of Red Power drew on all of these precedents and more at a time when subjugated Americans of all kinds were demanding justice and taking to the streets to claim it.[2]

Though there was no chance of AIM demonstrators at Wounded Knee winning a shoot-out with federal agents, few doubted their willingness to fight, given the violence that had characterized their short history of confrontation with white authorities. Over the previous three years AIM had grown from a small group of Indians in Minneapolis determined to end police brutality of their people, into a national organization of local cells throughout the country that confronted white oppression and asserted Indian sovereignty. AIM's first major public demonstration, a Day of Mourning held at Plymouth Rock on Thanksgiving in 1970, involved the protestors briefly occupying the *Mayflower II,* a replica of the "Pilgrims'" sailing ship. Two years later AIM staged a caravan to Washington, D.C., called the "Trail of Broken Treaties," in which it occupied the Bureau of Indian Affairs for six days on the eve of the 1972 presidential election, then trashed the building before abandoning it. AIM also confronted white authorities at the local level for their discriminatory treatment, particularly in Lakota country. The failure of the law to prosecute the white killers of Indians, or to address the factors that so often contributed to violence, such as racial prejudice and the exploitation of Indians by white liquor peddlers, led AIM to march on the towns of Gordon, Nebraska, and Custer, South Dakota. The latter featured a riot in which Indian protestors torched two police cars and the Chamber of Commerce building before suffering twenty-two arrests.

Yet it was the bungled federal response to these events that truly militarized AIM's tactics. Following the historic pattern of the colonial state enlisting Indian proxies to put down Indian resistance, Washington funneled tens of thousands of dollars to Chairman Dick Wilson of the Pine Ridge Reservation so he could raise a paramilitary force (known locally as "goons") to drum AIM off the reservation. In addition to welcoming funds that he could distribute to family and friends at his discretion, Wilson was eager to cooperate because AIM drew its greatest support from cultural traditionalists, many of whom were trying to have him impeached. Neither Wilson nor his federal sponsors anticipated how much the chairman's intimidation would stiffen the traditionalists' resolve, or draw them even closer to AIM. In a public meeting, two matrons, Gladys Bissonette and Ellen Moves Camp, called on AIM to revive the Lakotas' dormant warrior spirit. "For many years we have not fought any kind of battle, we have not fought any kind of war," Bissonette lamented, "and we have forgotten how to fight." Lest there was any question that masculine honor was at stake alongside politics, Moves Camp added, "Where are our men? Where are our defenders?" The takeover of Wounded Knee was supposed to answer these questions.[3]

Flaunting its armament was AIM's way of declaring that Indians still had men ready to protect their people. Indeed, they not only flaunted it, but exaggerated it. By the accounts of AIM members and newspaper reporters who visited the Indians' positions, the few dozen men who held Wounded Knee wielded a "pitiful" arsenal of .22 rifles, .30-06 hunting rifles, and .410 small-bore shotguns. Without small deliveries of ammunition carried by intrepid runners who slipped through the cordon of federal agents and reservation police, the Wounded Knee warriors probably would have run out within a couple of weeks. When the Indians heard of the government claiming that the occupiers possessed weapons "capable of wiping out a whole group before they can react," including an M60 machine gun mounted on a tripod, some of them laughed out loud, "We wish." Yet they did what they could to make those reports seem true. At night they would periodically shoot off their lone AK-47, contributed by a veteran of the Vietnam War, in different positions throughout their camp, knowing that federal marshals would recognize the report. This tactic was all the more manipulative because AIM expected federal officials to associate the AK-47 with the Soviet Union, which, given the state of the cold war, would raise fears that Moscow was funneling arms to the Indians. When media cameramen were around, the occupiers also staged displays of ammunition for sophisticated guns they did not possess. They wanted their opponents to believe they were much better armed than they actually were.[4]

It worked like a charm, particularly in an environment influenced by right-wing fears of Communist infiltration, militant people of color, and assorted longhairs. Bob Wiedrich, a conservative columnist from the *Chicago Tribune* declared with certainty that "a total of 63 modern rifles are in the hands of the militant Indians [at Wounded Knee], thanks to the radical Left," which he charged originated from behind the Iron Curtain and Fidel Castro's Cuba. The John Birch Society, always on the lookout for Communist conspiracies, agreed that red political agents were funneling weapons to the Red Power movement. Even South Dakota senator George McGovern, a favorite of the political left, was swept up in the panic, pronouncing that "Dr. King would be turning in his grave if he could see people claiming to be carrying on his tradition with automatic rifles." Taking no chances, federal marshals and FBI agents took positions around Wounded Knee equipped with M16s, M50s capable of firing bullets two inches in diameter, submachine guns, flak jackets, armored personnel carriers, and helicopters. They were backed up by armed men from Dick Wilson's goon squad. The next seventy-one days were marked by failed negotiations alternating with exchanges of gunfire in which federal troops unleashed more than half a million rounds of ammunition. Nevertheless, federal agents resisted calls to charge the Indians' lines. Certainly one factor was that they feared AIM's supposed firepower. The strongest restraint, however, was that they knew a public relations debacle would surely follow any killing of the occupiers. Headlines announcing "The Second Massacre at Wounded Knee" would only further diminish the sinking credibility of the federal government amid the Vietnam War, race riots, the shooting of Kent State student protestors, and the Watergate scandal.[5]

AIM Member Raising the Rifle. Pictures of AIM men triumphantly sporting rifles saturated print media and television news during the occupation of Wounded Knee. By AIM's design, these became iconic images of militant Indian demands for a restoration of their sovereignty and recognition of their basic dignity. Courtesy Associated Press Images.

Ultimately the occupiers surrendered without achieving their key demands, particularly the removal of Wilson and the restoration of the federal government dealing with Indian nations by treaty. Despite AIM's rhetoric that they would fight to the last man, their will was broken on April 25 by an immense barrage from federal guns that killed one of their people and injured several others. They were also desperately hungry despite their sympathizers having managed to deliver them some supplies through airlift as well as on foot. Quite simply, AIM had been unprepared for such a long standoff. Contrary to right-wing fears, the days were long gone in which foreign rivals armed Native Americans to resist U.S. imperialism. That time had passed along with indigenous people's economic influence and the international contest for dominance in North America. The members of AIM occupying Wounded Knee knew as much. Unwilling to become the victims of yet another U.S. massacre of Indians, on May 8, after seventy-one days of standoff, its members marched out of from behind their defenses and turned over their weapons to federal authorities. To the surprise of Attorney General Richard Hellstern, these amounted to just "a lot of old shotguns and rifles."[6]

A century earlier, Lakota heroes Crazy Horse and Sitting Bull had been reluctant to surrender their arms to U.S. forces both because it represented the beginning of a dispiriting new way of life and because they justifiably distrusted the Americans' promise to maintain their people's safety and welfare. This time was different. True, the government had retaken Wounded Knee, and afterward it managed to immobilize AIM by arresting most of its leaders, often on flimsy charges, and forcing them into expensive and timely court proceedings. Yet the showdown at Wounded Knee and the many demonstrations that preceded it had breathed new life into Indian politics centered on the goals of sovereignty and self-determination. This new politics played out less on the battlefield and more in courtrooms, legislative halls, academia, the media, and, of course, the reservations themselves.

Certainly it would be wrong to declare these campaigns an unmitigated success. They fell short in a number of ways that reflected indigenous people's long history of struggle with armed young men. Some people, particularly the elderly and cultural traditionalists, derided AIM as a bunch of showoffs from the city who showed little knowledge or respect for the old ways of the reservations they claimed to represent. More to the point, by provoking additional federal suppression, AIM made life more troublesome for people already struggling to get by, like too many warriors in days of old. Some Native women felt torn between their support for AIM's goals and their resentment toward AIM's male leaders for forcing women into the shadows whenever the cameras were on, and for expecting them to perform menial roles. In the mid-1970s these women would found WARN (Women of All Red Nations) to fight against Indian domestic violence and the adoption of indigenous children by non-Indians, issues that AIM had ignored. This organization also continued AIM's battle for Native cultural and political autonomy. For many people the most extreme example of AIM's male chauvinism was the murder of one of its most prominent women, Ann Mae Pictou-Aquash, whose lifeless body was discovered at Pine Ridge in the winter of 1975–1976 with a fatal gunshot wound to the head. Many people at the time and since believed that AIM's leadership ordered the murder out of the belief that Pictou-Aquash had become an FBI informant. Two low-level AIM members have since been convicted of the crime in federal and state courts. Pictou-Aquash might be seen as one of untold numbers of indigenous women during the gun era who sacrificed their lives in campaigns in which they exercised too little authority.[7]

It goes without saying that AIM also fell short in forcing the federal government and the American public to answer for the staggering rates of poverty, unemployment, suicide, low life expectancy, alcoholism, physical and sexual abuse, and diabetes that continue to plague many reservation communities and urban Indian neighborhoods. At the same time, signs of progress in Indian country are undeniable. They take the form of the growing authority of tribal governments over tasks that once fell to the Bureau of Indian Affairs. They can be measured in the recovery by some communities of a portion of the land stolen from them by state and federal governments. There are new entrepreneurial ventures ranging from casinos, to fish hatcheries, to ecological tourism. Not least of all, the activist politics represented by AIM helped to forge a critical mass of American public opinion, however tepid it might be, that Indians should enjoy all the rights of citizens, that their tribes should exercise the rights guaranteed to them in historic treaties with the United States, and that they have the right to deal with Washington on a government-to-government basis. In light of the long history of the United States trying to extinguish Indian tribes as sovereign and cultural entities, and bring their most valuable resources into the open market for whites to possess, these developments are real gains, even if far more progress is needed.[8]

It is a sad commentary on the history of the United States' treatment of Indians that these small victories probably would have been impossible without AIM militants raising the rifle and forcing the public and politicians to acknowledge, if not necessarily to address, the desperate state of Indian country. As men who understood the close relationship between fear and respect, and between the gun and power in modern times, Crazy Horse and Sitting Bull could have predicted this outcome.

ABBREVIATIONS

Amherst Papers	Jeffery Amherst Papers, William L. Clements Library, University of Michigan, Ann Arbor
Amherst Papers, microfilm	*America, Britain and the War of Independence: The Correspondence and Papers of Sir Jeffery Amherst, 1717–1797, in the Kent Archives Office,* 16 microfilm reels, arranged by date
AROIA	*Annual Report of the Office of Indian Affairs* (Washington, DC: Government Printing Office, by year)
Bexar Archives	Bexar Archives Online, Briscoe Center for American History, University of Texas, Austin, https://www.cah.utexas.edu /projects/bexar/index.php
Bouquet Papers	*The Papers of Henry Bouquet,* ed. S. K. Stevens, Donald H. Kent, Autumn L. Leonard, and Louis M. Waddell, 6 vols. (Harrisburg: Pennsylvania Historical and Museum Commission, 1972–1974)
Bouquet Papers, Ser. 21631, 21632	Sylvester K. Stevens and Donald H. Kent, eds., *The Papers of Col. Henry Bouquet, Series 21631 and 21632* (Harrisburg: Pennsylvania Historical and Museum Commission, 1941)
CR	Charles J. Hoadly, ed. *The Public Records of the Colony of Connecticut,* 15 vols. (Hartford, CT: Brown and Parsons, 1850–1890)
Critical Period	Clarence Walworth Alvord and Clarence Edwin Carter, eds., *The Critical Period, 1763–1765: Collections of the Illinois State Historical Library,* vol. 10 (Springfield: Trustees of the Illinois State Historical Library, 1915)
CSHSW	*Collections of the State Historical Society of Wisconsin*
DRCHNY	*Documents Relative to the Colonial History of the State of New York,* 15 vols. (Albany, NY: Weed, Parsons, and Co., 1853–87)
FHQ	*Florida Historical Quarterly*
Gage Papers	Thomas Gage Papers, William L. Clements Library, University of Michigan, Ann Arbor

HBCA	Hudson's Bay Company Archives, Archives of Manitoba, microfilm
Henry and Thompson Journals	Elliot Coues, ed., *New Light on the Early History of the Greater Northwest: The Manuscript Journals of Alexander Henry and David Thompson, 1799–1814,* 2 vols. (New York: F. P. Harper, 1897)
HNAI	*Handbook of North American Indians,* gen. ed. William C. Sturtevant, 20 vols. (Washington, DC: Smithsonian Institution Press, 1978–)
IHC	*Collections of the Illinois Historical Library*
JAH	*Journal of American History*
Johnson Papers	*Papers of Sir William Johnson,* 14 vols. (Albany: The University of the State of New York, 1921–1965)
JR	Reuben Gold Thwaites, ed., *The Jesuit Relations and Allied Documents: Travels and Explorations of the Jesuit Missionaries in New France, 1610–1791,* 73 vols. (Cleveland: Burrows Brothers, 1896–1901)
LROIA	Letters Received by the Office of Indian Affairs, 1824–1880, M234, National Archives, Washington, DC
Maryland Archives	*Archives of Maryland,* ed. William Hand Browne et al., 72 vols. (Baltimore: Maryland Historical Society, 1883–1972)
MBR	Nathaniel B. Shurtleff, ed., *Records of the Governor and Company of the Massachusetts Bay in New England,* 5 vols. (Boston: William White, 1853–1854)
MHS	Massachusetts Historical Society, Boston
MHSC	Massachusetts Historical Society, *Collections*
Mo. Hist. Soc.	Missouri Historical Society, St. Louis, Missouri
NYHS	New-York Historical Society, New York
PA Archives	*Pennsylvania Archives*
PCR	Nathaniel B. Shurtleff and David Pulsipher, eds., *Records of the Colony of New Plymouth,* 12 vols. (Boston, MA: William White, 1855)
PPLC	Papers of Panton, Leslie & Company, 1783–1847, University of West Florida Archives, microfilm
RICR	John R. Bartlet, ed., *Records of the Colony of Rhode Island and Providence Plantations in New England,* 10 vols. (Providence, RI: A. C. Greene and Bros., 1856–1865)
Russians in Tlingit America	Nora Marks Dauenhauer, Richard Dauenhauer, and Lydia T. Black, eds., *Anóoshi, Lingít Aaní Ká, Russians in Tlingit America: The Battles of Sitka, 1802 and 1804* (Seattle: University of Washington Press, 2008)
TIP	Dorman H. Winfrey and James M. Day, eds., *The Indian Papers of Texas and the Southwest, 1825–1916,* 5 vols. (1966; Austin: Texas State Historical Association, 1995)

UCR	*Acts of the Commissioners of the United Colonies of New England,* vols. 9 and 10 of *Records of the Colony of New Plymoth* (Boston, MA: W. White, 1859)
WHQ	*Western Historical Quarterly*
WMQ	*William and Mary Quarterly,* 3rd series

NOTES

INTRODUCTION

1 Jeffrey Ostler, *The Plains Sioux and U.S. Colonialism: From Lewis and Clark to Wounded Knee* (New York: Cambridge University Press, 2004), 1–62; Robert M. Utley, *The Indian Frontier of the American West, 1846–1890* (Albuquerque: University of New Mexico Press, 1984), 1–65; Elliott West, *The Contested Plains: Indians, Goldseekers, and the Rush to Colorado* (Lawrence: University Press of Kansas, 1998).

2 Charles E. Rankin, ed., *Legacy: New Perspectives on the Battle of the Little Bighorn* (Helena: Montana Historical Society Press, 1996); Richard Allan Fox Jr., *Archaeology, History, and Custer's Last Battle: The Little Bighorn Re-examined* (Norman: University of Oklahoma Press, 1997); Peter Cozzens, ed., *Eyewitnesses to the Indian Wars, 1865–1890,* vol. 2: *The Wars of the Pacific Northwest* (Mechanicsburg, PA: Stackpole Books, 2002), 31 (blades of grass).

3 Charles M. Robinson III, *A Good Year to Die: The Story of the Great Sioux War* (New York: Random House, 1995); Jerome A Greene, ed., *Lakota and Cheyenne Views of the Great Sioux War, 1876–1877* (Norman: University of Oklahoma Press, 1994); Ostler, *Plains Sioux,* 63–84; Utley, *Indian Frontier,* 99–202; Kingsley M. Bray, *Crazy Horse: A Lakota Life* (Norman: University of Oklahoma Press, 2006).

4 Royal B. Hassrick, *The Sioux: Life and Customs of a Warrior Society* (Norman: University of Oklahoma Press, 1964); Preston Holder, *The Hoe and the Horse on the Plains: A Study of Cultural Development among North American Indians* (Lincoln: University of Nebraska Press, 1970); James R. Walker, *Lakota Society,* ed. Raymond J. DeMallie (Lincoln: University of Nebraska Press, 1982); Anthony McGinnis, *Counting Coup and Cutting Horses: Intertribal Warfare on the Northern Plains* (Evergreen, CO: Cordillera Press, 1990).

5 Richard G. Hardorff, ed., *The Surrender and Death of Crazy Horse: A Source Book about a Tragic Episode in Lakota History* (Spokane, WA: Arthur H. Clarke, 1998), 165, 210 ("surrender their arms"; "neither Crazy Horse"), 203–206 ("chanting songs"; "sullen"); Castle McLaughlin, *A Lakota War Book from the Little Bighorn: The Pictographic "Autobiography of Half Moon"* (Cambridge, MA: Peabody Museum Press, 2013), 113–114; L. James Dempsey, *Blackfoot War Art: Pictographs of the Reservation Period, 1880–2000* (Norman: University of Oklahoma Press, 2007), 14.

6 Hardorff, *Surrender and Death of Crazy Horse,* 208, 212.

7 Ari Kelman, *A Misplaced Massacre: Struggling over the Memory of Sand Creek* (Cambridge, MA: Harvard University Press, 2013); Utley, *Indian Frontier,* 178–189. On dog feasts, see James R. Walker, *Lakota Society,* ed. Raymond J. DeMallie (Lincoln: University of Nebraska Press, 1982), 65.

8 Robert M. Utley, *Lance and Shield: The Life and Times of Sitting Bull* (New York: Henry Holt, 1993), 84–89.

9 Richard White, "The Winning of the West: The Expansion of the Western Sioux in the Eighteenth and Nineteenth Centuries," *JAH* 65, no. 2 (September 1978): 319–343; Utley, *Lance and Shield,* 183–198; David D. McCrady, *Living with Strangers: The Nineteenth-Century Sioux and the Canadian-American Borderlands* (Lincoln: University of Nebraska Press, 2009).

10 Utley, *Lance and Shield,* 199–210 (206 and 207 for prairie mice); John C. Ewers, *The Blackfeet: Raiders on the Northwestern Plains* (Norman: University of Oklahoma Press, 1958), 278–280.

11 Utley, *Lance and Shield,* 232.

12 R. Todd Romero, *Making War and Minting Christians: Masculinity, Religion, and Colonialism in Early New England* (Amherst: University of Massachusetts Press, 2011).

13 Theda Perdue, *Cherokee Women* (Lincoln: University of Nebraska Press, 1998), 17–40; Will Roscoe, *Changing Ones: Third and Fourth Genders in Native North America* (New York: St. Martin's Press, 1998), 23–38; Walter A. Williams, *Spirit and the Flesh: Sexual Diversity in American Indian Culture* (Boston, MA: Beacon Press, 1986), 233–251; Roger M. Carpenter, "Womanish Men and Manlike Women: The Native American Two-spirit as Warrior," in *Gender and Sexuality in Indigenous North America, 1400–1850,* ed. Sandra Slater and Fay A. Yarborough (Columbia: University of South Carolina Press, 2011), 146–164; Beatrice Medicine, " 'Warrior Women': Sex Role Alternatives for Plains Indian Women," in *The Hidden Half: Studies of Plains Indian Women,* ed. Patricia Albers and Beatrice Medicine (Washington, DC: University Press of America, 1983), 267–277.

14 Roger Williams, *A Key into the Language of America,* ed. John J. Teunissen and Evelyn J. Hinz (Detroit: Wayne State University Press, 1973), 158, 234; Eugene Buechel and Paul Manhart, eds., *Lakota Dictionary* (Lincoln: University of Nebraska Press, 2002), 197 (*mázawakan*); Joan M. Vastokas and Roman K. Vastokas, *Sacred Art of the Algonkians* (Petersborough, ON: Mansard Press, 1973), 93–94; Kathleen J. Bragdon, *Native People of Southern New England, 1500–1650* (Norman: University of Oklahoma Press, 1996), 187–188, 212.

15 Åke Hultkrantz, *The Religions of the American Indians,* trans. Monica Setterwall (Berkeley: University of California Press, 1979), 50–51; George R. Hammell, "The Panther in Huron-Wyandot and Seneca Myth, Ritual, and Material Culture," in *Icons of Power: Feline Symbolism in the Americas,* ed. Nicholas J. Saunders (London: Routledge, 1998), 258–291; William A. Fox, "Horned Panthers and Erie Associates," in *A Passion for the Past: Essays in Honour of James F. Pendergast,* ed. James V. Wright and Jean-Luc Palon (Gatineau, QC: Canadian Museum of Civilization, 2004), 283–304; Bragdon, *Native People of Southern New England, 1500–1650,* 185–189, 203–214; Christopher L. Miller and George R. Hammell, "A New Perspective on Indian-White Contact: Cultural Symbols and Colonial Trade," *JAH* 73, no. 2 (September 1986): 325; William S. Simmons, "Southern New England Shamanism: An Ethnographic Reconstruction," in *Papers of the Seventh Algonquian Conference,* ed.

William Cowan (Ottawa: Carleton University Press, 1976), 218–253; George Hammell and William A. Fox, "Rattlesnake Tales," *Ontario Archaeology,* no. 79/80 (2005): 127–149; Stephen Warren, *The Worlds the Shawnees Made: Migration and Violence in Early America* (Chapel Hill: University of North Carolina Press, 2014), 43.

16 On the side plates, see William A. Fox, "Dragon Sideplates from York Factory: A New Twist on an Old Tail," *Manitoba Archaeological Journal* 2, no. 2 (1992): 21–35; M. L. Brown, *Firearms in Colonial America: The Impact on History and Technology 1492–1792* (Washington, DC: Smithsonian Institution Press, 1980), 283–284; Charles E. Hanson Jr., *The Northwest Gun* (Lincoln: University of Nebraska Press, 1955), 2, 7; Carl P. Russell, *Guns on the Early Frontiers: A History of Firearms from Colonial Times through the Years of the Western Fur Trade* (Berkeley: University of California Press, 1957), 103, 108–109, 116–119, 127–130; S. James Gooding, *Trade Guns of the Hudson's Bay Company, 1670–1790* (Alexandria Bay, NY: Museum Restoration Service, 2003), 70–73; James A. Hanson, *Firearms of the Fur Trade* (Chadron, NE: Museum of the Fur Trade, 2011), 111, 140, 144, 146, 148, 168–180, 217; Dean R. Snow, *Mohawk Valley Archaeology: The Sites* (University Park: Matson Museum of Anthropology, Pennsylvania State University, 1995), 333. On French examples, see Russel Bouchard, *Les Armes de Traite* (Sillery, QC: Éditions du Boreál Express, 1976), 56, 77, 104; Kevin Gladysz, *The French Trade Gun in North America, 1662–1759* (Woonsocket, RI: Andrew Mowbray Publishers, Inc., 2011), 142–143, 146. On bags and pouches, see Roland Bohr, *Gifts from the Thunder Beings: Indigenous Archery and European Firearms in the Northern Plains and the Central Subarctic, 1670–1870* (Lincoln: University of Nebraska Press, 2014), 194–203. On blue finished barrels, see Gooding, *Trade Guns of the Hudson's Bay Company,* 31, and the following from the American Fur Trade Company Papers, NYHS: Bought of Joseph Child, Birmingham, March 1, 1841, Invoices Inward, 2:91; Bought of Joseph Child, July 1, 1845, Invoices Inward, 2:230; Memorandum of guns ordered from Mr. J. Joseph Henry, Outward Orders, 2:44; Memorandum of the Guns to be imported from England by Messrs. Tredwell Dissam, Outward Orders 2:69; American Fur Company to C. M. Lampson, Feb. 7, 1840, Letters, 11:406–407. On the significance of the color blue, see Miller and Hammell, "New Perspective," 324.

17 On "rogue colonialism," see Shannon Lee Dawdy, *Building the Devil's Empire: French Colonial New Orleans* (Chicago: University of Chicago Press, 2009), 4–5, 233–246.

18 Patricia Nelson Limerick, *The Legacy of Conquest: The Unbroken Past of the American West* (New York: Norton, 1987); Richard White, "Frederick Jackson Turner and Buffalo Bill," and Limerick, "The Adventures of the Frontier in the Twentieth Century," in *The Frontier in American Culture,* ed. James R. Grossman (Berkeley: University of California Press, 1994), 7–65, 67–102; Howard Lamar and Leonard Thompson, eds., *The Frontier in History: North America and Southern Africa Compared* (New Haven, CT: Yale University Press, 1981); William Cronon, George Miles, and Jay Gitlin, "Becoming West: Toward a New Meaning for Western History," in *Under an Open Sky: Rethinking America's Western Past,* ed. William Cronon, George Miles, and Jay Gitlin (New York: Norton, 1992), 3–27; Stephen Aron, "Lessons in Conquest: Towards a Greater Western History," *Pacific Historical Review* 63, no. 2 (1994): 125–147; Kerwin Lee Klein, "Reclaiming the 'F' Word, or Being and Becoming Postwestern," *Pacific Historical Review* 65, no. 2 (May 1996): 179–215.

19 On Indians accumulating power by harnessing the forces of colonialism, see Ewers, *Blackfeet;* White, "Winning of the West"; Kathleen DuVal, *The Native Ground: Indians and Colonists in the Heart of the Continent* (Philadelphia: University of Pennsylvania

Press, 2006); Brian DeLay, *War of a Thousand Deserts: Indian Raids and the U.S.-Mexican War* (New Haven, CT: Yale University Press, 2008); Pekka Hämäläinen, *The Comanche Empire* (New Haven, CT: Yale University Press, 2008); Michael Witgen, *An Infinity of Nations: How the Native New World Shaped Early North America* (Philadelphia: University of Pennsylvania Press, 2011); Julie A. Fisher and David J. Silverman, *Ninigret, the Niantic and Narragansett Sachem: War, Diplomacy, and the Balance of Power in Seventeenth Century New England and Indian Country* (Ithaca, NY: Cornell University Press, 2014).

1: LAUNCHING THE INDIAN ARMS RACE

1 Dean R. Snow, Charles T. Gehring, and William A. Starna, eds., *In Mohawk Country: Early Narratives about a Native People* (Syracuse, NY: Syracuse University Press, 1996), 1–13.

2 On the Champlain battle, see H. P. Biggar, ed., *The Works of Samuel de Champlain,* 6 vols. (Toronto: Champlain Society, 1922–1936), 2:65–107. On the formation of the League, see William N. Fenton, *The Great Law and the Longhouse: A Political History of the Iroquois Confederacy* (Norman: University of Oklahoma Press, 1998), 51–65, 128–131, 135–140; William A. Starna, "Retrospecting the Origins of the League of the Iroquois," *Proceedings of the American Philosophical Society* 152 (2008): 279–321; Robert D. Kuhn and Martha L. Sempowski, "A New Approach to Dating the League of the Iroquois," *American Antiquity* 66, no. 2 (April 2001): 301–314. On the "mourning wars," see Daniel K. Richter, "War and Culture: The Iroquois Experience," *WMQ* 40, no. 4 (October 1983): 528–559; James F. Pendergast, "The Confusing Identities Attributed to Stadacona and Hochelaga," *Journal of Canadian Studies* 32, no. 4 (Winter 1997/1998): 149–167. On the early spread of European materials and intertribal warfare, see John A. Dickinson, "Old Routes and New Wares: The Advent of European Goods in the St. Lawrence Valley," in *Le Castor Fait Tout: Selected Papers of the Fifty North American Fur Trade Conference, 1985,* ed. Bruce G. Trigger, Toby Morantz, and Louise Dechêne (Montreal: Lake St. Louis Historical Society, 1987), 31–41; James W. Bradley, *Evolution of the Onondaga Iroquois: Accommodating Change, 1500–1655* (Syracuse, NY: Syracuse University Press, 1987), 69–78, 89–103, 130–142, 146–153; Laurier Turgeon, "French Fishers, Fur Traders, and Amerindians during the Sixteenth Century: History and Archaeology," *WMQ* 55, no. 4 (October 1998): 584–610; Charles F. Wray and Harry L. Schoff, "A Preliminary Report on the Seneca Sequence in Western New York, 1550–1687," *Pennsylvania Archaeologist* 23, no. 2 (1953): 55–57; Dean R. Snow, *Mohawk Valley Archaeology: The Sites* (University Park: Matson Museum of Anthropology, Pennsylvania State University, 1995), 222, 230, 252–254, 269; Peter Bakker, "A Basque Etymology for the Word 'Iroquois,'" *Man in the Northeast* 40 (1990): 89–93.

3 For two recent accounts in this vein, see David Hackett Fischer, *Champlain's Dream: The European Founding of North America* (New York: Simon and Schuster, 2008), 2–4, 254–273; Fred Anderson and Andrew Cayton, *The Dominion of War: Empire and Liberty in North America, 1500–2000* (New York: Viking, 2005), 16–32.

4 Bruce G. Trigger, "The Mohawk-Mahican War (1624–1628): The Establishment of a Pattern," *Canadian Historical Review* 52, no. 3 (1971): 276–286; Starna and Brandão "From the Mohawk-Mahican War to the Beaver Wars," 725–770. The population figures are from Dean R. Snow, "Mohawk Demography and the Effects of Exogenous Epidemics on American Indian Populations," *Journal of Anthropological Archae-*

ology 15, no. 2 (1996): 164, 174. But see also the critique of Snow in William Howard Carter, "Chains of Consumption: The Iroquois and Consumer Goods, 1550–1880" (PhD diss., Princeton University, 2008), 195–208.

5 H. Ph. Vogel, "The Republic as an Exporter of Arms, 1600–1650," in *The Arsenal of the World: The Dutch Arms Trade in the Seventeenth Century,* ed. Jan Piet Puype and Macro van der Hoeven (Amsterdam: Batavian Lion International, 1996), 13–22.

6 Roger Pauly, *Firearms: The Life Story of a Technology* (Westport, CT: Greenwood Press, 2004), 28–38, 43; Geoffrey Parker, *The Military Revolution: Military Innovation and the Rise of the West, 1500–1800* (New York: Cambridge University Press, 1988), 17–24; Kenneth Chase, *Firearms: A Global History to 1700* (New York: Cambridge University Press, 2003), 60–61, 73–76; James A. Hanson, *Firearms of the Fur Trade* (Chadron, NE: Museum of the Fur Trade, 2011), 54–55.

7 Pauly, *Firearms,* 43–46; M. L. Brown, *Firearms in Colonial America: The Impact on History and Technology, 1492–1792* (Washington, DC: Smithsonian Institution Press, 1980), 68–69, 72; Snow, *Mohawk Valley Archaeology,* 300, 306.

8 Pauly, *Firearms,* 50–52; Bradley, *Before Albany: An Archaeology of Native-Dutch Relations in the Capital Region, 1600–1664* (Albany: University of the State of New York, 2007), 120 ("first-quality"), 125 ("up to date"); Snow, *Mohawk Valley Archaeology,* 39, 299; Jan Piet Puype, *Dutch and Other Flintlocks from Seventeenth Century Iroquois Sites* (Rochester, NY: Rochester Museum and Science Center, 1985), 76; Bradley, *Evolution of the Onondaga Iroquois,* 142–145; Joseph R. Mayer, *Flintlocks of the Iroquois, 1620–1687* (Rochester, NY: Rochester Museum and Science Center, 1943); Thomas B. Abler, "European Technology and the Art of War in Iroquoia," in *Cultures in Conflict: Current Archaeological Perspectives,* ed. Diana Claire Tkaczuk and Brian C. Vivian (Calgary: University of Calgary Archaeological Association, 1989), 275.

9 Puype, "Dutch Firearms from Seventeenth Century Indian Sites," in Puype and van der Hoeven, *Arsenal of the World,* 52–61, esp. 57; Puype, *Dutch and Other Flintlocks,* 50; Brown, *Firearms in Colonial America,* 153; Hanson, *Firearms of the Fur Trade,* 58; Harold Leslie Peterson, *Arms and Armor in Colonial America, 1526–1783* (Mineola, NY: Dover Publications, 2000), 14; Harold B. Gill, *The Gunsmith in Colonial Virginia* (Williamsburg, VA: Colonial Williamsburg Foundation, 1974), 4.

10 Roland Bohr, *Gifts from the Thunder Beings: Indigenous Archery and European Firearms in the Northern Plains and the Central Subarctic, 1670–1870* (Lincoln: University of Nebraska Press, 2014), 154–155, 159; Wayne E. Lee, "The Native American Military Revolution: Firearms, Forts, and Polities," in *Empires and Indigenes: Intercultural Alliance, Imperial Expansion, and Warfare in the Early Modern World* (New York: New York University Press, 2011), 57–58, 59; Abler, "European Technology," 274–275.

11 *JR,* 18:155, 32:29–31, 241, 49:45; Louis Hennepin, *A New Discovery of the Vast Country in America* [1698], ed. R. G. Thwaites (Chicago: A. C. McClurg and Co., 1903), 1:24–25, 2:77, 86–87; Snow, Gehring, and Starna, *In Mohawk Country,* 72, 121; Lahonton, *New Voyage,* 2:77; William Engelbrecht, *Iroquoia: The Making of a Native World* (Syracuse, NY: Syracuse University Press, 2002), 108; Elisabeth Tooker, *An Ethnography of the Huron Indians, 1615–1649* (Syracuse, NY: Syracuse University Press, 1991), 65–66.

12 *DRCHNY,* 1:282–283; *JR,* 21:33–35; Reuben Gold Thwaites, ed., *Early Western Travels, 1748–1846,* vol. 1 (Cleveland: Arthur H. Clark, 1904), 284; Brian J. Given,

A Most Pernicious Thing: Gun Trading and Native Warfare in the Early Contact Period (Ottawa: Carleton University Press, 1994), 91, 108; Bohr, *Gifts of the Thunder Beings,* 131, 133. On small musket balls at Iroquois archaeological sites, see Puype, *Dutch and Other Flintlocks,* 70. Numerous musket balls found at mid-seventeenth-century Seneca archaeological sites contain teeth marks. See items 12051–12071/100 from the Steele Site and items 12371–12397/25 from the Power House Site at the Rochester Museum and Science Center, Rochester, NY.

13 *JR,* 24:269–271; *DRCHNY,* 1:150, 182; *PCR,* 9:116; José António Brandão, *"Your Fyre Shall Burn No More": Iroquois Policy toward New France and Its Native Allies to 1701* (Lincoln: University of Nebraska Press, 1997), 87 ("great trade"); Denys Delâge, *Bitter Feast: Amerindians and Europeans in Northeastern North America, 1600–1664,* trans. Jane Brierley (Vancouver: University of British Columbia Press, 1993), 134–135; Bradley, *Evolution of the Onondaga,* 142–143; Puype, *Dutch and Other Flintlocks,* 9, 80; Charles F. Wray, "The Volume of Dutch Trade Goods Received by the Seneca Iroquois, 1600–1687," *New Netherland Studies,* nos. 2 and 3 (June 1985): 100–112; Snow et al., *In Mohawk Country,* 44 ("weapons in war"); Jon Parmenter, *Edge of the Woods: Iroquoia, 1534–1701* (Lansing: Michigan State University Press, 2010), 56 ("as well as"); *DRCHNY,* 1:282–283 ("excel").

14 Puype, *Dutch and Other Flintlocks,* 75–81; Snow, *Mohawk Valley Archaeology,* 39, 290, 299; G. W. Hagerty, *Wampum, War, and Trade Goods West of the Hudson* (Interlaken, NY: Heart of the Lakes Publishing, 1985), 248; Snow, "Mohawk Demography," 174.

15 Puype, *Dutch and Other Flintlocks,* 75–81; Snow, *Mohawk Valley Archaeology,* 39, 290, 299; Bradley, *Before Albany,* 124; *JR,* 18:157, 21:41, 31:30, 169–171, 32:175; Cadwallader Colden, *The History of the Five Indian Nations of Canada,* 2 vols. (London: Lockyer Davis, J. Wren, and J. Ward, 1755), 1:8.

16 Cathy Matson, *Merchants and Empire: Trading in Colonial New York* (Baltimore: Johns Hopkins University Press, 2002), 15–17; Ian K. Steele, *Warpaths: Invasions of North America* (New York: Oxford University Press, 1994), 114; A. J. F. van Laer, trans. and ed., *Van Rensselaer Bowier Manuscripts, Being the Letters of Kiliaen Van Rensselaer, 1630–1643* (Albany: University of the State of New York, 1908), 565–566; *PA Archives,* ser. 2, vol. 5 (Harrisburg, PA: State Printer, 1877), 96; *DRCHNY,* 182; Snow et al., *In Mohawk Country,* 210 ("gave everything"); Brandão, *"Your Fyre Shall Burn No More,"* 88; Allen W. Trelease, *Indian Affairs in Colonial New York: The Seventeenth Century* (1960; Lincoln: University of Nebraska Press, 1997), 60–61.

17 *PA Archives,* ser. 2, vol. 5 (Harrisburg, PA: State Printer 1877), 96, 189 ("contraband goods"), 192 ("sparing hand"); *DRCHNY,* 1:182, 311–312, 388–389, 392; Delâge, *Bitter Feast,* 134–135.

18 *DRCHNY,* 1:174, 282–283 ("overrun"), 311–312, 342, 373–374 ("greatest profit"), 427–428, 455, 499, 599, 2:155 ("contrivance"), 157; *PA Archives,* ser. 2, vol. 5 (Harrisburg, PA: State Printer, 1877), 162–164; Trelease, *Indian Affairs in New York,* 89, 97–98; *Records of the Colony and Plantation of New Haven, from 1638 to 1649* (Hartford, CT: Case, Tiffany, and Co., 1849), 508–509, 514–515; Charles T. Gehring, trans. and ed., *Correspondence, 1647–1653,* New Netherland Document Series (Syracuse, NY: Syracuse University Press, 2000), 37, 83 ("bad use"); Susanah Shaw Romney, *New Netherland Connections: Intimate Networks and Atlantic Ties in Seventeenth-Century America* (Chapel Hill: University of North Carolina Press for the Omohundro Institute of Early American History and Culture, 2014), 168 ("so many guns").

19 *PA Archives,* ser. 2, vol. 5 (Harrisburg, 1877), 840 ("chiefly"); Charles T. Gehring and Janny Venema, trans. and eds., *Fort Orange Records, 1654–1679* (Syracuse, NY: Syracuse University Press, 2000), 84–85 ("unbrotherly"); Lawrence H. Leder, ed., *The Livingston Indian Records, 1666–1723* (Gettysburg: Pennsylvania Historical Commission, 1956), 30; Matthew Dennis, *Cultivating a Landscape of Peace: Iroquois-European Encounters in Seventeenth-Century America* (Ithaca, NY: Cornell University Press, 1993), 177.

20 Daniel K. Richter, *Trade, Land, Power: The Struggle for Eastern North America* (Philadelphia: University of Pennsylvania Press, 2013), 68 ("trade and peace"); Bradley, *Before Albany,* 86–93; Richter, *The Ordeal of the Longhouse: The Peoples of the Iroquois League in the Era of European Colonization* (Chapel Hill: University of North Carolina Press for the Institute of Early American History and Culture, 1992), 93–95, 97–98, 103–104.

21 *JR,* 12:197–199, 18:231, 21:21–23, 59–61, 22:267, 275–277, 305 ("now use"), 23: 273–275, 24:271, 273–275, 287–289, 291, 25:23, 26:29–31, 33, 35, 53, 235, 27:61, 62, 29:147, 30:287, 31:19–23, 169–171, 35:209–211, 217, 36:105–107, 123–125, 133, 37:97, 105–107, 139–141, 38:173, 39:177, 40:85, 227–229, 233, 42:227–229, 43:105, 211, 47:163–165, 49:247; Brandão, *"Your Fyre Shall Burn No More,"* 169–278; Baron de La Hontan, *New Voyages to North America,* 2 vols. (London: H. Bonwicke, T. Goodwin, M. Wotton, B. Tooke, 1703), 1:32; Daniel Gookin, "Historical Collections of the Indians in New England," *MHSC,* ser. 1, vol. 1 (1792), 162; Delâge, *Bitter Feast,* 134–135.

22 *JR,* 24:269–271, 273–275; Brandão, *"Your Fyre Shall Burn No More,"* 53.

23 *JR,* 21:267–269, 24:298, 27:62 ("entirely naked"), 69 ("sharpest thorn").

24 *JR,* 20:287–289 ("afraid to arm"), 25:23, 26:30–31, 34, 32:173–175, 45:429–455; Delâge, *Bitter Feast,* 136. See also Russel Bouchard, *Les Armes à Feu en Nouvelle-France* (Sillery, QC: Septentrion, 1999), 72–75.

25 Alber, "European Technology," 275; James Hunter, "The Implications of Firearms Remains from Sainte-Marie among the Hurons, A.D. 1639–1649," in *Proceedings of the 1984 Trade Gun Conference, Part II,* ed. Charles F. Hayes III (Rochester, NY: Rochester Museum and Science Center, 1985), 1–9; Daniel K. Richter, *Before the Revolution: America's Ancient Pasts* (Cambridge, MA: Belknap Press of Harvard University Press, 2011), 149; Roger M. Carpenter, *The Renewed, the Destroyed, and the Remade: The Thought Worlds of the Iroquois and the Huron, 1609–1650* (East Lansing: Michigan State University Press, 2004), 108 ("we have told them").

26 Bruce G. Trigger, *The Children of Aataentsic: A History of the Huron People to 1660* (Montreal: McGill-Queen's University Press, 1976), 751–753, 762–766, 767, 776–777; Parmenter, *Edge of the Woods,* 72, 74.

27 Trigger, *Children of Aataentsic,* 753–754, 762; *JR,* 34:89–91, 121 ("well furnished"), 135, 215, 35:111–113, 115, 38:67 ("speak to the Captain").

28 *JR,* 36:115–117, 41:81, 179, 45:207, 249–255, 46:209; Trigger, *Children of Aataentsic,* 789–791; Craig S. Keener, "An Ethnohistorical Analysis of Iroquois Assault Tactics Used against Fortified Settlements of the Northeast in the Seventeenth Century," *Ethnohistory* 46, no. 4 (Fall 1999); Keener, "Ethnohistorical Analysis," 791–792, 794; Lee, "Military Revolution," 52–53.

29 Richter, *Ordeal of the Longhouse,* 53; Barry C. Kent, *Susquehanna's Indians* (Harrisburg: Pennsylvania Historical and Museum Commission, 1984), 17–18, 117; James D.

Rice, *Nature and History in the Potomac Country: From Hunter-Gatherers to the Age of Jefferson* (Baltimore: Johns Hopkins University Press, 2009), 49–50; Martha L. Sempowski, "Early Historic Exchange between the Seneca and the Susquehannock," in *Archaeology of the Iroquois: Selected Readings and Research Sources,* ed. Jordan E. Kerber (Syracuse, NY: Syracuse University Press, 2007), 194–218.

30 J. Frederick Fausz, "Merging and Emerging Worlds: Anglo-Indian Interest Groups and the Development of the 17th Century Chesapeake," in *Colonial Chesapeake Society,* ed. Lois Green Carr, Phillip Morgan, and Jean Russo (Chapel Hill: University of North Carolina Press for the Institute of Early American History and Culture, 1989), 58–63, 71–74; Brown, *Firearms in Colonial America,* 150; Clayton Colman Hall, ed., *Narratives of Early Maryland, 1633–1684* (New York: Barnes and Noble, 1910), 155.

31 Jean R. Soderlund, *Lenape Country: Delaware Valley Society before William Penn* (Philadelphia: University of Pennsylvania Press, 2015), 42–44; Richter, *Before the Revolution,* 150; Francis Jennings, "Susquehannock," *HNAI, Northeast,* vol. 15, ed. Bruce G. Trigger (Washington, DC: Smithsonian Institution Press, 1978), 364–365; Amandus Johnson, *The Swedish Settlements on the Delaware, 1638–1664,* 2 vols. (Philadelphia: Swedish Colonial Society, 1911), 190; DRCHNY, 12:41, 113; Albert Cook Myers, ed., *Narratives of Early Pennsylvania, West Jersey, and Delaware, 1630–1707* (New York: Barnes and Noble, 1912), 105; Karen Ordahl Kupperman, "Scandinavian Colonists Confront the New World," and Lorraine E. Williams, "Indians and Europeans in the Delaware Valley, 1620–1655," in *New Sweden in America,* ed. Carol E. Hoffecker et al. (Newark: University of Delaware Press, 1995), 89–111, 112–120; Mark L. Thompson, *The Contest for the Delaware Valley: Allegiance, Empire, and Identity in the Seventeenth Century* (Baton Rouge: Louisiana State University Press, 2013).

32 DRCHNY, 12:40, 47, 57, 59, 193, 233–234, 237; *PA Archives,* ser. 2, vol. 5 (Harrisburg, PA: State Printer, 1877), 78, 84, 119; Beauchamp Plantagenet, *A Description of the Province of New Albion* (London: n.p., 1648), 18; Peter Lindeström, *Geographia Americae, with an Account of the Delaware Indians, Based on Surveys and Notes Made in 1654–1656,* trans. Amandus Johnson (Philadelphia: Swedish Colonial Society, 1925), 227; Johnson, *Swedish Settlements on the Delaware,* 216; Hall, *Narratives of Early Maryland,* 317–318.

33 DRCHNY, 12:40 ("he could sell"), 67 ("will earn blame"); Myers, *Narratives of Early Pennsylvania,* 142, 147, 157 ("before our eyes").

34 Hall, *Narratives of Early Maryland,* 42, 136, 151. On Maryland-Susquehannock relations, see Fausz, "Merging and Emerging Worlds"; Francis Jennings, "Glory, Death, and Transfiguration: The Susquehannocks in the Seventeenth Century," *Proceedings of the American Philosophical Society* 112 (1968): 15–53; Cynthia J. Van Zandt, *Brothers among Nations: The Pursuit of Intercultural Alliances in Early America, 1580–1660* (New York: Oxford University Press, 2008), 166–185; *Maryland Archives,* 3:106–107, 117, 149–150; Holm, *Description of the Province of New Sweden,* 157–158 ("defend"); Myers, *Narratives of Early Pennsylvania,* 102; Plantagenet, *Description of the Province of New Albion,* 22–23.

35 Fausz, "Merging and Emerging," 83; *JR,* 37:95–97; 38:191; 43:143, 48:75 ("two bastions"); DRCHNY, 9:10, 12:346, 439; Kent, *Susquehanna's Indians,* 39; Francis Jennings, "Jacob Young: Indian Trader and Interpreter," in *Struggle and Survival in Colonial America,* ed. David G. Sweet and Gary B. Nash (Berkeley: University of

California Press, 1982), 347–361; Matthew Kruer, "The Susquehannock War: Anglo-Indian Violence and Colonial Rebellion in the Mid-Atlantic, 1675–1682" (PhD diss., University of Pennsylvania, 2015), chap. 2. By incorrectly identifying the fortress community of Atrakwae as Susquehannock, several historians have wrongly stated that the Iroquois captured between 500 and 600 Susquehannocks in 1651–1652. See David J. Sorg, "Problematic Tribal Names of Pennsylvania," *Pennsylvania Archaeologist* 76, no. 2 (Fall 2006): 49. I thank Matthew Kruer for this reference.

36 Francis Jennings, *The Ambiguous Iroquois Empire: The Covenant Chain Confederation of Indian Tribes with English Colonies* (New York: Norton, 1984), 123–125; *DRCHNY*, 12:346, 419, 430, 431, 439; Jennings, "Glory, Death, and Transfiguration," 28; *JR*, 48:75; Charles A. Hanna, *The Wilderness Trail, or, The Ventures and Adventures of the Pennsylvania Traders on the Allegheny Path*, 2 vols. (New York: G. P. Putnam's Sons, 1911), 1:47; Kent, *Susquehanna's Indians*, 22–23.

37 William A. Starna, *From Homeland to New Land: A History of the Mahican Indians, 1600–1830* (Lincoln: University of Nebraska Press, 2013), 77–98; Colin G. Calloway, *The Western Abenakis of Vermont, 1600–1800: War, Migration, and the Survival of an Indian People* (Norman: University of Oklahoma Press, 1990), 42; Alfred A. Cave, *The Pequot War* (Amherst: University of Massachusetts Press, 1996), 58; Sylvester Judd, "The Dutch House of Good Hope at Hartford," *New England Historic Genealogical Register* 6, no. 4 (October 1852): 368; Francis X. Moloney, *The Fur Trade in New England, 1620–1676* (Cambridge, MA: Harvard University Press, 1931), 46–66; William Iredell Roberts, "The Fur Trade of New England in the Seventeenth Century" (PhD diss., University of Pennsylvania, 1958), 46–48; Peter A. Thomas, "In the Maelstrom of Change: The Indian Trade and Cultural Process in the Middle Connecticut River Valley, 1635–1665" (PhD diss., University of Massachusetts at Amherst, 1979), 180, 263–266, 277–285.

38 David Wilton to John Winthrop Jr., December 10 and December 28, 1663, Winthrop Papers, MHS; *DRCHNY*, 13:355–356; *JR*, 49:139–141.

39 *JR*, 51:83, 169, 52:123, 129–131; Parmenter, *Edge of the Woods*, 111, 115–116.

40 Gookin, "Historical Collections," 162, 164 ("stout and lusty"); Neal Salisbury, "Toward the Covenant Chain: Iroquois and Southern New England Algonquians, 1637–1684," in *Beyond the Covenant Chain: The Iroquois and Their Neighbors in Indian North America, 1600–1800*, ed. Daniel K. Richter and James H. Merrell (Syracuse, NY: Syracuse University Press, 1987), 66–67; Calloway, *Western Abenakis of Vermont*, 70–74; Thomas, "Maelstrom of Change," 244–260.

41 *JR*, 53:137–145 ("advantageous spot" and "shower of balls" on 141), 155 ("weaken"); Gookin, "Historical Collections," 166 ("so furious"), 167.

42 Brandão, *"Your Fyre Shall Burn No More,"* 112, 118–119; Bouchard, *Les Armes à Feu*, 75; Brown, *Firearms in Colonial America*, 155; Richter, *Ordeal of the Longhouse*, 103–104; Parmenter, *Edge of the Woods*, 122.

43 *JR*, 49:139 ("surround"), 57:27, 29; Lee, "Military Revolution," 63–64; Parmenter, *Edge of the Woods*, 119, 127, 130; Brandão, *"Your Fyre Shall Burn No More,"* 98 ("kill the Algonquins"), 114; Matson, *Merchants and Empire*, 55; David Arthur Armour, *The Merchants of Albany, New York: 1686–1760* (New York: Garland, 1986), 41; Bradley, *Before Albany*, 183; Richter, *Ordeal of the Longhouse*, 105–132.

44 *Maryland Archives*, 3:549; *JR*, 53:155–157, 243, 247, 253, 56:55–57, 59:251, 60:173; Hanna, *Wilderness Trail*, 1:48; Richter, *Before the Revolution*, 151; James Rice, "Ba-

con's Rebellion in Indian Country," *JAH* 101, no. 3 (December 2014): 726–750; Parmenter, *Edge of the Woods,* 143–144.

45 Benjamin Franklin French, *Historical Collections of Louisiana,* 5 vols. (New York: Wiley and Putnam, 1846–1853), 2:288 ("harmless"); Hennepin, *New Discovery,* 88 ("more valiant"); John Gilmary Shea, ed., *Discovery and Exploration of the Mississippi Valley with the Original Narratives of Marquette, Allouez, Membré, Hennepin, and Anastase Douay* (New York: Redfield, 1853), 151, 158; Brandão, *"Your Fyre Shall Burn No More,"* 124 ("nine hundred"); Parmenter, *Edge of the Woods,* 165 ("fifteen hundred"); *JR,* 54, 167, 191, 59:127, 60:159, 62:163; Brett Rushforth, *Bonds of Alliance: Indigenous and Atlantic Slaveries in New France* (Chapel Hill: University of North Carolina Press for the Omohundro Institute of History and Culture, 2012); Steven Warren, *The Worlds the Shawnees Made: Migration and Violence in Early America* (Chapel Hill: University of North Carolina Press, 2014), 57–79.

46 La Hontan, *New Voyages,* 1:40–41 ("supplied the Illinese"), 2:63–65; Colden, *History of the Five Indian Nations,* 1:72; Parmenter, *Edge of the Woods,* 160, 172; *JR,* 62:71–73; Hennepin, *New Discovery,* 99, 101 ("none of the neighbors"), 285 ("all Fusilieres"); *Historical Collections of Louisiana,* 1:56–58, 66.

47 Warren, *Worlds the Shawnees Made,* 34, 50, 58–59, 66; Laura Keenan Spero, "'Stout, Bold, Cunning and the Greatest Travelers in America': The Colonial Shawnee Diaspora" (PhD diss., University of Pennsylvania, 2010), 45–51; James H. Merrell, "'Their Very Bones Shall Fight': The Catawba-Iroquois Wars," and Theda Perdue, "Cherokee Relations with the Iroquois in the Eighteenth Century," in Richter and Merrell, *Beyond the Covenant Chain,* 115–134, 135–150.

48 Richter, *Ordeal of the Longhouse,* 133–213; Richard White, *The Middle Ground: Indians, Empires, and Republics in the Great Lakes Region, 1650–1815* (New York: Cambridge University Press, 1991), 136.

49 Jan Gabrowski, "Les Amérindiens Domiciliés et la 'Contrabande' des Forrures en Nouvelle-France," *Reserches Amérindiennes au Québec* 24, no. 3 (1994): 45–52; Richter, *Ordeal of the Longhouse,* 214–254; Norton, *The Fur Trade in Colonial New York,* 121–151; Gilles Havard, *The Great Peace of Montreal of 1701: French-Native Diplomacy in the Seventeenth Century,* trans. Phyllis Aronoff and Howard Scott (Montreal: McGill-Queen's University Press, 2001).

50 Peter Wraxall, *An Abridgement of the Indian Affairs,* ed. Charles Howard McIlwain (Cambridge, 1915), 52, 63, 64, 81, 113, 117, 131; Hennepin, *New Discovery,* 56 ("we should provide"); Thomas Elliot Norton, *The Fur Trade in Colonial New York, 1686–1776* (Madison: University of Wisconsin Press, 1974), 30, 166–167; Richter, *Ordeal of the Longhouse,* 220–221; Parmenter, *Edge of the Woods,* 204–205, 261; Colden, *History of the Five Nations,* 1:160, 163; Kees-Jan Waterman, trans. and ed., *"To Do Justice to Him & Myself": Evert Wendell's Account Book of the Fur Trade with Indians in Albany, New York, 1695–1726* (Philadelphia, PA: American Philosophical Society, 2008), 21–22; Richard Aquila, *The Iroquois Restoration: Iroquois Diplomacy on the Colonial Frontier* (Detroit, MI: Wayne State University Press, 1983), 112–121; Wilbur R. Jacobs, *Diplomacy and Indian Gifts: Anglo-French Rivalry along the Ohio and Northwest Frontiers, 1748–1763* (Stanford, CA: Stanford University Press, 1950).

51 From the Archives Nationales de France, Paris, http://Heritage.canadiana.ca: Mémoire de Vaudreuil au comte de Toulouse, président du Conseil de Marine, 1716, C11A 36/fol. 100–113v; Délibération du Conseil de Marine à propos des présents à faire aux Sauvages, C11A 123/fol. 153–155; Lettre de Hocquart au ministre—

justification de certaines demandes dans l'état des munitions et marchandises à tirer de Rochefort l'an prochain, October 24, 1744, C11A 81/fol. 433–436v; Lettre de Beauharnois et Hocquart au ministre—les munitions reçues de France, Sept. 26, 1746, C11A 85/fol. 27–30v; Lettre de Beauharnois au ministre (chiffrée), Nov. 4, 1745, C11A 83/fol.114–118; Kevin Gladysz, *The French Trade Gun in North America, 1662–1759* (Blackstone, RI: Andrew Mowbray Publishers, 2011), 37, 39, 41; White, *Middle Ground,* 131–132, 136; Catherine M. Desbarats, "The Cost of Early Canada's Native Alliances: Reality and Scarcity's Rhetoric," *WMQ* 52, no. 4 (October 1995): 609–630; W. J. Eccles, "The Fur Trade and Eighteenth-Century Imperialism," *WMQ* 40, no. 3 (July 1983): 341–362; Dale Miquelon, *New France, 1701–1744: "A Supplement to Europe"* (Toronto: McLelland and Stewart, 1987), 155–156. In the Montreal Merchants' Records Project, Research Files, 1971–1975, Minnesota Historical Society, microfilm, 1 reel, see the following headings: "Guns (Fusils de chasse)"; "Guns (Fusils de traitte)"; "Guns (fusils)"; "Posts and Territories"; and "Trade Goods." Statistics on the number of warriors from allied nations can be found in "1736: Census of the Indian Tribes," *Collections of the State Historical Society of Wisconsin,* vol. 17 (1906), 245–251; and www.statcan.gc.ca/pub/98-187-x/4151278 -engl.htm#part1. I have included the following groups and their respective number of warriors in the figure of 4,000: Michilimackinac Ottawas (180); Mississaugas (50); Sauteurs (Ojibwas) at the Falls of St. Mary (30); Papinakois (Montagnais; 20); Keweenaw Sauteurs (Ojibwas; 40); Point Chequamegon Sauteurs (Ojibwas; 150); Folles Avoines (Menominees; 160); Potawatomis at La Baye (20); Kickapoos (80); Mascoutens (60); St. Joseph Potawatomis (100); St. Joseph Miamis (10); Ontationoue (Nottoway; 350); Illinois (250); Kaskaskias (100); Peorias (50); Cahokias (200); Detroit Hurons (200); Detroit Potawatomis (180); Detroit Ottawas (200); Lake St. Clair Mississaugas (80); Saginaw Ottawas (80); Kahnwake Iroquois (370); Lorette Hurons (260); Abenakis of St. John's River and St. Francis (590). These figures do not include the Sauks and Foxes, with whom the French were often at war during these years, or the Sioux, Assiniboines, or nations around Lake of the Woods, whose diplomacy and trade with the French were more sporadic than among the above-mentioned nations.

52 Brown, *Firearms in Colonial America,* 153 ("will not carry"); Colden, *History of the Five Nations,* 1:149–150 ("shall we throw"); Leder, *Livingston Indian Records,* 165, 227; Wraxall, *Abridgement,* 63, 83, 92, 99, 102–103, 116, 119.

53 Colden, *History of the Five Nations,* 2:15, 33, 78; Jennings, *Ambiguous Iroquois Empire,* 325–346; Laurence M. Hauptman, *Conspiracy of Interests: Iroquois Dispossession and the Rise of New York State* (Syracuse, NY: Syracuse University Press, 1999); Alan Taylor, *The Divided Ground: Indians, Settlers, and the Northern Borderland of the American Revolution* (New York: Knopf, 2006).

54 Richter, *Before the Revolution,* 151.

2: A VICIOUS COMMERCE

1 Her account appears in "Plans for the Colonization and Defense of Apalache, 1675," trans. and ed. Katherine Reding, *Georgia Historical Quarterly* 9, no. 2 (June 1925): 174–175. On the Yuchis' location, see John E. Worth, "Enigmatic Origins: On the Yuchi of the Contact Era," in *Yuchi Indian Histories before the Removal Era,* ed. Jason Baird Jackson (Lincoln: University of Nebraska Press, 2012), 33–42. On slave coffles, see Robbie Ethridge, *From Chicaza to Chickasaw: The European Invasion and*

the Transformation of the Mississippian World, 1540–1715 (Chapel Hill: University of North Carolina Press, 2010), 198; Brett Rushforth, *Bonds of Alliance: Indigenous and Atlantic Slaveries in New France* (Chapel Hill: University of North Carolina Press for the Omohundro Institute of Early American History and Culture, 2012), 3–14. On the Carolina-Barbados relationship, see Richard S. Dunn, *Sugar and Slaves: The Rise of the Planter Class in the English West Indies, 1624–1713* (Chapel Hill: University of North Carolina Press for the Institute of Early American History and Culture, 1972), 111–116.

2 Among the works grasping the slave/gun connection are John Phillip Reid, *A Better Kind of Hatchet: Law, Trade, and Diplomacy in the Cherokee Nation during the Early Years of European Contact* (University Park: Pennsylvania State University Press, 1976); Eric E. Bowne, *The Westo Indians: Slave Traders of the Early Colonial South* (Tuscaloosa: University of Alabama Press, 2005); Christina Snyder, *Slavery in Indian Country: The Changing Face of Captivity in Early America* (Cambridge, MA: Harvard University Press, 2010); Steven Warren, *The Worlds the Shawnees Made: Migration and Violence in Early America* (Chapel Hill: University of North Carolina Press, 2014); and Ethridge, *From Chicaza to Chickasaw*. On the changing role of captives in the Native Southeast, see Denise I. Bossy, "Indian Slavery in Southeastern Indian and English Societies, 1670–1730," in *Indian Slavery in Colonial America*, ed. Alan Gallay (Lincoln: University of Nebraska Press, 2010), 207–250. On the reach of colonial violence, see Ned Blackhawk, *Violence over the Land: Indians and Empires in the Early American West* (Cambridge, MA: Harvard University Press, 2006).

3 Bowne, *Westo Indians*, 21–53; Maureen Meyers, "From Refugees to Slave Traders: The Transformation of the Westo Indians," in *Mapping the Mississippian Shatter Zone: The Colonial Indian Slave Trade and Regional Instability in the American South*, ed. Robbie Ethridge and Sheri M. Schuck-Hall (Lincoln: University of Nebraska Press, 2009), 81–90; Warren, *Worlds the Shawnees Made*, 57–82.

4 Myers, "From Refugees to Slave Traders," 88–90; James F. Pendergast, *The Massawomeck: Raiders and Traders into the Chesapeake Bay in the Seventeenth Century* (Philadelphia: American Philosophical Society, 1991); Martha M. Sempowski, "Early Historic Exchange between the Seneca and Susquehannock," in *Archaeology of the Iroquois: Selected Readings and Research*, ed. Jordan E. Kerber (Syracuse, NY: Syracuse University Press, 2007), 196; Bowne, *Westo Indians*, 62, 74–75; April Lee Hatfield, *Atlantic Virginia: Intercolonial Relations in the Seventeenth Century* (Philadelphia: University of Pennsylvania Press, 2003), 25–56.

5 Bowne, *Westo Indians*, 2, 36, 49; C. S. Everett, "'They shalbe slaves for their lives': Indian Slavery in Colonial Virginia," in Gallay, *Indian Slavery in Colonial America*, 74–75.

6 David Weber, *The Spanish Frontier in North America* (New Haven, CT: Yale University Press, 1992), 92–121; Amy Turner Bushnell, "Ruling 'the Republic of Indians' in Seventeenth-Century Florida," in *Powhatan's Mantle: Indians in the Colonial Southeast*, ed. Peter H. Wood, Gregory A. Waselkov, and M. Thomas Hatley (Lincoln: University of Nebraska Press, 1989), 134–150; Bushnell, *Situado and Sabana: Spain's Support System for the Presidio and Mission Provinces of Florida* (Athens: University of Georgia Press, 1994); Jerald T. Milanich, *Laboring in the Fields of the Lord, Spanish Missions and Southeastern Indians* (Washington, DC: Smithsonian Institution Press, 1999); Gene Waddell, *Indians of the South Carolina Lowcountry, 1562–1751* (Spartanburg, SC: The Reprint Company, 1980).

7 John E. Worth, *The Struggle for the Georgia Coast: An Eighteenth-Century Spanish Retrospective on Guale and Mocama* (Athens: University of Georgia Press, 1995), 15–16 ("great number"), 17 ("much damage").

8 Worth, *Struggle for the Georgia Coast,* 18–20; Everett, "Indian Slavery in Colonial Virginia," 83; Ethridge, *From Chicaza to Chickasaw,* 116–193.

9 Robin Beck, *Chiefdoms, Collapse, and Coalescence in the Early American South* (New York: Cambridge University Press, 2013), 99–136; Everett, "Indian Slavery in Colonial Virginia," 72, 84; Clarence Walworth Alvord and Lee Bidgood, eds., *The First Explorations of the Trans-Allegheny Region by the Virginians, 1650–1674* (Cleveland: Arthur H. Clark, 1912), 149 ("volleys of shot"), 169–170, 185, 218–221; Meyers, "From Refugees to Slave Traders," 95; James H. Merrell, *The Indians' New World: Catawbas and Their Neighbors from European Contact through the Era of Removal* (Chapel Hill: University of North Carolina Press for the Institute of Early American History and Culture, 1989), 40 ("mart"); R. P. Stephen Davis Jr. and H. Trawick Ward, "The Ocaneechi in the Seventeenth-Century Virginia-North Carolina Trade Network," www.ibiblio.org/dig/html/part5/tab4.html; Paul Kelton, *Epidemics and Enslavement: Biological Catastrophe in the Native Southeast, 1492–1715* (Lincoln: University of Nebraska Press, 2007), 114 ("great Indian trade"); Steven Christopher Hahn, "A Miniature Arms Race: The Role of the Flintlock in Initiating Indian Dependency in the Colonial Southeastern United States, 1656–1730" (MA thesis, University of Georgia, 1995), 79–80.

10 *The Shaftesbury Papers and Other Records Relating to Carolina,* ed. Langdon Cheves (Charleston, SC: Home House Press in association with the South Carolina Historical Society, 2010), 166, 167–168, 194 ("eat them"), 224, 334 ("afraid"); Alan Gallay, *The Indian Slave Trade: The Rise of the English Empire in the American South* (New Haven, CT: Yale University Press, 2002), 49; Merrell, *Indians' New World,* 99–101, 106–109; Peter H. Wood, *Black Majority: Negroes in Colonial South Carolina from 1670 through the Stono Rebellion* (New York: Knopf, 1974), 25.

11 Everett, "Indian Slavery in Colonial Virginia," 82; Cheves, *Shaftesbury Papers,* 457, 459, 460 ("well provided"); Eric E. Bowne, "Dr. Henry Woodward's Role in Early Carolina Indian Relations," in *Creating and Contesting Carolina: Proprietary Era Histories,* ed. Michelle LeMaster and Bradford J. Wood (Columbia: University of South Carolina Press, 2013), 73–93.

12 "Plans for the Colonization and Defense of Apalachee, 1675," 174–175 ("teaching them"); Worth, *Struggle for the Georgia Coast,* 10, 27–28, 31, 34, 47; Bowne, *Westo Indians,* 86–87; Joseph M. Hall Jr., *Zamumo's Gifts: Indian-European Exchange in the Colonial Southeast* (Philadelphia: University of Pennsylvania Press, 2009), 89.

13 A. S. Salley, ed., *Records in the British Record Office Relating to South Carolina, 1663–1693,* 2 vols. (Atlanta: Historical Commission of South Carolina by Foote and Davies Co., 1928–1929), 1:257 ("ruined"); Gallay, *Indian Slave Trade,* 57–63.

14 Verner W. Crane, *The Southern Frontier, 1670–1732* (New York: Norton, 1981), 40–41; Ethridge, *From Chicaza to Chickasaw,* 160, 161; Warren, *Worlds the Shawnees Made,* 58–59, 74–75; Gallay, *Indian Slave Trade,* 60–61.

15 Gallay, *Indian Slave Trade,* 138 ("dealers"; "contemptuously"); Robert M. Weir, *Colonial South Carolina: A History* (Millwood, NY: KTO Press, 1983), 66–67; Robert M. Calhoon, *Dominion and Liberty: Ideology in the Anglo-American World, 1660–1801* (Arlington Heights, IL: Harlan Davidson, 1994), 23 ("Machiavelli"); *Collections of the*

South Carolina Historical Society, 5 vols. (Columbia: South Carolina Historical Society, 1857), 1:217.

16 *Records in the British Record Office Relating to South Carolina,* 1:258 ("induce them"), 2:27, 28, 33–34 ("brook it"; "best suited"); *The Carolina Chronicle of Dr. Francis Le Jau, 1706–1717,* ed. Frank. J. Klingberg (Berkeley: University of California Press, 1956), 41, 48, 62, 116; Gallay, *Indian Slave Trade,* 50; Weir, *Colonial South Carolina,* 86.

17 Merrell, *Indians' New World,* 110–111; Steven C. Hahn, *Invention of the Creek Nation, 1670–1763* (Lincoln: University of Nebraska Press, 2004), 242–243.

18 Warren, *World the Shawnees Made,* 98–99, 101–102.

19 Thomas Nairne, *Nairne's Muskogean Journals: The 1708 Expedition to the Mississippi River,* ed. Alexander Moore (Jackson: University of Mississippi Press, 2005), 75–76.

20 Worth, *Struggle for the Georgia Coast,* 38–47.

21 Steven J. Oatis, *A Colonial Complex: South Carolina's Frontiers in the Era of the Yamasee War* (Lincoln: University of Nebraska Press, 2008), 32; Hahn, *Invention of the Creek Nation,* 40–47, 49–51; Ethridge, *From Chicaza to Chickasaw,* 165–166; Gregory Waselkov, "The Macon Trading House and Early European-Indian Contact in the Colonial Southeast," in *Ocmulgee Archaeology, 1936–1986,* ed. David J. Hally (Athens: University of Georgia Press, 1994), 190–196; Kelton, *Epidemics and Enslavement,* 134–135.

22 Hahn, *Invention of the Creek Nation,* 53–54.

23 Gallay, *Indian Slave Trade,* 135–136, 148, 295–296; Weir, *Colonial South Carolina,* 76, 80–82; Hahn, *Invention of the Creek Nation,* 62–64; Ethridge, *From Chicaza to Chickasaw,* 207; Kelton, *Epidemics and Enslavement.*

24 Mark F. Boyd, Hale G. Smith, and John W. Griffin, *Here They Once Stood: The Tragic End of the Apalachee Missions* (Gainesville: University Press of Florida, 1951), 42, 49 ("lack of munitions"), 42, 54, 68, 90–91 ("become so expert"); John H. Hahn, *Apalachee: The Land between the Rivers* (Gainesville: University Press of Florida, 1988), 148, 246–247; Weber, *Spanish Frontier,* 178, 246; Hall, *Zamumo's Gifts,* 107 ("did not give them"); *Historical Collections of Louisiana,* 5 vols. (New York, 1846–1853), 3:29.

25 Ethridge, *From Chicaza to Chickasaw,* 160, 161; Kelton, *Epidemics and Enslavement,* 130–132; Charles L. Heath, "Catawba Militarism: Ethnohistorical and Archaeological Overviews," *North Carolina Archaeology* 53 (2004): 84; Vernon J. Knight Jr. and Sherée Adams, "A Voyage to the Mobile and Tomeh in 1700, with Notes on the Interior of Alabama," *Ethnohistory* 28, no. 2 (Spring 1981): 182 ("English were in"); *Mississippi Provincial Archives, French Dominion,* vols. 1–3, ed. and trans. Dunbar Rowland and Albert Godfrey Sanders (Jackson: Press of the Mississippi Department of Archives and History, 1927–1932), 3:22, 182; Oatis, *Colonial Complex,* 69, 96; Hall, *Zamumo's Gifts,* 105.

26 Ethridge, *From Chickaza to Chickasaw,* 49–53; Kelton, *Epidemics and Enslavement,* 139; *Historical Collections of Louisiana,* 3:16 ("carried off"), 20, 34; Claudio Saunt, "History until 1776," *HNAI, Southeast* 14 (Washington, DC: Smithsonian Institution Press, 2012), 136; *Nairne's Muskogean Journals,* 37 ("never to return"); Elizabeth N. Ellis, "The Many Ties of the Petites Nations: Relationships, Power, and Diplomacy in the Lower Mississippi Valley, 1685–1785" (PhD diss., University of North Carolina, Chapel Hill, 2014), 15–95.

27 *Nairne's Muskogean Journals,* 37–38, 47–48 ("no employment"); Ethridge, *From Chickaza to Chickasaw,* 168, 219, 235; *Iberville's Gulf Journals,* ed. and trans. Richebourg McWilliams (Tuscaloosa: University of Alabama Press, 2010), 174; Gallay, *Indian Slave Trade,* 297–298; Snyder, *Slavery in Indian Country,* 61.

28 Ethridge, *From Chicaza to Chickasaw,* 204; *Mississippi Provincial Archives,* 1:31, 90–91, 109–110, 156–157, 2:27, 33–34 ("most precious"), 126–127, 154, 612, 3:20, 31, 260–261, 327–328, 552.

29 Edmund S. Morgan, *American Slavery/American Freedom: The Ordeal of Colonial Virginia* (New York: Norton, 1975), 295–315; John C. Coombs, "A New Chronology for the Rise of Slavery in Early Virginia," *WMQ* 68, no. 3 (July 2011): 332–360.

30 William L. Saunders, ed., *The Colonial Records of North Carolina,* 16 vols. (Raleigh, NC: P.M. Hale, State Printer, 1886–1890), 1:812 ("better provided"), 874, 893–894, 2:26; "Journal of John Barnwell: Part I," *Virginia Magazine of History and Biography* 5 (April 1988): 397–398 ("twice a year"); "Journal of John Barnwell, Part II," *Virginia Magazine of History and Biography* 6 (July 1988): 52 ("Virginia furnished"); *The Secret Diary of William Byrd of Westover, 1709–1712,* ed. Louis B. Wright and Marion Tinling (Richmond, VA: The Dietz Press Inc, 1941), 521; David La Vere, *The Tuscarora War: Indians, Colonists, and the Fight for the Carolina Colonies* (Chapel Hill: University of North Carolina Press, 2013), 121; William Palmer, ed., *Calendar of Virginia State Papers,* 11 vols. (Richmond, VA: R. F. Walker, 1875–1893), 1:159, 163–164 ("greater quantity").

31 La Vere, *Tuscarora War,* 122–123 ("some great guns"); "Journal of John Barnwell: Part I," 397 ("great deal"); "Journal of John Barnwell, Part II," 44–45 ("enemy says"); http://blog.ecu.edu/sites/nooherooka/.

32 La Vere, *Tuscarora War,* 208–209; Wayne E. Lee, "Fortify, Fight, or Flee: Tuscarora and Cherokee Defensive Warfare and Military Culture Adaptation," *Journal of Military History* 68, no. 3 (2004): 713–770; Gallay, *Indian Slave Trade,* 259–287; Stephen Feeley, "'Before Long to Be Good Friends': Diplomatic Perspectives of the Tuscarora War," in LeMaster and Wood, *Creating and Contesting Carolina,* 140–163; and T. C. Paramore, "Tuscarora War (1711–1713)," in *Colonial Wars of North America, 1512–1763: An Encyclopedia,* ed. Alan Gallay (New York: Garland, 1996), 749–751.

33 Merrell, *Indians' New World,* 54; Gallay, *Indian Slave Trade,* 267–268; Hall, *Zamumo's Gifts,* 111; William L. Ramsey, *The Yamasee War: A Study of Culture, Economy, and Conflict in the Colonial South* (Lincoln: University of Nebraska Press, 2008), 25, 36; Hahn, *Invention of the Creek Nation,* 77.

34 Gallay, *Indian Slave Trade,* 133–134; Hahn, *Invention of the Creek Nation,* 77–78; Oatis, *Colonial Complex,* 83–139; Ramsey, *Yamasee War,* 79–97, 101–156; Merrell, *Indians' New World,* 66–75.

35 *Colonial Records of North Carolina,* 2:196–199, 246 ("extremely well armed"), 251; James Adair, *The History of the American Indians; particularly those nations adjoining to the Missisippi [sic], East and West Florida, Georgia, South and North Carolina, and Virginia* (London: Edward and Charles Dilly, 1775), 247; Oatis, *Colonial Complex,* 179; *Mississippi Provincial Archives,* 3:205 ("not seeing"); *Carolina Chronicle,* 162 ("bows and arrows"); Ramsey, *Yamasee War,* 150.

36 Daniel K. Richter, *The Ordeal of the Longhouse: The Peoples of the Iroquois League in the Era of European Colonization* (Chapel Hill: University of North Carolina Press for

the Institute of Early American History and Culture, 1992), 239–241; Merrell, *Indians' New World,* 78; Theda Perdue, "Cherokee Relations with the Iroquois in the Eighteenth Century," in *Beyond the Covenant Chain: The Iroquois and Their Neighbors in Indian North America, 1600–1800,* ed. Daniel K. Richter and James H. Merrell (Syracuse, NY: Syracuse University Press, 1987), 135–149, esp. 137; Reid, *Better Kind of Hatchet,* 56–73, 112; Oatis, *Colonial Complex,* 185; Ramsey, *Yamasee War,* 150–152; Hahn, *Invention of the Creek Nation,* 90; W. L. McDowell, ed., *Journals of the Commissioners of the Indian Trade, September 20, 1710–August 29, 1718* (Columbia: South Carolina Archives Department, 1955), 73, 84, 89, 96 ("for the public"), 269.

37 *Mississippi Provincial Archives,* 3:187 ("same advantages"); *Journals of the Commissioners of the Indian Trade,* 246, 249, 281; Oatis, *Colonial Complex,* 212; Hahn, *Invention of the Creek Nation,* 81–120.

38 Michael D. Green, *The Politics of Indian Removal: Creek Government and Society in Crisis* (Lincoln: University of Nebraska Press, 1982), 22 ("no one"); Oatis, *Colonial Complex,* 178.

39 *Mississippi Provincial Archives,* 1:57–58, 98 ("great deal"); James F. Barnett Jr., *The Natchez Indians: A History to 1735* (Jackson: University Press of Mississippi, 2007), 63–101, 112–113; Jean-François-Benjamin Dumont de Montigny, *The Memoir of Lieutenant Dumont, 1715–1747,* ed. Gordon M. Sayre and Carla Zecher, trans. Gordon M. Sayre (Chapel Hill: University of North Carolina Press for the Omohundro Institute of Early American History and Culture, 2012), 178–188, 210–213, 227–238.

40 *Memoir of Lieutenant Dumont,* 245–248 (245: "when they get"), (246: "white flag"); Barnett, *Natchez Indians,* 109–119.

41 Barnett, *Natchez, Indians,* 119–127; Claiborne A. Skinner, *The Upper Country: French Enterprise in the Colonial Great Lakes* (Baltimore: Johns Hopkins University Press, 2008), 131; Arrell M. Gibson, *The Chickasaws* (Norman: University of Oklahoma Press, 1971), 51–53; *Mississippi Provincial Archives,* 1:268–269, 307, 308, 313, 317–319, 322–323, 324 ("have the advantage"), 3:694; *Memoir of Lieutenant Dumont,* 251–252, 258–273 (267: "shower"); du Pratz, *History of Louisiana,* 1:174–176; Adair, *History of American Indians,* 356; Jean Bernard Bossu, *Travels through that part of North America formerly called Louisiana* (London: T. Davies, 1771), 311–312; De Crémont to the Minister, 1737 in Joseph L. Peyser, ed., *Letters from New France: The Upper Country, 1686–1783* (Urbana: University of Illinois Press, 1992), 160–161; James R. Atkinson, "The Ackia and Ougoula Tchetoka Village Locations in 1736 during the French-Chickasaw War," *Mississippi Archaeology* 20, no. 1 (June 1985): 53–72.

42 Richard White, *The Roots of Dependency: Subsistence, Environment, and Social Change among the Choctaws, Pawnees, and Navajos* (Lincoln: University of Nebraska Press, 1983), 11–12; Kathryn E. Holland Braund, *Deerskins and Duffels: Creek Indian Trade with Anglo-America, 1685–1815* (Lincoln: University of Nebraska Press, 1993), 70, 128; Daniel H. Usner Jr., *Indians, Settlers, and Slaves in a Frontier Exchange Economy: The Lower Mississippi Valley before 1783* (Chapel Hill: University of North Carolina Press for the Institute of Early American History and Culture, 1992), 246; *Mississippi Provincial Archives,* 1:261, 3:21.

43 Hall, *Zamumo's Gifts,* 162; Merrell, *Indians' New World,* 207; Braund, *Deerskins and Duffels,* 74; Allan D. Candler and Lucien L. Knight, eds., *The Colonial Records of the State of Georgia,* 26 vols. (Atlanta: University of Georgia Press, 1904–1916), 2:111, 190, 211, 236, 275, 291, 419.

44 *Mississippi Provincial Archives,* 1:32, 3:652–653, 4:208–209, 223; Wilbur R. Jacobs, ed., *Indians of the Southern Colonial Frontier: The Edmond Atkins Report and Plan of 1755* (Columbia: University of South Carolina Press, 1954), 9 ("judicious application"), 10–11 (10: "we furnish"); Khalil Saadani, "Gift Exchange between the French and Native Americans in Louisiana," in *French Colonial Louisiana and the Atlantic World,* ed. Bradley G. Bond (Baton Rouge: Louisiana State University Press, 2005), 43–64; Adair, *History of American Indians,* 294; *Mississippi Provincial Archives,* 4:67 ("all the warriors"), 144, 239–240; Gregory A. Waselkov, "French Colonial Trade in Upper Creek Country," in *Calumet and Fleur-de-Lys: Archaeology of Indian and French Contact in the Midcontinent,* ed. John A. Walthall and Thomas E. Emerson (Washington, DC: Smithsonian Institution Press, 1992), 36 ("currency").

45 James A. Hanson, *Firearms of the Fur Trade* (Chadron, NE: Museum of the Fur Trade, 2011), 79–92; White, *Roots of Dependency,* 53; Kevin Gladysz, *The French Trade Gun in North America, 1662–1759* (Woonsocket, RI: Andrew Mowbray Publishers, 2011), 63, 77–78; Gov. Vaudreuil to the Duke of Orleans, February 1716, under the heading "Guns (fusils)," Montreal Merchants' Records Project, Research Files, 1971–1975, Minnesota Historical Society, microfilm, 1 reel ("the best").

46 "Merchandise needed at Mobile for Indian presents in the year 1732," December 23, 1731, under the heading "Indians, Presents, 1731–32, for Louisiana Territory," Montreal Merchants' Records Project, Research Files ("ask for them"); *Colonial Records of the State of Georgia,* 21:213, 214 ("tributary"), 296; Adair, *History of American Indians,* 263; *Mississippi Provincial Archives,* 5:227–241.

47 Kelton, *Epidemics and Enslavement,* 105 ("get more hides"); John Lawson, *A new voyage to Carolina; containing the exact description and natural history of that country* (London: n.p., 1709), 27 ("always shot"), 207 ("not worth"); Gregory A. Waselkov and Kathryn E. Holland Braund, eds., *William Bartram on the Southeastern Indians* (Lincoln: University of Nebraska Press, 1995), 48.

48 Adair, *History of American Indians,* 60 ("firing off"), 65 ("they were warriors"), 151 ("imagine"); Brent Richards Weisman, *Like Beads on a String: A Culture History of the Seminole Indians in Northern Peninsular Florida* (Tuscaloosa: University of Alabama Press, 1989), 107–108; *William Bartram on the Southeastern Indians,* 129.

49 Lawson, *New Voyage,* 27 ("curious artists"), 172; Adair, *History of American Indians,* 425; Carol I. Mason, *The Archaeology of Ocmulgee Old Fields, Mason, Georgia* (Tuscaloosa: University of Alabama Press, 2005) 83–84, 87.

50 Braund, *Deerskins and Duffels,* 89–90.

51 White, *Roots of Dependency,* 44, 45; *Mississippi Provincial Archives,* 4:289 ("forced to take up"); Adair, *History of American Indians,* 314–317.

52 *Mississippi Provincial Archives,* 4:160, 274–275; Adair, *History of American Indians,* 320–321; Richard White, "Red Shoes: Warrior and Diplomat," in *Struggle and Survival in Colonial America,* ed. David G. Sweet and Gary B. Nash (Berkeley: University of California Press, 1981), 49–68; White, *Roots of Dependency,* 54–64; James Taylor Carson, *Searching for the Bright Path: The Mississippi Choctaws from Prehistory to Removal* (Lincoln: University of Nebraska Press, 2003), 32–33.

53 Lawson, *New Voyage,* 20.

54 David S. Jones "Virgin Soils Revisited," *WMQ* 60, no. 4 (2003): 703–742; Peter H. Wood, "The Changing Population of the Colonial South: An Overview by Race

and Region, 1685–1790," in Wood, Waselkov, and Hatley, *Powhatan's Mantle,* 35–103, esp. 38–39; Kelton, *Epidemics and Enslavement.*

55 James Axtell, *Beyond 1492: Encounters in Colonial North America* (New York: Oxford University Press, 1992), 125–151.

56 Wood, *Black Majority,* 151; Gregory E. O'Malley, "Diversity in the Slave Trade to the Colonial Carolinas," in LeMaster and Wood, *Creating and Contesting Carolina,* 234–255; Oatis, *Colonial Complex,* 294–295; R. A. Kea, "Firearms and Warfare on the Gold and Slave Coasts from the Sixteenth to the Nineteenth Centuries," *Journal of African History* 12, no. 2 (1971): 185–213; J. E. Inikori, "The Import of Firearms into West Africa, 1750–1807: A Quantitative Analysis," *Journal of African History* 18, no. 3 (1977): 339–368; Robin Law, "Warfare on the West African Slave Coast, 1650–1850," in *War in the Tribal Zone: Expanding States and Indigenous Warfare,* ed. R. Brian Ferguson and Neil L. Whitehead (Santa Fe, NM: School of American Research Press, 1999), 103–126; John K. Thornton, *Warfare in Atlantic Africa, 1500–1800* (New York: UCL Press, 1999).

3: RECOIL

1 William Bradford, "A Descriptive and Historical Account of New England," *MHSC,* ser. 1, vol. 3 (1794), 82–83.

2 Benjamin Thompson, *New England's Crisis* (Boston, 1676), in *So Dreadful a Judgment: Puritan Responses to King Philip's War, 1676–1677,* ed. Richard Slotkin and James K. Folsom (Middletown, CT: Wesleyan University Press, 1978), 220.

3 Douglas Edward Leach, *Flintlock and Tomahawk: New England in King Philip's War* (New York: Norton, 1966), 242–250; Shelburne F. Cook, "Interracial Warfare and Population Decline among the New England Indians," *Ethnohistory* 20 (1973): 1–24; James D. Drake, *King Philip's War: Civil War in New England, 1675–1676* (Amherst: University of Massachusetts Press, 1999), 168–197; Jill Lepore, *The Name of War: King Philip's War and the Origins of American Identity* (New York: Norton, 1998), 150–172; Margaret Ellen Newell, *Brethren by Nature: New England Indians, Colonists, and the Origins of American Slavery* (Ithaca, NY: Cornell University Press, 2015), 131–188; Colin G. Calloway, *The Western Abenakis of Vermont, 1600–1800: War, Migration, and the Survival of an Indian People* (Norman: University of Oklahoma Press, 1990), 79–89; Evan Haefeli and Kevin Sweeney, "Wattanummon's World: Personal and Tribal Identity in the Algonquian Diaspora, c. 1660–1712," in *Proceedings of the 25th Algonquian Conference,* ed. William Cowan (Ottawa: Carleton University Press, 1993), 212–224.

4 Harry M. Ward, *The United Colonies of New England, 1643–90* (New York: Vantage, 1961); Kevin A. McBride, "The Source and Mother of the Fur Trade: Native-Dutch Relations in Eastern New Netherland," in *Enduring Traditions: The Native Peoples of New England,* ed. Laurie Weinstein (Westport, CT: Bergin and Garvey, 1994), 31–51; Sylvester Judd, "The Dutch House of Good Hope at Hartford," *New England Historic Genealogical Register* 6, no. 4 (October 1852): 368.

5 Eric S. Johnson, "Released from Thraldom by the Stroke of War: Coercion and Warfare in Native Politics of Seventeenth-Century Southern New England," *Northeast Anthropology* 55 (1998): 1–13; Kathleen Bragdon, *Native Peoples of Southeastern New England, 1650–1775* (Norman: University of Oklahoma Press, 1996), 140–156.

6 William I. Roberts III, "The Fur Trade of New England in the Seventeenth Century" (PhD diss., University of Pennsylvania, 1958), 55–58 (56: "would give"); Alden T. Vaughan, *New England Frontier: Puritans and Indians 1620–1675,* 3rd ed. (Norman: University of Oklahoma Press, 1995), 89–91, 214; Neal Salisbury, *Manitou and Providence: Indians, Europeans, and the Making of New England, 1500–1643* (New York: Oxford University Press, 1982), 152–164; Michael Zuckerman, "Pilgrims in the Wilderness: Community, Modernity, and the Maypole at Merry Mount," *New England Quarterly* 50, no. 2 (June 1977): 255–277; William Bradford, *Of Plymouth Plantation,* ed. Samuel Eliot Morrison (New York: Knopf, 1952), 204 ("no laws"), 232–233; Virginia DeJohn Anderson, *New England's Generation: The Great Migration and the Formation of Society and Culture in the Seventeenth Century* (New York: Cambridge University Press, 1991); Bernard Bailyn, *The New England Merchants in the Seventeenth Century* (Cambridge, MA: Harvard University Press, 1953), 55–56, 59.

7 M. L. Brown, *Firearms in Colonial America: The Impact on History and Technology 1492– 1792* (Washington, DC: Smithsonian Institution Press, 1980), 122; *MBR* 2:986; *CR,* 1:1 ("heavy"), 2, 3; Robert Charles Anderson, *The Great Migration: Immigrants to New England, 1634–1635,* 7 vols. (Boston: New England Historic Genealogical Society, 1999–2011), 6:521–523; John Mason, *A Brief History of the Pequot War* (Boston, 1736), in *History of the Pequot War: The Contemporary Accounts of Mason, Underhill, Vincent, and Gardener,* ed. Charles Orr (Cleveland: Helman-Taylor Company, 1897), 21; Edward Johnson, *Johnson's Wonder-Working Providence, 1628–1651,* ed. J. Franklin Jameson (New York: Barnes and Noble, 1910), 149.

8 *MBR,* 1:92–93, 196, 203, 312, 2:16 ("indirect"); *CR* 1:79; Charles J. Hodley, ed., *Records of the Colony and Plantation of New Haven, from 1638 to 1649* (Hartford, CT: Case, Tiffany, and Co., 1849), 60, 206; *RICR,* 1:155; *UCR,* 1:21–22; *Records of the Particular Court of Connecticut, 1639–1663* (Hartford: Connecticut Historical Society, 1928), 63, 78, 130; Bradford, "Descriptive and Historical Account," 82 ("And of the English").

9 Walter W. Woodward, *Prospero's America: John Winthrop, Jr., Alchemy, and the Creation of New England Culture, 1606–1676* (Chapel Hill: University of North Carolina Press for the Omohundro Institute of Early American History and Culture, 2010); Eugene Cole Zubrinsky, "The Immigration and Early Whereabouts in America of Thomas Stanton of Connecticut: Challenging the Conventional Wisdom," *American Genealogist* (October 2006): 270; *CR,* 1:146–147 ("selling lead"); Thomas Stanton to John Mason, July 8, 1669, Yale Indian Papers, 1669.07.08.00 ("exceedingly furnished"); Anderson, *Great Migration,* 1:339–345.

10 *CR,* 1:200, 216–218 ("solitary"); Thomas Stanton to John Winthrop Jr., January 29, 1649/1650, *Winthrop Papers,* vol. 6, *1650–54* (Boston: Massachusetts Historical Society, 1992), 14–16; Frances Manwaring Caulkins, *History of New London, Connecticut: From the First Survey of the Coast in 1612 to 1852* (New London: published by author, 1852), 99–101.

11 William R. Carlton, ed., "Overland to Connecticut in 1645: A Travel Diary of John Winthrop, Jr.," *New England Quarterly* 13, no. 3 (September 1940), 506; *Narragansett Historical Register* 7 (1889): 287–288; Peter Allen Thomas, "In the Maelstrom of Change: The Indian Trade and Cultural Process in the Middle Connecticut River Valley, 1635–1665" (PhD diss., University of Massachusetts, Amherst, 1979), 377– 379; *UCR,* 1:148 ("trade of guns").

12 Roberts, "Fur Trade of New England," 61; Bradford, "Descriptive and Historical Account," 83 ("Indians are nurtured").

13 David J. Silverman, *Faith and Boundaries: Colonists, Christianity, and Community among the Wampanoag Indians of Martha's Vineyard, 1600–1871* (New York: Cambridge University Press, 2005), 41, 80; *UCR*, 1:105–106; *MBR*, 4:329–330; Richard W. Cogley, *John Eliot's Mission to the Indians before King Philip's War* (Cambridge, MA: Harvard University Press, 1999), 150; Michael Leroy Oberg, *Uncas: First of the Mohegans* (Ithaca, NY: Cornell University Press, 2003), 139–170; Shawn G. Wiemann, "Lasting Marks: The Legacy of Robin Cassacinamon and the Survival of the Mashantucket Pequot Nation" (PhD diss., University of New Mexico, 2011).

14 *The Journal of John Winthrop, 1630–1649,* ed. Richard S. Dunn, James Savage, and Laeititia Yeandle (Cambridge, MA: Belknap Press of Harvard University Press, 1996), 412, 602; Roger Williams, *A Key into the Language of America* [1643], ed. John J. Teunissen and Evelyn J. Hinz (Detroit: Wayne State University Press, 1973), 235; Susan G. Gibson, ed., *Burr's Hill: A 17th Century Wampanoag Burial Ground in Warren, Rhode Island* (Providence, RI: Haffenreffer Museum of Anthropology, 1980), 109–110; William A. Turnbaugh, *The Material Culture of RI-1000: A Mid-17th Century Narragansett Indian Burial Site in North Kingstown, Rhode Island* (Kingston: Department of Sociology and Anthropology, University of Rhode Island, 2004), 50–52; Patricia E. Rubertone, *Grave Undertakings: An Archaeology of Roger Williams and the Narragansett Indians* (Washington, DC: Smithsonian Institution Press, 2001), 150, 160, 193.

15 Christian Koot, *Empire at the Periphery: British Colonists, Anglo-Dutch Trade, and the Development of the British Atlantic, 1621–1713* (New York: New York University Press, 2011), 41–43; Benjamin Schmidt, "The Dutch Atlantic: From Provincialism to Globalism," in *Atlantic History: A Critical Reappraisal,* ed. Jack P. Greene and Philip D. Morgan (New York: Oxford University Press, 2009), 163–187; Charles T. Gehring, trans. and ed., *Correspondence, 1647–1653,* New Netherland Document Series (Syracuse, NY: Syracuse University Press, 2000), 37; Examination of William Baker and Mary Baker, April 29, 1653, *Winthrop Papers,* 6:287; McBride, "Source and Mother of the Fur Trade," 36; *UCR*, 1:112–113, 149–150 ("plentifully furnished"); Williams to the General Court of Massachusetts, November 15, 1655, *The Correspondence of Roger Williams,* ed. Glenn La Fantasie, 2 vols. (Hanover, NH: Brown University Press/University Press of New England, 1988), 445 ("insolency"); Cynthia Van Zandt, *Brothers among Nations: The Pursuit of Intercultural Alliances in Early America, 1586–1660* (New York: Oxford University Press, 2008), 88–115; Faren R. Siminoff, *Crossing the Sound: The Rise of Atlantic American Communities in Seventeenth-Century Eastern Long Island* (New York: New York University Press, 2004); Andrew Lipman, *The Saltwater Frontier: Indians and the Contest for the American Coast* (New Haven, CT: Yale University Press, 2015).

16 Thomas Peters to John Winthrop, May 1645, *Winthrop Papers,* 5:19 ("won them"); Oberg, *Uncas,* 149–150; Julie A. Fisher and David J. Silverman, *Ninigret, Sachem of the Niantics and Narragansetts: Diplomacy, War, and the Balance of Power in Seventeenth-Century New England and Indian Country* (Ithaca, NY: Cornell University Press, 2014), 83–84; *UCR*, 1:101–102 ("40 or 50").

17 *CR*, 1:318–319 ("Bullets shot"), 576–577, 2:227–228, 236–237, 248–249. From the Winthrop Family Transcripts, MHS: Report on the Indians at Farmington, May 26, 1658 ("armed with guns"); Thomas Welles to John Winthrop Jr., March, 25, 1659; John Winthrop Jr. et al. to John Endecott, March 27, 1659; Humphrey Atherton et al.

to John Winthrop Jr., Aug. 30, 1659; John Mason to Connecticut, Aug. 22, 1659; Francis Newman to Winthrop, July 5, 1660.

18 Cogley, *John Eliot's Mission,* 58 (apprentice); Patrick M. Malone, *The Skulking Way of War: Technology and Tactics among the New England Indians* (Lanham, MD: Madison Books, 1991), 72, 74; Newell, *Brethren by Nature,* 60–84; Michael L. Fickes, "'They Could Not Endure That Yoke': The Captivity of Pequot Women and Children after the War of 1637," *New England Quarterly* 73, no. 1 (March 2000): 58–81; Joshua Micah Marshall, "'A Melancholy People': Anglo-Indian Relations in Early Warwick, Rhode Island," *New England Quarterly* 68, no. 3 (September 1995): 402–428; Rubertone, *Grave Undertakings,* 162, 237–238n105.

19 Gloria L. Main, *Peoples of a Spacious Land: Families and Cultures in Colonial New England* (Cambridge, MA: Harvard University Press, 2001), 104; John S. Marr and John T. Cathey, "New Hypothesis for Cause of Epidemic among Native Americans, New England, 1616–1619," *Emerging Infectious Diseases* 16, no. 2 (February 2010), http://wwwnc.cdc.gov/eid/article/16/2/09-0276_article; Timothy Bratton, "The Identity of the New England Indian Epidemic of 1616–1619," *Bulletin of the History of Medicine* 62 (1988): 351–383; Salisbury, *Manitou and Providence,* 22–30, 190–192; Fisher and Silverman, *Ninigret,* 170n56.

20 Jenny Hale Pulsipher, *Subjects unto the Same King: Indians, English, and the Contest for English Authority in Colonial New England* (Philadelphia: University of Pennsylvania Press, 2005); Drake, *King Philip's War;* Virginia DeJohn Anderson, "King Philip's Herds: Indians, Colonists, and the Problem of Livestock in Early New England," *WMQ* 51, no. 4 (October 1994): 601–624; Fisher and Silverman, *Ninigret,* 87–112; Silverman, "'Natural Inhabitants, Time Out of Mind': Sachem Rights and the Struggle for Wampanoag Land in Colonial New England," *Northeast Anthropology* 70 (2005): 4–10; William Cronon, *Changes in the Land: Indians, Colonists, and the Ecology of New England* (New York: Hill and Wang, 1983); Laurie Weinstein, "Indian vs. Colonist: Competition for Land in Seventeenth-Century Plymouth Colony" (PhD diss., Southern Methodist University, 1983); Bradford, *Of Plymouth Plantation,* 296 (Sassacus warning).

21 *UCR,* 2:23–25 ("furnished with powder"), 94–95 ("forty or fifty Indians").

22 William Hubbard, *A Narrative of the Troubles with the Indians in New England* (Boston, 1677), in *The History of the Indian Wars in New England,* 2 vols., ed. Samuel G. Drake (Roxbury, MA: W. E. Woodward, 1865), 10 ("appalled"); Increase Mather, *A Brief History of the Warr with the Indians in New-England* [Boston, 1676], in Slotkin and Folsom, *So Dreadfull a Judgment,* 71 ("raging"; "send"); John Cotton Jr. to Increase Mather, March 20, 1677, *MHSC,* ser. 4, vol. 8 (1868), 233–234.

23 *PCR,* 5:63–64 ("many guns"), 79–80; Mather, *Brief History,* 73; Malone, *Skulking Way of War,* 95.

24 *CR,* 2:119; Malone, *Skulking Way of War,* 62–63; Vaughan, *New England Frontier,* 229–230; Fisher and Silverman, *Ninigret,* 104–112.

25 *PCR,* 5:173, 174 ("submissive"); Almon Wheeler Lauber, "Indian Slavery in Colonial Times within the Present Limits of the United States" (PhD diss., Columbia University, 1913), 146; Drake, *King Philip's War,* 117, 121; Daniel R. Mandell, *King Philip's War: Colonial Expansion, Native Resistance, and the End of Indian Sovereignty* (Baltimore, MD: Johns Hopkins University Press, 2010), 78–79; Pulsipher, *Subjects unto the Same King,* 210 ("Indians in those parts").

26 Richard R. Johnson, "The Search for a Usable Indian: An Aspect of the Defense of Colonial New England," *JAH* 64, no. 3 (March 1977): 626–627; Daniel Gookin, "An Historical Account of the Doings and Sufferings of the Christian Indians in New England in the Years 1675, 1676, 1677," *Transactions and Collections of the American Antiquarian Society* 2 (1836): 434 ("jealous"), 450, 454; Ephraim Curtis to the Massachusetts General Court, July 16, 1675, photostats, MHS ("destroy them"); Mather, *Brief History,* 93, 94–95; Hubbard, *Narrative of the Troubles,* 92 ("discover"), 111, 121–122; Solomon Stoddard, "An Account of the Reasons Alledged for Demanding the Armes of the Indians of Northampton and Hadley so far as can at present be recalled," Yale Indian Papers, 1675.09.15.00; Commissioners of the United Colonies to Anonymous, 12 November 1675, *Further Letters on King Philip's War* (Providence, RI: Society of Colonial Wars, 1923), 18–19; William Harris, *A Rhode Islander Reports on King Philip's War: The Second William Harris Letter of August, 1676,* ed. Douglas Leach (Providence: Rhode Island Historical Society, 1963), 66; Drake, *King Philip's War,* 84–90, 103.

27 *CR,* 2:353–354, 381, 387, 408–409; Wait Winthrop to John Winthrop Jr., July 9, 1675, Colonial War Series, ser. 1, vol. 1, doc. 6a, Connecticut State Archives; Brian Carroll, "From Warrior to Soldier: New England Indians in the Colonial Military, 1675–1763" (PhD diss., University of Connecticut, Storrs, 2009), 42–47; Johnson, "Search for a Usable Indian"; Oberg, *Uncas,* 171–203.

28 Matthew Mayhew, *The Conquests and Triumphs of Grace: Being a Brief Narrative of the Success which the Gospel hath had among the Indians of Martha's Vineyard* (London: Nathaniel Hiller, 1695), 40–41 ("mostly to be doubted"); Franklin B. Hough, ed., *Papers Relating to the Island of Nantucket . . . while under the Colony of New York* (Albany: J. Munsell, 1865), 88–89 ("ill consequence"); Silverman, *Faith and Boundaries,* 111.

29 Benjamin Church, *Entertaining Passages relating to Philip's War* (Boston, 1716), in Slotkin and Folsom, eds., *So Dreadfull a Judgment,* 402 ("Pilot"), 407 ("possessed themselves"); Hubbard, *Narrative of the Troubles,* 69, 85 ("ready to fire"); Armstrong Starkey, *European and Native American Warfare, 1675–1815* (Norman: University of Oklahoma Press, 1998), 22.

30 Hubbard, *Narrative of the Troubles,* 68, 84–85, 98–99, 111, 113 ("skulking"), 115, 121, 169, 195, 197, 204, 206–207; Noah Newman to John Cotton, March 14, 1676, Curwen Papers, box 1, folder 3, American Antiquarian Society, Worcester, MA; Mather, *Brief History,* 91, 94, 97, 98, 113–114; Church, *Entertaining Passages,* 407; Thomas Wheeler, *A Thankfull Remembrance of God['/]s Mercy to Several Persons at Quabaug or Brookfield* (Cambridge, MA: n.p., 1676), in Slotkin and Folsom, *So Dreadfull a Judgment,* 244; Gookin, "An Historical Account," 441; Malone, *Skulking Way of War,* 106–107, 115.

31 Hubbard, *Narrative of the Troubles,* 133–134; Thompson, *New England's Crisis,* 220; Williams to Leverett, October 11, 1675, *Correspondence of Roger Williams,* 795 ("such places"); Gookin, "An Historical Account," 441 ("it was found"); Starkey, *European and Native American Warfare,* 68 ("accurate marks men").

32 Hubbard, *Narrative of the Troubles,* 167–168 ("one half"), 169–170 ("under the sides"); Newman to Cotton, March 14, 1676, Curwen Papers; Eric B. Shultz and Michael J. Tougias, *King Philip's War: The History and Legacy of America's Forgotten Conflict* (Woodstock, VT: Countryman Press, 1999), 198. For similar attacks, see Neal Salisbury, ed., *The Sovereignty and Goodness of God, by Mary Rowlandson, with Related Documents* (Boston: Bedford Books, 1997), 68–70; Leach, *Flintlock and Tomahawk,*

90, 159–160, 165, 173–174; Lepore, *Name of War,* 71–96; Mandell, *King Philip's War,* 96–98, 105–108. Statistics from John M. Murrin, "Revolution and Social Hysteria: King Philip's War and Bacon's Rebellion," 13, manuscript in author's possession.

33 Salisbury, *Sovereignty and Goodness of God,* 100.

34 Roger Williams to John Leverett, October 11, 1675, *Correspondence of Roger Williams,* 705.

35 John Pynchon to John Winthrop Jr., April 9, 1674, in *The Pynchon Papers,* 2 vols., ed. Carl Bridenbaugh (Boston: Colonial Society of Massachusetts, 1982), 1:124; William A. Starna, *From Homeland to New Land: A History of the Mahican Indians, 1600–1830* (Lincoln: University of Nebraska Press, 2013), 47, 148–149, 158–159; Calloway, *Western Abenakis,* 82–83; Lisa Brooks, *The Common Pot: The Recovery of Native Space in the Northeast* (Minneapolis: University of Minnesota Press, 2008), 25–27; Ted J. Brasser, *Riding on the Frontier's Crest: Mahican Indian Culture and Culture Change* (Ottawa: National Museums of Canada, 1974), 22, 25; Shirley Dunn, *The Mohican World, 1680–1850* (Fleischmanns, NY: Purple Mountain Press, 1997), 53–54, 101; Gordon Day, "Missisquoi: A New Look at an Old Village," *Man in the Northeast* 6 (Fall 1973): 51; unidentified and undated testimony but clearly from New York, March 1676, Colonial War Series, doc. 44a ("most of them armed"); Franklin B. Hough, ed., *Narrative of the Causes Which Led to Philip's Indian War, of 1675 and 1676, by John Easton of Rhode Island* (Albany, NY: J. Munsell, 1858), 145; Gookin, "An Historical Account," 488; Examination and Relation of James Quannapaquait, January 24, 1675/76, *MHSC,* ser. 1, vol. 6 (1846), 205–207; Hubbard, *Narrative of the Troubles,* 203; Samuel Symonds to Sir Joseph Williamson, April 6, 1676, Colonial State Papers Online, CO 1/36, no. 43; Roger Williams to John Leverett, January 14, 1675/76, *Correspondence of Roger Williams,* 712; Mather, *Brief History,* 110; Governor and Council of Connecticut to Edmund Andros, October 6, 1675, Yale Indian Papers, 1675.10.06.01; Emerson Woods Baker II, "New Evidence on the French Involvement in King Philip's War," *Maine Historical Society Quarterly* 28, no. 2 (Fall 1988), 85–91.

36 *CR,* 2:397, 404, 478; Mather, *Brief History,* 113–114, 134; Samuel Symonds to Sir Joseph Williamson, April 6, 1676, Colonial State Papers Online, CO 1/36, no. 43; Hough, *Narrative of the Causes,* 178–179; Examination of Pessacus's Messenger, Wuttawawaigkeessuck Sucqunch, April 29, 1676, Yale Indian Papers Online, 1676.04.29.01; Donna Merwick, *Death of a Notary: Conquest and Change in Colonial New York* (Ithaca, NY: Cornell University Press, 1999); *DRCHNY,* 3:238, 254, 255; Answer of Edward Randolph to Several Heads of Query Concerning the Present State of New England, October 12, 1676, Colonial State Papers Online, CO 1/37, no. 70, and CO 5/903, pp. 114–116; Examination and Relation of James Quannapaquait; Examination of Menonwiet, a hostile Indian taken near Farmington, August 13 or 14, 1676, Colonial War Docs., no. 108; Daniel K. Richter, "Dutch Dominos: The Fall of New Netherland and the Reshaping of Eastern North America," *Trade, Land, Power: The Struggle for Eastern North America* (Philadelphia: University of Pennsylvania Press, 2013), 97–112.

37 Michael Leroy Oberg, *Dominion and Civility: English Imperialism and Native America, 1585–1685* (Ithaca, NY: Cornell University Press, 1999), 162–163 ("free market"), 164–166; Mather, *Brief History,* 128–129; Stephen Saunders Webb, *1676: The End of American Independence* (New York: Knopf, 1984), 367–371; Francis Jennings, *The Invasion of America: Indians, Colonialism, and the Cant of Conquest* (Chapel Hill: University of North Carolina Press for the Institute of Early American History and Culture, 1975), 314–315; Jon Parmenter, "After the Mourning Wars: The Iroquois as Allies in Colonial North American Campaigns, 1676–1760," *WMQ* 64, no. 1 (January 2007): 42.

38 Oberg, *Dominion and Civility,* 165–166; Webb, *1676,* 371–374; Jennings, *Invasion of America,* 323; Daniel K. Richter, *The Ordeal of the Longhouse: The Peoples of the Iroquois League in the Era of European Colonization* (Chapel Hill: University of North Carolina Press for the Institute of Early American History and Culture, 1992), 136–137, 221–223, 226–227, 229–234; Laurence M. Hauptman, "Refugee Havens: The Iroquois Villages of the Eighteenth Century," in *American Indian Environments: Ecological Issues in Native American History,* ed. Christopher Vecsey and Robert W. Venables (Syracuse, NY: Syracuse University Press, 1980), 128–139; Francis Jennings, " 'Pennsylvania Indians' and the Iroquois," in *Beyond the Covenant Chain: The Iroquois and Their Neighbors in Indian North America, 1600–1800,* ed. Daniel K. Richter and James H. Merrell (Syracuse, NY: Syracuse University Press, 1987), 75–92; Eric Hinderaker, *The Two Hendricks: Unraveling a Mohawk Mystery* (Cambridge, MA: Harvard University Press, 2010).

39 Examination and Relation of James Quannapaquait ("store of arms"); Leach, *Flintlock and Tomahawk,* 200–204; Malone, *Skulking Way of War,* 99.

40 *PCR,* 5:173; Benjamin Batten to Sir Thomas Allen, June 29–July 6, 1675, Colonial State Papers Online, CO 1/34, no. 108; *CR,* 2:271; John Noble and John F. Cronin, eds., *Records of the Court of Assistants of Massachusetts Bay, 1630–1692,* 3 vols. (Boston: County of Suffolk, 1901–1928), 1:102–103.

41 Hubbard, *Narrative of the Troubles,* 181–182 ("without the loss), 236, 240, 252–253; Mather, *Brief History,* 122–123; Mandell, *King Philip's War,* 114–115; Leach, *Flintlock and Tomahawk,* 205–207; Richard Greenwood, Doug Harris, Sarah Holmes, Albert Klyberg, David Naumec, and Paul Robinson, "The Battles of Nipsachuck: Research and Documentation," National Park Service, American Battlefield Protection Program, Final Technical Report, GA-2255-09-023, pp. 61–64 (my thanks to Charlotte Taylor for providing me with a copy of this study).

42 Gookin, "An Historical Account," 511–513 ("it was observed").

43 Mandell, *King Philip's War,* 115–116; Jenny Hale Pulsipher, "Massacre at Hurtleberry Hill: Christian Indians and English Authority in Metacom's War," *WMQ* 53, no. 3 (July 1996): 459–486; Church, *Entertaining Passages,* 442 ("Indians gain'd").

44 Hubbard, *Narrative of the Troubles,* 193, 257, 261, 262, 264, 266–267; Church, *Entertaining Passages,* 434, 440, 446–447, 451; Drake, *King Philip's War;* Pulsipher, *Subjects Unto the Same King;* William Harris to Joseph Williamson, Aug. 12, 1676, *Rhode Island Historical Society Collections,* vol. 10 (1902), 162–163, 178 ("want of powder").

45 Mather, *Brief History,* 124 ("shaking"); Hubbard, *Narrative of the Troubles,* 67–68, 262, 275 ("shot twice"); James Drake, "Symbol of a Failed Strategy: The Sassamon Trial, Political Culture, and King Philip's War," *American Indian Culture and Research Journal* 19, no. 2 (1995): 131; John Callender, *An Historical Discourse, on the Civil and Religious Affairs of the Colony of Rhode-Island,* rev. ed. (1739; Providence, 1838: Knowles, Vose, and Co.), note on 127–128.

4: INDIAN GUNMEN AGAINST THE BRITISH EMPIRE

1 George Croghan to Sir Jeffrey Amherst, April 30, 1763, *Bouquet Papers, Ser. 21631, 21632,* 1:159; Amherst to William Johnson, May 29, 1763 ("not in their power"), Amherst to Bouquet, June 6, 1763 ("fully convinced"), *Amherst Papers,* microfilm.

2 Howard H. Peckham, *Pontiac and the Indian Uprising* [1947] (Detroit, MI: Wayne State University Press, 1994), 252; Michael N. McConnell, *A Country Between: The Upper Ohio Valley and Its Peoples, 1724–1774* (Lincoln: University of Nebraska

Press, 1992), 196; Richard Middleton, *Pontiac's War: Its Causes, Course, and Consequences* (New York: Routledge, 2007), 144, 145; Colin G. Calloway, *The Scratch of a Pen: 1763 and the Transformation of North America* (New York: Oxford University Press, 2006), 74.

3 "Des Savages" [1759], France Fonds des Colonies, Série C11A, Correspondance Générale; Canada: C-2402, Archives Nationales de France, Paris, http://Heritage .canadiana.ca; Joseph L. Peyser, trans. and ed., *On the Eve of the Conquest: The Chevalier de Raymond's Critique of New France in 1754* (East Lansing: Michigan State University Press, 1997); *Adventures in the Wilderness: The American Journals of Louis-Antoine de Bougainville, 1756–1760,* ed. and trans. Edward P. Hamilton (Norman: University of Oklahoma, 1964), 150–151; Peter D. McLeod, "Microbes and Muskets: Smallpox and the Participation of Amerindian Allies of New France in the Seven Years' War," *Ethnohistory* 39, no. 1 (Winter 1992): 42–64; Fred Anderson, *Crucible of War: The Seven Years' War and the Fate of Empire in British North America, 1754–1766* (New York: Knopf, 2000), 338–339, 394–395.

4 Peckham, *Pontiac and the Indian Uprising,* 72 ("purchasing"); Gregory Evans Dowd, *War under Heaven: Pontiac, the Indian Nations, and the British Empire* (Baltimore, MD: Johns Hopkins University Press, 2002), 70–71.

5 Stuart to Amherst, June 2, 1763, Amherst Papers, 3:51 ("ideas"); Johnson to Amherst, August 25, 1763, *Amherst Papers,* microfilm ("remarkably"); Amherst to William Johnson, August 9, 1761 ("impolitic"), *Johnson Papers,* 3:115. On Johnson, see James Thomas Flexner, *Mohawk Baronet: A Biography of Sir William Johnson* (New York: Harper, 1959); and Michael J. Mullin, "Personal Politics: William Johnson and the Mohawks," *American Indian Quarterly* 17, no. 3 (Summer 1993): 350–358.

6 John Oliphant, *Peace and War on the Anglo-Cherokee Frontier, 1756–63* (London: Palgrave, 2001); Anderson, *Crucible of War,* 457–471; Tom Hatley, *The Dividing Paths: Cherokees and South Carolinians through the Revolutionary Era* (New York: Oxford University Press, 1995), 119–178.

7 Richard White, *The Middle Ground: Indians, Empires, and Republics in the Great Lakes Region, 1650–1815* (New York: Cambridge University Press, 1991), 50–93, 256–268; "George Croghan's Journal, 1759–1763," ed. Nicholas Wainwright, *Pennsylvania Magazine of History and Biography* 71 (1947): 388 ("expressed"), 394–395 ("while the French"); Johnson to Amherst, June 16, 1763, *Amherst Papers,* microfilm ("wealthy people").

8 Johnson to Amherst, January 21, 1763, and March 21, 1761, Extract from George Croghan, October 8, 1762, *Johnson Papers,* 10:246–247 ("jealousy"), 279 ("alliance"), 548–549, 612 ("proof of friendship"); Mercer to Bouquet, January 19, 1759, Croghan to Bouquet, November 25, 1762, *Bouquet Papers,* 1:136 ("sulky") 2:14–15 ("blacksmith"); Middleton, *Pontiac's War,* 49 ("think hardest").

9 Journal of Indian Affairs, March 8–15, 1761, and Journal of James Gorrell, October 12, 1761–June 14, 1763, *Johnson Papers,* 10:239 (French gunpowder), 697–705; Eucyer to Bouquet, January 8, 1763, *Bouquet Papers, Ser. 21631, 21632,* 141–142 ("which foot"), 165; "Croghan's Journal," 416, 419, 420, 422, 423–424, 437; Keith R. Widder, *Beyond Pontiac's Shadow: Michilimackinac and the Anglo-Indian War of 1763* (East Lansing: Michigan State University Press, 2013), 85 (Etherington gifts), 116–120 (Gorrell gifts); McConnell, *Country Between,* 162–163 ("brothers and friends").

10 Peter C. Mancall, *Valley of Opportunity: Economic Culture along the Upper Susquehanna, 1700–1800* (Ithaca, NY: Cornell University Press, 1991); David L. Preston, *The Texture of Contact: European and Settler Communities on the Frontiers of Iroquoia,*

1667–1783 (Lincoln: University of Nebraska Press, 2009); "Croghan's Journal," 410 ("these steps"), 430–431, 432–433, 435; *Johnson Papers,* 10:221–222, 681; Indian Intelligence from Fort Pitt, January 30, 1763, *Bouquet Papers,* 4:156; Extracts of Letters, etc., Regarding Some Bad Dispositions of Indians in the Western Department, 1763, *Amherst Papers,* microfilm ("better attempt").

11 Gregory Evans Dowd, *A Spirited Resistance: The North American Indian Struggle for Unity, 1745–1815* (Baltimore, MD: Johns Hopkins University Press, 1992), 23–46.

12 Milo Milton Quaife, ed., *The Siege of Detroit in 1763: The Journal of Pontiac's Conspiracy and John Rutherfurd's Narrative of a Captivity* (Chicago, IL: R. R. Donnelley, 1958), 14–15 ("live by the bow and arrow"); Middleton, *Pontiac's War,* 62; Daniel K. Richter, *Trade, Land, Power: The Struggle for Eastern North America* (Philadelphia: University of Pennsylvania Press, 2013), 174 ("trouble your lands").

13 Johnson to Amherst, July 11, 1763, *Amherst Papers,* microfilm ("scarcity and dearness"). The size of the garrisons is charted in Timothy J. Todish and Todd E. Harburn, *A "Most Troublesome Situation": The British Military and the Pontiac Indian Uprising of 1763–1764* (Fleischmanns, NY: Purple Mountain Press, 2006), 175–176.

14 Instructions to Capt. Lt. Gardiner, August 10, 1763, *Amherst Papers,* microfilm.

15 Generally, see Wilbur R. Jacobs, *Diplomacy and Indian Gifts: Anglo-French Rivalry along the Ohio and Northwest Frontiers, 1748–1763* (Stanford, CA: Stanford University Press, 1950), 115–185.

16 Jacobs, *Diplomacy and Indian Gifts;* Mancall, *Valley of Opportunity;* Preston, *Texture of Contact;* McConnell, *Country Between;* White, *Middle Ground,* 186–222; Yoko Shirai, "The Indian Trade in Colonial Pennsylvania, 1730–1768: Traders and Land Speculation" (PhD diss., University of Pennsylvania, 1985); Charles A. Hanna, *The Wilderness Trail, or, The Ventures and Adventures of the Pennsylvania Traders on the Allegheny Path,* 2 vols. (New York: G. P. Putnam's Sons, 1911), 2:317, 326–343; Nicholas Wainwright, *George Croghan: Wilderness Diplomat* (Chapel Hill: University of North Carolina Press for the Institute of Early American History and Culture, 1958), 29; James H. Merrell, *Into the American Woods: Negotiators on the Pennsylvania Frontier* (New York: Norton, 1999), 79–83; John Armstrong to William Denny, September 14, 1756, and [George Croghan?], Account of the Beginning of the Seven Years' War, Mss. on Indian Affairs, pp. 410 ("explosion"), 500, American Philosophical Society, Philadelphia; Raymond to La Jonquière, January 5, 1750, *IHC,* vol. 29 (1940), 149–150 ("great quantity"); White, *Middle Ground,* 186–222; McConnell, *Country Between,* 47–88; *Early American Indian Documents: Treaties and Laws, 1607–1789,* vol. 2, *Pennsylvania Treaties, 1737–1756,* ed. Donald H. Kent (Washington, DC: University Publications of America, 1984), 174–193; Ian K. Steele, *Setting All the Captives Free: Capture, Adjustment, and Recollection in Allegheny Country* (Montreal: McGill-Queen's University Press, 2013), 102–105.

17 Kevin Gladysz, *The French Trade Gun in North America, 1662–1759* (Blackstone, RI: Andrew Mowbray Publishers, 2011), 70 (Mercier quotes); "Memoir of Bougainville," 1757, and Vaudreuil to the Minister, June 24, 1760, *CSHSW,* vol. 18 (1908), 195, 218; Pouchot, *Memoirs on the Late War in North America,* 94, 98, 117, 127; Sylvester K. Stevens, Donald H. Kent, and Emma Edith Woods, eds., *Travels in New France by J.C.B.* (Harrisburg: Pennsylvania Historical Commission, 1941), 43; Lettre de François-Marc-Antoine Le Mercier au ministre, October 20, 1755, C11A 100/fols. 178–179, Archives Nationales de France, Paris, http://Heritage.canadiana.ca; James Axtell, *The Indians' New South: Cultural Change in the Colonial Southeast* (Baton

Rouge: Louisiana State University Press, 1997), 64; *Adventure in the Wilderness: The American Journals of Louis Antoine de Bougainville, 1756–1760,* trans. and ed. Edward P. Hamilton (Norman: University of Oklahoma Press, 1964), 150–151; Pierre Pouchot, *Memoirs on the Late War in North America between France and England,* ed. Brian Leigh Dunnigan, trans. Michael Cardy (Youngstown, NY: Old Fort Niagara Association, 1994), 133–134; Steele, *Setting All the Captives Free,* 139.

18 *DRCHNY,* 10:311 ("considerable plunder"); Pouchot, *Memoirs on the Late War in America,* 82; Anderson, *Crucible of War,* 94–107, 185–201; Steele, *Setting All the Captives Free,* 88–96, 129; Steele, *Betrayals: Fort William Henry and the "Massacre"* (New York: Oxford University Press, 1990), 109–128; Dowd, *War under Heaven,* 143; Mc-Connell, *Country Between,* 122.

19 Anderson, *Crucible of War,* 330–339; Johnson to Amherst, May 24, 1759, December 26, 1758 ("good light arms"), May 6, 1759 ("good powder"), December 8, 1759, *Amherst Papers,* microfilm.

20 Walter S. Dunn Jr., *Frontier Profit and Loss: The British Army and the Fur Traders, 1760–1764* (Westport, CT: Greenwood Press, 1998), 49, 50; James Sterling Letter Book, 53, Clements Library ("three thousand weight"); Middleton, *Pontiac's War,* 84 ("£300 worth").

21 Johnson to the Earl of Egremont, May 1762, *Johnson Papers,* 10:463; List of Indian Traders and Their Servants Killed or Captured by Indians, September 30, 1763, *Bouquet Papers,* 4:412–413; Steele, *Setting All the Captives Free,* 20, 21, 33, 34, 49–50, 148–151, 172; Dowd, *War under Heaven,* 77, 133; Gladwin to Amherst, May 14, 1763, Lt. Cuyler's Report of Being Attacked and Routed by a Party of Indians on Lake Erie, and Amherst to Egremont, June 27, 1763, *Amherst Papers,* microfilm; Gladwin to Amherst, July 26, 1763, Amherst Papers, 2:7 ("sufficient supply"); William Winepress to Thomas Gage, June 15, 1763, Gage Papers, vol. 9, American Series; Jehu Hay Journal, entries of May 13 and May 30, 1763, William L. Clements Library, University of Michigan; Quaife, *Siege of Detroit,* 110–116; Middleton, *Pontiac's War,* 72; James MacDonald, Detroit, to Horatio Gates, August 8, 1763, Michigan Collection, William L. Clements Library, University of Michigan; Hay Journal, entry for June 19, 1763; Widder, *Beyond Pontiac's Shadow,* 182.

22 Dowd, *War under Heaven;* Dowd, "The French King Wakes Up in Detroit: 'Pontiac's War' in Rumor and History," *Ethnohistory* 37, no. 3 (Summer 1990): 254–278; Anderson, *Crucible of War,* 541; Middleton, *Pontiac's War,* 25–26, 85; Quaife, *Siege of Detroit,* 36.

23 Quaife, *Siege of Detroit,* 151–153, 200; Hay Journal, entry for June 26, 1763; Relation of the Gallant Defense Made by the Crew of the Schooner on Lake Erie, *Amherst Papers,* microfilm; Dowd, *War under Heaven,* 134, 137.

24 Amherst to Bouquet, October 3, 1763, *Bouquet Papers,* Ser. 21631, 21632, 282; Dowd, *War under Heaven,* 137–138; Middleton, *Pontiac's War,* 119–120, 122.

25 Hay Journal, entry of June 26, 1763 ("annoy"); Sterling Letter Book, 112; Quaife, *Siege of Detroit,* 204–205; Account of Alexander Duncan, *Johnson Papers,* 10:762–766; James MacDonald to Horatio Gates, August 8, 1763, Michigan Collection, Clements Library. On the siege at Pitt, see Dowd, *War under Heaven,* 143; McKee to Croghan, June 16, 1763, Ecuyer to Bouquet, June 26, 1763, and Ecuyer to Bouquet, August 2, 1763, *Bouquet Papers,* 4:252–253, 260, 332; Bouquet to Amherst, August 11, 1763, *Amherst Papers,* microfilm.

26 William Smith, *An Historical Account of the Expedition against the Ohio Indians, in the Year 1764* (Philadelphia: William Bradford, 1765), vi ("very bad"), vii; Blane to Bouquet, June 28, 1763, *Bouquet Papers*, 4:268 ("1,000").

27 Bouquet to Amherst, August 5 and 6, 1763 ("heavy fire"), August 11, 1763 ("boldness"), *Amherst Papers*, microfilm ("heavy fire), and *Bouquet Papers*, 4:339, 342–345.

28 Proceedings of a Court of Inquiry, Fort Pitt, September 1, 1763, *Bouquet Papers, Ser. 21631, 21632*, 257; Middleton, *Pontiac's War*, 123.

29 Jon William Parmenter, "Pontiac's War: Forging New Links in the Covenant Chain," *Ethnohistory* 44, no. 4 (Autumn, 1997): 617–654; *Johnson Papers*, 11:32, 33, 34, 108, 111, 161, 188; Steele, *Setting All the Captives Free*, 169–170.

30 Anderson, *Crucible of War*, 620 ("fill their canoes"); Steele, *Setting All the Captives Free*; Middleton, *Pontiac's War*, 153–154.

31 Anderson, *Crucible of War*, 621.

32 Dowd, *War under Heaven*, 153–168.

33 Steele, *Setting All the Captives Free*, 163–184. Generally, see Peter Silver, *Our Savage Neighbors: How Indian War Transformed Early America* (New York: Norton, 2008).

34 Ecuyer to Bouquet, June 2, 1763, Bouquet to Amherst, June 5, 1763, Amherst to Bouquet, June 16, 1763, Amherst to Bouquet, July 2, 1763, *Bouquet Papers*, 4:202–203, 207, 209 ("while we ourselves"), 274n1, 284 ("utmost"); Amherst to Bouquet, October 16, 1763, *Bouquet Papers, Ser. 21631, 21632*, 286 ("exhausted"); Dunn, *Frontier Profit and Loss*, 119; Deposition of La Salle, arrived at Montreal November 14 with a pass from Detroit, Gage Papers, vol. 9, American Series ("draw out").

35 Gladwin to Gage, January 9, 1764, Gage Papers, vol. 12, American Series ("enemy have lost"); Colden to Johnson, December 19, 1763, and Gage to Johnson, April 30, 1764, and May 3, 1764, *Johnson Papers*, 10:959 ("want of ammunition"), 11:168 ("every quarter"; "want of ammunition"), 11:173 ("want of supplies"; "hostile design"); Testimony of Matthias Warren, March 30, 1764, Gage Papers, vol. 16, American Series ("hunted"); Deposition of Corporal James Berry and Five Private Men, Gage Papers, vol. 14, American Series; Gage to Bradstreet, May 16, 1764, Gage Papers, vol. 18, American Series ("masters of their country").

36 Gage Instructions to Colonel Bradstreet, April 2, 1764, Gage Papers, vol. 16, American Series ("much animated"); Gage to Bouquet, June 20, 1764, Gage Papers, American Series, vol. 20 ("do not want"); Middleton, *Pontiac's War*, 171; Croghan to Johnson, May 13, 1765, *Johnson Papers*, 11:738 ("does not appear").

37 Calloway, *Scratch of a Pen*, 133–149; Dunn, *Frontier Profit and Loss*, 124–125; Robert Michael Morrissey, *Empire by Collaboration: Indians, Colonists, and Government in Colonial Illinois Country* (Philadelphia: University of Pennsylvania Press, 2015), 194–123; Johnson to Amherst, September 14, 1763, *Amherst Papers*, microfilm ("I well know"); Deposition of Gershom Hicks, April 14, 1764, and a reexamination of Gershom Hicks, April 26, 1764, Gage Papers, vol. 17, American Series; Gage to Halifax, June 8, 1764, in *The Correspondence of General Thomas Gage with the Secretaries of State, 1763–1775*, 2 vols., ed. Clarence Edwin Carter (New Haven, CT: Yale University Press, 1931), 1:31 (hereafter *Gage Correspondence*); Gage to Johnson, December 30, 1765, *Johnson Papers*, 11:988.

38 Deposition of Gershom Hicks, April 14, 1764, and a reexamination of Gershom Hicks, April 26, 1764, Gage Papers, vol. 17, American Series; Smith, *Historical Ac-*

count, 2; William Dunbar to Gage, September 22, 1763, Gage Papers, vol. 9, American Series; Thomas Smallman to Bouquet, November 8, 1764, *Bouquet Papers,* 706–707; Smallman to Thomas McKee, November 8, 1764, and Gage to Johnson, April 3, 1765, *Johnson Papers,* 11:404, 664; Gage to Halifax, December 13, 1764, *Gage Correspondence,* 1:53; Samuel Wharton to Benjamin Franklin, December 19, 1764, *Critical Period,* 376; Gage to Gladwin, January 9, 1764, Gage Papers, vol. 12, American Series; Gage, Instruction to Col. Bradstreet, April 2, 1764, Gage Papers, vol. 16, American Series; Gage to Lt. Gov. Bull, July 22, 1764, Gage Papers, American Series, vol. 22; Dowd, *War under Heaven,* 226–227.

39 Johnson to the Lords Commissioners for Trade and Plantations, *Critical Period,* 377 ("exorbitant"); Dunn, *Frontier Profit and Loss,* 62 (85,000); Gage to Bull, July 22, 1764, Gage to Burton, August 7, 1764, and Gage to Stuart, August 10, 1764, Gage Papers, vol. 22, American Series.

40 Deposition of Gershom Hicks, April 14, 1764, and a reexamination of Gershom Hicks, April 26, 1764, Gage Papers, vol. 17, American Series; Court of Inquiry held by order of Maj. Henry Gladwin, September 8, 1763, Amherst Papers, 2:20; Proceedings of a Court of Inquiry held at Detroit, October 1, 1763, *The Gladwin Manuscripts* (Lansing, MI: Robert Smith, 1897), 650; Testimony of Matthias Warren, March 30, 1764, Gage Papers, vol. 16, American Series.

41 D'Abbadie to the Minister, September 10, 1764, *Critical Period,* 312; Charles-Philippe Aubry to the Minister, February 4, 1765, *Critical Period,* 429–430 ("continually visited"); Journal of Indian Affairs, July 4–August 4, 1763, Indian Proceedings, December 2–16, 1764, Journal of William Howard, November 3, 1764–April 16, 1765, *Johnson Papers,* 10:767, 11:500–508, 696, 739–740; Gage to John Stuart, June 19, 1764, Gage Papers, vol. 20, American Series ("powder and ball"); Amherst to Halifax, April 14, 1764, Gage to Halifax, June 8, 1764, and Gage to Halifax, September 21, 1764, *Gage Correspondence,* 1:25–26, 31, 36; Bouquet to Gage, May 27, 1764, and Gage to Bouquet, June 5, 1764, Gage Papers, vol. 19, American Series.

42 Johnson to Gage, March 9, 1765, Extract from Letter of Alexander Fraser, May 18, 1765, Campbell to Johnson, June 3, 1765, Johnson to Gage, July 25, 1765, *Johnson Papers,* 11:625 ("universally believe"), 743 ("desired them"), 764 ("will never listen"), 868–870 ("lower order"); Fraser, Report on Indians in Illinois Country, April 27, 1765, Gage Papers, vol. 137, Indian Treaties and Congresses; Fraser to Campbell, May 17 and May 20, 1765, *Critical Period,* 493–494, 495 ("vast quantities").

43 Gage to Halifax, June 8, 1764, April 13, 1765, August 10, 1765, *Gage Correspondence,* 1:31 ("without the assistance"), 53, 63 ("no easy matter"); Report to Lord Barrington, December 18, 1765, *Gage Correspondence,* 2:320; Van Schaak and Other Traders, Detroit, to Jehu Hay, September 4, 1767, Clarence Walword Alvord and Clarence Edwin Carter, eds., *Trade and Politics, 1767–1769, IHC,* vol. 16 (Springfield, 1921), 4; Bradstreet's Opinion on Indians and their Affairs, December 7, 1764, Gage Papers, vol. 28, American Series ("strict justice").

44 Gage to Conway, July 15, 1766, Gage to Shelburn, January 17, 1767, and February 22, 1767, *Gage Correspondence,* 1:119, 121–122, 2:320; M. L. Brown, *Firearms in Colonial America: The Impact on History and Technology, 1492–1792* (Washington, DC: Smithsonian Institution Press, 1980), 260–264, 272; James A. Hanson, *Firearms of the Fur Trade* (Chadron, NE: Museum of the Fur Trade, 2011), 363–391; Charles E. Hanson Jr., *The Northwest Gun* (Lincoln: Nebraska State Historical Society, 1955), 45; Johnson to the Lords Commissioners of Trade and Plantations, ca. 1764–1765, *Critical Period,*

334 ("very fond"). For another statement on the drawbacks of rifles, see Joan B. Townsend, "Firearms against Native Arms: A Study in Comparative Efficiencies with an Alaskan Example," *Arctic Anthropology* 20, no. 2 (1983): 6–8.

45 Conference between Governor Denny, Governor Bernard, Governor DeLancey, George Croghan, Col. Montrosen, Col. Robinson, on the one hand, and Canawaga [*sic*] (Andrew Montour and Thomas King, deputies), on the other, April 10, 1759, Mss. on Indian Affairs, American Philosophical Society, Philadelphia; Colonel Bradstreet's Opinion on Indians and Their Affairs, December 7, 1764, Gage Papers, vol. 28, American Series; Morgan to Baynton and Wharton, July 20, 1768, *Trade and Politics,* 358–359; Dunn, *Frontier Profit and Loss,* 103, 104, 133–134; *DRCHNY,* 7:692 ("all the Shawnee"); Morgan to Baynton and Wharton, July 20, 1768, *Trade and Politics,* 358–359 ("all white persons"); Hanson, *Firearms of the Fur Trade,* 364.

46 Patrick Kehoe Spero, "Creating Pennsylvania: The Politics of the Frontier and the State, 1682–1800" (PhD diss., University of Pennsylvania, 2009), 257–272; Dowd, *War under Heaven,* 203–212.

47 Journal of Indian Affairs, May 17–June 4, 1765, *Johnson Papers,* 11:769 ("desired"); Johnson to the Commissioners of Trade and Plantations, Gage to Halifax, April 27, 1765, *Critical Period,* 338, 489 ("proof").

48 Campbell to Gage, October 3, 1764, Gage Papers, American Series, vol. 25 ("thought necessary"); Campbell to Gage, November 10, 1764, Gage Papers, American Series, vol. 26 ("very well convinced"); Major Forbes to Gage, July 15, 1764, Gage Papers, American Series, vol. 27 ("inconceivable"); James Covington, "English Gifts to the Indians, 1765–66," *Florida Anthropologist* 13, nos. 2–3 (September 1960): 71–75; White, *Middle Ground,* 310–312.

49 Gage to Johnson, *Johnson Papers,* 12:710 ("too numerous"); Dowd, *War under Heaven,* 174–212; Woody Holton, *Forced Founders: Indians, Debtors, Slaves and the Making of the American Revolution in Virginia* (Chapel Hill: University of North Carolina Press for the Omohundro Institute of Early American History and Culture, 1999), 3–38; Calloway, *Scratch of a Pen,* 92–111; Jack Sosin, *Whitehall in the Wilderness: The Middle West in British Colonial Policy* (Lincoln: University of Nebraska Press, 1961).

50 Colin G. Calloway, *The American Revolution in Indian Country: Crisis and Diversity in Native American Communities* (New York: Cambridge University Press, 1995), 3; Bernard Bailyn, *The Peopling of British North America: An Introduction* (New York: Knopf, 1986); Bailyn, *Voyagers to the West: A Passage in the Peopling of America on the Eve of the Revolution* (New York: Knopf, 1986), statistics on 26; Calloway, *Scratch of a Pen,* 59; Nathaniel Shiedley, "Hunting and the Politics of Masculinity in Cherokee Treaty-Making," in *Empire and Others: British Encounters with Indigenous Peoples, 1600–1850,* ed. Martin Daunton and Rick Halpern (Philadelphia: University of Pennsylvania Press, 1999), 167–185; Richter, *Trade, Land, Power,* 177–201; McConnell, *Country Between,* 239–246; White, *Middle Ground,* 315–517.

51 James L. Hill, "'Bring Them What They Lack': Spanish-Creek Exchange and Alliance Making in a Maritime Borderland," *Early American Studies* 12, no. 1 (Winter 2014): 36–67; Colin G. Calloway, *Crown and Calumet: British-Indian Relations, 1783–1815* (Norman: University of Oklahoma Press, 1987); Alan Taylor, *The Divided Ground: Indians, Settlers, and the Northern Borderland of the American Revolution* (New York: Knopf, 2006); Claudio Saunt, *A New Order of Things: Property, Power, and the Transformation of the Creek Indians, 1733–1816* (New York: Cambridge University Press, 1999); Dowd, *Spirited Resistance*; William S. Cooker, *Indian Traders of the*

Southern Borderlands: Panton, Leslie, and Company and John Forbes and Company, 1783–1847 (Gainesville: University Presses of Florida, 1986); Stephen Warren, *The Shawnees and Their Neighbors, 1795–1870* (Urbana: University of Illinois Press, 2005), 69–96; John Mack Faragher, "'More Motley than Mackinaw': From Ethnic Mixing to Ethnic Cleansing on the Frontier of the Lower Missouri, 1783–1833," in *Contact Points: American Frontiers from the Mohawk Valley to the Mississippi, 1750–1830,* ed. Andrew R. L. Cayton and Fredrika J. Teute (Chapel Hill: University of North Carolina Press for the Omohundro Institute of Early American History and Culture, 1998), 304–326.

5: OTTERS FOR ARMS

1 Eugene Arima and John Dewhirst, "Nootkans of Vancouver Island," *HNAI, Northwest,* vol. 7, vol. ed. Wayne Suttles (Washington, DC: Smithsonian Institution Press, 1990), 399, 400; Arrell Morgan Gibson, *Yankees in Paradise: The Pacific Basin Frontier* (Albuquerque: University of New Mexico Press, 1993), 29; James R. Gibson, *Otter Skins, Boston Ships, and China Goods: The Maritime Fur Trade of the Northwest Coast, 1785–1841* (Seattle: University of Washington Press, 1992), 3–4; Thomas F. Thornton, "The Ideology and Practice of Pacific Herring Cultivation among the Tlingit and Haida," *Human Ecology* 43, no. 2 (April 2015): 213–223.

2 Gibson, *Otter Skins,* 15; Claudio Saunt, *West of the Revolution: An Uncommon History of 1776* (New York: Norton, 2014), 34–53; Lydia Black, *Russians in Alaska, 1732–1867* (Fairbanks: University of Alaska Press, 2004), 65–67; Francis Ross Carpenter, *The Old China Trade: Americans in Canton, 1784–1843* (New York: Coward, Mc-Cann, and Geoghegan, 1976), 80; John R. Brockstoce, *Furs and Frontiers in the Far North: The Contest among Native and Foreign Nations for the Bering Strait Fur Trade* (New Haven, CT: Yale University Press, 2009), 117–118.

3 Gibson, *Yankees in Paradise,* 67, 69–70, 109–110; Gibson, *Otter Skins,* 23, 39, 57, 112; Carpenter, *Old China Trade,* 29–30; Robin Fisher, *Contact and Conflict: Indian-European Relations in British Columbia, 1774–1890,* 2nd ed. (Vancouver: University of British Columbia Press, 1992), 3, 13; Hiram Chittenden, *The American Fur Trade of the Far West: A History of Pioneer Trading Posts and Early Fur Companies of the Missouri Valley and Rocky Mountains and of the Overland Commerce with Santa Fe,* 2 vols. (New York: F. P. Harper, 1902), 95; "List of Vessels upon the Northwest Coast of America in the Year 1792," Magee Papers, MHS; Cecil Jane, trans. and ed., *A Spanish Voyage to Vancouver and the Northwest Coast of America, Being the Narrative of the Voyage Made in the Year 1792 by the Schooners Sutil and Mexicana to Explore the Strait of Fuca* (London: Argonaut Press, 1930), 90; Mary Malloy, *"Boston Men" on the Northwest Coast: The American Maritime Fur Trade, 1788–1844* (Fairbanks, AK: Limestone Press, 1998), 25–26, 30; William Sturgis, Three Lectures Dealing with his Voyages, 1:17, MHS.

4 *Russians in Tlingit America,* 34, 50n1 ("iron spear point"); William Beresford, *A Voyage Round the World; but More Particularly to the North-west coast of America: performed in 1785, 1786, 1787, and 1788* (London: George Goulding, 1789), 171 ("perfectly quiet"), 184; John Hoskins, "Memoir of Trade at Nootka Sound," undated, Ship *Columbia,* 1787–1817, MHS; *The Journal of Captain James Colnett Aboard the Argonaut from April 26, 1789 to Nov. 3, 1791* (Toronto: The Champlain Society, 1940), 202 ("ordnance stories"); Hoskins "Narrative of a Voyage," Log of the Ship *Columbia* (photostats), MHS, 131–132.

5 George Vancouver, *A Voyage of Discovery to the North Pacific Ocean, and Round the World,* 3 vols. (London: G. G. and J. Robinson, 1798), 2:364–365 ("means of signs"); Gibson, *Otter Skins,* 120 ("cunning savages"), 215 ("muskets need not be sent"); "Sullivan Dorr Letters," *Proceedings of the Massachusetts Historical Society,* ser. 3, vol. 67 (October 1941–May 1944): 231–232 ("good"); Sturgis Lectures, 1:14, MHS ("thorough examination"); John D'Wolf, *A Voyage to the North Pacific and a Journey throughout Siberia More than a Half Century Ago* (Cambridge, MA: Welch, Bigelow, 1861), 19; *Russians in Tlingit America,* 313 ("best English arms"); John Suter to James and Thomas Lamb, July 15, 1808 ("French arms") and "A Cargo Suitable for the Northwest Coast of America, July 1808," John Suter Papers, MHS.

6 Shipping Papers, oversized, account dated October 2, 1799, Thomas Lamb Papers *(Alert),* MHS; Sturgis Lectures, 1:12, MHS; Gibson, *Yankees in Paradise,* 111; Gibson, *Otter Skins,* 6, 315 (trade statistics from table 7).

7 Daniel W. Clayton, *Islands of Truth: The Imperial Fashioning of Vancouver Island* (Vancouver: University of British Columbia Press, 2000), 119, 168–169; John Edwin Mills, "The Ethnohistory of Nootka Sound, Vancouver Island" (PhD diss., University of Washington, 1955), 1–3; Jane, *Spanish Voyage to Vancouver,* 95–96; Arima and Dewhirst, "Nootkans," 393; Richard I. Inglis and James C. Haggarty, "Cook to Jewitt: Three Decades of Change in Nootka Sound," in *"Le Castor Fait Tout": Selected Papers of the Fifth North American Fur Trade Conference,* ed. Bruce G. Trigger, Toby Morantz, and Louise Dechêne (Montreal: Lake St. Louis Historical Society, 1985), 208; Beresford, *Voyage Around the World,* 146 ("go around").

8 Inglis and Haggarty, "Cook to Jewitt," 202 ("port dues"; "agents"); Clayton, *Islands of Truth,* 128; Gibson, *Otter Skins,* 110; Jasper Lesage, "The European-Nootkan Maritime Fur Trade in the Late Eighteenth Century" (PhD diss., University of Toronto, 1983), 115–122.

9 Arima and Dewhirst, "Nootkans," 401–402.

10 Joyce Annabell Wyke, "The Effect of the Maritime Fur Trade on Northwest Coast Indian Society" (PhD diss., Columbia University, 1951), 85–86 ("thirteen fine skins"), 99; John R. Jewitt, *A Narrative of the Adventures and Sufferings of John R. Jewitt* (New York: Daniel Fanshaw, 1816), 160 ("quantity of cloth").

11 Clayton, *Islands of Truth,* 119, 125, 154; Vancouver, *Voyage of Discovery,* 1:332; Gibson, *Otter Skins,* 8–9, 221–222; Hoskins, "Narrative of a Voyage," Log of the Ship *Columbia,* 144–145 ("trifling"); Wyke, "Effect of the Maritime Fur Trade," 50.

12 John Meares, *Voyages Made in the Years 1788 and 1789, from China to the Northwest Coast of America,* 2 vols. (London: J. Walter, 1791), 1:317 ("animated"; "more powerful"), 336; Jane, *Spanish Voyage to Vancouver,* 117 ("know well").

13 Robert H. Ruby and John A. Brown, *Indian Slavery in the Pacific Northwest* (Spokane, WA: A.H. Clark, 1993), 130–171; Leland Donald, *Aboriginal Slavery on the Northwest Coast of North America* (Berkeley: University of California Press, 1997).

14 Gibson, *Otter Skins,* 234 ("nine blankets"); Edward Sapir and Morris Swadesh, "Native Accounts of Nootka Ethnography," *International Journal of American Linguistics* 21, no. 4 (October 1955): 416, 417; Ruby and Brown, *Indian Slavery,* 67 ("nearly fifty"); Gary Coupland, "Warfare and Social Complexity on the Northwest Coast," in *Cultures in Conflict: Current Archaeological Perspectives,* ed. Diana Claire Tkaczuk and Brian C. Vivian (Calgary: University of Calgary Archaeological Association, 1989), 205–215.

15 Meares, *Voyages,* 1:182, 348; Vancouver, *Voyage of Discovery,* 3:308 ("muskets"); Jane, *Spanish Voyage to Vancouver,* 118; Jewitt, *Narrative,* 124–125.

16 Yvonne May Marshall, "A Political History of the Nuu-chah-nulth People: A Case Study of the Mowachaht and Muchalaht Tribes" (PhD diss., Simon Fraser University, 1993), 268–269; Clayton, *Geographies of Truth,* 137, 143 144, 146; Meares, *Voyages,* 1:234–236; *Journal of Captain James Colnett,* 191, 202; Jewitt, *Narrative,* 98; Jane, *Spanish Voyage to Vancouver,* 18.

17 Gibson, *Otter Skins,* 164, 166 ("considerable slaughter"); *The John Boit Log and Captain Gray's Log of the Ship Columbia,* ed. F. W. Howay and T. C. Elliott (Portland, OR: Ivy Press, 1921), 299–300, 303 ("fine village"); Jane, *Spanish Voyage to Vancouver,* 22 ("natives had not wished"); Log of the Ship *Columbia,* 155–156 ("conspiracy"), 161–162; Bernard Magee Logbooks, 1790–1794, entry of June 13, 1793, MHS; "The Voyage of the Hope, 1790–1792," *Washington Historical Quarterly* 11 (January 1920): 25–26.

18 Jewitt, *Narrative,* 117–118.

19 Ibid., 32–33 ("peshank"); Gibson, *Otter Skins,* 206 (curses).

20 Jewitt, *Narrative,* 19–20, 43–44, 45 ("muskets"; "rendering"), 55 ("attentive").

21 Ibid., 48–49 (all quotes); *Russians in Tlingit America,* 394.

22 Jewitt, *Narrative,* 51–52 ("no less"; *"Wocash"*); Vancouver, *Voyage of Discovery,* 1:396.

23 Jewitt, *Narrative,* 155–56, 176 ("respective ranks").

24 Ibid., 56 ("train oil"), 100–101 ("pelpeth"), 102 ("tributary offering"), 103–104 ; Inglis and Haggarty, "Cook to Jewitt," 103.

25 Jewitt, *Narrative,* 183–201.

26 Washington Irving, *Astoria: Or, Anecdotes of an Enterprise beyond the Rocky Mountains,* 2 vols. (Philadelphia: Carey, Lea, and Blanchard, 1836), 1:114; James P. Ronda, *Astoria and Empire* (Lincoln: University of Nebraska Press, 1990), 235–237; Gibson, *Otter Skins,* 168.

27 *Russians in Tlingit America,* xxiii; Gibson, *Otter Skins,* 222 ("plenty"; "first demand"); Samuel Curson, "My First Voyage; Experiences in the Ship *Eliza* from August 15, 1798 to February 19, 1799," 53, MHS; Jonathan Ritchie Dean, " 'Rich Men,' 'Big Powers,' and Wastelands: The Tlingit-Tsimshian Border of the Northern Pacific" (PhD diss., University of Chicago, 1993), 65; Wyke, "Effect of the Maritime Fur Trade," 17 ("farther back"); Urey Lisiansky, *A Voyage Round the World, in the Years 1803, 4, 5, & 6* (London: John Booth, 1814), 148, 239 ("former").

28 Curson, "My First Voyage," 52; Sturgis Lectures, 1:14; Sergei Kan, "The 19th-Century Tlingit Potlatch: A New Perspective," *American Ethnologist* 13, no. 2 (May 1986): 191–212. It is possible that Sturgis accurately related an attempt by Haida men to bond with the foreigners through misogyny. See Nancy Shoemaker, "An Alliance between Men: Gender Metaphors in Eighteenth-Century American Indian Diplomacy East of the Mississippi," *Ethnohistory* 46, no. 2 (1999): 239–264.

29 Gibson, *Otter Skins,* 13; *Russians in Tlingit America,* 135 ("I myself saw"); *Colonial Russian America: Kyrill T. Khlebnikov's Reports, 1817–1832,* trans. Basil Dmytryshyn and E. A. P. Crownhart-Vaughan (Portland: Oregon Historical Society, 1976), 35.

30 *Russians in Tlingit America*, xxvi, xxx, xxxiii, 56–57, 157–160, 383; Andrei Val'Terovich Grinev, *The Tlingit Indians in Russian America, 1741–1867,* trans. Richard L. Bland and Katerina G. Solovjova (Lincoln: University of Nebraska Press, 2005), 103–104, 117, 123–124; Gibson, *Otter Skins,* 14.

31 *Russians in Tlingit America*, xxxiii, 180, 198 ("provided much powder"); Grinev, *Tlingit Indians,* 131.

32 *Russians in Tlingit America*, 180, 192–193 ("heavy fire"; "plenty of firearms").

33 Ibid., 176 ("guns, spears"), 177 ("strong gunfire"), 179, 383–384.

34 *The Russian American Colonies, 1798–1867: A Documentary Record,* eds. and trans. Basil Dmytryshyn, E. A. P. Crownhart-Vaughan, and Thomas Vaughan (Portland: Oregon Historical Society, 1989), 159 ("firearms"), 160–161, 179, 223–224, 226.

35 *Russians in Tlingit America*, xxxvii, 234, 249, 257; William J. Hunt Jr., *Sitka National Historical Park: The Archaeology of the Fort Unit,* 2 vols. (Lincoln, NE: Midwest Archaeological Center, 2010).

36 *Russians in Tlingit America*, xxxvi–xxxvii, 231–232; Lisiansky, *Voyage,* 155; Ted C. Hinckley, *The Canoe Rocks: Alaska's Tlingit and the Euramerican Frontier, 1800–1912* (Lanham, MD: University Press of America, 1996), 24.

37 *Russians in Tlingit America*, xxx–xxxi, 157, 161,167, 231 ("awesome fire"; "every one . . . wounded"), 232–233, 334, 341–342, 345–346, 397–398; Lisiansky, *Voyage,* 158; *Russian American Colonies,* 160–162; John Dusty Kidd, "The Battle of Sitka: Generals and Soldiers," in *Over the Near Horizon: Proceedings of the 2010 International Conference on Russian America,* ed. Kidd (Anchorage, AK: Sitka Historical Society, 2011), 113–120.

38 *Russians in Tlingit America*, xxxvii–viii, 260–261 ("chief cause").

39 Ibid., 236, 240, 299–303; G. H. von Langsdorff, *Voyages and Travels in Various Parts of the World: During the Years 1803, 1804, 1805, 1806, and 1807,* 2 vols. (London. H. Colburn, 1814), 125–126; Grinev, *Tlingit Indians,* 141–144; Dean, "'Rich Men,'" 162.

40 *Russian American Colonies,* 13 ("in truth"), 143; Hinckey, *Canoe Rocks,* 27–28, 31 ("without hesitation"); *Khlebnikov's Reports,* 55; Gibson, *Otter Skins,* 17; Grinev, *Tlingit Indians,* 152–154 ("local peoples").

41 Gibson, *Otter Skins,* 61–63, 179, 208.

42 *Russian American Colonies,* lxviii; Gibson, *Yankees in Paradise,* 117; Archibald Campbell, *A Voyage Round the World, from 1806 to 1812* (Edinburgh: Archibald Constable and Co., 1816), 110–111; Malloy, *"Boston Men,"* 35–36, 39; Fisher, *Contact and Conflict,* 25–26; John Dunn, *History of the Oregon Territory and British North-America Fur Trade* (London, 1844), 244 ("company's vessels"); Laura F. Klein, "Demystifying the Opposition: The Hudson's Bay Company and the Tlingit," *Arctic Anthropology* 24, no. 1 (1987): 101–114; E. Palmer Patterson, "'The Indians Stationary Here': Continuity and Change in the Origins of the Fort Simpson Tsimshian," *Anthropologica* 36, no. 2 (1994): 181–203; Katherine L. Reedy-Maschner and Herbert D. G. Maschner, "Marauding Middlemen: Western Expansion and Violent Conflict in the Subarctic," *Ethnohistory* 46, no. 4 (Autumn 1999): 703–743.

43 Gibson, "European Dependence upon American Natives: The Case of Russian America," *Ethnohistory* 25, no. 4 (Autumn 1978): 359–385; Hinckley, *Canoe Rocks,*

32; Clayton, *Islands of Truth,* 126, 145; Dean, "'Rich Men,'" 181, 195, 205, 247; Fisher, *Contact and Conflict,* 31–32; Gibson, *Otter Skins,* 11.

44 Dean, "'Rich Men,'" 201 ("thousands"), 493–497, 503; Grivev, *Tlingit Indians,* 170–171 ("slaves").

45 Gibson, *Otter Skins,* 273; Arima and Dewhirst "Nootkans," 400; Grivev, *Tlingit Indians,* 173–174; Robert Thomas Boyd, "The Introduction of Infectious Diseases among the Indians of the North West Coast" (PhD diss., University of Washington, 1985), 147–152; Boyd, *The Coming of the Spirit of Pestilence: Introduced Infectious Diseases and Population Decline among Northwest Coast Indians, 1774–1874* (Vancouver: University of British Columbia Press, 1999); David Igler, "Diseased Goods: Global Exchanges in the Eastern Pacific Basin, 1770–1850," *American Historical Review* 109, no. 3 (2004): 693–719.

6: THE SEMINOLES RESIST REMOVAL

1 http://hsus.cambridge.org/HSUSWeb/table/showtable_essay.do?id=Aa9-14&seriesid=Aa9&swidth=1366; *Abstract of the Returns of the Fifth Census,* House Doc. no. 268 (Washington, DC: Government Printing Office, 1832), available at http://www2.census.gov/prod2/decennial/documents/1830a-01.pdf.

2 Daniel Walker Howe, *What God Hath Wrought: The Transformation of America* (New York: Oxford University Press, 2007), 517; John Missall and Mary Lou Missall, *The Seminole Wars: America's Longest Indian Conflict* (Gainesville: University Press of Florida, 2004), 125, 204–205. The army reported the death of 1,466 of its men but did not keep track the many militia and volunteer groups that fought in the war. On federal spending, see Susan B. Carter et al., eds., *Historical Statistics of the United States: Earliest Times to the Present* (New York, 2006), Series Ea, 584–587, 5–80.

3 On Seminole origins, see Edwin C. McReynolds, *The Seminoles* (Norman: University of Oklahoma Press, 1957), 3–21; J. Leitch Wright Jr., *Creeks and Seminoles* (Lincoln: University of Nebraska Press, 1986), 217–219; William C. Sturtevant and Jessica R. Cattelino, "Florida Seminole and Miccosuke," *HNAI, Southeast,* vol. 14, ed. Raymond Fogelson (Washington, DC: Smithsonian Institution Press, 2004), 431–432 ("simaló ni" on 431). On the Seminoles' political and cultural relationship to the Creeks and settlement patterns, see Brent Richards Weisman, *Like Beads on a String: A Culture History of the Seminole Indians in North Peninsular Florida* (Tuscaloosa: University of Alabama Press, 1989). On the Red Stick movement, see Gregory Evans Dowd, *A Spirited Resistance: The North American Indian Struggle for Unity, 1745–1815* (Baltimore: Johns Hopkins University Press, 1992), 148–190; Joel W. Martin, *Sacred Revolt: The Muskogees' Struggle for a New World* (Boston: Beacon Press, 1991); Claudio Saunt, "Taking Account of Property: Social Stratification among the Creek Indians in the Early Nineteenth Century," *WMQ* 57, no. 4 (October 2000): 733–760; and Saunt, *A New Order of Things: Property, Power, and the Transformation of the Creek Indians, 1733–1816* (New York: Cambridge University Press, 1999), 249–272.

4 On the Black Seminoles, see Kenneth W. Porter, *The Black Seminoles: History of a Freedom-Loving People,* rev. ed., ed. Alcione M. Amos and Thomas P. Senter (Gainesville: University Press of Florida, 1996); Kevin Mulroy, "Seminole Maroons," *HNAI, Southeast,* 465–466; Daniel F. Littlefield Jr., *Africans and Seminoles: From Removal to Emancipation* (Westport, CT: Greenwood Press, 1977); Nathaniel

Millett, *The Maroons of Prospect Bluff and Their Quest for Freedom in the Atlantic World* (Gainesville: University Press of Florida, 2013).

5 Colin G. Calloway, *The American Revolution in Indian Country: Crisis and Diversity in Native American Communities* (New York: Cambridge University Press, 1995), 244–271; Gregory A. Waselkov and Kathryn E. Holland Braund, *William Bartram on the Southeastern Indians* (Lincoln: University of Nebraska Press, 1995), 52; Wright, *Creeks and Seminoles*, 56, 59; William S. Coker and Thomas D. Watson, *Indian Traders of Southeastern Spanish Borderlands: Panton, Leslie, and Company and John Forbes and Company, 1783–1847* (Gainesville: University Press of Florida, 1986), 35; David J. Weber, *Bárbaros: Spaniards and Their Savages in the Age of Enlightenment* (New Haven, CT: Yale University Press, 2005), 178–220, esp. 204; John Leslie to Panton, Leslie, and Company, March 7, 1800, reel 12, PPLC.

6 Richard K. Murdoch, "Indian Presents: To Give or Not to Give, Governor White's Quandary," *FHQ* 35, no. 4 (April 1957); 329–330, 336; Jane Landers, *Black Society in Spanish Florida* (Urbana: University of Illinois Press, 1999), 72. From PPLC: Arturo O'Neill to Baron de Carondelet, January 30, 1793, and Carondelet to William Panton, February 5, 1793, reel 8; Carondelet to Duque de Alcudia, September 27, 1797, reel 9; Carondelet to Juan Ventura Morales, May 16, 1797, and Morales to Pedro Varela y Ulloa, June 30, 1797, reel 10; Salvador de Alva to Bartolome Garcia, January 28, 1809, reel 17.

7 James G. Cusick, *The Other War of 1812: The Patriot War and the American Invasion of East Florida* (Gainesville: University Press of Florida, 2003), 213–222, 224–225, 256–257; Landers, *Black Society in Spanish Florida,* 220–227.

8 J. Leitch Wright Jr., *William Augustus Bowles: Director General of the Creek Nation* (Athens: University of Georgia Press, 1967); Gilbert C. Din, *War on the Gulf Coast: The Spanish Fight against William Augustus Bowles* (Gainesville: University Press of Florida, 2012); Coker and Watson, *Indian Traders,* 112–119, 148–156, 226–242; Elizabeth Howard West, ed., "A Prelude to the Creek War of 1813–1814: In a Letter of John Innerarity to James Innerarity," *FHQ* 18, no. 4 (April 1940): 247–266; Owsley, *Struggle for the Gulf Borderlands,* 99–100, 103, 134–135, 181; Millett, *Maroons of Prospect Bluff*; Jim Piecuch, *Three Peoples, One King: Loyalists, Indians, and Slaves in the American Revolutionary South, 1775–82* (Columbia: University of South Carolina Press, 2008); Sylvia R. Frey, *Water from the Rock: Black Resistance in a Revolutionary Age* (Princeton, NJ: Princeton University Press, 1991).

9 Anthony F. C. Wallace, *The Long Bitter Trail: Andrew Jackson and the Indians* (New York: Hill and Wang, 1993), 94–97; Millett, *Maroons of Prospect Bluff*; Wright, *Creeks and Seminoles,* 184; Missall and Missall, *Seminole Wars,* 70–76; Adam Rothman, *Slave Country: American Expansion and the Origins of the Deep South* (Cambridge, MA: Harvard University Press, 2007); Edward E. Baptist, *The Half Has Never Been Told: Slavery and the Making of American Capitalism* (New York: Basic Books, 2014); Christopher Leslie Brown, *Moral Capital: Foundations of British Abolitionism* (Chapel Hill: University of North Carolina Press for the Omohundro Institute of Early American History and Culture, 2006).

10 Wright, *Creeks and Seminoles,* 199; *American State Papers,* 38 vols. (Washington, DC: Government Printing Office, 1832–1861), *Military Affairs,* 7 vols., 1:723; Martin, *Sacred Revolt,* 150–168; Karl Davis, "'Remember Fort Mims: Reinterpreting the Origins of the Creek War," *Journal of the Early Republic* 22, no. 4 (Winter 2002): 611–636; Kathryn E. Holland Braund, ed., *Tohopeka: Rethinking the Creek War and*

the *War of 1812* (Tuscaloosa: University of Alabama Press, 2012); Missall and Missall, *Seminole Wars*, 185–215; Saunt, *New Order of Things*, 249–290; Robert V. Remini, *Andrew Jackson and His Indian Wars* (New York: Viking, 2001), 130–162; Landers, *Black Society in Spanish Florida*, 229–237.

11 McReynolds, *Seminoles*, 114 ("nineteen-twentieths"); Wallace, *Long Bitter Trail*, 94–97.

12 George Klos, "Blacks and the Seminole Removal Debate, 1821–1835," in *The African American Heritage of Florida*, ed. David R. Colburn and Jane L. Landers (Gainesville: University Press of Florida, 1995), 128–156; Wallace, *Long Bitter Trail*, 94–97.

13 Hugh Young, "A Topographic Memoire on East and West Florida with Itineraries of General Jackson's Army, 1818," *FHQ* 13, no. 2 (October 1934): 94; Weisman, *Like Beads on a String*, 85–92; James Dell et al. to President Jackson [undated; received October 1828], *Territorial Papers of the United States,* comp. and ed. Clarence Edwin Carter (Washington, DC: Government Printing Office, 1934–1975), *Territory of Florida*, 24:282 ("buying up"); John T. Sprague, *The Origin, Progress, and Conclusion of the Florida War* (New York: D. Appleton and Co., 1848), 81 ("unusually large"), 85–86; Woodburne Potter, *The War in Florida: Being an Exposition of Its Causes and an Accurate History of the Campaigns of General Clinch, Gaines, and Scott* (Baltimore, MD: Lewis and Coleman, 1836), 74; John K. Mahon, *History of the Second Seminole War, 1835–1842,* rev. ed. (Gainesville: University Press of Florida, 1985), 89, 135; Missall and Missall, *Seminole Wars*, 90; McReynolds, *Seminoles*, 152.

14 Sprague, *Florida War*, 97–100; James W. Covington, *The Seminoles of Florida* (Gainesville: University Press of Florida, 1993), 83–84; Missall and Missall, *Seminole Wars*, 90; Mahon, *History of the Second Seminole War*, 99–101.

15 Mahon, *History of the Second Seminole War*, 101–102.

16 Ibid., 102–111; Covington, *Seminoles of Florida*, 79–80; Missall and Missall, *Seminole Wars*, 96–99; Ethan Allen Hitchcock, *Fifty Years in the Camp and Field*, ed. W. A. Croffut (New York: G.P. Putnam's Sons, 1909), 87 (quotes), 91; Frank Laumer, ed., *Amidst a Storm of Bullets: The Diary of Lt. Henry Prince in Florida, 1836–1842* (Tampa, FL: University of Tampa Press, 1998), 12 (hereafter *Prince Diary*).

17 *Annual Report of the Secretary of War, 1836* (Washington, DC: Government Printing Office, 1836); Mahon, *History of Second Seminole War*, 110–111; Missall and Missall, *Seminole Wars*, 98–99.

18 *Annual Report of the Secretary of War, 1832* (Washington, DC: Government Printing Office, 1832), 817–818; Mahon, *History of the Second Seminole War*, 146–150; Missall and Missall, *Seminole Wars*, 105–110.

19 *Prince Diary*, 5–6 (dog; false alarm; friendly fire), 8 (bear), 12 (scene of massacre), 15 (first ambush), 18 (second ambush).

20 Ibid., 19–22.

21 Sprague, *Florida War*, 460 ("first discharge"); M. L. Brown, "U.S. Arsenals, Depots, and Martial Firearms of the Second Seminole War," *FHQ* 61, no. 4 (April 1983): 445–458; Charles Edward Chapel, *Guns of the Old West* (New York: Coward-McCann, 1961), 152; Mahon, *History of the Second Seminole War*, 120; George E. Buker, *Swamp Sailors: Riverine Warfare in the Everglades, 1835–1842* (Gainesville: University Press of Florida, 1975), 13; *Prince Diary*, 18; Meyer M. Cohen, *Notices*

of Florida and the Campaigns (Charleston, SC: Burges and Honour, 1836), 173 ("imperfect loading").

22 *Annual Report of the Secretary of War, 1836,* 813; *Annual Report of the Secretary of War, 1837* (Washington, DC: Government Printing Office, 1837), 587; Cohen, *Notices of Florida,* 194–195; Missall and Missall, *Seminole Wars,* 115, 117–118, 125–126.

23 Jacob Rhett Motte, *Journey into Wilderness: An Army Surgeon's Account of Life in Camp and Field during the Creek and Seminole Wars, 1836–1838,* ed. James F. Sunderman (Gainesville: University Press of Florida, 1953), 124, 146 ("espionage"); Cohen, *Notices of Florida,* 222 ("prize ox"), 231 (Dade); McReynolds, *Seminoles,* 218 ("blunders").

24 Sprague, *Florida War,* 454 ("young men"), 498–499 ("you have guns"); *Prince Diary,* 42.

25 *Prince Diary,* 70 ("white men"); Motte, *Journey into Wilderness,* 183–184.

26 Toni Carrier, "Trade and Plunder Networks in the Second Seminole War in Florida, 1835–1842" (MA thesis, University of South Florida, 2005), 92–95, 137; Potter, *War in Florida,* 117; Governor Reid to the Secretary of War, August 22, 1840, and John T. McLaughlin to the Secretary of the Navy, August 11, 1840, *Territorial Papers of the United States, Territory of Florida,* 26:194, 203; William C. Sturtevant, "Chakaika and the 'Spanish Indians': Documentary Sources Compared with Seminole Tradition," *Tequesta* 13 (1953): 48–50; Baker, *Swamp Soldiers,* 13, 105–107, 134.

27 Carrier, "Trade and Plunder," 45, 96, 102, 128, 154; Robert Fitzpatrick, William Wyatt, and Cedar Keys, to William J. Worth, July 9, 1849, *Territorial Papers of the United States, Territory of Florida,* 26:509; James W. Covington, "Trade Relations between Southwestern Florida and Cuba, 1600–1840," *FHQ* 38, no. 2 (October 1959): 114–128; James L. Hill, "'Bring Them What They Lack': Spanish-Creek Exchange and Alliance Making in a Maritime Borderland," *Early American Studies* 12, no. 1 (Winter 2014): 36–67; Dorothy Dodd, "Captain Bunce's Tampa Bay Fisheries, 1835–1840," *FHQ* 25, no. 3 (January 1947): 246–256.

28 Buker, *Swamp Sailors,* 110–111 ("three Spaniards"), 115, 135 ("half breed"); Carrier, "Trade and Plunder," 124; *Prince Diary,* 70 ("mixture"); Sprague, *Florida War,* 454 ("down the country"; "along the keys"); Covington, "Trade Relations," 116.

29 Carrier, "Trade and Plunder," 22, 175 ("constant"); Kenneth W. Porter, "Notes on Seminole Negroes in the Bahamas," *FHQ* 24, no. 1 (July 1945): 56–60; John M. Goggin, "The Seminole Negroes of Andros Island," *FHQ* 24, no. 3 (1946): 201–206.

30 Reid to Secretary of War, August 22, 1840, *Territorial Papers of the United States, Territory of Florida,* 26:203 ("naval force"); Buker, *Swamp Sailors,* 4, 15, 35–56, 79; Missall and Missall, *Seminole Wars,* 125–126; Dallas to the Secretary of the Navy, Dept. 18, 1837, and Dallas to Edward B. Babbit, September 24, 1838, and Sec. of War to Commanding General, March 18, 1839, *Territorial Papers of the United States, Territory Florida,* 25:422 ("any was obtained"), 539–540 ("fishing smacks); *Annual Report of the Secretary of War, 1839* (Washington, DC: Government Printing Office, 1839), 44.

31 Missall and Missall, *Seminole Wars,* 126; Porter, *Black Seminoles,* 73; Jane G. Landers, *Atlantic Creoles in the Age of Revolutions* (Cambridge, MA: Harvard University Press, 2010), 175–178; *Prince Diary,* 48 ("miscreants"); Mahon, *History of the Second Seminole War,* 261; Sprague, *Florida War,* 187, 255–256 ("obtain"), 303 ("declared").

32 *Prince Diary,* 92 ("buried"); Carrier, "Trade and Plunder," 155; Sprague, *Florida War,* 466–467 ("hollow trees").

33 Sprague, *Florida War,* 318.

34 *Annual Report of the Secretary of War, 1837,* 588; Missall and Missall, *Seminole Wars,* 126–128; Porter, *Black Seminoles,* 71–72.

35 Missall and Missall, *Seminole Wars,* 134–141, 143; John W. Hall, "'A Reckless Waste of Blood and Treasure': The Last Campaign of the Second Seminole War," in *Between War and Peace: How America Ends Its Wars,* ed. Col. Matthew Moten (New York: Free Press, 2011), 79 ("ends"); Wright, *Creeks and Seminoles,* 264; Porter, *Black Seminoles,* 84 ("Napoleon"), 85–86; Motte, *Journey into Wilderness,* 180–181; Sprague, *Florida War,* 214; McReynolds, *Seminoles,* 201–202.

36 Missall and Missall, *Seminole Wars,* 132–133, 142, 151–152; Porter, *Black Seminoles,* 95; McReynolds, *Seminoles,* 210; Sprague, *Florida War,* 181–182; Covington, *Seminoles of Florida,* 97.

37 Wright, *Creeks and Seminoles,* 261; George R. Adams, "The Caloosahatchee Massacre: Its Significance in the Second Seminole War," *FHQ* 48, no. 4 (April 1970): 368–380.

38 Covington, *Seminoles of Florida,* 107–112; Missall and Missall, *Seminole Wars,* 204–205; Daniel L. Schafer, "U.S. Territory and State," in *The History of Florida,* ed. Michael Gannon (Gainesville: University Press of Florida, 2013), 220–243; Charlton W. Tebeau, *A History of Florida* (Coral Gables, FL: University of Miami Press, 1971), 181–198; Edward E. Baptist, *Creating an Old South: Middle Florida's Plantation Frontier before the Civil War* (Chapel Hill: University of North Carolina Press, 2002); F. Evan Nooe, "'Zealous in the Cause': Indian Violence, the Second Seminole War, and the Formation of a Southern Identity," *Native South* 4 (2011): 55–81.

39 Covington, *Seminoles of Florida,* 109; Brent R. Weisman, *Unconquered People: Florida's Seminole and Miccosukee Indians* (Gainesville: University Press of Florida, 1999).

40 Porter, *Black Seminoles,* 102–103, 111–158; Susan A. Miller, *Coacoochee's Bones: A Seminole Saga* (Lawrence: University Press of Kansas, 2003), 73–198; Kevin Mulroy, *Freedom on the Border: The Seminole Maroons in Florida, the Indian Territory, Coahuila, and Texas* (Lubbock: Texas Tech University Press, 1993); David La Vere, *Contrary Neighbors: Southern Plains and Removed Indians in Indian Territory* (Norman: University of Oklahoma Press, 2000), 114–117; Gary Clayton Anderson, *The Conquest of Texas: Ethnic Cleansing in the Promised Land* (Norman: University of Oklahoma Press, 2005), esp. 242; *Annual Report of the Office of Indian Affairs* (Washington, DC: Government Printing Office, 1846), 67. On the status of free and enslaved blacks among the Creeks, see Claudio Saunt, *Black, White, and Indian: Race and the Unmaking of an American Family* (New York: Oxford University Press, 2005).

7: INDIAN GUNRUNNERS IN A WILD WEST

1 For a recent example, see Eric Jay Dolin, *Fur, Fortune and Empire: The History of the Fur Trade in America* (New York: Norton, 2010).

2 Kathleen DuVal, *The Native Ground: Indians and Colonists in the Heart of the Continent* (Philadelphia: University of Pennsylvania Press, 2006), 76–77 ("almost all armed"), 79, 82.

3 Willard H. Rollings, *The Osage: An Ethnohistorical Study of Hegemony on the Prairie-Plains* (Columbia: University of Missouri Press, 1992), 84, 91, 102, 108–109, 116–120; Stephen Aron, *American Confluence: The Missouri Frontier from Borderland to Border State* (Bloomington: Indiana University Press, 2009), 8–9, 24–25; F. Todd Smith, *The Wichita Indians: Traders of Texas and the Southern Plains, 1540–1845* (College Station: Texas A&M University Press, 2000), 24–25, 26.

4 David J. Weber, *The Spanish Frontier in North America* (New Haven, CT: Yale University Press, 1992), 154–156, 158, 162–163, 167, 191–195.

5 Anna Lewis, ed., "La Harpe's First Expedition in Oklahoma, 1718–1719," *Chronicles of Oklahoma* 2, no. 4 (1924): 334 ("no fire arms"), 347 ("control the trade"); Weber, *Spanish Frontier,* 170–171; Smith, *Wichita Indians,* 19–22; *Iberville's Gulf Journals,* ed. and trans. Richebourg McWilliams (Tuscaloosa: University of Alabama Press, 2010), 144; Mildred Mott Wedel, *The Deer Creek Site, Oklahoma: A Wichita Village Sometimes Called Ferdinandina, An Ethnohistorian's View* (Oklahoma City: Oklahoma Historical Society, 1981), 34; Paul W. Mapp, *The Elusive West and the Contest for Empire, 1713–1763* (Chapel Hill: University of North Carolina Press for the Omohundro Institute of Early American History and Culture, 2011), 29–53.

6 Daniel H. Usner Jr., *Indians, Settlers, and Slaves in a Frontier Exchange Economy: The Lower Mississippi Valley before 1783* (Chapel Hill: University of North Carolina Press for the Institute of Early American History and Culture, 1992), 46–60, 155–165, 174–181; Paul La Chance, "The Growth of the Free and Slave Populations of French Louisiana," in *French Colonial Louisiana in the Atlantic World,* ed. Bradley G. Bond (Baton Rouge: Louisiana State University Press, 2005), 204–243.

7 The following discussion draws primarily on Dan Flores, "Bison Ecology and Bison Diplomacy: The Southern Plains from 1800 to 1850," *JAH* 78, no. 2 (September 1991): 465–485; Andrew Isenberg, *The Destruction of the Bison: An Environmental History, 1750–1920* (New York: Cambridge University Press, 2000); Preston Holder, *The Hoe and the Horse on the Plains: A Study of Cultural Development among North American Indians* (Lincoln: University of Nebraska Press, 1970); Pekka Hämäläinen, "The Rise and Fall of Plains Indian Horse Cultures," *JAH* 90, no. 3 (December 2003): 833–862; Colin G. Calloway, *One Vast Winter Count: The Native American West before Lewis and Clark* (Lincoln: University of Nebraska Press, 2003), 68–72, 267–312.

8 Alan Klein, "The Political-Economy of Gender: A 19th Century Plains Indian Case Study," and Patricia Albers, "Sioux Women in Transition: A Study of Their Changing Status in a Domestic and Capitalist Sector of Production," both in *The Hidden Half: Studies of Plains Indian Women,* ed. Patricia Albers and Beatrice Medicine (Washington, DC: University Press of America, 1983), 143–174, 175–136; Juliana Barr, "From Captives to Slaves: Commodifying Indian Women in the Borderlands," *JAH* 92, no. 1 (June 2005): 19–46; James Brooks, "'This Evil Extends Especially to the Feminine Sex': Negotiating Captivity in the New Mexico Borderlands," *Feminist Studies* 22, no. 2 (Summer 1996), 279–309.

9 These transitions are surveyed in Isenberg, *Destruction of the Bison.*

10 Pekka Hämäläinen, *The Comanche Empire* (New Haven, CT: Yale University Press, 2008); Hämäläinen, "The Politics of Grass: European Expansion, Ecological Change, and Indigenous Power in the Southwest Borderlands," *WMQ* 67, no. 2 (April 2010): 184; Thomas W. Kavanaugh, *The Comanches: A History, 1706–1875* (Lincoln: University of Nebraska Press, 1996); James F. Brooks, *Captives and Cousins:*

Slavery, Kinship, and Community in the Southwest Borderlands (Chapel Hill: University of North Carolina Press for the Omohundro Institute of Early American History and Culture, 2002); Weber, *Spanish Frontier,* 195–198.

11 DuVal, *Native Ground,* 109; Smith, *Wichita Indians,* 16–17; Juliana Barr, *Peace Came in the Form of a Woman: Indians and Spaniards in the Texas Borderlands* (Chapel Hill: University of North Carolina Press, 2007), 80, 87, 90, 103; Wedel, *Deer Creek Site,* 42–44; Dan L. Flores, ed., *Jefferson and Southwest Exploration: The Freeman and Custis Accounts of the Red River Expedition of 1806* (Norman: University of Oklahoma Press, 1984), 36; Elizabeth A. H. John, *Storms Brewed in Other Men's Worlds: The Confrontation of Indians, Spanish, and French in the Southwest, 1540–1795* (College Station: Texas A&M University Press, 1975), 317; Pekka Hämäläinen, "The Western Comanche Trade Center: Rethinking the Plains Indian Trade System," *WHQ* 29, no. 4 (Winter 1998): 485–513; Kavanaugh, *Comanches,* 128.

12 Hämäläinen, "Western Comanche Trade Center," 491 ("barter"), 494, 499; David La Vere, *Contrary Neighbors: Southern Plains and Removed Indians in Indian Territory* (Norman: University of Oklahoma Press, 2000), 34–35; On Louisiana's German population, see Usner, *Indians, Settlers, and Slaves,* 33, 51. Generally on the far-reaching violence of colonialism, see Ned Blackhawk, *Violence over the Land: Indians and Empires in the Early American West* (Cambridge, MA: Harvard University Press, 2006); Elizabeth A. Fenn, *Pox Americana: The Great Smallpox Epidemic of 1775–82* (New York: Hill and Wang, 2001).

13 Hämäläinen, "Western Comanche Trade Center," 491, 492; Hämäläinen, *Comanche Empire,* 65–66; John, *Storms Brewed,* 317; Barr, *Peace Came,* 180–196; Rollings, *Osage,* 148.

14 Barr, *Peace Came,* 180–183 ("most of the enemy" on 182); Hämäläinen, *Comanche Empire,* 59–60 ("1,000 French muskets"; "in firearms"); Elizabeth Ann Harper [John], "The Taovayas Indians in Frontier Trade and Diplomacy, 1719–1768," *Chronicles of Oklahoma* 31, no. 3 (1953): 281–282.

15 Barr, *Peace Came,* 189; John, *Storms Brewed,* 350–352; Smith, *Wichita Indians,* 31–33; Certified Copy of the Proceedings Concerning the Return of Antonio Treviño by the Taovaya Indians, March 20, 1765, Bexar Archives.

16 Hämäläinen, *Comanche Empire,* 45 ("this kingdom"), 53, 57–58; Kavanaugh, *Comanches,* 71–72, 74, 129.

17 Theodore Calvin Pease, ed., *Illinois on the Eve of the Seven Years' War, 1747–1755, IHC* 29 (1940): 357–358; Bucareli y Usura to Ripperdá, May 24, 1775, Bexar Archives; Hämäläinen, "Western Comanche Trade Center," 492, 494, 496 ("they sell"), 498; Hämäläinen, *Comanche Empire,* 93–97; DuVal, *Native Ground,* 116; Harper, "Taovaya Indians in Frontier Trade and Diplomacy," 279.

18 Weber, *Spanish Frontier,* 223; Rollings, *Osage,* 136 ("concourse"). From the Bexar Archives: Certified copy of proceedings concerning the return of Antonio Treviño by the Taovaya Indians, March 20, 1765 ("established"); Antonio Buscareli y Ursua to Juan María Ripperdá, January 6, 1773; Comingo Cabello to Felipe de Neve, March 29, 1784 ("million men"); Domingo Cabello to Jacob de Ugarte y Loyola, November 20, 1786; Muñoz to Códorba, November 16, 1793; Cortés to Muñoz, December 23, 1793; Nava to Muñoz, June 5, 1794; Códorba to Muñoz, July 2, 1794.

19 From the Bexar Archives: Antonio Buscareli y Ursua to Juan María Ripperdá, December 9, 1772, January 6, 1773 ("prejudicial equipment"), May 8, 1774; Domingo

Cabello to Teodoro de Croix, October 12, 1780 ("great resentment"); Report of Indian Presents made during 1786, [dated September 20, 1787]; Kavanaugh, *Comanches*, 185; Gary Clayton Anderson, *The Indian Southwest, 1580–1830: Ethnogenesis and Reinvention* (Norman: University of Oklahoma Press, 1999).

20 John, *Storms Brewed*, 338; DuVal, *Native Ground*, 122; Aron, *American Confluence*, 109; Rollings, *Osage*, 137; Smith, *Wichita Indians*, 44, 48, 50, 65–66, 71, 73, 88, 103–106; Anderson, *Indian Southwest*, 175–176; Jay Gitlin, "Constructing the House of Chouteau: St. Louis," *Common-place* 3, no. 4 (July 2003), http://www.common-place.org/vol-03/no-04/st-louis/.

21 Hämäläinen, *Comanche Empire*, 75, 95–96, 101.

22 Aron, *American Confluence*, 49; Hämäläinen, "Western Comanche Trade Center," 500, 504, 507–508; Hämäläinen, *Comanche Empire*, 72–73; Elizabeth A. Fenn, *Encounters at the Heart of the World: A History of the Mandan People* (New York: Hill and Wang, 2014), 203–204; Jean Louis Berlandier, *The Indians of Texas in 1830*, ed. John C. Ewers (Washington, DC: Smithsonian Institution Press, 1969), 119; Dan L. Flores, *Journal of an Indian Trader: Anthony Glass and the Texas Trading Frontier, 1790–1810* (College Station: Texas A&M University Press, 1985), 56; George E. Hyde, *A Life of George Bent, Written from his Letters* (Norman: University of Oklahoma Press, 1968), 53; Kavanaugh, *Comanches*, 205–206, 280–281.

23 Smith, *Wichita Indians*, 89–90 ("great commerce"); Flores, *Journal of an Indian Trader*, 10–11, 14–15, 16.

24 Aron, *American Confluence*, 88; John Mack Faragher, "'More Motley than Mackinaw': From Ethnic Mixing to Ethnic Cleansing on the Frontier of the Lower Missouri, 1783–1833," in *Contact Points: American Frontiers from the Mohawk Valley to the Mississippi, 1750–1830*, ed. Andrew R. L. Cayton and Fredrika J. Teute (Chapel Hill: University of North Carolina Press for the Omohundro Institute of Early American History and Culture, 1998), 304–326; La Vere, *Contrary Neighbors*, 44–47; Dianna Everett, *The Texas Cherokees: A People between Two Fires* (Norman: University of Oklahoma Press, 1990), 40; Gary Clayton Anderson, *The Conquest of Texas: Ethnic Cleansing in the Promised Land* (Norman: University of Oklahoma Press, 2005), 26; Rollings, *Osage*, 237; Anthony F. C. Wallace, *Jefferson and the Indians: The Tragic Fate of the First Americans* (Cambridge, MA: Belknap Press of Harvard University Press, 1999).

25 James A. Hanson, *Firearms of the Fur Trade* (Chadron, NE: Museum of the Fur Trade, 2011), 393, 395; Carl P. Russell, *Guns on the Early Frontiers: A History of Firearms from Colonial Times through the Years of the Western Fur Trade* (Berkeley: University of California Press, 1957), 136; Smith, *Wichitas*, 111–134; Everett, *Texas Cherokees*, 51; Anderson, *Conquest of Texas*, 74–75; Hämäläinen, *Comanche Empire*, 173–174; Mary Whatley Clarke, *Chief Bowles and the Texas Cherokees* (Norman: University of Oklahoma Press, 1971).

26 *Treaties and Laws of the Osage Nation* (Cedar Vale, KS: Press of the Cedar Vale Commercial, 1895), 1, 5, 10, 12, 18; La Vere, *Contrary Neighbors*, 50–51 ("few muskets"); Hyde, *Life of George Bent*, 89 ("good rifles"); DuVal, *Native Ground*, 184–84, 224; Rollings, *Osage*, 180–181, 184–188, 220–221, 224, 229, 233, 237–241, 244–251, 262–267; Everett, *Texas Cherokees*, 60–61; Brian DeLay, *War of a Thousand Deserts: Indian Raids and the U.S.-Mexican War* (New Haven, CT: Yale University Press, 2008), 43; Anderson, *Conquest of Texas*, 86.

27 *AROIA* (1854), vol. 90 (1855), 11, 117; Aron, *American Confluence,* 151, 159, 198; DuVal, *Native Ground,* 228–229; Anderson, *Conquest of Texas,* 3–4; Hämäläinen, *Comanche Empire,* 152–153.

28 *TIP,* 1:25 ("continual communication"); Grant Foreman, ed., *Adventure on Red River: Report on the Exploration of the Headwaters of the Red River by Captain Randolph B. Marcy and Captain G. B. McClellan* (Norman: University of Oklahoma Press, 1937), 173; *AROIA* (1856), 175 ("depradating").

29 Anderson, *Conquest of Texas,* 222; La Vere, *Contrary Neighbors,* 118; Report of Captain R. B. Marcy, October 20, 1849, U.S. Senate, 31st Congress, 1st Session, Senate Executive Doc. 64, 1849–1859, Congressional Serial Set 562, pp. 214–215 ("good rifles").

30 Janet Lecompte, *Pueblo, Hardscrabble, Greenhorn: Society on the High Plains, 1832–1856* (Norman: University of Oklahoma Press, 1978), 39–40; Anne F. Hyde, *Empires, Nations, and Families: A History of the North American West, 1800–1860* (Lincoln: University of Nebraska Press, 2011), 315–317; John M. Richardson to Samuel M. Rutherford, September 1, 1848, U.S. House, 30th Congress, 2nd Session, H. Exec. Doc. 1, Congressional Serial Set 437, pp. 541–542 ("tendency to cement"); Rollings, *Osage,* 270; *AROIA* (1854), 90 ("fine rifles").

31 Anderson, *Conquest of Texas,* 3 and passim; David J. Weber, *The Mexican Frontier: The American Southwest under Mexico, 1821–1846* (Albuquerque: University of New Mexico Press, 1982).

32 Kavanaugh, *Comanches,* 284; Lecompte, *Pueblo, Hardscrabble, Greenhorn,* 16–17, 79–80; DeLay, *War of a Thousand Deserts,* 101–103; Flores, *Journal of an Indian Trader,* xv; Hämäläinen, *Comanche Empire,* 151. On the area's tradition of long-distance trade, see Calloway, *One Vast Winter Count.*

33 Kavanaugh, *Comanches,* 176–177 ("quite expert"); Berlandier, *Indians of Texas in 1830,* 48; DeLay, *War of a Thousand Deserts,* 61–108.

34 *TIP,* 2:167–168, 2:192, 3:349; *AROIA* (1857), 263–264 ("depredating"), (1859), 383, (1860), 193, (1868), 86–69; Letter of Secretary of War Edwin Stanton, January 13, 1867, U.S. House, 39th Congress, 2nd Session, H. Misc. Doc. 40, Congressional Serial Set 130, p. 2 ("absurdity"); George Armstrong Custer, *My Life on the Plains, or, Personal Experiences with Indians* (New York: Sheldon, 1874), 26 ("fair play"); *Annual Report of the Secretary of War* (Washington, DC: Government Printing Office, 1868), 11–12; Isaac Cowie, *The Company of Adventurers: A Narrative of Seven Years in the Service of the Hudson's Bay Company during 1867–1874 on the Great Buffalo Plains* (1913; Lincoln: University of Nebraska Press, 1993), 257; Robert W. Utley, *The Indian Frontier of the American West, 1846–1890* (Albuquerque: University of New Mexico Press, 1984), 122–123.

35 *TIP,* 3:93; Colonel Richard Irving Dodge, *Our Wild Indians: Thirty-three Years Personal Experience among the Red Men of the Great West* (Hartford, CT: A.D. Worthington and Co., 1882), 450–451 ("magnificent"); Foreman, *Adventure on Red River,* 126 ("provided with rifles"); Charles Edward Chapel, *Guns of the Old West* (New York: Coward-McCann, 1961), 261; Hanson, *Firearms of the Fur Trade,* 393–424; Joseph G. Bilby, *A Revolution in Arms: A History of the First Repeating Rifles* (Yardley, PA: Westholme, 2006).

36 Dodge, *Our Wild Indians,* 290, 422 ("connoisseurs"); Dodge letter included in Letter of Edwin Stanton, February 1, 1867, U.S. House, 39th Congress, 2nd Session, H. Misc. Doc. 41, Congressional Serial Set 130, p. 2 ("issue and sale").

37 *TIP,* 4:107, 113 ("raiders"), 114 ("depot"), 175 ("opened with"), 200–201, 345–346.

38 Dodge, *Our Wild Indians,* 423.

39 Anderson, *Conquest of Texas,* 3, 4, 7; Smith, *Wichita Indians,* 16, 111–112; Hämäläinen, *Comanche Empire,* 179, 339–340; Isenberg, *Destruction of the Bison,* 123–163.

8: THE RISE AND FALL OF THE CENTAUR GUNMEN

1 *Henry and Thompson Journals,* 526 ("notorious thieves"); Edmonton Post Journals, October 26, 1823 ("greatest thieves"), November 1823 ("infernal itching"), December 12, 1834 ("damned fellows"), HBCA; W. I. Christie to Alexander Grant Dallas, August 16, 1833, Edmonton Correspondence Book, 1863–1864, B/60/b/1, HBCA.

2 William Gordon to William Cass, October 3, 1831, in *Chadron's Journal at Fort Clark, 1834–1839,* ed. Annie Heloise Abel, new ed. with intro. by William R. Swagerty (Lincoln: University of Nebraska Press, 1997), 346 ("dangerous, warlike, and formidable"); F. A. Wislizenius, *A Journey to the Rocky Mountains in the Year 1839* (St. Louis: Missouri Historical Society, 1912), 158; Edwin A. C. Hatch Journal, November 6, 1855, Ayer MS 3060, Newberry Library, Chicago ("warlike"); *AROIA* (1853) 116 ("terror to all the tribes"), (1854), 209.

3 Hugh A. Dempsey, "Blackfoot," *HNAI, Plains,* vol. 13, ed. Raymond DeMallie (Washington, DC: Smithsonian Institution Press, 2001), 604–628; John C. Ewers, *The Blackfeet: Raiders on the Northwestern Plains* (Norman: University of Oklahoma Press, 1958); Theodore Binnema, *Common and Contested Ground: A Human and Environmental History of the Northwestern Plains* (Norman: University of Oklahoma Press, 2001), 15; Hana Samek, *The Blackfoot Confederacy 1880–1920: A Comparative Study of Canadian and U.S. Indian Policy* (Albuquerque: University of New Mexico Press, 2011).

4 F. V. Hayden, *Contributions to the Ethnography and Philology of the Indian Tribes of the Missouri Valley* (Philadelphia, PA: The Society, 1862), 250; Binnema, *Common and Contested Ground,* 21; Dempsey, "Blackfoot," 604; Paul F. Sharp, *Whoop-Up Country: The Canadian-American West, 1865–1885* (Helena: Historical Society of Montana, 1960), 10.

5 Colin G. Calloway, *One Vast Winter Count: The Native American West before Lewis and Clark* (Lincoln: University of Nebraska Press, 2003), 267–312.

6 *David Thompson's Narrative of his Explorations in Western America, 1784–1812,* ed. J. B. Tyrrell (Toronto: Champlain Society, 1916), 330–331 ("Big Dogs"); Colin G. Calloway, "Snake Frontiers: The Eastern Shoshones in the Eighteenth Century," *Annals of Wyoming* 63 (1981), 82–92; John S. Milloy, *The Plains Cree: Trade, Diplomacy, and War, 1790–1870* (Winnipeg: University of Manitoba Press, 1998), 6; Pekka Hämäläinen, "The Rise and Fall of Plains Indian Horse Cultures," *JAH* 90, no. 3 (December 2003): 833–862.

7 Arthur J. Ray, *Indians in the Fur Trade: Their Role as Trappers, Hunters, and Middlemen in the Lands Southwest of Hudson Bay, 1660–1870* (Toronto: University of Toronto Press, 1974), 11–14, 68–69, 72, 87; Milloy, *Plains Cree,* 5, 16–19; Ann M. Carlos and Frank D. Lewis, "Trade, Consumption, and the Native Economy: Lessons from York Factory, Hudson Bay," *Journal of Economic History* 61, no. 4 (December, 2004): 1044, 1048; Binnema, *Common and Contested Ground,* 97–99; Roland Bohr, *Gifts from the*

Thunder Beings: Indigenous Archery and European Firearms in the Northern Plains and the Central Subarctic, 1670–1870 (Lincoln: University of Nebraska Press, 2014), 366n6; *York Factory to the Blackfeet Country: The Journal of Anthony Henday, 1754–55,* ed. Lawrence J. Burpee (Ottawa: Royal Society of Canada, 1908), 312.

8 *Thompson's Narrative,* 330–331.

9 Ibid., 329–330 ("great mischief"), 331 ("terror of that battle"), 335–356; Frank Raymond Secoy, *Changing Military Patterns on the Great Plains: 17th Century through Early 19th Century* (Seattle: University of Washington Press, 1953), 52; Milloy, *Plains, Cree,* 16–17, 24–25; *Journal of Matthew Cocking, from York Factory to the Blackfeet country, 1772–73,* ed. Lawrence J. Burpee (Ottawa: Royal Society of Canada, 1909), 111.

10 *Thompson's Narrative,* 336 ("fine Plains"); Milloy, *Plains Cree,* 10–11 ("our people").

11 Oscar Lewis, *The Effects of White Contact upon Blackfeet Culture, with Special Reference to the Role of the Fur Trade* (Seattle: University of Washington Press, 1942), 10–11, 13–14; Hugh A. Dempsey, "Sarcee," and Loreta Fowler and Regina Flannery, "Gros Ventres," both in *HNAI, Plains,* 629–637, 677–694; Hämäläinen, "Rise and Fall of Plains Indian Horse Cultures."

12 *Thompson's Narrative,* 338–339 (quotes). On this outbreak's manifestations throughout the hemisphere, see Elizabeth A. Fenn, *Pox Americana: The Great Smallpox Epidemic of 1775–82* (New York: Hill and Wang, 2001). On previous epidemics on the Plains, see Linea Sundstrom, "Smallpox Used Them Up: References to Epidemic Disease in Northern Plains Winter Counts, 1714–1920," *Ethnohistory* 44, no. 2 (1997): 305–329.

13 *Thompson's Narrative,* 338–339.

14 Ibid., 339–341.

15 Binnema, *Common and Contested Ground,* 129 ("unacquainted"); *Thompson's Narrative,* 339, 367, 370–371; Calloway, "Snake Frontiers," 88; Bohr, *Gifts from the Thunder Beings,* 273; *Henry and Thompson Journals,* 722 ("about 20 years").

16 Lewis, *Effects of White Contact,* 16–17.

17 Ibid.; *Journal of Anthony Henday,* 338 ("far off").

18 *The Journal of Duncan M'Gillivray of the North West Company at Fort George on the Saskatchewan, 1794–5* (Toronto: Macmillan Company of Canada, 1929), 41–42, 46–47; Lewis, *Effects of White Contact,* 16–17; Hiram Chittenden, *The American Fur Trade of the Far West: A History of Pioneer Trading Posts and Early Fur Companies of the Missouri Valley and Rocky Mountains and of the Overland Commerce with Santa Fe* (New York: F.P. Harper, 1902), 89–92; *The Journal of Alexander Henry the Younger, 1799–1814,* ed. Barry M. Gough, vol. 1: *Red River and the Journey to the Missouri* (Toronto: The Champlain Society, 1988), xxviii.

19 James A. Hanson, *Firearms of the Fur Trade* (Chadron, NE: Museum of the Fur Trade, 2011), 156–158; Charles E. Hanson Jr., *The Northwest Gun* (Lincoln: Nebraska State Historical Society, 1955), 2, 15–16; Carl P. Russell, *Guns on the Early Frontiers: A History of Firearms from Colonial Times through the Years of the Western Fur Trade* (Berkeley: University of California Press, 1957), 116–119; Russell, *Firearms, Traps and Tools of the Mountain Men* (New York: Knopf, 1967), 68–69; M. L. Brown, *Firearms in Colonial America: The Impact on History and Technology, 1492–1792* (Washington, DC:

Smithsonian Institution Press, 1980), 367; Bohr, *Gifts from the Thunder Beings,* 288; Clark Wissler, *Societies and Dance Associations of the Blackfoot Indians* (New York: American Museum of Natural History, 1913), 399–402; Adolf Hungry Wolf, *Blackfoot Papers,* vol. 1: *Pikunni History and Culture* (Skookumchuck, BC: Good Medicine Cultural Foundation, 2006), 140.

20 Bohr, *Gifts from the Thunder Beings,* 128 ("above all"), 144; *Saskatchewan Journals and Correspondence: Edmonton House, 1795–1800, Chesterfield House, 1800–1802,* ed. Alice M. Johnson (London: Hudson's Bay Record Society, 1967), 132 ("guns, powder, tobacco"); Edmonton Post Journals, April 5, 1799, March 2, 1800, April 15, 1807, HBCA.

21 *Henry and Thompson Journals,* 727–731 ("tedious"); Peter Fidler, *A Journal of a Journey over Land from Buckingham House to the Rocky Mountains in 1792 & 3,* ed. Bruce Haig (Lethbridge, AB: Historical Research Centre, 1992), 10; Edward Umfreville, *The Present State of Hudson's Bay: Containing a Full Description of that Settlement, and the Adjacent Country; and Likewise of the Fur Trade* (London: Charles Stalker, 1790), 63–64 ("take pity"); *Saskatchewan Journals,* 24, 28, 30, 148; Edmonton Post Journals, see the activities of gunsmith Gilbert Langthorn on November 8, 1798 and December 10, 1798, HBCA.

22 Fidler, *Journal of a Journey,* 20 ("it was of no use").

23 Ibid., 40 ("Pound Master"); *Henry and Thompson Journals,* 762; Ross Cox, *Adventures on the Columbia River: Including the Narrative of a Residence of Six Years on the Western Side of the Rocky Mountains,* 2 vols. (London: J. and J. Harper, 1831), 1:237–238 ("great advantage"); Bohr, *Gifts from the Thunder Beings,* 128 ("reckons"), 219.

24 Binnema, *Common and Contested Ground,* 99–100, 145, 155–159; Ray, *Indians in the Fur Trade,* 104; Milloy, *Plains Cree,* 26, 31–37; Edwin Thompson Denig, *Five Indian Tribes of the Upper Missouri: Sioux, Arikaras, Assiniboines, Crees, Crows,* ed. John C. Ewers (Norman: University of Oklahoma Press, 1961), 77.

25 On the wars with the Crees and Assiniboines, see, for instance, Edmonton Post Journals, August 25, 1806, September 22, 1806, James Bird to John McNabb, December 23, 1806, HBCA; Dempsey, "Blackfoot," 608; Milloy, *Plains Cree,* 85–86; Binnema, *Common and Contested Ground,* 155–159. On the Cree blockade, see Milloy, *Plains Cree,* 36 ("had determined"). On Blackfeet attacks on Edmonton, Pitt, and Carlton, see William Francis Butler, *The Great Lone Land: A Narrative of Travel and Adventure in the North-west of America,* 2nd ed. (London: Sampson, Low, Marston, Low and Searle, 1872); Isaac Cowie, *The Company of Adventurers: A Narrative of Seven Years in the Service of the Hudson's Bay Company during 1867–1874 on the Great Buffalo Plains* (1913; Lincoln: University of Nebraska Press, 1993), 206; Paul Kane, *Wanderings of an Artist among the Indians of North America* (London: Longman, Brown, Green, Longman, and Roberts, 1859), 113–114; Edmonton Post Journals, October 28, 1815, HBCA ("intimate allies").

26 *Henry and Thompson Journals,* 390–391, 399, 652, 726 ("easy prey"); Cox, *Adventures on the Columbia River,* 1:237–238 ("great object"); Peter Skene Ogden, *Traits of American-Indian Life and Character* (London: Smith, Elder, 1853), 24–25.

27 Milloy, *Plains Cree,* 36, 53 ("two hundred guns"), 84–85; Elizabeth A. Fenn, *Encounters at the Heart of the World: A History of the Mandan People* (New York: Hill and Wang, 2014), 203–204; Lewis, *Effects of White Contact,* 18–20; Lawrence J. Burpee, ed., *Journal of Larocque from the Assiniboine to the Yellowstone, 1805* (Ottawa: Govern-

ment Printing Bureau, 1910), 64, 72–73; Henry and Thompson Journals, 652 ("warlands"); *Journal of Alexander Henry the Younger,* li, lii; Cox, *Adventures on the Columbia River,* 1:199 ("idea of the profit").

28 *Henry and Thompson Journals,* 547, 566, 643–644 ("all the relations"); Cox, *Adventures on the Columbia River,* 1:234; *Thompson's Narrative,* 375; Edmonton Post Journals, October 31, 1810 ("intercept him"), May 13, 1811 ("again meet with a white man"), HBCA.

29 Edmonton Post Journals, April 28, 1813 ("Blood Indians and the Blackfeet"), HBCA; Lewis, *Effects of White Contact,* 18–21; Thomas F. Schilz, "Robes, Rum, and Rifles: Indian Middlemen in the Northern Plains Fur Trade," *Montana: The Magazine of Western History* 40, no. 1 (Winter, 1990): 9.

30 Butler, *Great Lone Land,* 281, 283–284, 377; H. M. Robinson, *The Great Fur Land, or Sketches of Life in the Hudson's Bay Territory* (New York: G. P. Putnam's Sons, 1879), 196–201 ("wily" on 197), 205–206; Kane, *Wanderings of an Artist,* 409; John Palliser, *The journals, detailed reports, and observations relative to the exploration . . . of that portion of British North America . . . between the western shore of Lake Superior and the Pacific Ocean during the years 1857, 1858, 1859, and 1860* (London: G. E. Eyre and W. Spottiswoode, 1863), 18.

31 Cox, *Adventures on the Columbia,* 1:237–239 ("overjoyed").

32 HBC District Reports, Flathead District, 1824–1825, B69/e/1, HBCA ("generally tent"); *Thompson Narrative,* 411; Edmonton Post Journals, October 16, 1827, HBCA.

33 Richard Edward Oglesby, *Manuel Lisa and the Opening of the Missouri Fur Trade* (Norman: University of Oklahoma Press, 1963).

34 On the Lewis and Clark encounter, see Patrick Gass, *A Journal of the Voyages and Travels of a Corps of Discovery: Under the Command of Capt. Lewis and Capt. Clarke* (Pittsburgh: Zadok Cramer for David M'Keehan, 1807), 245; Ewers, *Blackfeet,* 48–49; James P. Ronda, *Lewis and Clark among the Indians* (Lincoln: University of Nebraska Press, 1984), 238–243. On Piikani trade with Edmonton, see Edmonton Post Journals, November 12, 1808, HBCA; HBC District Reports, Edmonton District, Report of 1815, B60/e/1, HBCA. On trapper-tramontane Indian relations, see Lewis, *Effects of White Contact,* 23–24; Edmonton Post Journals, January 22, 1808, HBCA. On the Blackfeet trading and displaying American plunder, see Edmonton Post Journals, October 2, 1808, October 31, 1808, HBCA; *Henry and Thompson Journals,* 541. On the reasons behind Blackfeet raids against the Americans, see Mark A. Judy, "Powder Keg on the Upper Missouri: Sources of Blackfeet Hostility, 1730–1810," *American Indian Quarterly* 11, no. 2 (Spring 1987): 127–144; and Theodore Binnema, "Allegiances and Interests: Niitsitapi (Blackfoot) Trade, Diplomacy, and Warfare, 1806–1831," *WHQ* 37, no. 3 (Autumn 2006): 327–349.

35 On rendezvous, see Chittenden, *American Fur Trade,* 273; Ewers, *Blackfeet,* 56–55.

36 On estimates of American losses to the Blackfeet, see Chittenden, *American Fur Trade,* 8; George Catlin, *Letters and Notes on the Manners, Customs, and Condition of the North American Indians,* 2 vols. (London: G. Catlin, 1852), 1:51. For a higher estimate, see Ewers, *Blackfeet,* 55. Edmonton Post Journals, entry for September 19, 1825 ("tormented"), HBCA; George Simpson, *Fur Trade and Empire: George Simpson's Journal, Entitled, Remarks Connected with the Fur Trade in the Course of a Voyage from York Factory to Fort George and Back to York Factory 1824–25,* ed. Frederick Merk (Cam-

bridge, MA: Belknap Press of Harvard University Press, 1968), 307 ("dangerous service").

37 Warren Angus Ferris, *Life in the Rocky Mountains, 1830–1835* (Salt Lake City, UT: Rocky Mountain Book Shop, 1940), 72, 80, 87, 93, 94–95, 99 ("could not dislodge us"), 103, 124, 141–142 ("lightning and thunder"). For similar accounts, see Deposition of Hugh Johnson, January 13, 1824, St. Louis Superintendency, LROIA; *Chadron's Journal*, 344; Peter Skene Ogden, *Ogden's Snake Country Journals, 1824–26,* ed. E. E. Rich (London: Hudson's Bay Record Society, 1950), 15, 23, 35; Alexander Ross, *The Fur Hunters of the Far West: A Narrative of Adventures in the Oregon and Rocky Mountains,* 2 vols. (London: Smith, Elder and Co., 1855), 2:57–59, 85; William S. Lewis and Paul C. Phillips, eds., *The Journal of John Work: A Chief-Trader of the Hudson's Bay Company* (Cleveland: Arthur H. Clark, 1923), 6, 97, 107, 112, 122–123, 127–128, 129, 137–138, 180; Denig, *Five Indian Tribes,* 175–176; Prince Maximilian Wied, *Travels in the Interior of North America,* trans. H. Evans Lloyd (London: Ackermann and Co., 1843), 246; Chittenden, *American Fur Trade,* 150, 152–153, 298, 660–661; Milloy, *Plains Cree,* 92.

38 Edmonton Post Journals, October 22–23, 1823 ("W.G.C.K.R.I.J.M,"), March 16, 1824 ("Arabian Knights"), December 23, 1833 ("no end"), HBCA; Ferris, *Life in the Rocky Mountains,* 116; John C. Jackson, *The Piikani Blackfeet: A Culture Under Siege* (Missoula, MT: Mountain Press, 2000), 93.

39 Simpson, *Fur Trade and Empire,* xxxvi; Sanford to William Clark, July 26, 1833, William Clark Papers, Mo. Hist. Soc. ("if you send"); Chittenden, *American Fur Trade,* 33–34, 337; Lewis and Phillips, *Journal of John Work,* 36; Milloy, *Plains Cree,* 92–93; Jackson, *Piikani Blackfeet,* 101.

40 Ferris, *Life in the Rocky Mountains,* 105 ("white chief"), 117; Milloy, *Plains Cree,* 94 ("consult your own interests").

41 On gun and gunpowder orders, see AFC to G. M. Lampson, August 23, 1837, and AFC to Lacy and Reynolds, March 31, 1838, AFC Papers, 5:238 and 7:176, NYHS. On shipments to Blackfeet country, see vol. Y, ledger, AFC, Western, Upper Missouri Outfit, Fur Trade Ledgers, Mo. Hist. Soc. On the profit margin, see *AROIA* (1834), 96–97.

42 Edmonton Post Journals, November 1, 1823 ("think themselves entitled"), February 3, 1828 ("decorated"), April 21, 1828, December 12, 1834 ("talk much"), HBCA; *Report from the Select Committee on the Hudson's Bay Company* (London: House of Commons, 1857), 159 ("gratuitously if they require"); Russell, *Firearms, Traps, and Tools,* 66–69.

43 George Colpitts, "Provisioning the HBC: Market Economies in the British Buffalo Commons in the Early Nineteenth Century," *WHQ* 43, no. 2 (Summer 2012): 183–184; Secoy, *Changing Military Patterns,* 60.

44 Kipp to Kenneth McKenzie, September 5, 1834, Chouteau Collection, Mo. Hist. Soc.; Wied, *Travels,* 263.

45 On gun orders, see Memorandum of goods to be purchased by GMF and Co. and Delivered by December 1832, Orders Outward, AFC Papers, 2:189, NYHS ("precisely the same gun"); AFC to Joseph Henry, April 19, 1838, AFC Papers, 7:231, NYHS; William Gordon to William Clark, October 27, 1831, *Chadron's Journal,* 350. On blue barrels, see AFC to C. M. Lampson, February 7, 1840, AFC Papers, 11:406–407, NYHS. On molds, see Orders Outward, 3:13–14, AFC Papers,

NYHS. On uniform parts, Memorandum on guns to be purchased by Messrs. Tredwell, Kissam, and Co., 1833, Orders Outward, 2:200, AFC Papers, NYHS. On solid stocks, see Memorandum on guns to be purchased by Messrs. Tredwell, Kissam, and Co., 1833, Orders Outward, 2:200, AFC Papers, NYHS; John Evans to Pierre Chouteau, December 4, 1850, Fort Pierre Letter Book, Chouteau Collection, Mo. Hist. Soc. On inspections, see AFC to C. M. Lampson, March 31, 1838, and June 7, 1838, AFC Papers, 1:84, 7:177 ("so important"), 8:14 ("we spare no pains"), 12:127, NYHS. AFC to C. M. Lampson, March 7, 1840, AFC Papers, 12:90, NYHS ("for at least the season").

46 *AROIA* (1854), 205 ("file off a piece"), (1856), 76 ("out of his lodge"); Dodge, *Our Wild Indians,* 416 ("a rule"); Ewers, *Blackfeet,* 139; L. James Dempsey, *Blackfoot War Art: Pictographs of the Reservation Period, 1880–2000* (Norman: University of Oklahoma Press, 2007), 14, 15, 18, 47.

47 Dempsey, "Blackfoot," 616.

48 Ibid.; Arni Brownstone, *War Paint: Blackfoot and Sarcee Painted Buffalo Robes in the Royal Ontario Museum* (Toronto: Royal Ontario Museum, 1993), 10–11, 18; James D. Keyser, "Writing-on-Stone: Rock Art on the Northwestern Plains," *Canadian Journal of Archaeology,* no. 1 (1977): 15–80; Bohr, *Gift from the Thunder Beings,* 123–124, 312.

49 Dempsey, *Blackfoot War Art,* 81; James Carnegie Southesk, *Saskatchewan and the Rocky Mountains: A Diary and Narrative of Travel, Sport, and Adventure, During a Journey through the Hudson's Bay Company's Territories, in 1859 and 1860* (Edinburgh: Edmonston and Douglas, 1875), 329 ("certain herbs"); Charles Wissler, *Ceremonial Bundles of the Blackfoot Indians,* Anthropological Papers of the Museum of Natural History, vol. 7, no. 2 (New York: American Museum of Natural History, 1912), 270.

50 Hyde, *Empires, Nations, and Families,* 318–327; John E. Sunder, *The Fur Trade on the Upper Missouri, 1840–1865* (Norman: University of Oklahoma Press, 1965); Barton H. Barbour, *Fort Union and the Upper Missouri Fur Trade* (Norman: University of Oklahoma Press, 2001).

51 HBC District Reports, Edmonton District, Report of 1820, B60/e/3/, HBCA ("impossible to describe"); Edmonton Post Journals, January 29, 1819, February 6, 1820, March 5, 1820, HBCA; Joshua Pitcher to William Clark, February 27, 1838, Upper Missouri Agency, LROIA ("literally depopulated"; "graveyard"); Fenn, *Encounters at the Heart of the World,* 266–279, 311–325.

52 Jacob Hasley to Pratte, Chouteau, and Co., November 2, 1837, and D. D. Mitchell to P. D. Paquin, December 1, 1837, Chouteau Collection, Mo. Hist. Soc.; Pratte, Chouteau, and Co. to AFC, February 25, 1838, "Letters," p. 4041, reel 26, AFC Papers, NYHS ("less than four hundred lodges"); Clyde D. Dollar, "The High Plains Smallpox Epidemic of 1837–38," *WHQ* 8, no. 1 (January 1977): 15–38. On Blackfeet population counts: J. B. Brant to Jessup, December 1, 1834, Army Papers, Mo. Hist. Soc.; *AROIA* (1854), 194, and (1858), 81; Palliser, *Exploration,* 200–201; Henry Youle Hind, *Narrative of the Canadian Red River Exploring Expedition of 1857, and of the Assinniboine and Saskatchewan Exploring Expedition of 1858* (London: Longman, Green, Longman and Roberts, 1860), 157.

53 Report of H. G. Cummings, February 8, 1853, Central Superintendency, LROIA; Denig, *Five Indian Tribes,* 145–148, 163, 172–184 ("Blackfeet were their enemies," 172); *AROIA* (1856), 76 (1859), 118, (1860), 83, (1862), 179, (1864), 300; Palliser, *Exploration,* 18, 84; HBC District Reports, Edmonton Report, 1862, B60/e/9,

HBCA; W. I. Christie to Alexander Grant Dallas, August 16, 1863, Edmonton Correspondence Book, 1863–1864, B/60/b/1, HBCA; Milloy, *Plains Cree,* 111; Jackson, *Piikani Blackfeet,* 148.

54 Robert W. Utley, *The Indian Frontier of the American West, 1846–1890* (Albuquerque: University of New Mexico Press, 1984), 51–54; Ray H. Glassley, *Pacific Northwest Indian Wars* (Portland, OR: Binfords and Mort, 1953), 53–150; Schilz, "Indian Middlemen," 11; Dempsey, "Blackfoot," 617–668; Sunder, *Fur Trade of the Upper Missouri,* 167–168.

55 "List of Indian goods transported by the Steamship boat St. Mary to Fort Benton for the Blackfeet, 6/6/1856," Chouteau Collection, Mo. Hist. Soc.; Ewers, *Blackfeet,* 230; *AROIA* (1859), 14, (1866), 202–203; Henry Reed to H. P. Dole, January 14, 1863, Dakota Superintendency, LROIA; William T. Hamilton, "A Trading Expedition among the Indians in 1858, from Walla Walla to the Blackfoot Country and Return," in *Contributions to the Historical Society of Montana,* vol. 3 (Helena, MT: Rocky Mountain Publishing Co., 1900), 62 ("sparkled," "bounded").

56 Sharp, *Whoop-Up Country,* 5, 145; Bohr, *Gifts from the Thunder Beings,* 296 (Plenty Coups); *AROIA* (1864), 300, (1865), 511–512, (1866), 202–203, (1867), 256, (1868), 215, 221–222; Edmonton Post Journals, March 24, 1865, May 17, 1865, HBCA; Cowie, *Company of Adventurers,* 314–315; Milloy, *Plains Cree,* 113–114; *Annual Report of the Secretary of War* (1868), 34; Lewis, *Effects of White Contact,* 63–65.

57 On the smallpox, *AROIA* (1870), 190; Butler, *Great Lone Land,* 202, 386, 372; Journal of Major Alexander Culbertson of the American Fur Company, July 10, 1870, to August 18, 1870, pp. 10–11, Mo. Hist. Soc.; Robinson, *Great Fur Land,* 189. On the massacre, Ewers, *Blackfeet,* 236–253; Sharp, *Whoop-Up Country,* 145–148; Andrew R. Graybill, *The Red and the White: A Family Saga of the American West* (New York: Liveright, 2013), esp. 105–152; *AROIA* (1870), 190–191 ("subdued"); *Annual Report of the Secretary of War* (1870), 30.

58 A. Johnston, ed., *Battle at Belly River: Stories of the Last Great Indian Battle* (Lethbridge: Historical Society of Alberta, 1966); Milloy, *Plains Cree,* 115–118; Cowie, *Company of Adventurers,* 305–306; Robinson, *Great Fur Land,* 186, 196; Cowie, *Company of Adventurers,* 418, 425; Margaret Irvin Carrington, *Ab-sa-ra-ka, Home of the Crows: Being the Experience of an Officer's Wife on the Plains* (Philadelphia, PA: J. B. Lippincott and Co, 1868), 189, 191.

59 Ewers, *Blackfeet,* 258–262; Sharp, *Whoop-Up Country,* 58–59, 51, 54, 78–106; Hugh Dempsey, *Firewater: The Impact of the Whisky Trade on the Blackfoot Nation* (Markham, ON: Fifth House, 2002).

60 Butler, *Great Lone Land,* 377–378; Dempsey, "Blackfoot," 618; Daniel Miner Gordon, *Mountain and Prairie: A Journey from Victoria to Winnipeg via Peace River Pass* (Montreal: Dawson Brothers, 1880); Lewis, *Effects of White Contact,* 68.

EPILOGUE

1 This account draws primarily on Paul Chaat Smith and Robert Allen Warrior, *Like a Hurricane: The Indian Movement from Alcatraz to Wounded Knee* (New York: New Press, 1996), esp. 171–268; Peter Matthiessen, *In the Spirit of Crazy Horse,* new ed. (New York: Penguin Books, 1991); Stephen Cornell, *The Return of the Native: American Indian Political Resurgence* (New York: Oxford University Press, 1988); and

Joane Nagel, *American Indian Ethnic Renewal: Red Power and the Resurgence of Identity and Culture* (New York: Oxford University Press, 1996), esp. 158–212.

2 Troy R. Johnson, "The Roots of Contemporary Native American Activism," *American Indian Culture and Research Journal* 20, no. 2 (1996): 127–154; Johnson, *The Occupation of Alcatraz Island: Indian Self-Determination and the Rise of Indian Activism* (Champaign: University of Illinois Press, 1996); Fay G. Cohen, *Treaties on Trial: The Continuing Controversy over Northwest Indian Fishing Rights* (Seattle: University of Washington Press, 1986).

3 Smith and Warrior, *Like a Hurricane,* 198 ("For many years"; "Where are our men").

4 Russell Means and Marvin Wolf, *Where White Men Fear to Tread: The Autobiography of Russell Means* (New York: St. Martin's Press, 1995), 280–282 ("pitiful"); John Kifner, "Wounded Knee Is a Tiny Armed Camp," *Special to the New York Times,* March 5, 1973 ("we wish").

5 Bob Wiedrich, "How Guns Got to Wounded Knee," *Chicago Tribune,* April 10, 1973 ("63 modern rifles); "McGovern Hits Indian Militants," *Washington Post,* September 1, 1973.

6 "Wounded Knee Siege Ends as Indians Disarm," *Chicago Tribune,* May 9, 1973 ("old shotguns").

7 Devon A. Mihesuah, "Anna Mae Pictou-Aquash: An American Indian Activist," in *Sifters: Native American Women's Lives,* ed. Theda Perdue (New York: Oxford University Press, 2001), 204–219; Eric Konigsberg, "Who Killed Anna Mae?," *New York Times Magazine,* April 25, 2014.

8 Frederick E. Hoxie, *This Indian Country: American Indian Activists and the Place They Made* (New York: Penguin Press, 2012), 393–403.

ACKNOWLEDGMENTS

The research and writing of this book was possible because of generous outside financial support from a number of institutions. I was the fortunate beneficiary of two long-term awards providing time, scholarly resources, and vibrant intellectual communities: a National Endowment for the Humanities Residential Fellowship at the Library Company of Philadelphia, where I began this project, and a Barra Sabbatical Fellowship at the McNeil Center for Early American Studies at the University of Pennsylvania, where I did the bulk of the writing. Also invaluable were short-term fellowships at the American Antiquarian Society, Massachusetts Historical Society, Winterthur Museum and Library, American Philosophical Society, and Buffalo Bill Historical Center. Several summer grants from George Washington University and an award from the Phillips Fund for Native American Research permitted me to visit archives, museums, and historic sites across the continent, including the Glenbow Museum, Library of Congress, Missouri Historical Society, Museum of the Fur Trade, National Archives of the United States, Newberry Library, New-York Historical Society, Rochester Museum and Science Center, Royal Museum of Alberta, Sitka National Historical Park, William L. Clements Library at the University of Michigan, and Writing-on-Stone Provincial Park. For helping to make these trips a success, I pay special thanks to my former department chairman, William Becker, to George Washington University Department of History administrators, Michael Weeks and Johnny Vail, and to George Hamell, who devoted two full days to guiding me through the archaeological collections of the Rochester Museum and Science Center, all the while sharing his exquisite knowledge of Iroquois culture and history. George Washington University's Department of History and Columbian College of Arts and Sciences also made subventions to meet the cost of maps and illustrations.

The critiques I've received from audiences at conferences and public talks and from readers of my drafts have made this a much better book. I've presented portions of this work at the annual meetings of Organization of American Historians and the American Society for Ethnohistory, the Washington Area Early American Seminar at the University of Maryland, the Atlantic Seminar at New York University, the David Library of the American Revolution, the Buffalo Bill Historical Center, Jefferson Patterson Park (Maryland), Historic St. Mary's City, the Aquinnah Cultural Center, Sitka National Historical Park, Sealaska (Juneau), Michael Zuckerman's deservedly famous salon, and two seminars and two brown bags of the McNeil Center for Early American Studies. Generous friends and colleagues who have read my work-in-progress, in whole or in part, and offered penetrating criticisms (as well as some measure of encouragement) include Lindsay Beach, William Carter, Robbie Ethridge, Andrew R. Graybill, James L. Hill, Michael Oberg, Daniel K. Richter, James Rice, Chuck Smythe, Jessica Stern, my unparalleled editor, Joyce Seltzer, and two anonymous readers for Harvard University Press. Denver Brunsman suggested the epilogue. Not the least of all, I've imposed drafts on my students at George Washington University and received many helpful responses in return. To all of the above people and institutions, and to the others whom I regret to have overlooked, I offer my deepest gratitude. It goes without saying, all remaining errors of fact and interpretation and shortcomings of style in this book are my sole responsibility.

Family has been the foundation of this project. My parents, Richard and Julia Silverman, and parents-in-law, Dennis and Mary Fisher, have provided unflagging support. My children, Aquinnah and Bela Silverman, have (mostly) patiently suffered through extended visits to numerous historic sites and museums related to this work, and even longer stories.

Above all, there is my wife and fellow historian, Julie A. Fisher, whose love and influence wend their way through each and every page I've written. In heartfelt appreciation, I dedicate this work to her.

INDEX

Abbadie, Jean-Jacques-Blaise d', 146
Abenakis, 44, 113
Abraham, 201, 213
Ackia, 80–81
Akoi, 180
Alabama (state), 191, 192, 197, 204, 220
Alabamas (tribe), 70, 72, 78, 89
Alachua Savannah, 192, 196, 201, 207
Alaska, 15, 156, 175–187, 257
Albany (NY): founding of, 15, 21, 24; English conquest and, 47, 48; smuggling economy of, 51; Iroquois diplomacy in, 52, 53; gun trade of during King Philip's War, 113–114, 115, 120
Alberta, 6, 252, 256, 284
Aleutian Islands, 158
Aleuts, 158, 179, 180, 181, 182, 184
Alexander (Wamsutta), 105
Algonquian language family, 44, 45, 46, 48, 59, 96, 113, 256, 260
Algonquins (tribe), 22, 25, 36, 39
Alibamon Mingo, 83
Alligator. See Halpatter Tustenuggee
Alutiit (plural of Alutiiq, of Kodiak), 178, 179, 180
Ambrister, Robert, 198, 212
ambush: gun use in, 8, 22–23, 26, 28–30; by Iroquois, 35–36, 37, 46; by New England Algonquians, 45, 93, 107, 109–111; by Natchez, 79; by Chickasaws, 80; by Indians during Pontiac's War, 136, 138; by Seminoles, 196, 201–202, 207; by Pawnees and Otos, 226; by Blackfeet, 255, 268

American Fur Company, 15, 221, 270, 271, 272, 274
American Indian Movement (AIM), 287–294
American Revolution, 53, 152, 153, 149, 193, 194, 197
Amherst, Jeffrey, 121–122, 123, 124–128, 130, 133, 135, 140, 142, 144
Andros, Edmund, 114, 115
Anglo-Dutch Wars, 104–105
Apaches, 222, 225, 226, 228, 231, 232
Apalachee (province), 61, 69
Apalachees (tribe), 68, 69, 75
Apalachicola River, 192, 194, 196, 197, 198
Apalachicolas (tribe), 68
Appalachian Mountains, 50, 151, 153
Aquinnah, 109
Arapahos, 4, 228, 229, 244
Arbuthnot, Alexander, 198, 212
Arikaras, 228, 265, 279
Arkansas (territory and state), 222, 240
Arkansas River: as site of gun trade, 19, 222–223, 224, 226, 227, 229–231; as Quapaw territory, 224; as Wichita territory, 225; as site of intertribal trade, 228, 229–231; Comanche expansion along, 229–231; Osage expansion along, 235, 242; removed Indian expansion along, 238, 241; white American expansion along, 241, 244
arms embargos: ineffectiveness of, 15, 17, 81; during Yamasee War, 77; during King Philip's War, 117, 120; as part of Jeffrey Amherst's policies, 125–126;